Religion in Global Politics

Religion in Global Politics

Jeff Haynes

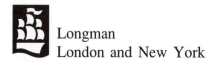

Longman
London and New York

Addison Wesley Longman Limited
Edinburgh Gate
Harlow
Essex CM20 2JE
United Kingdom
and Associated Companies throughout the world

*Published in the United States of America
by Addison Wesley Longman, New York*

First published 1998

ISBN 0 582–29312–X

British Library Cataloguing-in-Publication Data

A catalogue record for this book is available from the British Library

Library of Congress Cataloging-in-Publication Data

A catalogue record for this book is available from the Library of Congress.

Set by 35 in 10/12pt Times
Produced through Longman Malaysia, PP

Contents

Acknowledgements

I would like to thank all those who took the time to read and comment on draft chapters: Iwan Morgan, Andrew Moran, Stephen Carter, Dermot McCann and, above all, my friend and colleague, James Chiriyankandath. Thanks to you all. The errors? Mine, all mine.

Acknowledgements

Chapter 1

Introduction

Examples of religion's recent political impact abound in countries at varying levels of economic and political development. For example, there is the crucial role of Christian Churches in the 'Third Wave' of democracy in southern and eastern Europe, Latin America and Africa from the early 1970s; the overthrow of the Shah of Iran in 1979 and the contemporaneous growth of Islamist movements across the Muslim world from Morocco to Malaysia; the New Christian Right in the USA demanding fundamental political, social, and moral changes; long-running hostility between Protestants and Catholics in Northern Ireland and between Muslims and Christians in Africa; Hindu and Sikh political radicalism in India and Buddhist activism in South-east Asia; and Jewish extremism in Israel. The result is that, around the world, the mass media, social scientists, professional politicians and many 'ordinary' people feel compelled to pay increased attention to religion as a socio-political actor.

Religious organizations of various kinds seem openly to be rejecting the secular ideals dominating national policies, appearing as champions of alternative, confessional options. In keeping faith with what they interpret as divine decree, increasingly they refuse to render to non-religious power either material or moral tribute. They are increasingly concerned with political issues, challenging the legitimacy and autonomy of the primary secular spheres, the State, political organization and the market economy. They are also refusing to restrict themselves to the pastoral care of individual souls, instead raising questions about, *inter alia*, the interconnections of private and public morality and the claims of states and markets to be exempt from extrinsic normative considerations. Intent on retaining social importance, many religious organizations seek to elude what they regard as the cumbersome constraints of temporal authority, threatening to usurp constituted political functions. In short, refusing to be condemned to the realm of privatized belief, religion is once again reappearing in the public sphere, thrusting itself into issues of moral and political contestation. (Religious privatization means that religious organizations shall not have the right to be actively engaged with matters of public concern or to play a role in public life.) As Casanova (1994: 6) puts it, 'what was new and became "news" in the 1980s was the widespread and simultaneous refusal of the so-called "world religions" – that is, Islam, Christianity, Hinduism and Buddhism – to be restricted to the private sphere'.

This book examines the relationship between religion and politics since the early 1970s in a variety of countries.[1] Its title, *Religion in Global Politics*, aims to capture its goal, a general survey of the interaction of religion and politics in four regions: the Americas, Europe, Asia and Africa. Because this is obviously an ambitious task for one book, it cannot hope to be definitive. Nevertheless, by focusing on key issues, I seek to provide a commentary on what has taken place, and is currently happening, to the spheres of religion and politics throughout the world. Most chapters feature case studies of several countries, providing specific geographical foci to put empirical flesh on the theoretical bones outlined in the introduction. Overall, the aim is to offer a comparative treatment so that the reader can appreciate some of the rich variety of particular national situations involving religion and politics since the early 1970s.

Given the range of religious traditions – that is, the 'world religions' – and countries examined, it is necessary to establish at the outset what will and will not be focused upon. I am primarily concerned with the political relationships between states and leading religious institutions and organizations. Sometimes – as for example in Europe and the Americas – the main religious actors are various Christian Churches, while elsewhere – for example, the Middle East and Asia – non-Christian religions are the main focus. I do not focus on transnational religious actors except where they impact upon the domestic scene, as in Central Asia.[2]

The principal argument of the book is that religion is leaving, or refusing to accept, its assigned place in the private sphere. This is true, I believe, even in highly secular societies like England where mainline Christian Churches have re-emerged as important social, moral and – to a degree – political voices. There, building on a tradition established during the premiership of Margaret Thatcher in the 1980s, the publication in October 1996 of the Catholic Church's 13,000-word pamphlet, *The Common Good and the Catholic Church's Social Teaching*, was an important intervention in the political debate between the Labour and Conservative parties. Politicians – especially of the latter party – saw it as an endorsement of Labour's policies. Six months later – in April 1997 – 11 Churches collectively published a further report entitled, *Unemployment and the Future of Work*, an outspoken attack on the inability of the main parties in Britain to focus upon the amelioration of the suffering of the underprivileged. The report accused them of putting tax cuts before solutions to poverty and unemployment in the battle for victory in the May 1997 general election (Bellos and White 1997).

Concerned with overtly political issues, *The Common Good* and *Unemployment and the Future of Work* were both manifestations of the contemporary process of repolitization of the hitherto increasingly private religious and moral spheres in

---

1. Not convinced that 'value-free social science' is achievable, I should make it plain that I am a religious nonbeliever. While respecting the spiritual functions of religious organizations, my main interest in this book is in their socio-political purposes vis-à-vis the State.

2. For a recent and interesting book concerned with transnational religious actors, see Rudolph and Piscatori (1997).

England. The reports repesented an attempt to re-establish ethical norms of behaviour and activities in public and political spheres and to present a political case for so doing. In the publications, mainline Churches endorsed what were clearly political goals, expressing opposition to the dualism between religion and politics, and arguing that the concerns of social justice were, in fact, not only scripturally rooted, but also wedded to the defence of liberal democracy, pluralism and the market economy (Watson 1994: 149, Huntington 1991, 1993). In short, the central issue for the Churches was the degree to which the consumerist version of politics should be modified or balanced by the social dimension (Edwards 1990, Glasman 1996).

However, it is not only Churches in England that are becoming concerned with social, economic and political issues. Numerous religious organizations and institutions around the world also share a desire to change their societies in a direction where religious standards would be more central than before. In pursuit of such objectives, they use a variety of tactics and methods: some, like the British Churches, lobby, protest and publish reports at the level of *civil society* (see pp. 68–71); others seek desired changes via *political society* (see pp. 28–33), for example, the American New Christian Right regularly endorses electoral candidates with the most 'pro-religion' policies; a few – such as Islamists in Algeria and Egypt – even resort to violence and terrorism to achieve their goals. However, the means to achieve goals are perhaps less important than the ends pursued: whatever the chosen modes of political interaction, what is new and unexpected in all this is the remodelling and reassumption of public roles by religion which theories of secularization had long condemned to social and political marginalization.

Secularization can be thought of as a fivefold process, involving: (a) *constitutional secularization*, whereby religious institutions cease to be given special constitutional recognition and support by the State; (b) *policy secularization*, that is, when the State expands its policy domains and service provisions into areas previously reserved to the religious sphere; (c) *institutional secularization*, that is, when religious structures lose their political saliency and influence as pressure groups, parties and movements; (d) *agenda secularization*, which occurs when issues, needs and problems deemed relevant to the political process no longer have an overtly religious content; and (e) *ideological secularization*, that is, when 'the basic values and belief-systems used to evaluate the political realm and to give it meaning cease to be couched in religious terms' (Moyser 1991: 14).

To state the main argument of the book briefly, what I believe is happening in the sphere of religion and politics, on the one hand, involves a widespread, if patchy, 'deprivatization'[3] of previously privatized religions in the Western world – that is, Europe, North America and Israel.[4] These are regions and countries where

---

3. 'Deprivatization' – a neologism coined by Casanova (1994) – refers to the fact that many religions are not content with such a compartmentalized existence and instead try to influence things in the public sphere.

4. The inclusion of Israel among Western countries is somewhat controversial, yet it seems to me appropriate because it exhibits many of the general characteristics of 'Western-ness': a well-established democratic structure, a welfare state, relatively high levels of GNP per capita (for Jewish Israelis at least), and a theoretically clear division between the State, political society and civil society.

there is a more or less clear tripartite division of democratic polities into State, political society and civil society; according to conventional social science wisdom such an arrangement should – inevitably – lead to religion's privatization and corresponding decline in social and political importance. On the other hand, where the process of religious privatization is not so far advanced – that is, in most Third World[5] countries – it is the fear of imminent or creeping privatization which, I believe, provides the stimulus for religion to act politically to prevent its social marginalization.

Religion and politics defined

Before proceeding, it may be useful to define two of the key terms used in the book: religion and politics. Defining politics is simple: it is about the pursuit of power. But when it is won – by a class, faction, group or whatever – politics is also about how to exercise power and to regulate the inevitable conflicts that emerge between the various interest groups within a polity.

Explaining the term religion satisfactorily is more difficult. For the sociologist, two main approaches are common. Religion is either (a) a system of beliefs and practices related to an ultimate being, beings, or to the supernatural or (b) that which is sacred in a society, that is, ultimate beliefs and practices which are inviolate (Aquaviva 1979). For purposes of wider social analysis, religion is normally approached (a) from the perspective of a body of ideas and outlooks, that is, as theology and ethical code; (b) as a type of formal organization, that is, the ecclesiastical 'Church'; or (c) as a social group, that is, religious groups and movements. There are two basic ways in which religion can affect the temporal world: by what it says and by what it does. The former relates to religion's doctrine or theology, the latter to its importance as a social phenomenon and mark of identity, working

5. The term, 'Third World', was invented in the 1950s to refer, on the one hand, to the large group of economically underdeveloped, then decolonizing countries in Africa, Asia and the Middle East and, on the other, to Latin American states, mostly granted their freedom in the early nineteenth century, but still economically weak. Despite a shared history of colonization there are important differences between Third World states. For example, such economically diverse countries as the United Arab Emirates (1993 GNP per capita: $21,430), South Korea ($7,660) and Mozambique ($90), or politically singular polities such as Cuba (one-party communist State), Nigeria (military dictatorship), and India (multi-party democracy), are all members of the Third World. To many, the economic and political – not to mention cultural – differences between Third World countries outweighs their supposed similarities. While the blanket term 'Third World' obscures cultural, economic, social and political differences between states, it has advantages over alternatives like 'the South' or 'developing countries'. The expression 'the South' is essentially a geographic expression which ignores the fact that some 'Western' countries – such as Australia and New Zealand – are in the geographical south. The idea of the 'South' does, however, have the advantage of getting away from the connotation of developing towards some preordained end state or goal which is explicit in the idea of '*developing* countries'. It is by no means clear, however, what the idea of a 'developed' State looks like: does it connote only a certain (high) degree of economic growth or is there an element of redistribution of the fruits of growth involved? What of widely divergent social conditions in a 'developed' country? In this book I will use the term 'Third World', still the standard terminology in the absence of a better alternative (GNP figures from World Bank 1995: Table 1, pp. 162–3).

through a variety of modes of institutionalization, such as political parties and Church–State relations.

It is necessary to distinguish between religion at the individual and group levels: only the latter is normally of political importance. From an individualist perspective, religion may be thought of as 'a set of symbolic forms and acts which relates man [sic] to the ultimate conditions of his existence' (Bellah 1964: 359). This is its *private*, spiritual side. However, I am concerned with *group* religiosity, whose claims and pretensions are *always* to some degree political; there is no such thing as a religion without consequences for value systems (Ramet 1995: 64). Group religiosity, like politics, is a matter of collective solidarities and, frequently, of inter-group tension and conflict, focusing either on shared or disagreed images of the sacred, or on cultural and class, in short, political, issues. To complicate matters, however, such influences may well operate differently and with 'different temporalities for the same theologically defined religion in different parts of the world' (Moyser 1991: 11).

To try to bring together political and religious spheres in all their varied aspects and then to discern significant patterns and trends is not a simple task. But, in attempting it, three points are worth emphasizing. First, there is something of a distinction to be drawn between looking at the relationship in terms of the impact of religion on politics, and that of politics on religion. At the same time, they are interactive: the effects of one stimulates and is stimulated by the other. In other words, because I am concerned with the way in which power is exercised in society, and the way(s) in which religion is involved, the relationship between religion and politics is both dialectical and interactive: each shapes and influences the other. Both causal directions need to be held in view.

Second, religions are creative and constantly changing; consequently their relationships with politics also vary over time. Although I am concerned with the interactions of religious organizations and the State since the early 1970s, the picture is not static. Associations between religion and secular power may suddenly change. For example, in Eastern Europe, Latin America and Iran in recent times, leading religious institutions and figures shifted – apparently abruptly – from support to opposition of incumbent regimes.

Finally, religious organizations as political actors can only be usefully discussed in terms of specific contexts; I believe interactions involving the State provide the most fruitful area. Yet, the model of responses, while derived from and influenced by specific aspects of particular religions, is not necessarily inherent to them. Rather this is a theoretical construct suggested by much of the literature on State–society relations, built on the understanding that religion's specific role is largely determined by a broader context. The assumption is that there is an essential core element of religion shaping behaviour in, for example, Christian, Islamic, or Buddhist societies. I question this assumption in the chapters which follow. The focus of many earlier studies has been to seek to analyse how an existing religious belief or affiliation affects political action. In this book, however, I am equally concerned with the reverse process: how specific political contexts affect religious organizations.

Church and State in comparative perspective

To understand the political importance of religious actors, we need to compre-
hend what they say and do in their relationship with the State. Following Stepan
(1988: 3), I mean something more than 'mere' government when referring to the
State: it is the continuous administrative, legal, bureaucratic and coercive system
that attempts not only to manage the State apparatus but in addition to 'structure
relations between civil and public power and to structure many crucial relationships
within civil and political society'. Almost everywhere, states seek to reduce religion's political influence, that is, they seek to privatize it, significantly to reduce its
political importance. Sometimes, in countries at differing levels of economic development – for example, the USA, Nigeria, Tanzania, Indonesia, Israel, Burma and
Poland – the State will attempt to erect an arrangement called 'civil religion' where
a certain designated religious format 'functions as the cult of the political community' (Casanova 1994: 58). The purpose is to create forms of consensual, corporate
religion, claiming to be guided by general, culturally appropriate, societally specific
religious beliefs, not necessarily tied institutionally to any specific religious tradition (Hallencreutz and Westerlund 1996, Liebman and Eliezer 1983). The main
point is that the development of civil religion in a polity is a strategy to avoid social
conflicts and promote national coordination, especially in countries with serious
religious or ideological divisions. However, civil religions are often perceived by
minority religious persuasions as aiming to install and perpetuate the hegemony of
one religious tradition at the expense of others.

But religion's relationship with the State is not only bounded by attempts to build
civil religions; it has become of greater public salience in a wide range of State–
religion relationships. That relations between religious organizations and the State
have become more visible and often increasingly problematic in many countries in
recent years does not, of course, constitute in itself evidence against the idea that
states in the contemporary era do not need the kind of religious legitimation exemplified by civil religion. One certainly has, for example, to entertain the possibility
that the recent proliferation of religious-based challenges to the authority of the
State are merely transitory reactions to the onward march of secularization. Moreover, even if – as some significant figures in social science have claimed – the
modern State is particularly vulnerable to legitimation crises, that does not in itself
mean that religion is becoming again *automatically* relevant to the functioning
of the State machinery. Normally, religion-based challenges have their roots in
endeavours by the State to assert a monitoring role vis-à-vis religion, in effect to
control it. We can see such a development at three levels: political society, civil
society and at the level of the State itself.

Religion and political society

Many believe that religion is being liberated from providing slavish legitimacy for
secular authority because religious officials and activists increasingly criticize
government. Yet, if heightened concern about the State's policies is held up as

evidence of the regeneration of the socio-political power of religion, one must still ask further questions. The issues are themselves secular and in so far as religious agencies are active in these areas, this is a radical shift of concern from the super-natural, from devotional acts, to what are largely secular goals to be pursued by secular means. However, a note of caution may be in order: we need to bear in mind that when religious interests act as pressure groups – rather than as prayer bodies – they are not necessarily particularly effective. As Wilson (1992: 202–3) points out, the more secularized a society, the less likely religion will have a politically significant role.

At the level of political society – that is, the arena in which the polity specifically arranges itself for political contestation to gain control over public power and the State apparatus – we can see a range of religious responses which are in part dependent upon the degree of secularization. These include (a) resistance to the disestablishment and the differentiation of the religious from the secular sphere, that is, the goals of many so-called 'fundamentalist' religious groups;[6] (b) the mobilizations and countermobilizations of religious groups and confessional parties against other religions or against secular movements and parties; (c) religious groups' mobilization in defence of religious, social and political freedoms, that is, demanding the rule of law and the legal protection of human and civil rights, protecting the mobilization of civil society and/or defending the institutionalization of democratic regimes. In pursuit of such goals, there has been in recent times Christian mobilization in Ghana and Kenya (Gyimah-Boadi 1994: 141, Gifford 1994) and in communist Poland, Spain and Brazil (Casanova 1994). Buddhist groups in Thailand (McCargo 1992) and Islamist groups in a variety of countries (Haynes 1993) have also sought to influence State policies at the level of political society.

Religion and civil society

I once again follow Stepan (1988: 3): civil society is the arena where multifold social movements – neighbourhood associations, women's groups, religious groupings, intellectual currents and the like – join with civic organizations – such as those mobilizing lawyers, journalists, trade unions and entrepreneurs – to constitute themselves in an ensemble of arrangements to express themselves and seek to advance their interests. The concept of *civil* society is sometimes used in contrast to *political* society. Unlike the latter, civil society refers to institutions and movements – not political parties – not involved in the business of government or in overt political management. But this does not prevent organizations in civil society

6. The continuing debate about the contours, characteristics and objectives of 'religious fundamentalism' has delivered more heat than light. Ultimately, perhaps, as Berger (1997: 32) notes, what we are really talking about here is merely 'any passionate religious movement'. In this book, I shall refer to religious 'fundamentalists' in three contexts only: in the USA, where those passionate about injecting 'Christian' values into politics, society and morality use this nomenclature, in Israel where the commonly accepted term for right-wing, Judaist fanatics is 'Jewish fundamentalists' and in Northern Ireland where a brand of fundamentalism is relevant to politics. Elsewhere, I shall refer to Hindu nationalists, Islamists, and so on. This is in line with what such activists call themselves.

from sometimes exercising profound political influence, on matters ranging from single issues to national constitutions.

When it comes to religion, at the civil society level one may distinguish between hegemonic civil religions – such as evangelical Protestantism in nineteenth-century America – and the public intervention of religious pressure groups, either concerned with single issues such as abortion or with a morally determined view of wider societal development. In trying to influence public policy – without seeking to become political office-holders – religious organizations may employ a variety of tactics, including (a) lobbying the executive apparatus of the State; (b) going to court; (c) building links with political parties; (d) forming alliances with like-minded groups, whether secular or from other religions; (e) mobilizing their followers to protest, and/or (g) seeking to sensitize public opinion through the mass media. The overall point is that religious actors may use a variety of methods to achieve their objectives.

Religion and the State

Interactions between the State and the leading religious organization – if there is one – are usually referred to as 'Church–State' relations. It is necessary to point out, however, that one of the difficulties in seeking to prepare a survey of Church–State relations in the contemporary world is that the very concept of *Church* is a somewhat parochial Anglo-American standpoint with most relevance to the Christian tradition. It is derived primarily from the context of British establishmentarianism, that is, the maintenance of the principle of 'establishment' whereby one Church is legally recognized as the established Church. In other words, when we think of Church–State relations we tend to assume a single relationship between two clearly distinct, unitary and solidly but separately institutionalized entities. In this implicit model built into the conceptualization of the religio-political nexus there is *one* State and *one* Church; both entities' jurisdictional boundaries need to be carefully delineated. Both separation and pluralism must be safeguarded, because it is assumed the leading Church – like the State – will seek institutionalized dominance over rival organizations. For its part, the State is expected to respect individual rights even though it is assumed to be inherently disposed toward aggrandizement at the expense of citizens' personal liberty. In sum, the conventional concept of State–Church relations is rooted in prevailing Western conceptions of the power of the State of necessity being constrained by forces in society, including those of religion.

The traditional European-centred perspective is that both Church and State have a fair degree of power in relation to each other. Yet, when we look at the situation in, for example, Eastern Europe under communism, a different situation pertained. There the communist States presided over – and rigorously enforced – a monolithic unity with an institutional interpenetration of political–administrative and religio-ideological orders. Even in Western Europe it is possible to trace a declining position for the Church in most countries over time. In France, for example, when the dominant Catholic Church placed itself on the wrong side of the French Revolution it eventually lost a great deal of its power, privilege and moral authority. By the mid-twentieth century, the Church in France was greatly lacking in political clout (Martin 1978: 16). The point is that in much of contemporary Europe State prevails over Church, while the political saliency of Church–State issues has declined in importance as secularization has dug ever deeper into the social fabric.

Expanding the problem of Church–State relations to non-Christian contexts necessitates some preliminary conceptual clarifications – not least because the very idea of a prevailing State–Church dichotomy is culture-bound. *Church* is a Christian institution, while the modern understanding of *State* is deeply rooted in the post-Reformation European political experience. In their specific cultural setting and social significance, the tension and the debate over Church–State relationships are uniquely Western phenomena, present in the ambivalent dialectic of 'render therefore unto Caesar the things which be Caesar's and unto God the things which be God's (Matthew 22:21). Overloaded with Western cultural history, these two concepts cannot easily be translated into non-Christian terminologies. Some religions – for example, Hinduism – have no ecclesiastical structure at all. Consequently, there *cannot* be a clerical challenge to India's secular State comparable to that of Buddhist monks in South-east Asia or Shiite mullahs in Iran. However, political parties and movements energized by religious notions – especially Hinduism and Sikhism – are of great importance in contemporary India.

Regarding Third World regions, only in Latin America is it pertinent to speak of Church–State relations along the lines of the European model. This is so because of the historical regional dominance of the Roman Catholic Church and the creation of European-style states in the early nineteenth century. But the traditional Eurocentric Christian conceptual framework of Church–State relations appears alien within and with respect to nearly all African and Asian societies, whether predominantly Christian, Islamic, Buddhist or Hindu or involving religious mixes of various kinds.

The differences between Christian conceptions of State and Church and those of other world religions are well illustrated by reference to Islam. In the Muslim tradition, mosque is not Church. The closest Islamic approximation to 'State' – *dawla* – means, as a concept, either a ruler's dynasty or his administration (Vatikiotis 1987: 36). Only with the specific Durkheimian stipulation of *Church* as the generic concept for *moral community, priest* for the *custodians of the sacred law*, and *State* for *political community* can we comfortably use these concepts in Islamic and other non-Christian contexts. On the theological level, the command–obedience nexus that constitutes the Islamic definition of authority is not demarcated by conceptual categories of religion and politics. Life as a physical reality is an expression of divine will and authority (*qudrah'*). There is no validity in separating the matters of piety from those of the polity; both are divinely ordained. Yet, although both religious and political authorities are legitimated Islamically, they invariably constitute two independent social institutions. They do, however, regularly interact with each other (Dabashi 1987: 183).

While there is a variety of Church–State relations in the contemporary world, Table 1.1 indicates five common relationships. It does not aim to be exhaustive but to identify some of the more common arrangements.

Table 1.1 Policies of religion: A comparative model

Confessional	'Generally religious'	Established faith	Liberal secular	Marxist secular
		(often with highly secular societies)		
Iran	Indonesia	England	Netherlands	China
Saudi Arabia	USA	Denmark	Turkey	Albania (until 1991)
Afghanistan		Norway	India	USSR (until 1991)
Sudan			Ghana	North Korea

The *confessional* Church–State relationship has ecclesiastical authority pre-eminent over secular power. A dominant religion – Islam in the countries in the table – seeks to shape the world according to its leadership's interpretations of God's plan for humankind. However, confessional states are rare in the late twentieth century: one of the most consistent effects of secularization is to separate religious and secular power almost – but not quite – regardless of the religion or type of political system. However, as events in Saudi Arabia after the country's creation in 1932, in Iran since the 1979 Islamic revolution, and in Sudan and Afghanistan from the 1970s indicate, several Muslim countries are attempting to build confessional polities.

Second, there are the 'generally religious' states, like the USA and Indonesia. They are guided by religious beliefs in general where the concept of civil religion is important, but are not tied to any specific religious tradition. Both have a belief in God as one of the bases on which the nation should be built. In Indonesia, such a belief is one of the five pillars of the State ideology, *Pancasila*. This position is very similar to the notion of civil religion in the USA. However, whereas the generally religious policy of religion in Indonesia is an official policy, civil religion in the USA is not formally recognized.

Third, there are the Scandinavian countries and England, examples of countries that have an officially established faith but are also socially highly secular. The result is that, over time, the voices of the established Churches in public policy issues became increasing marginalized. However, in England at least, the Anglican Church has – quite recently – begun once again to add its voice to demands for greater social justice. Yet, just as the Danish Folk Church, the established Church in Denmark, was criticized by the Danish Government (Gustafsson 1989), when the Anglican Church in England began publicly to express its views on socio-political issues from the late 1970s it was strongly criticized by the Conservative Government of Margaret Thatcher.

Fourth, frequently encountered in the modern era, the *liberal secular* model encapsulates the notion of secular power holding sway over religion; there is distance, detachment and separation between Church and State (Weber 1978: 1159–60, Hallencreutz and Westerlund 1996: 2). The State strives to use religion for its own ends, to 'legitimate political rule and to sanctify economic oppression and the given system' of social stratification (Casanova 1994: 49). Secularization policies are widely pursued as a means of national integration in post-colonial multi-religious states, like India (Hallencreutz and Westerlund 1996: 3). No religion is given official predominance. In fact, in aggressively modernizing countries including India and post-Ottoman Turkey, modernization was expected to lead inevitably to a high degree of secularization; hence, their constitutions are neutral towards religion. Things turned out differently, however: democratization and secularization worked at cross-purposes. Increasing participation in the political arena drew in new social forces – in India, religious Hindus, Sikhs and Muslims – who, in demanding greater formal recognition of their religions by the State, were responsible for making religion the central issue in contemporary Indian politics. In Turkey, the accession to power of the Islamist Welfare Party (*Refah Partisi*) in 1996 – the party of the poor and the alienated – suggests that even when secularization is aggressively pursued over a long period – more than 70 years – there is no certainty that, for important constituencies, the socio-political appeal of religion will wither.

Finally, we come to the declining numbers of *Marxist secular* states. Before the overthrow of communism in 1989–90, Eastern Europe was filled with anti-religious polities: religion was stifled by the State or even, in Albania between 1947 and 1990, 'abolished'. Most Marxist regimes were less hardline than Enver Hoxha's Albania: religion was permitted to exist but only as the private concern of the individual, constituting a kind of promise that the authorities would respect the people's religious faith and practice as long as they did it behind closed doors as a solitary vice and not for public view. Skeletal religious organizations were allowed to exist, but only so the State could use them for their objectives of social control. They were reduced to liturgical institutions, with no other task than the holding of divine services. Numbers of permitted places of worship were greatly reduced.

Paradoxically, however, even the most strident and prolonged Marxist anti-religion campaigns failed to secularize societies. When measured by the high levels of religiosity and the pivotal role of the Christian Churches in the return to democracy in Eastern Europe in the 1980s or the contemporary revival of Islam in formerly communist Central Asia it is clear that popular religiosity retained immense social importance. Incidentally, we should not take it for granted that the Marxist, anti-religion State is a thing of only historical interest: in late 1996, China – home to a billion people – launched a fierce campaign to 'teach atheism to Tibetan Buddhists', necessary, the State argued, so that Tibetans could 'break free of the bewitchment of religion' (Gittings 1996).

The overall point of describing some of the extant State–Church relations is that none has been permanently able to resolve the tension between religion and the secular world. The chief manifestation of this tension in recent times is the desire of religious organizations not to allow the State to sideline them as – almost everywhere – secular administration bites ever deeper into social life. There are widespread attempts either to reverse or prevent religious privatization which are taking place in numerous countries, apparently irrespective of what form of relationship pertains between Church and State. But I need to justify such a sweeping remark. In the next section, I seek to explain why religion is seeking to deprivatize – that is, involving itself in political, social and moral contestation – even in countries hitherto believed to be irredeemably secular.

Explaining religious deprivatization

Once it was believed axiomatic that modernization would lead to religious privatization and, ineluctably, to secularization. In other words, it was believed *inevitable* that a *global* decline was occurring in religion's social and political importance. But the 1979 revolution in Iran burst onto the scene, suggesting not only that there was more than one interpretation of modernization but also that it could be that religion plays a leading role. Since then, religion in politics seems to be everywhere. Three questions are central in seeking to account for religion's current impact on politics. First, why should religious organizations become political actors? I contend that this normally occurs when religion feels under serious threat from secular policies. Second, how widespread is the phenomenon? My starting assumption is that it is widespread, although case-by-case study in the following chapters will verify or falsify this conjecture. Third, what are the political consequences of religion's intervention? The short answer is: they are variable. Sometimes religion appears to have a pivotal influence on political outcomes – for example, the role of the Catholic Church in the return to democracy in Latin America and Eastern Europe in the 1980s – while elsewhere – for example, in the attempts by Algerian Islamists to force the government to stand down despite a civil war costing a reported 60,000 lives – it seems unable to influence political outcomes definitively, at least in the short term.

For analytical reasons I will divide the world into two parts, the West and the Third World, with Eastern Europe – the former 'Second World' – treated as part of the former because of State-imposed secularization over decades during the communist era.

The West

Two phenomena are simultaneously taking place in the West: (a) there is an increase in various forms of spirituality and religiosity and (b) leading Churches are articulating viewpoints on political and social issues more readily and openly than in the past. I have already suggested that the latter phenomenon is because many Churches are no longer willing to be sidelined as states' jurisdictions expand into areas previously under their control. But are people becoming personally more religious while their societies are becoming collectively more secular? Three main arguments are offered in this regard: (a) religion takes the place of secular ideologies which no longer have wide appeal; (b) religion becomes popular on a cyclical basis, and (c) religion, expressed in new religious movements, emerges in response to the impact of modernity. Let us look at each argument.

First, people are believed to be turning to religion in the West in response to a decline in the attraction of secular ideologies, especially communism and socialism: people *need* something to believe in, and religion fits the bill, in the context of the 'New World Disorder' of the 1990s (Jowitt 1993). During this period of uncertainty, many people are thought to be rediscovering the religious dimension to group identity. Religiously pluralistic societies – especially the USA – have increased emphasis on religion as a basis of group identity which is, it is argued, politically destabilizing. The main problem with this explanation is that religion has not returned *only* in the 1990s. Rather, in some countries – the USA is the archetypal example – political religion has been a feature since the 1960s, with a decline of the influence of civil religion.

Second, we are said to be witnessing what is merely a cyclical phenomenon: periodically there is a collective 'thirst' for religion (Martin 1994). Shupe (1990: 20) argues that religion has been a significant factor in a number of political mass movements in the West since the 1960s, including 'the American civil rights movement, the Northern Ireland struggle of independence . . . and the Moral Majority in the United States'. The conclusion he draws is that this-worldly answers to the meaning and purpose of life periodically appear alienating and unsatisfying to many people: as a result, religious beliefs periodically find fresh relevance and power, perhaps within new structures and patterns of belief. Yet what needs to be explained is why religion should enjoy a periodic resurgence. What set of factors needs to be in operation to trigger this development? This is not satisfactorily answered by the proponents of the cyclical theory of religious resurgence.

Third, it is suggested that statistics indicate that people are becoming 'more' religious in the West, rather than less: secularization is being reversed. The argument hinges partly on surveys purportedly showing growing attendance at religious services and more religious book buying (Duke and Johnson 1989, Martin 1994). It is also dependent on the large numbers of new religious movements emerging, including the fast-growing 'charismatic' Christian phenomenon, unattached to any strong doctrinal tradition. Charismatics are Christians who believe in the 'power of present manifestations of the holy spirit but, unlike Pentecostalists, choose to remain in mainline congregations' (Coleman 1996: 30). Charismatic Christianity is a widespread non-denominational tendency based on a belief in the divinely in-spired gifts of speaking in tongues, healing, prophecy, and so on, offering devotees spiritual excitement. Charismatics are often thought to eschew politics, because, they believe, religion and politics should be kept separate.

There are many other new religious and spiritual phenomena in the West, includ-ing various manifestations of what is known as 'New Age' spirituality, various 'exotic' Eastern religions like the Hare Krishna cult, 'televangelism', renewed inter-est in astrology, and new sects like the Scientologists. Yet, such religious groups, Casanova (1994: 5) points out, are 'not particularly relevant for the social sciences or for the self-understanding of modernity', because they do not present 'major problems of interpretation . . . They fit within expectations and can be interpreted within the framework of established theories of secularization.' The point is that they are *normal* phenomena, examples of *private* religion which do not challenge – nor wish to – the dominant political and social structures. Such religious phenomenon are very often *apolitical*; 'all' they really show is that many people are interested in spiritual issues. Yet, in many Western Catholic countries – for example, Italy and Spain – the Church has lost much of its moral appeal for many people, especially the young (Hooper 1996a). In sum, it is correct to stress that the multi-plicity of extant religious phenomena belie any popular loss of interest in religious meaning – even in apparently highly secular countries – and that innovative religious forms are gaining ground, often at the expense of traditional religions. But from a *political* perspective new religions are not of importance.

To assess religion's socio-political role in the West it is necessary to separate two linked – yet analytically autonomous – phenomena, which are often unwarrantedly conflated. First, as already noted, there is said to be a widespread revival of religious belief in the West. Woollacott (1995) writes that 'anybody who had prophesied 30 years ago that the 20th century would end with a resurgence of religion, with great new cathedrals, mosques, and temples rising up, with the symbols and songs of faith everywhere apparent, would, in most circles, have been derided'. Second, many religious organizations in the West are involving themselves in political, social and moral questions to a considerable degree. These two developments may well be connected *but they are not the same thing*. Woollacott says nothing about the political impact of perceived religious resurgence, nor what has caused it. Given that one of the areas in the throes of an apparent religious revival – Eastern Europe – is a region where religion was, until recently, strongly controlled by the State, it is not that surprising that once restraints are withdrawn religion will assume a higher profile. But does this mean that religion then *necessarily* assumes a higher political profile, just because there are more openly religious people than before? My tentative answer is no. For example, the Russian Orthodox Church has failed to involve itself extensively in political controversies despite a popular shift to religion in the post-communist era. In other words, Russian society may now be highly religious at the level of individual belief, but this has not led to an institutionalized political role for the Orthodox Church, probably because the Church cannot easily shake off the behaviour of the last 80 years.

The point is that Russia was a highly secular society during the communist era. More generally, it has long been believed that as society modernizes it secularizes, that is, it becomes more complex with a division of labour emerging whereby institutions become more highly specialized and increasingly in need of their own technicians. When this happens, religious agencies – once concerned with a variety of activities including heath delivery, government and the interplay of gender relations – are forced, like the Russian Orthodox Church during communism, to withdraw to the core area of expertise: the spiritual realm. The end result of secularization is of course a secular society: that is, where the pursuit of politics takes place irrespective of predominant religious interests.

Secularization has been one of the main social and political trends in Western Europe since the Enlightenment (1720–80). In 1970, Smith, following such senior figures of nineteenth-century social science as Marx, Durkheim and Weber, declared secularization 'the most fundamental structural and ideological change in the process of political development' (Smith 1970: 6), a global trend, a universal facet of modernization. As Shupe (1990: 19) puts it, the 'demystification of religion inherent in the classic secularization paradigm posited a gradual, persistent, unbroken erosion of religious influence' as societies modernized.

The existence of a stubbornly significant role for religion in two Western environments – the USA and Northern Ireland – casts doubt on the secularization thesis. Additionally, while *most* Western countries are to a large degree secularized, in some of them Churches are involving themselves in political controversies in a manner unthinkable 20 or 30 years ago. The point is that 'when religion finds or retains work to do other than relating people to the supernatural' it is likely to have a public voice and a concern with socio-political issues (Bruce 1993: 51). I posit that *only* when religion does something other than intercede between the individual and God does it keep a high place in people's attentions and in their politics in otherwise highly secular societies.

Both Northern Ireland and the USA fit the bill in this regard. In the former, religion is an integral component of local communities' strategies of *cultural defence*. When 'culture, identity, and a sense of worth are challenged by a source promoting either an alien religion or rampant secularism and that source is negatively valued' then religion will serve as an important facet of group solidarity (Wallis and Bruce 1992: 17–18). In Northern Ireland, religion furnishes resources for asserting a group's claim to a sense of worth, where differing religious interpretations not only form the basis of group identity but also amount to an ideology of defence from encroachment from the feared 'other'. Both sets of believers – Catholics and Protestants – believe that the other lot is out to crush them and their religious (and ethnic) identity, hence, the retention of religion helps not only to bolster one's *personal* sense of identity but also helps to maintain a strong *collective* ethos against outside attack.

In the USA, religion has a continuing high social and political profile because it helps those engaged in the prolonged process of *cultural transition*. Cultural transition refers to the notion that when a religious group's identity is threatened by modernization it will turn to its theology to furnish the means to fight back, serving as an ideology of group solidarity (Wallis and Bruce 1992, Walker 1996, Abramsky 1996). Fundamentalist Christians – an important feature of the political scene in the USA for several decades – exhibit the desire to stop the encroachment of secularization, perceived as the work of the Devil. The overall point is that in both the USA and Northern Ireland religion furnishes the resources either for dealing with the effects of modernization and cultural transitions or for asserting a group's claim to a sense of worth during times of profound social change.

The Third World

Surveys indicate that most people in nearly all Third World countries are religious believers (Duke and Johnson 1989). Some argue that there is widespread growth of religious movements with political goals in the Third World which emerged in the 1980s (Thomas 1995, Casanova 1994). Many are grass roots movements led or coordinated by middle- or low-ranking religious professionals. Sometimes, as in Guatemala, the perceived secularization of the Catholic Church 'seems to bear a direct and inverse correlation to the strength of popular religious movements and organizations, especially in indigenous sectors' (Garrard-Burnett 1996: 98).

Why should there be an increase in numbers of Third World religious groups with political goals? Sahliyeh (1990: 15) maintains that social upheaval and economic dislocation connected to the processes of modernization have sent people *back* to religion in the Third World. Miles (1996: 525) argues that in the 1990s, a period of social, economic and political transition in many countries, 'populations throughout the developing world . . . are *rediscovering* the religious dimension to group identity and statist politics' (emphasis added). Sahliyeh and Miles are claiming that there has been a 'return' to religion in the Third World, the consequence of inconclusive or unsatisfactory modernization, disillusionment with secular nationalism, problems of State legitimacy, political oppression and incomplete national identity, widespread socio-economic grievances, and the perceived erosion of traditional morality and values. The simultaneity of these crises is said to provide a fertile milieu for the growth of political religion.

I do not doubt that such factors provide an enabling environment for religion's political prominence in the Third World. I am equally sure that unwelcome developments prod many people to look to religion to provide answers to existential angst. But religion has *always* fulfilled such a role; it is highly unlikely that there is 'more' religion now than in the past in the Third World. Why then do religious groups with political goals *seem* more common? It is possible that they are simply more visible due to the global communications revolution; there are not more of them, just that we can see them – and their consequences – more easily. Smith (1990: 34) claims that 'what has changed in the present situation . . . is mainly the growing awareness of' manifestations of political religion in the Third World 'by the Western world, and the perception that they might be related to our interests' (also see Huntington 1991, 1993).

It is important to understand that there are numerous historical examples of political religion in the Third World, especially during Western colonization and after it. In the colonial era, Western powers sought to introduce secularism, in many cases resulting in a religious backlash. 'Non-Western' religions, such as Hinduism, Buddhism and Islam had periods of intense political activity (Smith 1990: 34, Haynes 1993, 1995, 1996a). In the years immediately after World War I, religion was widely employed in the service of anti-colonial nationalism in Africa, Asia and the Middle East (Engels and Marks 1994, Furedi 1994, Haynes 1993, 1995, 1996a). After World War II, in 1947, Pakistan was founded as a Muslim State, religiously and culturally distinct from Hindu-dominated India, while Buddhism was of great political importance in Burma and Vietnam in the struggle for liberation from colonial rule. During the 1960s in Latin America, Christian democracy and liberation theology were of widespread political significance. In the 1970s and 1980s, political religion was of great importance in the varying contexts of Iran and Nicaragua. What this all points to is that political religion in the Third World has a long history of opposition to unacceptably secular regimes; it is not *ab initio* in the contemporary period, but rather should be seen as a series of historical responses to attempts by the State to reduce religion's political influence.

In the immediate aftermath of independence after World War II, Third World modernizing politicans, influenced by Western ideologies, often Western-educated, and impressed by Western countries' order and progress, filled the void left by colonial administrators. However, the secularization process promoted by nationalist leaders did not, for the most part, bring development. Instead, secularization resulted in the attempted transplantation of alien Western institutions, laws and procedures which aimed to erode, undermine and eventually displace traditional and holistic religio-political systems. The putative modernizers saw their countries as politically, socially and economically backward; what was needed was to emulate the secular model of progress pursued so successfully by Western countries. Consequently, political modernizers sought to enforce policies and programmes of modernization, which also, to them, meant secularization. However, within a few years, the credibility and legitimacy of 'secular socialism, secular capitalism, or a mixture of both' (Husain 1995: 161) was often seriously undermined, as they widely failed to deliver on promises of economic development and national integration.

Poorly implemented modernization programmes also proved incompatible with traditional religious practices, as growing numbers of people left the rural areas for urban locales because of land and employment shortages. While the social, political and economic impact of displacement and urban migration is extensive and complex, it seems highly likely that dislocations of large numbers of people from local communities, and the reforging of personal relations in urban areas, 'opened the way to renegotiation of allegiances to traditional institutions' (Garrard-Burnett 1996: 102). Where modernization was particularly aggressively pursued – in, for example, India, Thailand, Egypt, Algeria, Brazil – religious backlashes occurred, in protest at unpopular State policies.

In summary, post-colonial governments in the Third World often followed policies of nation-building and expansion of State power, equating secularization with modernization. However, by undermining traditional value systems, often allocating opportunities in highly unequal ways, modernization produced in many ordinary people a deep sense of alienation, stimulating a search for an identity that would give life some purpose and meaning. Many believed they might deal with the unwelcome effects of modernization if they presented their claims for more of the 'national cake' as part of a group. Often the sense of collectivity was rooted in the epitome of traditional community: religion. The result was a focus on religiosity, with far-reaching implications for social integration and political stability. This is not a 'return' to religion, but the utilization of religious belief to help pursue the pursuit of social, political and economic goals.

Clearly, for religion to be useful as a defence against secularization, it must be able to focus and coordinate popular dissatisfaction. There must be what Bellah (1965: 194) calls a 'creative tension between religious ideals and the world' where 'transcendent ideals, in tension with empirical reality, have a central place in the religious symbol system, while empirical reality itself is taken very seriously as at least potentially meaningful, valuable, and a valid sphere for religious action'. This is a way of saying that when the secular world seeks to impose on religion's space, at a certain somewhat variable stage it will fight back, aiming to reduce secular influence and to regain its autonomy.

Fighting back against encroaching secularization explains the strong profile of political religion in the Third World. For example, the radicalism of Catholic priests and liberation theology in Latin America, the growth of Islamism[7] in the Middle East and of Sikh separatism in India, are all explicable in this way. Smith (1990: 33) claims that overt links between such phenomena are 'weak or nonexistent. Liberation theologians and revolutionary ayatollahs may be aware of each other's existence but have not influenced each other very much.' What he means by this, I take it, is that empirical evidence of direct, personal relationships are absent. But this is not the point: virtually all post-colonial Third World countries share the historical desire of political elites to secularize, to modernize, to 'improve' their 'backward' societies. In my view, we do not need to look further for 'causes' of political religion in the Third World: it is a common response from those who value their religious milieu and who do not wish to see it undermined by the advance of secularized 'progress'. If people of different religious backgrounds employ broadly similar tactics it does not mean they have had to learn from each other, only that they collectively respond in similar ways.

Third World states seek to prevent, or at the least make it very difficult for, political religion to organize. In most Muslim countries, for example, Islamist parties are either proscribed or, at least, infiltrated by State security services. Algeria's Islamic Salvation Front (FIS), the Islamic Tendency Movement of Tunisia, *Hamas* and *Islamic Jihad* in Palestine, the Islamic Party of Kenya, and Tanzania's *Balukta* were all banned in the early 1990s. Others – including the Partai Persatuan Pembangunan of Indonesia, the Parti Islam Se Malaysia and Egypt's Muslim Brothers – are controlled or infiltrated by the State. On the rare occasions when Islamist parties *are* allowed openly to seek electoral support they are often successful. Examples include the FIS electoral victories in 1990–1 and that of Turkey's Welfare Party (*Refah Partisi*). The latter won the largest share of the vote (21 per cent) of any party in the 1995 election. Later, in 1996, *Refah* achieved power in coalition with a right-wing secular party, the True Path, before being ousted by the military in mid-1997. Parties like the FIS and *Refah* are electorally popular because they offer the disaffected, the alienated and the poverty-stricken a vehicle to pursue beneficial change.

On the other hand, in India, there is strong electoral support for Hindu nationalist parties – and not only from the poor and marginalized. Shiv Sena jointly rules Bombay and Maharashtra State with the Bharatiya Janata Party (BJP). Nationally, the BJP has emerged as the largest political party in India, eclipsing the country's traditionally dominant Congress (I) Party. In Buddhist Thailand, on the other hand, a Buddhist reformist party, Santi Asoke, had some electoral success in the early 1990s. The point is that parties like Shiv Sena, the BJP and Santi Asoke all have a wide appeal as viable alternatives to ruling parties often characterized as both

---

7. Often called erroneously 'Islamic fundamentalism', although the term is a tautology. *All* Muslims accept the fundamentals, the five pillars, of Islam: that there is but one God, and that the Prophet Muhammad was the last, and greatest, messenger; to pray five times a day; *zakat*, the contribution of 2.5 per cent of one's income to charitable institutions or the poor; fasting during the month of Ramadan; the *hajj*, the pilgrimage to Mecca; thus the use of the term to depict Islamist radicals makes no sense. In this book, I use the term 'Islamists' to refer to Muslims whose political agenda is chiefly moulded by religious, rather than secular, issues.

corrupt and inefficent. In sum, when Third World people lose faith in the trans-formatory abilities of secular politicians, religion often appears a viable alternative for the pursuit of beneficial change. It has widely re-emerged into the public arena as a mobilizing normative force.

Conclusion

My main argument is that the political impact of religion will fall into two main – not necessarily mutually exclusive – categories. First, if the mass of people are not especially religious, organized religion will often seek a public role as a result of the belief that society has taken a wrong turn and needs an injection of religious values to put it back on the straight and narrow. Religion will try to deprivatize itself, so that it has a voice in contemporary debates about social and political direction. The aim is to be a significant factor in political deliberations so that religion's voice is taken into account. Religious leaders seek support from ordinary people by addressing certain crucial issues, including not only the perceived decline in public and private morality but also the insecurities of life in an undependable market where 'greed and luck appear as effective as work and rational choice' (Comaroff 1994: 310). In sum, in the West religion's return to the public sphere is moulded by a range of factors, including the proportion of religious believers in society and the extent to which religious organizations perceive a decline in public standards of morality and compassion.

In Third World societies, on the other hand, most people are already religious believers. Following widespread disappointment at the outcomes of modernizing policies, however, religion often focuses and coordinates opposition, especially – but not exclusively – the poor and ethnic minorities. Attempts by political leaders to pursue modernization leads religious traditions to respond. What this amounts to is that in the Third World in particular religion is often well placed to benefit from any strong societal backlash against the perceived malign effects of modernization.

I commence the survey – looking from left to right, as it were, on a conventional map of the world – with the Americas, then move on to Europe, Africa, the Middle East and, finally, Asia. In the chapters that follow I will describe and account for the varying and various relationships between religion and politics in countries at diverse levels of economic development and differing political systems. The final chapter will summarize and discuss the conclusions that emerge.

Chapter 2

The United States of America: bucking the trend of Western secularization?

The language of the first amendment of the US constitution – 'Congress shall make no law respecting an establishment of religion or prohibiting the free exercise thereof' – seems to restrict politics and religion to separate realms, forever dividing them. Nonetheless, argument over the allowable limits of 'religious expression by public authority' continues to generate lively debate among Americans (Wald 1991: 238). Such controversy is not new: the US political system has long presented a fertile environment for the expression of religious differences in the public realm. The prospects for a religious presence in public life seem high owing to several factors: first, unlike people in virtually all other Western countries, a large minority of Americans – over 40 per cent – regularly attend religious services, attesting to the high popular regard with which religion is held; second, there is a strong tie between religious affiliation and ethnic identity; and, third, there is a remarkable diversity of religious opinion in the country. Because of these factors, religion is an important ingredient in defining the terms of political conflict in America.[1]

According to Wald (1991: 241), religion in America retains political significance 'through such diverse paths as the impact of sacred values on political perceptions, the growing interaction between complex religious organizations and State regulatory agencies, the role of congregational involvement in political mobilization and the functionality of Churches as a political resource for disadvantaged groups'. This is not to imply that things have remained static: America's progress towards modernity has greatly affected the pattern of people's religious commitment: it has encouraged tendencies towards both religious *differentiation* – that is, there are a great many extant religions *and* divisions within religions – and religious *voluntarism*, that is, people increasingly feel that their religious choices are less an ascriptive trait, conferred by birth, and more a matter of choice and discretionary involvement.

Given such circumstances it is not surprising that the role of religion in politics is a controversial issue, especially since the 1970s. Every four years, at the time of the US presidential elections, American and foreign journalists seem to rediscover religion, or more precisely they scent the electoral possibilities of what is often

---

1. For the objective of stylistic conciseness, 'America' refers in this chapter to the United States

called the New Christian Right, that is, the growing corpus of born-again, conservative Christian evangelicals.[2] Attention was initially focused on this group at the time of the election of the born-again Jimmy Carter in 1976. Since then, the public re-emergence of religion as a political actor in the United States raises three important questions, issues I shall examine in this chapter. The first question, 'why America and not elsewhere among Western industrial countries?', springs from the fact that only in the United States has there appeared three religious groupings of political importance in recent times: born-again, conservative, Christian – predominantly Protestant – evangelicals, Catholic leaders and, most recently, the radical Muslims of Louis Farrakhan's Nation of Islam.[3] Second, why at the current time? This question stems from the fact that for nearly half a century – from the 1930s to the 1970s – these groups were characterized by high levels of piety, yet they were effectively privatized and, often ignored, they lacked sustained political impact. This is not to deny that a number of religious groups had intermittent political impact from the 1950s: for example, the Nation of Islam achieved some visibility via Malcolm X in the late 1950s and early 1960s. Some Christian Churches played a significant part in the Civil Rights movements of the 1950s and the early 1960s. One of its leaders, Martin Luther King, assassinated in 1968, was a Baptist minister and figure-head of the Southern Christian Leadership Conference. Finally, various Christian leaders were prominent in the anti-Vietnam war peace protests.[4] The third question is: what are the likely political implications and consequences of the unexpected re-entry of these religious groups into American politics?

Civil religion and Church–State relations

Before I move to an analysis of the three religious groups' political impact, it is necessary both to examine the concept of *civil religion* and to describe the main features of Church–State relations.

Civil religion and politics

Until recently, because the language of civil religion is intended to be used by all in political society, religion was not associated with any single political position in America. Since the 1970s, however, the contribution of religion to political culture and the judicial sphere has undergone significant change; increasingly, certain religio-political groups have defined their *raison d'être* in primarily or exclusively

2. Being 'born again' refers to having received a new spiritual life, that is, being converted to evangelical Christianity.
3. I am not including America's five to seven million Jews in this survey although it is widely agreed that they have exercised considerable influence through the strength of their organizations and leadership, as well as a political focus that concentrates on protection of Israel vis-à-vis its enemies. There is much less of a discernible Jewish position in relation to American domestic political issues, the focus of this chapter; this is because America's Jews are firmly established in political circles in the country.
4. I am indebted to my colleague, Andrew Moran, for this information.

religious terms. Religious cleavages have not disappeared as America has modernized, as secularization theory predicted: rather, religious alignments have been
redefined and group differences have extended to new social and political issues.

The American State historically attempted to create civil religion as the cult of
the political community. The term was originally used by Jean-Jacques Rousseau
in *The Social Contract*, published in 1762. To Rousseau, civil religion referred to
the religious dimension of a polity; more recently, the term has become an important concept in the sociology of religion, largely through the work of Robert Bellah.
In an influential article published in 1967, 'Civil religion in America', Bellah
attempted to define the notion of a civic faith and assess its significance in the
history of post-colonial America. To Bellah, civil religion is the *generalized* religion of the 'American way of life', existing with its own integrity alongside the
more particularistic faiths of Judaism and the various Christian denominations. Civil
religion has been summarized as the 'complex of shared religio-political meanings
that articulate a sense of common national purpose and that rationalize the needs
and purposes of the broader community' (Robbins and Anthony 1982: 10). American civil religion postulates the idea that a democratic United States is the prime
agent of God in history, implying a collective faith that the American nation serves
a transcendent purpose in history. While the political and religious spheres are
differentiated structurally in America, civil religion nonetheless furnishes a symbolic way to unite the two.

In the 1960s, Bellah, like de Tocqueville (1969) two centuries earlier, saw civil
religion as essential to restrain the self-interested elements of American liberalism,
turning them toward public-spirited forms of citizenship that allowed republican
institutions to survive. He perceived civil religion as a fundamental requisite for
stable democracy, given the context of the United States' pluralistic and individualistic culture. Bellah believed it made a positive contribution to societal integration
by binding a fractious people around a common goal, imparting a sacred character
to civic obligation. Civil religion provided a public manifestation of religion, as
opposed to the more privatized orientations of particular faiths. Of specific interest
is the problem posed both by the increasing structural differentiation of private
from public sectors and by growing religious diversity which together make the
general acceptance of a shared conception of moral order and cosmos increasingly
unlikely. Bellah argued that civil religion in America is the medium through which
people perceive common values in a society built, on the one hand, on ideals of
mutual tolerance and unity and, on the other, on cultural and religious pluralism.
Ironically, just as Bellah was relaying his views vis-à-vis civil religion, he began
to realize that something was changing in this regard.

The title of his 1975 book, *The Broken Covenant*, reflected his belief that
social changes had both virtually destroyed public confidence in US intentions and
weakened the religious tradition that historically had sustained faith in the republic:
the social consensus that was central to civil religion had been shattered by a
number of national reverses and scandals, especially the Vietnam War and Watergate.
Societal unity had also been undermined by the growth of disputes over a large
number of moral and ethical issues, including decriminalization of 'soft' drugs,

State prohibitions on gender- and race-based discrimination, abortion rights, increased rates of cohabitation, permissiveness towards sexual expression in art and literature, reduced sanctions against homosexuality and the Supreme Court decision prohibiting prayers in school. These perceived shifts from traditional Judaeo-Christian morality suggested to many that civil religion was fatally undermined.

While it is possible that the civil religion proposition has been overstated, it nonetheless does point to an important moralistic strain in American public life that was seriously shaken by national political setbacks and scandals. While some argue that civil religion has now disappeared, others maintain that it is still a force with which to be reckoned. Wald (1991: 256) argues that 'if the core of the concept [is] the tendency to hold the nation accountable to divine standards, then the case can be made that US political culture has actually been revitalized by the rise of the "New Christian Right" (NCR)' which attacked liberalism as the engine of moral decay. The NCR's theme of repentance has sounded loud in recent political rhetoric; it is the voice of theologically conservative Christians who regard America's travails as punishment for alleged departure from traditional Judaeo-Christian morality.

Church–State relations

'American civil religion has a complex relationship with the polity – a relationship that reflects the history of the United States' (Coleman 1996: 27). For many observers of the United States, 'religion and politics' connotes interaction between the main institutional forms of Church and State. (In the current chapter – and in the book generally – the concept of 'religion' is broadened beyond 'the' Church to take in the numerous voluntary associations and informal networks of interaction that bind congregations of believers.) The separation of Church and State specified in the Constitution guarantees the freedom of religion. The USA is probably the most religious of countries in the Western world when measured in the proportion of adults regularly attending religious services. Yet, in contrast to European countries, such as Britain or Sweden, there are no established symbols of the polity, such as a monarchy or State Church; instead, the values and rituals of civil religion sought to provide diffuse, unofficial means of articulating national identity.

Religious pluralism and politics

In the late 1990s it seems to many observers that America is a country torn by economic, political and cultural insecurities. Angry white people blame African–Americans and immigrants for taking their jobs. Unemployed African–Americans look to blame the Hispanics. Forty million Americans have no health insurance, while blue-collar wages have fallen by nearly 20 per cent in real terms since the 1970s. Middle management is regularly 'downsized', while manufacturing jobs relocate to low-wage countries in Asia and Latin America. Meanwhile, the richest 2 per cent of the population control the majority of the wealth (Abramsky 1996: 18). A single company, communications giant AT &T shed 40,000 jobs in the mid-1990s, while its chief executive enjoyed a $5 million (£3.2 million) rise in the value of his share options. In short, the USA is racked by scapegoating and chronic insecurity in the 1990s.

What was once a left–right vertical split in American politics is now something different: a horizontal split between the elites and the educated and those who believe in the global economy, and those farther down the socio-economic pyramid who fear it. What has been the impact of such developments upon religion in politics? Once a speechwriter for the discredited president, Richard Nixon, the economic nationalist Pat Buchanan was able to gain some credible early victories in Republican caucuses and primaries in 1996. He managed this not only by stressing his strongly religious viewpoint but also his economic nationalism: he claimed that, if elected, he would pull America back from the North American Free Trade Association and the World Trade Organization (the replacement to the post-war GATT) in a manner reminiscent of the nineteenth-century populists who feared the economic power of the eastern establishment. Given the manifest insecurities affecting many millions of Americans, it is unsurprising that such populism is widely appealing. Buchanan's economic guru is Ludwig Erhard, the architect of Germany's post-war economic reconstruction, who devised the thesis that economics is not simply a series of equations but a philosophy which takes note of the human soul, an idea enshrined in Buchanan's 'conservatism of the heart'. In the 1996 presidential race Buchanan was able to attract – at least initially – many of the so-called 'Reagan Democrats', the disaffected blue-collar workers then fearing for their jobs in Bill Clinton's new world of fierce competition and local free trade. On the other hand, he ran best in 1996, as in 1992, in areas of the country where evangelicals were most numerous, notably the South.

Despite Buchanan's ephemeral electoral success, it is implausible to argue that perceptions of growing material insecurity have persuaded Americans to *return* to religion, because they have never left it. Rooted in a unique historical legacy, there is both religious pluralism and vibrancy in the United States. As Bruce (1992: 5) notes, this is contrary to what the secularization thesis proposes: religious pluralism is associated in the United States with increased – rather than diminished – religious adherence. To understand why this is the case, we need to bear in mind that, to a considerable degree, the nation was forged by religious dissenters from Europe. Such people understood that elimination of State-established Churches and a guarantee of religious freedom were the price of a reasonable degree of civil cordiality in a pluralistic society. Ironically, Churches thrived when cut loose from the paternalistic hand of government; evangelical activism became – and continues to be – a regular phenomenon of society, boosted by television evangelists. Statistics measuring religiosity confirm the deep-rootedness – the longevity – of religious adherence, not its revival. As Wald (1991: 244) notes, temporal comparisons underline continuity over time in this regard. Like their parents and grandparents, most Americans are decidedly Church-rooted and believing people: over 40 per cent attend a religious service in a given week,[5] 70 per cent are members of a Church and affirm the divinity of Jesus Christ, while over 90 per cent express a belief in God (Hertzke 1989: 298).

Over the last few years, pollsters and scholars have begun to focus on the politically salient religious cleavages in American society, in part because they seem to be changing fast. There is a traditional tripartite split among Christians. A 1978 poll indicated that Catholics comprised approximately 30 per cent of the population; 'mainline', that is, moderate or liberal, Protestant Churches – the Episcopalian (the US equivalent of the Church of England), the Lutheran and the Methodist – encompassed 35 per cent; while 22 per cent identified themselves as evangelical Christians. Jews amounted to 5–7 per cent, while Muslims, Hindus, and Sikhs numbered about 4 per cent each. Nine per cent regarded themselves as 'secularists' (Kepel 1994: 104).

The 1978 poll was conducted in the middle of a 25-year decline in membership of the mainline Protestant denominations – which eventually led to a loss of one-third of members – which did not level off until the late 1980s. Theologically conservative evangelical Churches, on the other hand, saw dramatic growth in the same period, reflecting a major restructuring of religious alignments. The evangelical Southern Baptist Convention, for example, is now by far the largest Protestant denomination. Other fast growing Churches include the Assemblies of God, Nazarenes, Seventh Day Adventists, and Mormons. The fastest-growing Church in the South is the New Covenant Fellowship, an evangelical interdenominational group. Sociologist Dean Kelley (1986: xxv) explains the trend towards such Churches in the following way: 'while the mainline Churches have tried to support the political and economic claims of [US] society's minorities and outcasts, it is the sectarian groups that have had most success in attracting new members from these very sectors of society'.

Michael Barone, editor of the *Almanac of American Politics*, identified four distinct and roughly equal religious groupings in the USA in the mid-1990s: (a) mainline Protestants; (b) evangelical Christians; (c) Catholics and (d) 'others' (Walker 1996). These data suggest that religious adherence has not remained static, that the proportion of mainline Protestants and Catholics has declined, and that both evangelical Christians and 'others' have grown swiftly.

What does this changing pattern of religious alignment mean for politics? First, it seems clear that the traditional, politically salient Protestant–Catholic divide that once defined society has been replaced by a split between, on the one hand, conservative evangelical Christians and, on the other, theological liberals (Hertzke 1989: 298). Until the 1940s, the politically salient division between early and later immigrants had principally hinged on the fact that the former were solidly Protestant and the latter firmly Catholic (Casanova 1994: 168). Yet division was not expressed in religious terms *per se*, rather it focused largely on questions about social welfare and labour policy: that is, the chief electoral issue was the clash between the 'haves' – mainline Protestants – and the 'have nots' – recent Catholic

---

5. This is about four times as many as in England or France.

immigrants. At this time, the Democratic Party bound together most Catholics, Jews and evangelical Protestants – white and black alike – because they were outsiders, prompting them to form a *de facto* coalition to contest the electoral ground with their rivals, 'mainline' Protestant Republicans. Until about 1960 this electoral equation held; after that date it was increasingly likely that Catholics, Protestants and, to a certain degree, African–Americans and Jews would enter politics under the banner of either party (Wald 1991: 265).

In 1992 mainline Protestants voted narrowly for the Democratic challenger Bill Clinton with 42 per cent, while 37 per cent went for the incumbent Republican president, George Bush. Twenty per cent voted for the 'third force' maverick, Ross Perot. This closely reflected the overall national vote. Born-again Christians are thought to have provided core support for Jimmy Carter's presidential campaign of 1976, Ronald Reagan's in 1980 and 1984, that of the 'televangelist' Baptist preacher, Pat Robertson in 1988, and the conservative Catholic Pat Buchanan's in 1992 and 1996. The psephological point is that even though the number of evangelical Christians continues to grow, they have not demonstrated a particularly high level of electoral solidarity. The consequence is that the right-wing Christian vote has been unable to determine the outcome of recent presidential elections in the 1990s. However, born-again Christians have been extremely effective at the local level, campaigning against, and removing, pro-abortion choice senators like George McGovern, Frank Church and Birch Bayh.[6]

Then there are the moderate Catholics, by no means monolithically anti-abortion. For 30 years, since the Second Vatican Council of Pope John XXIII in 1965, Catholics have been divided between the devout and regular worshippers who accept the teachings of the Church on birth control and abortion, and those whose Church attendance is casual and who live with little regard to papal encyclicals. In 1992 Catholics voted for Clinton over Bush by 44 to 36 per cent, slightly more pro-Clinton than the national average.

The final group are the 'others', a nonspecific category including Hindus, Jews, Muslims and secularists, who have always been the most loyal Democratic base. In 1992 they went for Clinton over Bush by a heavy margin of 63 to 26 per cent, with an additional 10 per cent voting for Perot (Walker 1996). Whereas the Jews have traditionally been of political importance, 'exercis[ing] impressive influence through robust organizations, eminent leadership, and focused political agendas', they have recently been out of the political spotlight; instead, Muslims, have 'emerged as a visible [political] force', the result both of immigration and conversions of inner city African–Americans (Hertzke 1989: 299). With an important political vehicle in the controversial Nation of Islam (discussed below), African–American Muslim converts have begun to exercise political clout in such strategic cities as Detroit, Washington and Chicago.

The second general point is that the traditional Protestant–Catholic division has been replaced by a fragmentation of religious–political alignments: new patterns of group affiliation focusing primarily on moral and social issues: including, *inter*

6. Once again, thanks to Andrew Moran for this information.

alia, recreational drug use, pornography, homosexuality, abortion and marital fidelity. The result is that there is 'a pronounced attitudinal gap between practising Christians and non-believers', revealing distinctive religious preferences which do not conform to the historical dimension previously defining religious conflict on public issues (Wald 1991: 265–6). To what extent has secularization altered political perspectives in America?

Secularization and politics in America

Secularization is often thought to be a natural tendency of industrializing societies.[7] The theory has most often been applied to societies in the process of transformation from an agricultural to an industrial base; yet there is no reason why it should not be applied to modern societies, like the USA. Can one find evidence that religion has ceased to inform the culture and the political order there? Certainly, the USA is a secular State: the government apparatus is formally independent of religion; Churches do not enjoy a favoured role in governance; the rights of citizenship are not reserved for the religious; law, not religious norms, regulate citizens' conduct. Yet secularization is not *only* about a formal divorce of Church and State; in a secular society, public attitudes to religion can range from indifference to outspoken hostility.

How should we regard the USA in this regard? Has religion been relegated to the periphery? The answer depends to a great extent how one chooses to judge the hold that religious sensibilities retain in modern societies. If the health of religion is measured by the breadth of commitment to religious institutions and the persistence of ritualized behaviour, then it appears that the US experience – judged by figures of religious adherence referred to above – falsifies modernization theory. However, it is now commonplace for observers to note the inadequacies of this rather naive form of the secularization hypothesis as applied to the USA. This is because, as Wald (1991: 244–5) notes, Americans continue in reporting 'strong loyalties to their faiths and experience religion as a significant force in their lives . . . Religious enthusiasm in the United States may ebb and flow but it has *not* followed the steady downward spiral predicted by the naive version of the modernization model.'

A more sophisticated version of the secularization hypothesis focuses on the *depth* and *quality* of commitment as the suitable index of religiosity in a society. From this perspective, the impact and extent of modernization and secularization in America is apparent in the degree to which religion has become 'a private matter for individuals, compartmentalized in the form of conscience, rather than as a vital

7. In a political sense, the USA should be regarded as a rather secularized society because, as we shall see, the Moral Majority effected little, whether the issues were open – and by no means exclusively religious – as in the case of abortion, or were narrower attempts to defend religion (as in the case of 'creation science'). The appearance and evidence suggest that the influence of religious leaders is far less than they themselves presume and hope it to be; nevertheless, very many Americans would classify themselves as religious believers.

force in public arenas' (Wald 1991: 243). The apparent institutional strength of religion – reflected in the numbers of self-proclaimed believers and their regular attendance at religious services – would seem to cast doubt on the idea of a weakened state of faith. Yet poll data, reported by Wald (1991: 245–6), 'suggests that formalized religion commitment vastly overstates religious consciousness in the American mind': many Americans – between one third and three quarters – feel that religion is losing influence in their society. Moreover, other studies also show signs of the substantial modification of religious belief, and the attenuation of supernaturalism in the contemporary USA (Wallis and Bruce 1992: 20). By these indicators – that is, in terms of the central role many Americans *wish* religion to play in their culture – the position of faith appears far more precarious than the naive secularization thesis would indicate.

The declining hold of religion upon the minds of many Americans – even those who regularly attend Church – suggests that voluntarism, that is, the principle that individuals should be free to choose their own denomination or to have none at all, has reached the point for many that the definition of proper or appropriate faith within a religious tradition is the prerogative of the individual believer and no one else. Because of this, 'America is the paradigm case of such attenuation of distinctive belief' (Wallis and Bruce 1992: 20). What this amounts to is that in some mainline denominations the supernatural has been virtually evacuated from religion; what remains for many who regularly attend liberal denominations, it is argued, is a practice that primarily serves social and psychological – rather than religious – functions. It is hard to imagine such an individualized perspective in an age when religion was inculcated, virtually taken in with the mother's milk, as a fundamental aspect of a near-tribal inheritance of what amounted to ethnic enclaves. Geographic mobility and social development undermined the erstwhile homogeneity of traditional urban villages populated by Irish, Jews, Italians, and so on. Individuals are now much freer than before to choose a new religious identity and to define a personal moral universe. The consequence is that religious traditions exert much less political relevance while the more immediate religious perspective – the product of personal values, the congregation and social networks within the religious community – count for more. However, it is important to note that these cleavages represent a change in the form of linkage between religion and politics rather than a desacralization of the mass political realm. In sum, both fragmentation and voluntarism shape the manner in which religion intersects mass political life in America.

To examine and shed light on this issue, next I focus upon the politics of three religious groups: the New Christian Right, Catholics, and the Nation of Islam. What they have in common is that each group pursues particularistic political goals with a religious dimension to them.

The New Christian Right

The New Christian Right (NCR), comprising several strands of conservative – predominantly Protestant – Christianity, can be divided into fundamentalist, evangelical and Pentecostalist strands. Christian fundamentalism in the USA – in common with 'fundamentalisms' in other religious traditions – involves a scripturalist form of religious piety affirming the central relevance of holy books for day-to-day activities and the regulation of all aspects of individual and social behaviour (Haddad 1985: 277). Caplan (1987) argues that such 'fundamentalism' is quintessentially modern, offering responses to contemporary conditions and events, including perceived threats from rival religions. In the United States, Christian fundamentalists are reacting not only against old enemies – evolutionary theory and communism – but also against unwelcome social changes as a result of modernization which threatens them and their ideas of morality. The very *pace* of change is important: traditional habits, beliefs, cultures and communities are under considerable pressure to adapt to a swiftly changing world. Casanova (1994: 151) explains that 'fallen nature, a covenant broken beyond repair, an American nation forsaken by God and turned into Babylon, a world beyond redemption in this dispensation until the Second Coming' are the very core of separatist fundamentalism. In sum, the external, taken-for-granted sinful world is changing beyond recognition; external forces are encroaching upon the separatist lifeworld, and they must be stopped.

Most evangelicals, on the other hand, believe in the inerrancy of the Bible but may interpret it slightly more flexibly. Neither they nor the Pentecostalists separate themselves from the rest of society like the fundamentalists. Pentecostalists share fundamentalist and evangelical attitudes to the Bible but also stress the possibility of gaining the gifts of the Spirit such as glossolalia or 'speaking in tongues', abnormal utterances under religious emotion.

Taken together, Christian conservatives strive to uphold what they perceive as desirable 'traditional values', regarding as anathema manifestations of unwelcome liberalism: legal abortion, the absence of prayers in State-run schools, and science teaching which adopts a rationalist, as opposed to a 'Creationist', perspective.[8] They are united theologically by a shared born-again experience. The NCR is dominated numerically by white Protestants: around 20–22 per cent of the adult population, 35–40 million people.[9] Hunter (1987: 362) notes there has been a remarkable upsurge in the disaffection and politicization of theologically conservative Protestants since the early 1970s; many seem to act on their beliefs – especially in relation to attempts to trying to prevent legal abortion – with growing militancy (Hertzke 1989: 299, Kepel 1994: 104, Vulliamy 1995).

Christian conservatives were regarded in the past as a 'swing' voting group, turning out against the liberal John Kennedy in 1960, but the decisive force in the 1976 election of Jimmy Carter. Strongly supportive of Ronald Reagan in 1980 and 1984, in 1992 they went heavily for Bush by a margin over Clinton of 55 per cent to 20 per cent. In the 1996 election, however, it appears that the born-again vote was split almost evenly between Bob Dole and Bill Clinton (Walker 1996).

8. A Creationist view of humankind's development insists that people were placed on the earth by God at a particular time in the historical past.

9. The US population in 1993 was 257.9 million people. Recent polls indicate that one in four born-again Christians are now African–Americans whose cultural conservatism often blends with liberalism on other matters.

Whatever their preferences when it comes to choosing presidents, what stands out is that for one important strand of the NCR in particular – the fundamentalists – it is the attempt to defend their culture from secular encroachment which is the key to understanding their political choices: it explains the shift from reactive defence to active offence in the early 1970s. From this time, Christian fundamentalism ceased to be a privatized, separate religious enclave, re-entering 'American public life as a public religion with claims upon the public sphere of civil society' (Casanova 1994: 156). Four main concerns underpin the fundamentalists' political campaigns: (a) as already noted, it is a defensive reaction to protect their interests and culture from undesirable outside influences, which developed into (b) an offensive to restore a theologically correct 'American way of life', exemplified by (c) a crusade to (re)impose biblical morality on the nation via (d) the programmes of the Republican Party.

In explaining the emergence and nature of the fundamentalists in particular and the NCR in general, two points should be stressed. First, the culture of the core constituency of the NCR – Sun Belt and other geographically peripheral conservative Christians – has been increasingly encroached upon since the end of World War II by a liberal centre identified with the East Coast, Ivy League universities and the eastern elite. 'The more socially peripheral and culturally distinct the region, the more likely religion is to provide a focus of resistance, particularly when language no longer provides a viable basis for the assertion of cultural defence' (Wallis and Bruce 1992: 17–18). Since the 1960s southern states have been under constant political, judicial and legislative pressure to promote racial integration and equality. As Casanova (1994: 148) argues, 'the greater attachment of southern and midwestern states to traditional Protestant religious forms has represented an element of a nativist defence of the culture of native-born Anglo-Saxon Protestants'. Influxes of Catholics and Jews, coupled with the attempts of a secularistic establishment to impose unwanted social and cultural patterns throughout the country, have served to provoke a cultural defence from Christian conservatives, especially in the republic's peripheries. This leads to a second, related area of concern: accompanying this process were the strongly expressed claims to rights by members of disadvantaged groups, including African–Americans, women, gays. These campaigns induced apoplexy among the fundamentalists: why should such people enjoy benefits – via taxation – at their expense? Because conservative Christians found intolerable the spread of the values of the permissive culture they fought back by creating their own organizational structures and communication networks and by linking up with the conservative secular right wing of the Republican Party. This was necessary because, being a minority in a culturally plural democracy, conservative Christians were forced to camouflage the openly religious elements of their political agenda in a 'secularized' form with the goal of becoming electorally popular.

Professional Republican Party activists perceived the Christian conservatives as a potentially important bloc in a new populist conservative grouping which would seek to mobilize voters not only around shared social and moral concerns but also in relation to a conservative secular agenda vis-à-vis the welfare state, the economy, business regulation, and foreign policy. In the 1970s, they managed to persuade a number of leading Christian conservatives – notably Jerry Falwell, leader of the Moral Majority – to become politically active. There was, however, a drawback to this entryism: 'The relative neutrality of the Republican Party on socio-moral issues and its unwillingness to become identified with a particular religious position is not an accident but a sensible response to the problems of maximizing voter support in a culturally plural society' (Bruce 1993: 61). The veracity of Bruce's point is illustrated by the highly disappointing – for them – performance of politicians associated with the NCR in recent presidential elections: both Pat Robertson in 1988 and 1992 and Pat Buchanan in 1992 and 1996 remained aggressively fundamentalist but failed, after an initially satisfactory beginning, to take off electorally.

Electoral failure in recent presidential elections might appear to suggest that the long-term political impact of the NCR is destined to be less than once expected. While some maintain the Christian conservatives are unlikely to have enduring political significance, others believe that they have – and will continue to enjoy – a profound, durable political influence. At the very least, the modernizing processes that were supposed to eliminate conservative Christianity have instead propelled it to new strength. Bearing in mind the huge amount of journalistic and social-scientific commentary it has stimulated, one could perhaps concur with Hadden's (1989: 238) assessment that Christian conservatism 'is destined to become the major social movement in America during the last quarter of the twentieth century'. Certainly, at the local level Christian conservatives have been effective, particularly regarding education and the teaching of Creationist theory.

It seems to me that the electoral potential of the NCR is overestimated. The main reason is that it has what seems to be an insurmountable problem: it represents only a small minority of the American people. If we accept that conservative Protestants are one-quarter of the US electorate, it indicates that three-quarters of voters are not. To have any national effect and to be able to claim national legitimacy, the NCR must work in alliance with conservative Catholics, Jews, conservative African–American Christians, Mormons and secular conservatives. Even though the NCR controlled the 1992 Republican Convention and forced George Bush to the right on many issues, his failure to win the election against a heart-on-the-sleeve liberal like Bill Clinton strongly suggests that the values of the Christian conservatives are not those of many Americans. The trick, then, would be to link up with right-wing populists, which Buchanan appeared to be doing early in the 1996 electoral race when he won Republican caucuses and primaries in New Hampshire, Louisiana and Alaska, but not, as it turned out, with any lasting success.

Buchanan's failure underlines how important it is for electoral success (a) to be ready to adjust strategically to the rules and dynamics of electoral politics, and (b) to make ideological compromises; the problem in relation to the latter, however, is that it would unacceptably dilute principles and identities, which would be unacceptable for many conservative Christians. As the emphatic victory for Pat Buchanan in Louisiana indicates[?] – he took an astonishing 62 per cent of the 30,000 votes – a well-organized militant minority may be able to exploit the element of surprise to score a few early victories. But this will eventually lead to counter-mobilization, especially when, like Buchanan, a candidate seeks to underline his credentials as the standard bearer of the Christian right wing. Buchanan's early successes suggested that in 1996 the battle lines were drawn up between, on the one hand, the born-again Christians and, on the other, the much larger numbers of socially liberal Christians and the 'others', non-believers, Jews, and so on. Democrats always get a large majority among the latter category. Republican victories thus depend on mobilizing conservatives, both Christian and other varieties. The more they get, the more likely they are to win, which explains why the activists of the Christian Coalition were so important to Dole in 1996.

The problem, however, is that to build a majority among voters in a plural society it will always be necessary to enter into electoral alliances; it will sooner or later become apparent that the goal of melding the religious vote with that of the secular will *only* be possible with the kind of normative compromises and parliamentary horse trading required for legislative success. Bob Dole was well aware of this: he very reluctantly agreed to drop his 'tolerance clause' – emphasizing there was a place in the Republican Party for those who supported abortion rights – from the Republican manifesto. This served to rally the 'born agains', but at the cost of mainstream support, especially among women. When he then tried to play down his links to the religious right the Christian Action Network (CAN) turned against him; he was saying so little about abortion and prayer in schools that the organization's activists said they would boycott the polls to protest (Walker 1996). In the end the Dole campaign fell between two stools: it failed either to win the lion's share of the born-again vote – polls a week before voting indicated that it was split more or less evenly between Dole and Clinton – *or* to attract sufficient numbers of the other three religious groupings: mainstream Protestants, Catholics and 'others'.

It is appropriate to conclude this section by emphasizing that, although politically interesting, the NCR has not been electorally successful. Its failure is predictable because its exclusively religion-centred electoral programme contrasted rather starkly with the ideals and values of a large section of America's modern democratic society. The chief political lesson of the failure of the NCR to make great political headway is that in a religiously pluralistic democracy, religious particularisms have to be confined to the private world of the family and the home; they *cannot* attain enough broad electoral support for victory by mobilizing the Christian battalions alone. As Bruce (1993: 65) puts it: 'The only religious values which can be allowed in the public square are the most general and benign banalities which everyone can endorse' even though 'the federal and decentralized nature of American public administration' offers subcultures an unusual degree of autonomy. This circumstance allowed the Christian conservatives an opportunity to initiate an attempt to turn America towards a Christiancentric worldview, but the attempt failed because the electoral cards are – and will remain – stacked against it.

The failure of the NCR underlines a second, wider electoral point: there are in fact fundamental dilemmas facing *any* religion – whether Christianity, Islam, Hinduism, Buddhism or Judaism – aiming to score political victories in the competitive electoral field in modern or modernizing democratic polities. When religious dogmatists seek electoral victories they have to validate their claims through public argument and debate. Claims that their policies and programmes will be best for the electorate will be 'exposed to open appraisal, to the typical plausibility tests' in the 'open pluralist market of ideas' (Casanova 1994: 166). Most of those who do not ascribe to an exclusivist religious world view will not be attracted by what they see, a conclusion that will be underlined when we look later at other religious parties in a variety of countries with varying degrees of modernity.

US Catholicism: from private to public denomination

When we turn to America's largest religious institution, the Catholic Church, we see a fundamentally different strategy to achieve distinct political goals. Whereas leaders of the mainly Protestant religious right entered the electoral arena, Catholic religious leaders have instead protested against certain specific federal policies and programmes: especially, the legal right of women to have abortions, the perceived lack of concern for social justice at home and abroad, and the nuclear arms race and deterrence. As far as the abortion issue is concerned, some Catholics have allied themselves with the NCR: consecutive presidential candidates have stated their opposition to abortion under any circumstances. Yet, apart from the abortion issue, much Catholic opinion is more liberal than that of the NCR. For example, in 1992 Catholics voted for Clinton over Bush by 44 to 36 per cent, slightly more pro-Clinton than the national average. Colombo (1984: 79) claims this is because, 'the social culture promoted by Catholicism is on a collision course with fundamentalism over the issues of charity and aid to the poor'.

Because mainline Protestant denominations now claim only a quarter of the population, barely on a par with their fast-growing evangelical competitors, Catholics, comprising about 28 per cent of Americans, hold the balance of power in a keen cultural and political struggle. Although once aliens in a Protestant land, the vast majority of Catholics now feel comfortable in American society. Catholics, once heavily Democratic, now vote in roughly equal proportions for them and the Republicans, although still with a slim Democratic majority. Political divisions between ordinary Catholics are reflected in their leaders' political pronouncements. On the one hand, bishops' pastoral letters on nuclear arms and the economy give ammunition to social gospel liberals, while, on the other, anti-abortion pronouncements and support for public accommodation of faith buoy cultural conservatives. The point is that the pluralism of American Catholicism shapes and constrains the Church's political influence.

American Catholicism has been shaped by consecutive waves of immigration – Irish, Italians, Central and Latin Americans – to become a multi-ethnic, territorially organized national Church. The Catholic Church underwent swift Americanization after World War I; within 50 years – that is, by the 1960s – the assimilation of American Catholics of Irish and Italian origin into the mainstream of US life was virtually complete. However, the American Catholic Church has had to live with two specific sources of tension, the result of being a member of the universal Roman Catholic Church, that is, it is *both* Roman and American. For this reason, it is caught between the traditional Church principle of prescribed membership and the voluntary denominational principle dominant in the American religious environment. The result is conflict between the traditional episcopal, clerical and authoritarian governance structures of the Church and the democratic, lay and participatory principles permeating America's polity (Casanova 1994: 176).

In terms of Church–State relations, American Catholicism has stood to the left and the right of government at different times. It has demanded more from a 'right wing' position than any administration in the 1980s or 1990s has been willing to offer – that is, a constitutional amendment equating abortion with murder – while, from the left, it has been open in its opposition both to US support for Latin American dictators and the nuclear arms race. The basic point, however, is that such stances on political and social issues indicate that the Church has moved away from its formerly privatistic orientation.

During the first half of the twentieth century, however, Catholic devotion became less communitarian and more privatistic, moving toward progressively higher levels of generality: from the village to the ethnic neighbourhood to American Catholic community to American national community to world community. Catholics learnt to compartmentalize rigidly two spheres of life, the religious and the secular. As Casanova (1994: 181) puts it: Catholicism became 'restricted to the religious sphere, while Americanism was restricted to the secular sphere'. In the 1950s, however, the anti-Communist crusade of the Cold War secured the end of the tension of being both Catholic and American. 'This was a crusade all freedom-loving people could join, those fighting for republican freedom and those fighting for the freedom of the Church. Rome and the republic could at last be allies' (Casanova 1994: 183). Yet, from the late 1960s, according to public opinion surveys, lay Catholics were consistently and increasingly more dovish than their religious leaders, Protestants and the general population vis-à-vis the Vietnam War; only in 1971, after most other religious leaders and most Americans had condemned the war, did the Catholic bishops argue that it was no longer a just war (Wald 1991: 264).

Liberalizing Catholic attitudes on a range of social issues stemmed to a large degree from the Second Vatican Council (Vatican II) of 1965. Vatican II led to a radical transformation of American Catholicism, a radical reform from *above* coming from *abroad*, moulded by the American political context. The consequence was that a new and activist intellectual stratum emerged within American Catholicism, manifested among bishops, priests, nuns and laity alike. It centred on greater concern for social justice, and in 'offer[ing] broader, more universalistic perspectives which challenged the nationalist particularism of the American civil religion' (Casanova 1994: 178).

Vatican II was the main doctrinal event of the twentieth century for the Church. It was there that the Pope and other senior Catholic figures rather belatedly expressed concern with human rights and democracy. Its main concern, however, was the issue of religious flexibility within the corpus of Catholic doctrine. The results of its deliberations included the idea that the Church should seek to reduce the uniformity of its spiritual guidance policy in order to allow for cultural distinctiveness outside of Europe where the majority of the Church's followers were found; second, it also underlined the Church's support for religious liberty, its opposition to racism and colonialism, and its commitment to social and economic development and peace.

Prior to this the Church was often characterized as an opponent of liberalism and democracy. In the 1920s and 1930s, for example, it dealt with the rise of fascism in Germany, Spain and Italy by giving it at least tacit support. After World War II the Church enjoyed a close relationship with Christian Democratic parties in Western Europe, as the latter sought to defeat socialism (and those generally advocating socially progressive measures) electorally. In the wake of Vatican II, however, it became clear that a new style of public Catholicism was emerging among many Catholics, both religious and lay alike: private faith could no longer leave secular public matters alone. Nor could spiritual truths any longer be immune to freedom of inquiry. As a result of these developments – which had no precedent in the history of American Catholicism – Catholics dared to challenge the status quo in public affairs.

Three discrete issues – abortion, nuclear weapons, and economic and social justice – exemplify the new type of public Catholicism. Having already referred to the Catholic institutional position on abortion, I shall restrict myself to a survey of the Catholic stance on nuclear weapons and the economy, turning to the bishops' politically assertive pastoral letters which appeared from the early 1980s. Here there is evidence of the Janus-face of the Church on political and social issues: letters on nuclear weapons and the economy and social justice give ammunition to social gospel liberals; those relating to abortion buoy the conservatives. Roman Catholic leaders have condemned liberal, pro-Choice politicians – such as Mario Cuomo in New York – as sinners damned to hell.

A June 1983 pastoral letter, *The Challenge of Peace: God's Promise and Our Response*, was the first systematic moral evaluation of nuclear warfare and nuclear military policies from the perspective of the Catholic moral tradition. It was specifically concerned with nuclear weapons, deterrence and the arms race and disarmament. It helped to initiate debate on the morality of nuclear arms by formally declaring the position of the Catholic Church in America. The bishops, who had previously been accused of being concerned only with one issue – abortion – put forward the controversial view that nuclear war could never be morally justified, a position wholly contradicting that of the government (Colombo 1984: 109).

Three years later, in 1986, another pastoral letter – *Economic Justice for All: Catholic Teaching and the US Economy* – was issued. Like the 1983 letter which followed in the tradition of the Church's concern for just war, the 1986 offering was the latest in a series of statements concerned with economic policy. What made *Economic Justice for All* unique was its 'detailed, systematic, and thorough application of Catholic social thought to a concrete, particular economy', that of America (Casanova 1994: 191). Two aspects of the letter are especially noteworthy: first, the claim that all governmental economic decisions should be judged not only in relation to 'instrumental rational criteria' but also according to whether it protects or undermines the dignity of the human person. Second, the bishops presented their letter as a contribution to a public debate over the nature of what they called 'a New American Experiment'. They perceived the economic challenges facing America in the late twentieth century as similar to the political challenges facing the nation's founding figures some 200 years earlier; at that time they had been compelled to develop political institutions *de novo*. To complete the 'unfinished business' of the American experiment, it would be necessary to expand economic participation and broaden economic power while making economic decisions for the common good. It is not important for our analysis whether the ideas of the bishops in relation to economic justice were taken up by the government (they were not); what is significant is that the contents of the letter were evidence of the willingness 'to extend public ethical discourse to the economic sphere' (Casanova 1994: 192).

The accounts of the politics of public Catholicism and of the NCR suggest that extant religious–political conflicts in US life do not neatly fall into denominational compartments; instead, they create what has been called 'unlikely alliances' between Christians of different denominations (Wuthnow 1988). Three conclusions emerge from the account of public Catholicism: first, because there is no longer a bloc Catholic vote in the US, dividing as it does relatively equally between Democratic and Republican candidates, the bishops do not represent any particular political constituency. Second, Catholic religious leaders, like their Protestant counterparts, are divided between *theologically* liberal and conservative positions; third, Catholic religious leaders are uniformly conservative on moral and sexual issues. For example, all eight US cardinals joined the National Conference of Catholic Bishops in condemning a presidential decision when Bill Clinton refused in April 1996 to ban a controversial late-term abortion procedure (Freedland 1996). On the other hand, Catholic religious leaders tend to be more socially progressive on issues of social justice, both domestically and internationally. Given that such positions tend to be universal among Catholic leaders – as we shall see when we examine the political position of the Church in Latin America and Eastern Europe – then it is entirely plausible that they derive principally from global Catholic positions, not from those of American electoral party preferences. Rather than being a question of support or not for one partisan political position or another, it is perhaps most appropriate to see the recent 'political' pastoral letters of the Catholic bishops in terms of the evolving position of the Church more widely: since Vatican II there has been a much greater willingness to make political statements than hitherto on a wide range of issues. This could be thought of as a global deprivatization of the Church, no longer to keep silent in the face of political, social and economic developments it abhors.

The most relevant aspect of the US bishops' pastoral letters and speeches is that the Catholic religious leaders have entered what Neuhaus (1984) calls the 'naked public square', probably not in order to establish their Church as the pre-eminent Church but to take part in public debate. By proposing their normative positions they contribute to rational public debate; there is no obvious reason why in America, notwithstanding the traditional fear of religious involvement in politics, religion should not contribute *as long as it plays by the rules of open public debate*, which the Catholic Church does. This is not to claim that Church leaders will necessarily have a great impact upon the debate; surveys indicate that Catholics in America resent being told what to do by their religious professionals and that the latter's powers of political mobilization are rather limited. For example, survey data released just before the November 1996 poll indicate that Catholics – notwithstanding their religious leaders' thundering denunciation of Clinton's abortion policy – were leaning to him rather than Dole by a margin of 10 points (Walker 1996). The implication of this is that the Catholic religious leaders have less power of political mobilization than might be expected.

The Nation of Islam

Islam is said to be the swiftest growing religion in the United States. It is 'expected to pass Judaism as the second largest' religious faith in the latter half of the 1990s. In the early 1990s there were between three and five million Muslims in the USA (Gardell 1996: 48, Nyang 1988: 520). Such growth is in large part due to conversions from other religions, especially Christianity. Most American Muslims maintain a low political profile, for example, very few openly express sympathies with Islamic radicals in Iran and elsewhere. However, outspoken exceptions do exist – mainly in the African–American community – where Islam has made significant inroads. The subject of this section of the chapter is the Nation of Islam (NOI), led by the controversial Louis Farrakhan. The NOI is like the NCR and Catholics in two important ways: (a) the NOI has become politically strident in recent years, following decades of non-involvement in politics, and (b) current political activism is primarily a reaction to governmental policies and programmes judged detrimental to members' interests.

The Nation of Islam was founded in Detroit in 1930 by W. D. Fard – also known as Farad Muhammad – an itinerant salesman and religious teacher. Fard, who seems to have regarded himself as God, met one Elijah Poole, a Southern man with a rural background, who he 'anointed' as his divine messenger, dubbing him Elijah Muhammad. Fard died in 1933, leaving his people in Elijah Muhammad's care. Under Muhammad's stewardship, the NOI prospered, forging its way as a variant under the general umbrella of Islam. Although the NOI's early efforts in the name of Islam were both denied and rejected by most mainstream Muslims, the organization was able to gain members both during the 1930s – a period of economic and social instability characterized by the Great Depression – and after World War II. During the 1950s and early 1960s it gained notoriety under the inspirational leadership of Malcolm X, an advocate of black separatism, black nationalism and black pride.

During the 1970s, the NOI went through a thorough-going theological transformation: under the leadership of Elijah Muhammad's son, Imam Warith Deen Muhammad, it moved swiftly towards mainstream Sunni Islam (Gardell 1996: 54), becoming the 'largest body of Sunni Muslims in the United States' (Nyang 1988: 526). Imam Muhammad strove to hasten the assimilation of the members of the NOI into the mainstream of American society, to realize, like all other American citizens, the fruits and benefits of the American Dream. Under his leadership, the NOI tried to achieve for its predominantly African–American constituency what many

Protestants, Catholics and Jewish Americans had achieved: prosperity and status. Assimilation into mainstream USA society was to be achieved through 'emphasis on self-pride and on the dignity of self-help and self-development within the framework of their community' (Nyang 1988: 526). By starting small businesses, NOI members were to become increasingly self-confident, propelling them towards greater involvement with the American Dream.

The assimilationist agenda of Imam Muhammad met opposition from a strand of opinion in the NOI. As a result, in 1977, Louis Farrakhan started a politically militant counter-movement from within the NOI, which developed into a separate group; I shall refer to it as the radical NOI. Unlike the mainstream of the NOI, Farrakhan's group does not believe in the American Dream. Farrakhan states that 'Elijah Muhammad never intended for us to follow completely what is called orthodox Islam' (Gardell 1996: 55). The theology of Farrakhan's group is rather different from mainstream Islam, with its roots more in the tradition of African–American religious nationalism. Nonetheless, during the 1990s Farrakhan developed working relations with radical Muslim organizations and states, including Libya. In effect, Farrakhan's faction has sought 'outward accommodation to Islamic orthopraxy while refining the reasons for rejecting Islamic orthodoxy' (Gardell 1996: 57).

Preaching a virulent mixture of anti-Semitism, anti-corruption, pro-community, self-help and African–American separatism, Farrakhan aims to focus alienated African–Americans' frustrations for political purposes. Estimates of the numbers of members of Farrakhan's radical NOI range between 10,000 and 30,000, with up to 500,000 additional 'sympathizers' (Fletcher 1994). Farrakhan's main idea is for African–Americans to work together in common pursuit of group self-interest and solidarity, but not to seek assimilation within the mainstream of American society. The Nation's ideologists 'focus on the prime symbols of American civil religion, which are given a revised and reversed meaning in order to expose the diabolical nature of American society' (Gardell 1996: 63). Like born-again Christian evangelicals, members of Farrakhan's faction of the NOI believe that America is on the road to self-destruction, a declining civilization where the social fabric is falling apart. Drugs, criminality, unemployment, poverty and pornography are all regarded as signs of the Final Days. While awaiting Armageddon, NOI radicals demand a separate black State 'in an area fertile and rich in minerals, as compensation for all the centuries of unpaid slave labour' (Gardell 1996: 63).

Besides stressing the desirability of autonomous development in separate enclaves, the radical NOI strives to promote the building of a separate African–American infrastructure. Until the 1970s, that is, during the regime of Elijah Muhammad, the Nation had prospered economically, establishing hundreds of business enterprises, becoming, according to one source, 'the most potent organized economic force in the black community' (Lincoln 1973: 97). In the late 1970s, the NOI's assets were estimated at $60–80 million (Mamiya 1982: 144). When Imam Muhammad took over the organization's leadership from his father, he dismantled the financial empire in order to facilitate the transition into the Muslim mainstream. The consequence of declining economic power is that Farrakhan must seek to rebuild the organization's financial base, to be accomplished through the People Organized and

Working for Economic Rebirth (POWER) programme. In pursuit of this goal, radical NOI has, since the mid-1980s, undertaken a variety of business enterprises including 'shampoo and skin care ranges, publishing firms, restaurants, hotels, agribusinesses, food importers and banking' (Gardell 1996: 64–5). In addition, it organizes its own welfare agencies (Smart 1989: 374).

Having sought to address the economic and welfare aspirations of the radical NOI members, Farrakhan's parallel objective is nothing less than fundamental reform of the social and political arrangements of society. His influence within some sections of the African–American community is especially high in several declining northern industrial cities, including Detroit and Chicago, the original support bases for Malcom X. Wider influence was demonstrated in October 1995 when he managed to mobilize around one million African–American men – women were not invited – to the 'Million Man March' through the city of Washington to protest at the lowly socio-economic position of many African–Americans. Yet, Farrakhan does not seem satisfied with making the radical Nation of Islam a socio-political force in the USA alone; he also appears to have international aspirations, aiming to build links between the NOI and black people elsewhere. The purpose of Farrakhan's January 1996 visit to South Africa was to present his message of black liberation from white domination to the volatile young men of the townships. In such places, despite the end of the white-minority dominated State, unemployment is at crisis levels and many young people are turning to Islam. Farrakhan's visit alarmed many South African whites: not least, because his deputy made a speech in early 1994 – which Farrakhan endorsed – calling for the slaughter of white people by blacks (McGreal 1996). Farrakhan is also strongly anti-Semitic.

Despite the militant, separatist rhetoric that characterizes the message of Farrakhan, the social values he and the NOI champion are actually rather similar to those of the born-again Christians. Both groups applaud such pillars of the nation as God and the nuclear family. Whereas the born-again Christians target the State for criticism because they believe it is presiding over a serious decline in moral and ethical standards, radical NOI has begun to take the law into its own hands. Believing that the State's law enforcement officers are unable to rid the streets of drug dealing and prostitution, the Nation's own 'soldiers' – 'the Fruit of Islam' – have intervened. Calling themselves 'Dopebusters', they operate in several rundown African–American neighbourhoods, including Washington DC, acting to 'clear the streets of dealers and prostitutes' (Gardell 1996: 65).

The programmes and policies of radical NOI suggest strongly that its leaders and followers believe that the State is quite unable to deal with the problems of the African–American community. Rejecting the privatization of Islam put forward by Imam Muhammad, Farrakhan's view is that the 'African–American has divine potential', *if* he is freed from 'the grip of the [white] devil'. Addressing the Congress in 1989, Farrakhan pleaded, 'Let our black brothers out of prison.' He argued that the NOI should replace the State's efforts in seeking to reform African–American criminals, alcoholics, drug addicts and prostitutes. The strategy is to take them and 'give them hope by making them do something for themselves' (Farrakhan quoted in Gardell 1996: 65). The NOI has also intervened in a second important issue of community concern for many African–Americans: gang warfare. Farrakhan also seems to have built a degree of support among African–American youth, exemplified by his ability to get two leading Los Angeles street gangs – the 'Bloods' and 'Crips' – to agree to a truce in their 'war' in mid-1992 (Gardell 1996: 66).

When it comes to institutional politics, the NOI has so far not been successful. Having endorsed the Christian minister Jesse Jackson's unsuccessful presidential campaign in 1984 – because he is an African–American nationalist concerned with the problems of the black community – Farrakhan became convinced that the next step was to run the Nation's own candidates for political office. As a result, two of Farrakhan's right-hand men ran for Congress in 1990. However, George X. Cure gained a mere 5 per cent of the votes in Washington DC, while Abdul Alim Muhammad managed a respectable 21 per cent of the ballot in the Fifth district of Maryland.

Conclusion

The radical NOI is an example of a religiously defined community which has become politically active in recent times. Like the NCR and Catholic religious leaders, the radical NOI deems it necessary to pursue its aspirations by involvement in secular politics. It is like the NCR in at least two respects: (a) it has put forward its candidates for political office, and (b) it has had less electoral impact than it would have liked. Although differing greatly in terms of their political aspirations, what these groups have in common is that they have deprivatized for broadly the same reasons: they believe successive governments are taking the country in an unacceptable anti-religious, anti-social and amoral direction. Both the NCR and the NOI believes that it is necessary to seek change through theologically appropriate progammes and policies. More generally, the combined political impact of the NCR, the NOI and Catholic bishops falsifies the secularization thesis: in contemporary America the drive towards modernity has not marginalized religion politically; rather, it has been stimulated to enter the public arena. Although the religious actors examined in this chapter have not been able to dominate the political agenda to the extent they would no doubt like, they are far from marginal figures.

At the start of the chapter I posed three questions: (a) why has religion been a fairly important relogous actor in America and not elsewhere among Western industrial countries? (b) why has this happened at the current time? (c) what are the likely political implications and consequences? We are now in a position to provide some answers. Taking the last question first, it seems from the evidence presented that the political implications so far have not been that great: the religious right is unable to enlist enough support from the secular right or from religious moderates because its putative policies are seen as too extreme; Catholic leaders offer advice vis-à-vis socio-political questions, but most Catholics ignore it; Farrakhan's radical NOI has achieved a level of support, predominantly among young, alienated Africans, but has been unable to build on it. I conclude from this that the political impact of the religious groups examined is quite significant but not important enough to warrant a wholesale reinterpretation of American politics.

Second, the main reason why religion is a political actor at the current time differs from actor to actor: for the NCR it is linked to perceptions of an increasingly meddling State; Catholic leaders' concerns stem both from the changing views of the Catholic Church – exemplified by Vatican II from the mid-1960s – and by the stubborn refusal of successive governments to act on abortion. For Farrakhan's NOI, the – so far minor – political role is linked both to the inability of many African–Americans to prosper as well as to the State's apparent uninterest in ameliorating the position.

Chapter 3

Latin America: Catholic hegemony under attack

The contemporary interaction of religion and politics in Latin America[1] reflects (a) the importance of various interpretations of Christianity as sources of legitimation and inspiration for political ideas, and (b) the development of competing political ideas, ideologies and political movements explicitly based on the Christian message. Three developments are of particular importance and form the subject matter of the chapter: the rise and decline of the progressive or popular Catholic Church in the 1960s; the withdrawal of national Catholic Churches from overt political involvement after the return to democracy in the 1980s; and the challenge to Catholicism's hegemony from the Protestant surge.

First, there was the emergence of socially progressive, politically involved Catholic Churches in the 1960s and 1970s. Encouraged by the Vatican's *aggiornamento*[2] (literally, 'updating'), there was a discernible 'shift to the left' in many of the region's national Catholic Churches.[3] Manifested in concern with human rights, education and empowerment of poor laypeople and the socially damaging consequences of economic policies, it posed a strong challenge to 'the traditional authoritarian conservatism that dominated the continent for so many centuries' (Sigmund 1993: 329).

Second, following the regional return to democracy in the 1980s there was another ideological shift, this time back to a more conservative outlook. Now there was political plurality was it still appropriate, Catholic figures asked, for the Churches to express strongly stated political views? Many senior figures, including the Pope, thought the answer should be 'no'. The net effect was that the Church

1. The term 'Latin America' was invented in the nineteenth century by French writers anxious to promote French influence in the Roman Catholic world. It now commonly refers to all of the Western hemisphere south of the Mexico–United States frontier, particularly to those countries where French, Spanish or Portuguese are widely spoken. Traditionally, the region has been Catholic, but recently there have been mass conversions to Protestantism.

2. For an account of the *aggiornamento* process, see Papousek (1993).

3. In most respects, the individual countries of Latin America are rather diverse, and this is no less true in terms of the socio-political orientations of the national Catholic Churches. This chapter seeks to identify trends over time, but makes no pretensions to follow the twists and turns of every one of the 23 national Catholic Churches.

withdrew from the public realm, at least in terms of overtly expressing political preferences and working for their attainment. But this was not only the result of soul-searching about whether it was correct for the institutional Church strongly to proclaim – and work towards – political goals. It was also connected to a quite separate issue: the swift regional growth of evangelical Protestantism which, in many countries, threatens to displace the Catholic Church from 500 years of hegemony.

This third issue, the growth of evangelical Protestantism, is seen in some quarters – not least in the Catholic Church – to be closely connected to American imperialistic interference in the region. However, the evidence suggests that the bulk of the region's fast-growing Protestant Churches – the great majority are evangelical, many are Pentecostal – are *indigenous*, responding to *local* people's spiritual and material needs. They are primarily the religious result of decades of profound socio-economic change to which the national Catholic Churches have often been rather slow to respond.

In Latin America, like elsewhere in the world, modernization has dislocated millions of people from ties to local communities, necessitating the reforging of personal relations, including religious ones, thus opening the way to renegotiation of allegiances to traditional institutions. Put another way, the strong growth of Protestantism is tied to the regional phenomena of urban migration and social dislocation. Politically, the Protestant Churches have a variety of stances: from a disinclination to participate in politics to strong involvement, sometimes to the extent of sponsoring candidates for political office. More generally, they seek to achieve parity with the Catholic Church, battling with it for space in civil religion.

Catholic Church–State relations

Until recently, the Catholic Church enjoyed hegemony in *all* countries of the region. Latin America emerged as a Catholic area following the European discovery of the Americas in the late fifteenth century. From this time, Church and State cooperated closely in the task of imperial conquest and administration (Medhurst 1991: 190). The Church looked to the State to create and then maintain a stable political framework so that evangelistic work could proceed with a minimum of opposition, counting on the State to uphold its doctrinal monopoly.

The historical maintenance of mutually supportive relationships between the Church and colonial administrations helps to explain why the former rarely threw institutional weight behind independence struggles in the early nineteenth century.[4] After independence was won, however, there emerged many of the usual kinds of conflicts relating to the role of hegemonic religious organizations in modernizing societies, for instance, the Church's 'economic status, its educational influence and its impact on law-making processes' (Medhurst 1991: 192). The general point is

4. Most of the 23 Latin American countries gained independence from colonial rule in the 15 years after 1811.

that, notwithstanding such squabbles, the Church robustly defended its institutional interests and integrity through collaboration with economic and political elites, nearly always the same people.

However, in most respects, the Latin American region is extremely diverse, and this is no less true in terms of Church–State relations. At one extreme there is Colombia, where a still extant Concordat, initially signed in 1887, guarantees the Catholic Church a privileged and legally established position. At the other is Mexico where the post-revolution Church was until 1991 politically marginalized. During the revolutionary period – the first decades of the twentieth century – the State sought to crush the Church's traditional power and wealth by nationalizing its property, banning religious processions and barring priests from voting, owning property or wearing clerical dress in public. Only in 1992, when President Carlos Salinas de Gortari re-established diplomatic relations with the Vatican, were restrictions on the Church and priests finally lifted. In the middle is Chile where, although the Church was officially disestablished in 1925, it has managed to retain considerable *de facto* political and social influence. Feeling relatively secure, it has lacked 'incentives radically to question inherited alliances, assumptions, structures and practices' (Medhurst 1991: 192). This was made clear during the Pinochet dictatorship (1973–90) when the Church showed itself to be 'politically conservative, corporatist, and hostile to liberal democracy' (Sigmund 1993: 330).

However, it would be inaccurate to suggest that the national Churches have always been unified in their responses to secular power initiatives. Like in most religious hierarchies, there have been divisions within them which became pronounced after World War II. The catalyst was not only theological but also economic and political: on the one hand, the post-1945 regional economic boom polarized the 'haves' and the 'have nots', while, on the other, the tenets of Christian democracy[5] were coming to the fore, suggesting alternative – and better – ways of ordering society. Some Church figures began to champion the concerns of the socially disadvantaged – becoming active in support of social movements and programmes designed to improve the lot of the poor – and urging Church hierarchies to abandon the historical ties to elites. In Chile, for example, the Christian Democratic Party led by a future national president, Eduardo Frei, featured many Catholic figures among its membership. The aim of the Party was social reform (Sigmund 1993: 330). Several senior leaders of Venezuela's COPEI (*Comité de Organización Política Electoral Independiente*, or the Social Christian Party) came from the Catholic student movement. COPEI was the principal opposition party to the ruling Accíon Democratica in 1946–8. Similar parties were to be found throughout the region in the late 1940s and 1950s. Although many were small, 'exercising influence mainly on intellectuals and students', some – especially those in El Salvador, Panama and Costa Rica – had significant electoral successes (Sigmund 1993: 331–2).

The overall point is that after World War II it became increasingly common for socially progressive Catholics to involve themselves in burgeoning Christian

---

5. The core of Christian democracy is the subordination of both State and market to a self-governing society through the cultivation of solidarity based on Christian principles.

Democratic parties and movements. Their emergence signified a decisive break with the old integralist hierarchical model that had predominated for centuries, providing a focus for social reform and democracy via programmes based on populist welfare-State liberalism. Especially after 1959 (the year of the Cuban Revolution), Christian Democratic programmes tried to project themselves as an achievable 'third position' (*tercerismo*) between the 'extremes' of liberal individualism and socialist collectivism. Frightened by the prospect of communist revolution in their backyard, Church hierarchies – particularly in Chile, Brazil and Venezuela – announced a corporate interest in social and agrarian reform in the early 1960s. No doubt they believed it imperative to win the hearts and minds of the marginalized – the peasantry, the slum dwellers, and the poor – to turn them from the path of revolutionary change *à la* Cuba (Gott 1973).

However, such expressed aspirations could do little to hide the growing polarization between advocates and opponents of social reform. Especially important among the latter were national armed forces which normally did not welcome a focus upon social injustice. Following growing political instability, a wave of military coup d'états – Brazil (1964), Argentina (1966 and 1976), Peru (1968),[6] Ecuador (1972), Uruguay (1973), Chile (1973) – ousted elected governments. Military-dominated 'bureaucratic–authoritarian regimes' replaced them (O'Donnell 1973).

The assumption of power by the military did nothing to end the polarization within the Churches between those welcoming the prospect of socio-political change and those that found it abhorrent. In Brazil, for example, the armed forces were seen by conservative Church leaders to be rescuing society from the disorder, political instability and economic mismanagement that they associated with pluralist politics. Perceived Marxist threats in Chile worked to the same end. In the early 1970s, most of the Church hierarchy initially maintained an officially neutral attitude to the elected left-wing government. But, when President Salvador Allende sought to wrest control of education from the Church, many believed it time to take the gloves off: Church–State relations became progressively more fraught. However, the Church in Chile also had an important left wing strand – focused in the 'Christians for Socialism' movement – that not only offered support to Allende, but also openly challenged the position of the ecclesiastical conservatives, normally their superiors. Following the 1973 coup, however, the left wing strand was marginalized, with the conservatives forging a close relationship with the Pinochet regime (Medhurst 1991: 204).

Military governments were not new to the region: historically, the armed forces have widely – if, for the most part, temporarily – intervened for the stated purpose of restoring political order. We must not forget that in Latin America, rebellion, revolutions and other kinds of political upheavals have been common for 200 years. This time, however, there was something new: the post-1960 wave of military takeovers led to permanent regimes, some for two decades. Claiming to be acting on behalf of the national interest, the stated aim was swift modernization: the development of stable political systems and the delivery of rapid economic progress.

6. The military takeover in Peru was the exception: a leftist coup d'état.

These were to be accomplished through a depoliticization of society in the name of 'economic efficiency, the nation and social order' (Carnoy 1984: 199).

These objectives were, however, sought with little apparent regard for the economic well-being of the poorest sectors of society, and in an atmosphere of severe repression (Boron 1995: 16–24). The mass of people was excluded from political decision: there were no democratically elected political institutions, while civil society was denied a voice. Political opponents, including many within the Church, were jailed, deported or killed, and human rights were widely abused. As a result, some leading Church figures openly opposed military rule, proclaiming their support for those most disadvantaged by postcoup governmental policies. This led, eventually, to the emergence of the popular Church.

The Medellín conference and the popular Church

Just as Christian Democracy became an important strand in Church thinking after World War II, so the Medellín (Colombia) bishops' conference of 1968 articulated a form of progressive Catholicism which, for a decade or more, became a highly important current of thought in the Latin American Church.[7] The term, 'progressive Catholicism', encompasses the notion of a 'preferential option for the poor', for solidarity and collective commitment, for a Church in which 'the people' of God hold power rather than the bishops, for a reading of the Bible through the eyes of the poor, and for the pursuit of the Kingdom of God on earth and in society, rather than in heaven and in individual isolation; in short, this amounted to a 'popular Church', where the hierarchy is only as important as the mass of ordinary members (Lehmann 1994). Around the time of Medellín, socially critical Church leaders were mounting protests against violations of human rights and socially damaging consequences of economic policies. Church bodies were also publishing reports detailing the errors and harm caused by government policies. Churches enunciated a strident advocacy of the cause of the poor and the marginalized, campaigning for political, economic and social change via pastoral letters, statements, critiques, position papers and concrete action strategies and programmes. In Chile, the Church took the lead in providing legal and other services for the victims of State oppression and in organizing relief for impoverished people. In Brazil, Church leaders went on the offensive in support of workers, peasants and Indians, groups whose welfare was being sacrificed in the interests of rapid capital accumulation and growth. The Church endorsed various agencies and commissions to support the rights of peasants (the Pastoral Land Commission) and Indians (Indigenous Missionary Council), as well as human rights more generally via the Peace and Justice Commission (Medhurst 1991: 205).

The Medellín conference served, as Casanova (1994: 119) notes, 'to legitimate and to give official impetus to a process which had already started from below but

7. On the emergence and development of the socially progressive Catholic Church, see Lernoux (1982), Mainwaring (1986) and Burdick (1993).

now assumed a dynamic of its own'. It also facilitated the emergence of a specifically *Latin American* Church, a continent-wide institution, albeit with a differentiated regional identity. The regional popular Church amounted to a transnational social movement made up of activists and collective actors with a common discourse and a collective project of historical transformation. The process whereby many official Church leaders moved to a socially progressive position was complex. Three sets of explanations have been advanced. The first see the changes in the Church's stance as the result of bottom-up pressure: Church innovations in the political sphere were sparked by activism at the grass roots stemming from popular dissatisfaction with the political, social and economic status quo. Liberation theologians,[8] such as Gutiérrez (1981), Boff[9] (1981), and Betto (1983), perceived the increase in Church-based activism in this way. Others, focusing upon the Church as 'institution', drew upon a Weberian conception of organizational structure, power and interest. In this view, the Church's political activism was the result of a dynamic agenda set primarily by institutional leaders in response not only to the prevailing socio-economic and political circumstances but also in an attempt to enhance their own institutional power (Bruneau 1974, 1982). A few 'synthetic' approaches attempted to improve upon these 'grass roots' and 'institutional' perspectives, pointing to a dynamic relationship between community-level demands and institutional interests in the Church in the late 1960s (Lima 1979, Mainwaring 1986).

Whatever is the 'correct' way to understand the shift in the Church's position, four factors seem important. First, it was – at least in part – a matter of reacting to pressure from below, from priests, members of religious orders and lay activists. Such people often found themselves caught up with the victims of social, economic and political crises. Many were radicalized by their experiences. Second, it was partly a consequence of conservative ecclesiastical leaders redefining their attitudes following the Second Vatican Council of 1965 (Vatican II) and partly a result of unfolding political events at home. State-sanctioned attacks on Church staff probably led leaders to sympathize with radical causes. Third, the State turn to authoritarianism gave radical figures, such as Helda Camara in Brazil, new credibility within the Church and helped to create a climate of opinion where figures like Camara could seize the initiative within Church decision-making bodies. Finally, the shift in Church thinking was also, in some measure, the product of encouragement or pressure from the international ecclesiastical community after Vatican II. International Church networks were a means of communicating fresh ideas and disseminating reinterpreted values. The Vatican was generally supportive of hierarchies engaged in conflict with repressive military regimes, except when Catholic figures appeared to be leaning towards communist ideals.

8. Central to the concept of liberation theology are dependence and underdevelopment, the use of a class struggle perspective to explain social conflict and justify political action, and the exercise of a political role to achieve religious as well as secular goals. For a discussion of liberation theology, see Haynes (1995).

9. Leonardo Boff resigned from the priesthood and the Franciscan order in July 1992 due to Vatican criticism of his allegedly 'Marxist' brand of liberation theology and because of disillusionment with the Church's new conservative ideological turn. He is now a professor at Rio and Harvard universities.

The emergence of the popular Church was, rather predictably, not welcomed by Church conservatives. In Colombia, several bishops vigorously attacked moves towards greater democratization within the Church, the concept of the popular Church, and radical base Christian communities (Levine 1990: 26). Conservative Church leaders in Nicaragua attacked Ernesto Cardenal (a prominent member of Nicaragua's Sandinista Government) for aligning himself with the secular left. In Brazil, Leonardo Boff, among others, faced up to the same charge from Catholic conservatives. Several prominent liberation theologians paid with their lives for their support for socially progressive causes: the Brazilian, Camilo Torres, was assassinated in 1965 while Archbishop Romero of El Salvador was gunned down in his own Church in 1980.

Base Christian communities

At the grass roots level the main result of Medellín was to give the Church's seal of approval to the burgeoning base Christian communities[10] (*comunidades eclesiales de base* or CEBs). The CEBs gave strong voice to those excluded from the political arena during the period of the military regimes, representing the most concrete sign of progressive Catholicism's socio-political significance. In many of the region's countries, they became an important force for institutional activism. During their heyday (from the late 1960s to the early 1980s), three to four million people were active in tens of thousands of CEBs; most were located in rural areas or on the outskirts of the region's larger towns and cities (Cleary 1985: 104).[11] Some directed themselves towards principally devotional ends (prayer, baptism, etc.); others had political goals: participatory democracy, workers' strikes, and organizing mass rallies; while still others sought better developmental outcomes: electricity, schools, health posts, clean water, roads and latrines for their local communities.

Many CEBs produced leaders for mass movements, such as trade unions and political parties, especially in Brazil. Such people often became important figures in the popular mobilization that ultimately undermined the credibility and viability of military dictatorships (Medhurst 1989: 25). On the other hand, socialist-oriented Nicaragua was also the home of numerous CEBs, with many wedded to a vision of a Christian-socialist future, while others were strongly opposed to the regime. The Sandinistas saw the CEBs as political allies and encouraged them (Serra 1985). In Chile, politically repressive and economically stringent measures had the effect of seriously disadvantaging the poor. This helped to radicalize the country's CEBs, which often became vehicles for objectives of wholesale socio-political change. Attacks against them first appeared in the government-controlled media in 1977, charging that their umbrella group, the *Vicaria de la Solidaridad* (Vicariate of Solidarity), not only harboured communist sympathizers but also received foreign money for political subversion. Many CEB members were harassed while

---

10. There is a huge literature on the CEBs. See the bibliography of Haynes (1993) for a selection.
11. If the figure of three to four million is correct this represents only a tiny fraction of adults in Latin America: between 1 and 2 per cent.

400 foreign priests – perceived as politically undesirable – were expelled between 1973 and 1979, precipitating a net decline of over 10 per cent in the total clergy (Smith 1982: 343). In conclusion, CEBs were an important focus of opposition to military regimes which did not, however, manage to sustain their political activism once democracy returned.

Ideological conflict in the Catholic Church in the 1980s

The post-Medellín period was notable for serious divisions within the national Churches. While of pivotal importance in the mobilization of opposition to military regimes, the political significance of progressive Catholicism was ultimately short-lived: it only thrived during military rule. Conceived after Vatican II, the popular Church prospered under the shadow of dictatorship, reaching a kind of maturity in 1979, when progressive priests found themselves in power in Nicaragua. During the 1980s, however, 'expansion and utopian hope[s] were replaced by retrenchment and, in many places, decline' (Della Cava 1989: 144). A combination of factors contributed, including the inner tensions of the liberationist model which divided the Church among itself, more conservative Vatican policy, redemocratization, and the growth of evangelical Protestantism. I examine these issues next.

Tensions in the Church

The return to institutional conservatism in the 1980s was in part a response to the success of liberation theology and the popular Church (Medhurst 1991: 209). Church conservatives argued that it should be less obviously committed to political argumentation because this deflected from the Church's main role of pastoral care. They also stressed the danger of Christianity being 'watered down' through the influence of Marxist ideas and of being betrayed as a result of involvement in revolutionary politics. The conservative point was that while the Church ought to urge the claims of social justice, these should be accomplished through its conventional preaching ministry rather than via political activism. Evangelism, rather than a direct challenge to existing socio-political structures, was, for the conservatives, first priority for the Church-as-institution, although it was accepted that some politically conscious Catholics in their *individual* capacity would wish to take part in politics and attack the status quo.

The Vatican's shift to a more conservative position

From 1978 – the onset of the papacy of Karol Wojtyla, John Paul II – conservatives received overt support from the Vatican. Some senior officials – such as Cardinal Joseph Ratzinger, Prefect of the Sacred Congregation for the Doctrine of the Faith – openly attacked liberation theology and the popular Church. John Paul II made clear his opposition to clerical involvement in revolutionary politics and made plain his support for traditional understandings of clerical authority. As noted above, he silenced influential liberation theologians, such as Leonardo Boff (Medhurst 1991: 210, Casanova 1994: 133).

Redemocratization and the Church

When Latin America redemocratized in the 1980s,[12] and electoral competition assumed a dynamic of its own, leaders of the national Catholic Churches began to distance themselves from the political process. While the Church encouraged political participation, urging people to vote and to help publicize different political opinions, 'there was certainly pressure on the Church from the Vatican to depoliticize, to leave politics to the politicians, and to concentrate on its pastoral duties' (Casanova 1994: 132). Vatican pressure – open support for moderate and conservative sectors of the hierarchy through episcopal nominations and appointments – was instrumental in helping to silence many progressive Church voices at this time. In short, the Church privatized itself, making the decision to leave politics to the politicians, to concentrate on pastoral concern for souls.

The phase of democratic consolidation in the late 1980s coincided with the withdrawal of most national Churches – that of Mexico was an exception – from political society, leaving this realm to professional politicians. This was not a uniquely Latin American phenomenon but also apparent in two other democratizing regions – Eastern Europe and sub-Saharan Africa – at this time. In both regions the Catholic Church was active in pressurizing incumbent regimes to democratize but faded from the political scene once democracy arrived; political society took over. This points to the fact that, because there is always an accompanying institutionalization of political society in a democratic environment, with its characteristic elitist structures of mediation and representation, religious organizations will be excluded – or choose to exclude themselves – from the new political order, irrespective of how active they have been during the struggle for democracy. Put another way, once democratic consolidation occurs, civil society, united in opposition to an authoritarian State, quickly loses its political importance. Even if the Church in Latin America had wanted to resist this structural trend – and it appears that under a variety of pressures it did not – it is very unlikely that it would have been able to continue with its formerly highly prominent political role once democracy was restored.

12. The return to democracy was the result of both domestic and international pressure. Military governments were unable for the most part to maintain satisfactory economic growth rates during a period of global recession. Markets for Latin American exports shrank while rising fuel costs cut deeply into profits, workers' wages and State tax revenues. By the early 1980s, most countries had built up a massive debt load, possessing few resources to help them repay creditors (Haynes 1996b: 79–87). The financial crisis, coupled with domestic and international pressure against human rights abuses, led to the delegitimization of most military regimes. Consequently, the militaries' authoritarian structures were scrapped and power handed back to elected civilians.

In sum, three sets of factors – intra-Church tensions, Vatican hostility to Church political involvement and the democratic consolidation – coalesced, leading to a common, if not quite uniform, withdrawal of the national Churches from political society. Is such a condition likely to be permanent? Having noted periodic Church political activism since at least the 1940s, privatization represents a strategic orientational shift conditioned by new sets of realities within both the institution and the wider religio-political domain. However, it seems unlikely that the Church will withdraw permanently to the privatized sphere of the spiritual care of souls. Why? Because the main factors that led to the emergence of the Christian democracy after World War II and the popular Church in the 1960s – a seriously declining economic position for many poor people – is still widely apparent. During the 1980s and early 1990s, Latin America experienced a negative per capita GNP growth rate of 0.1 per cent a year, while an estimated three-quarters of the region's population – some 300 million people – suffer from indications of malnutrition (Black 1993: 545). Under such circumstances, it is plausible that the Church may again venture to become the 'voice of the voiceless', the champion of the poor and marginalized who cannot normally find institutional representation in the national political societies.

However, there is a serious religious challenge to the Church which if sustained, as seems likely, will undermine the plausibility of any future claim to be the corporate voice of the marginalized or the conscience of society. Currently, there is a surge of conversions to evangelical Protestantism, especially strong among both rural and urban poor and the marginalized. The inroads evangelical Protestantism is making constitute an important part of the background against which Catholic debates are being conducted as the dynamics of religious competition impel the Church to concentrate on its pastoral role.

The evangelical Protestant challenge

Protestantism, especially evangelical[13] and Pentecostal varieties, has grown at a steady pace in Latin America for decades, becoming indigenized and self-reproducing to such an extent that nowadays it needs to rely less than Catholicism on religious personnel from abroad. New Pentecostal Churches are the fastest growing of the evangelical Protestant family, although several historic Churches – Baptists, Mormons, Methodists, and Jehovah's Witnesses – are also present. In the late 1960s, Protestants amounted to only 2 or 3 per cent of the population in many Latin American countries; growth since then has been swift. Many estimates now put them at 10– 15 per cent, some 50 million people (Freston 1996: 1, Berryman 1994: 7, Stoll 1990: 337–8). Because of this growth, Lernoux (1989) argues that Latin America is rapidly 'de-Catholicizing'. Every hour, she estimates, some 400 Latin Americans convert to Protestant Churches, that is, about 3.5 million people a year. Stoll (1990: 9, 337–8) claims that Protestant Churches are set to claim the majority of the

---

13. Derived from a Greek word meaning 'good news', evangelism is spreading the good news of salvation. In Latin America, this tends to mean Protestants.

population by 2010 in Brazil, El Salvador, Puerto Rico, Honduras and Guatemala and more than one-third of the people of Bolivia, Chile, Costa Rica and Haiti. What is happening, Lehmann (1994) maintains, is nothing less than a long, slow cultural revolution, a revolution from which Catholics – even progressive Catholics – are excluded because of the symbolic association of Catholicism, in all Latin American societies, with power.

However, there are wide variations between countries. Rocha (1991) estimates that nearly 30 per cent of Brazil's 160 million people belong to more than 4,000 extant Protestant Churches. In Chile, Protestants, mostly evangelicals, account for about 21 per cent of the population, while Peru is thought to have 5–7 per cent (Klaiber, 1992: 94, Stoll 1990: 333, 337). Crahan (1990) estimates that Honduras is approximately 8 per cent Protestant, while Guatemala is three or four times greater, around 25–35 per cent. Daudelin (1992) estimates that Nicaragua is 20 per cent Protestant and Stein (1992) contends that El Salvador has 15–20 per cent Protestant believers.

Evangelical Protestantism, especially Pentecostalism, is often perceived as a 'me religion' where politics and religion belong in distinct spheres, often emphasizing a materialist 'gospel of prosperity' where personal economic success is a sign of God's favour (Deiros 1992). By giving money to the Church *you* will become richer, while conversion will solve *your* problems, and those of *your* family. Obedience to Church authority is a condition of full membership. Salvation comes *exclusively* through faith, and good 'works' do not count for much; in this respect it is at the opposite extreme to progressive Catholicism. New Protestant Churches, especially those with roots in North America, are said to bring to Latin America a crusading anti-Communist, millennialist theology and philosophy. Some see the imperialistic hand of US foreign policy behind them: many Catholic officials regard the growth of Protestantism as a new form of Yankee imperialism, the most recent attempt to submerge Latin American culture beneath a layer of alien propaganda (D'Antonio 1990: 148–9). In Chile in the 1980s new Protestant Churches were known as 'Reagan cults' because they promoted right wing American values and interests. Serra (1985) reports that in Nicaragua such Churches were opponents of the Sandinistas' social change agenda; some clergy were reputedly involved with the Contras. Stein's (1992) research points to a general tendency towards the right wing among the new Protestant Churches in Central America. Stoll (1990: 19) suggests that such a pattern exists for Latin America as a whole.

However, such a one-dimensional picture is misleading. It is inadvisable to make sweeping generalizations about Latin American Protestants' political affiliations and choices as there is too much diversity and ambiguity among them (Boudewijinse *et al.* 1991, Freston 1996, Peterson 1996). Even Pentecostalism is not a unitary phenomenon: some Brazilian Pentecostals are left wing, while others are apolitical or politically conservative (Burdick 1994).

There is growing evidence that most evangelical Protestantism in Latin America is national in origin, that is, it is expanding from local, *not* foreign, roots, and is rapidly becoming a religion appealing to people from many walks of life. Millions of Latin Americans are joining the Protestant Churches, not necessarily as a result of persuasion by American preachers, but because they offer a *better* religious experience than the Catholic Church can offer: Protestant worship is a way of getting close to God, unmediated by a hierarchy of religious officials. In short, the growth of Protestant Churches in the region is much more to do with local than foreign factors. While some Protestant Church leaders may well acquire some social cachet from their association with the USA, this does not in itself explain why so many Latin Americans convert. What's in it for them?

In the late 1960s, most analyses of Protestantism in Latin America focused on its role in relation to the social consequences of modernization (Roberts 1968, Willems 1967, Lalive d'Epinay 1969). Heavily influenced by Weber, it was predicted that the construction of Protestantism in Latin America would be identical to that of Europe: that is, it would be symbiotically fused to modernization in general and to the progressive development of capitalism and social secularization. By the late 1970s, however, the expansion of Protestantism was being perceived differently: it was now a consequence of *failed* modernization. With Latin American economies faltering, its expansion was understood to be tied to the declining position of the poor and marginalized who turned to Protestantism as a consequence of anomie and marginalization. However, by the late 1980s, a third interpretation was emerging: Protestantism was booming, it was said, but not only among the poor and marginalized; in some countries it was also the upwardly mobile middle classes changing religious allegiance (Boudewijnse *et al.* 1991, Aguilar *et al.* 1993, Bastian 1993). Three separate strands – spiritual, social and political – are believed to be important in explaining contemporary conversions across a range of social classes.

Spiritually, it seems beyond dispute that evangelical Protestantism holds considerable appeal for many Latin Americans, especially – but by no means exclusively – the poor and marginalized. Many converts live in countries not only racked in recent times by civil war and commotion but also strongly stratified along racial lines. For many, Protestantism may well provide a safe spiritual haven away from traumatic reality.

Socially, the appeal of Protestantism is thought to be heightened by the failure of modernization. The context is the pace and direction of change, especially since World War II: traditional habits, beliefs, cultures and communities have been under considerable pressure to adapt to multifaceted processes of change. Since the late 1940s, tens of millions of people have left their rural homes to seek a better life in the urban areas. Once, 'economies of affection' were of considerable importance to such people, yet when they flocked to the cities they found traditional support networks sundered. Uprooted from families, moral codes and religio-cultural norms, living in slums and at the mercy of criminals, the newly arrived urban poor were a fertile seed bed for Protestant proselytization. It is argued that in Central America, a region racked by civil war, Protestantism, especially Pentecostalism, is a kind of 'therapy' – a response to multiple crises.[14] Pro Mundi Vita, a Belgian Catholic research body, notes that 'many peasants and slum inhabitants need religion as a

---

14. On the other hand, Protestant growth has also been swift in Costa Rica, one of the most stable countries in Central America. This underlines the impossibility of pinpointing any single cause in such a diverse region.

refuge in a society in permanent and progressive disintegration in order to deal with fear, threats, repression, hunger and death'. Too often, the agency claims, the Catholic Church is unable to respond because it lacks sufficient religious professionals, money and imagination (quoted in Lernoux 1989: 52). The Vatican came to a similar conclusion in a report entitled, 'Sects or new religious movements: pastoral challenges', published in 1986. While arguing that the new Protestant Churches were created and sustained by powerful American ideological, economic and political interests, it acknowledged that they were fulfilling 'needs and aspirations which are seemingly not being met in the mainline Churches. The Church is often seen simply as an institution, perhaps because it gives too much importance to structures and not enough to drawing people to God in Christ' (Lernoux 1989: 52). The Vatican's conclusion hints that it is not only the poor and marginalized who look to the new Churches, but also those who want a bit of religious excitement and spiritual – and social – independence from the 'dead hand' of Catholicism.

It is, however, the poor and marginalized who seem most attracted to Protestantism. Four groups stand out: the urban poor, especially women; people of African descent; Indians; and *mestizos* (persons of mixed race). Protestantism is a vehicle for helping such people to deal with the highly destabilizing impact of modernization, industrialization and urbanization. It is particularly attractive to the alienated and marginalized because it is a significant source of social change, helping to build religious communities of 'discontinuity and transformation' (Burdick 1993). Protestantism confronts a number of social issues and crises, including *machismo* and the role of women in society, where traditional notions of male domination seem to be undermined by Protestant ideas stressing the equality of believers, whatever their gender. It also offers an alternative to the endemic drug cultures in the shanty towns of Latin America (Freston 1996: 3). The general point is that, rather than reflecting a Christian self-abnegation and denial of the world, Protestant spirituality helps many in the increasingly cut-throat and competitive market economy of the modern city; it is a means to help fulfil individual potential.

It is also reported that Protestants often manage to escape a traditional Latin American tradition: the universe of clientelist relations governing millions of peoples' lives. Protestants strive to form 'clean' communities of believers tied together in a nexus of spiritual, moral and ethical beliefs. Conversion helps people hitherto regarded as 'no hopers' to metamorphosize into respected members of the community by their own efforts with the support of their religious fellows. 'Once a man surrenders his life to Jesus,' proclaims the Argentinian Protestant evangelist preacher Luis Palau, 'he finds he can stop drinking [alcohol] and chasing women' (Lernoux 1989: 51). Protestant Churches may evolve into a kind of counter-society, governed by rigid conceptions of morality, where telling lies, cheating, stealing, bribing (or being bribed), adultery and fornication are frowned upon. In short, many converts seem to develop strongly moralistic world views reflecting a belief that the well-being of society is dependent upon good standards of personal morality (Shepard 1987: 364).

Burdick (1993) reports that in Brazil, Pentecostals in particular recruit well among the poorest people and those of African descent, especially among women. The latter claim they are empowered by membership in their Church, finding space to express themselves emotionally, while gaining company and security which offers them both material and spiritual support. In other words, Protestant converts appear to find spiritual comfort in the immediacy, closeness and concern of the services in their Churches. Yet women largely remain absent from positions of leadership in the Pentecostalist Churches in Brazil. While socially progressive Catholics take up militant positions in the name of poor women and of the black population in Brazil, Pentecostals are often silent on such matters. In sum, Pentecostalism helps poor Latin Americans of both sexes to cope with the hardships of poverty; it helps them to *survive* it, useful when nothing available helps them *actually to escape it*. For those facing personal and financial crises, it encourages behaviour and creates networks that stabilize individuals in extreme situations.

Many among the poor and marginalized turn to Protestantism to help them cope with the hardships of poverty. It will be recalled that it was the (Catholic) CEBs that were long thought to offer such people a natural home. Yet the influence and popularity of the CEBs has waned in recent times. Burdick (1994) suggests a plausible reason for this: they are often dominated by the relatively powerful. His survey of CEBs in Rio de Janeiro in the early 1990s found they predominantly helped *not* the poorest of the poor but the 'working poor' and the slightly better off, that is, those with some degree of stability, who were interested in medium-term changes that would materially improve their neighbourhoods. Living for two years in a working-class suburb of Rio de Janeiro, he found local CEBs to be dominated by white, middle-class men, closely controlled by the local priest and rather unsympathetic to the emotional and social problems of the very people – the poor and women – they were supposed to mobilize. Local Pentecostal Churches, he discovered, provided what he calls 'a cult of affliction', that is, solace to help deal with spiritual and existential dilemmas.

In summary, as far as it is possible to generalize among such diversity, it seems that Protestant Churches in Latin America offer uprooted people new religious communities to help them cope. Millions of Latin Americans have joined Protestant Churches since the late 1960s because of the spiritual experience and sense of community they offer, the intensity of the prayer experience, the attraction of a simple and comprehensible message that seems to make sense of the chaos which many perceive all around them, a moral code that offers guidance and the resuscitation of community values, and, finally, the provision of a sense of group solidarity.

Becoming an evagelical Protestant (*evangélico*) offers poor Latin Americans a chance to gain enhanced self-esteem and perhaps social status through a concern with individual and collective morality rather than politics *per se*. Their main concerns are probably not political in a conventional, institutional interpretation of the term, but they do touch upon political concerns in a wider sense. An interest in community development and well-being eventually shades into overtly political concerns, such as the nature of the government, the health of the economy, the best form of State, and so on. For this general reason, many Protestants, like their Catholic counterparts, engage in politics as a way of delivering a better community, especially in urban surroundings of shortages and the breakdown of public services.

Protestants and politics

Some accounts suggest that members of the new Protestant Churches tend to be politically conservative, and that they tend to submit willingly to those in authority (Stoll 1990, Moran and Schlemmer 1984, Roberts 1968). They are said, in addition, to assimilate easily to the norms of consumer capitalism, helping to defuse putative attacks on the social order (Martin 1990: 160). However, it is not clear whether members of Protestant Churches are actually more politically conservative than others. Evangelical Protestantism may actually incorporate a critique of powerful elites, as in Brazil. There is no concrete evidence to suggest that they are less likely to vote; that they will vote more to the right than to the left; or that their members are indifferent to political or union activism. Rather the contrary: once they are committed, Burdick (1993) claims, they are loyal and reliable in the business to which they have put their hand.

Two factors seem to be of particular importance in the growth of Protestantism: self-interested conversions, already discussed, and governmental encouragement. New Protestant Churches are sometimes overtly encouraged by political leaders determined to break the influence of the Catholic Church. As with an earlier spurt of Protestant conversions and Church expansion in the the late nineteenth century, some contemporary regimes encourage Protestantism. In Guatemala, for example, President (General) Ríos Montt persecuted the Catholic Church in the early 1990s but promoted Protestant rivals (Garrard-Burnett 1996). Like Ríos Montt, his successor, Jorge Serrano, was also an *evangélico*, and continued the policy. The same pattern was also apparent in Peru where evangelical Protestants played an important role in the election of President Alberto Fujimori in 1990 (Reid 1990, Freston 1996: 2). Fujimori, like his Guatemalan counterparts, was also keen to reduce the influence of the Catholic Church (Rostas and Droogers 1993).

When it comes to the politics of the Protestants, as Crahan (1990: 2) notes, 'the role of Churches and Church people . . . today is highly complex, and does not lend itself to easy categorization'. While Guatemala is often regarded as a hotbed of right-wing Protestantism, in fact the social involvement of some Churches is not welcomed by the secular right or some sections of the military (Garrard-Burnett 1996: 96). Serra (1985) points to political divisions within Protestant groups in Nicaragua, as does Klaiber (1992: 94) in Peru, where some have moved toward social action. In Brazil, there is an active and growing evangelical left wing whose champion is Benedita da Silva, the first black woman senator ever in the country, elected in 1994. Da Silva is both a member of the Assemblies of God Church and the radical Workers Party. Freston (1996: 5) calculates that approximately one-fifth of her two million votes came from Protestants. Regarding Chile, it would be wrong to assume that Protestants there are clearly and uniformly conservative. Many were reported to take exception to statements made by the American televangelist Jimmy Swaggart during his visit to Santiago in 1987. Swaggart effusively praised the right wing military regime of General Augustus Pinochet (1973–90), congratulating him on having expelled the 'devil' – meaning the political left – following his coup d'état (Haynes 1993: 120). In sum, there is lack of political uniformity among the

Protestant Churches in Latin America; it is simplistic to see them as necessarily on the political right. The fact that there are two distinct Protestant Church conferences, one for the socially involved Churches, the Latin American Council of Churches, the other for conservatives, the Latin American Confraternity, implies that the Protestant universe is politically and socially fragmented (O'Shaughnessy, 1990: 99).

To illustrate the political diversity of Protestantism in Latin America, I will briefly examine the situation in Brazil, Peru and Guatemala. In each country, Protestants played a significant role in electing presidents: Collor (Brazil), Fujimori (Peru) and Serrano (Guatemala) in the late 1980s and early 1990s. Only Serrano was actually an evangelical. Once elected, however, both Collor and Fujimori ignored the *evangélicos*. None of the trio was an exemplar of democratic government: Collor was impeached for corruption; Fujimori made an 'auto-coup' with the help of the military; and Serrano, attempting the same, was deposed.

Peru

In Peru – and in the Andes and in Central America more generally – the extraordinary growth of indigenous Protestantism is a key factor in politics. With their presence in areas where the State, political parties and Catholic priests are often conspicuous by their absence, the Protestant Churches provide an alternative route to mass politics. The Protestant world is relatively united in a National Evangelical Council (CONEP). Protestants make up 5–7 per cent (between 1.5 and 1.6 million people) of the population of 23 million, while the Catholic Church traditionally is rather socially and politically conservative. Converts to Protestantism are strongly clustered among Peru's indigenous inhabitants. Indians form half of a population whose cultural identity was long suppressed, initially by Spanish colonial regimes and latterly by post-colonial governments. The Adventist Church is the largest Protestant Church, providing 'a new collective faith' for many Indians, and – in the absence of adequate State provision – some 'basic infrastructure[s] of health and education' (Martin 1990: 86).

Like many other countries in the region, the social context of the growth of Protestantism is swift urbanization,[15] conflict between State and society in the form of guerrilla warfare, acute impoverishment of large sectors of the population, and a long-term economic crisis. During the 1980s and early 1990s, there was very high price inflation – the average *annual* rate was 316.6 per cent – and plummeting GNP per capita: *minus* 2.7 per cent a year (UNDP 1996: Table 25, p. 186). It is this context of urbanization, poverty and societal conflict which sets the scene for the recent swift growth – from a very low base – of Protestantism in Peru. Numerous new Churches, as well as historic groups like Mormons and Jehovah's Witnesses, have recorded swift growth, especially in burgeoning urban areas; one working-class district of Lima, Agustino, is 12 per cent Protestant. Converts are mostly from the poor and

15. The proportion of Peru's population living in urban areas grew from 46 per cent in 1960 to 71 per cent in 1993 (UNDP 1996: Table 20, p. 176).

Indians. Martin (1990: 87) claims that such converts 'are still sometimes identified as political subversives and shot impartially by [both] guerrillas and the army'.

The entry of Protestants into politics in 1990 – at the time of the electoral campaign of Fujimori – should be seen in the light of the foregoing: Protestants are generally marginalized and often brutalized by rebels and security personnel. Freston (1996: 2) reports that the Protestants' corporate appearance on the political scene was in response to a clear initiative from the Fujimori campaign, a secular political source. Pro-Fujimori activists' main interest seems to have been access to the strongly Protestant indigenous vote through the tightly knit *evangélico* network. Once elected, however, Fujimori not only ignored the *evangélicos* but also became increasingly authoritarian.

Guatemala

In common with Peru, Guatemala has a burgeoning Protestant community. It is estimated that, before long, Guatemala will become 'the first Latin American country to have a professing evangelical majority' (Wiebe 1989: 89). Freston estimates that currently 30 per cent of Guatemala's 10 million people are Protestants, probably the largest national proportion in Latin America. About 80 per cent are Pentecostals. On the one hand, conversions were facilitated from the 1950s by large influxes of North American missionaries from the US Latin American Mission. On the other hand, indigenous Presbyterian and Nazerene Churches also grew in the Mayan highlands. The expansion of evangelical Protestantism suggests that Mayan culture is not only being reformed in non-Catholic terms but also that their communal organizations are being renewed in their thousands of chapels (Martin 1990: 92). Overall, Protestants are divided into over 300 denominations and sects, a mixture of both new and historic Churches; some of the latter have been present since the late nineteenth century. As in Peru, Protestants are widely suspected of subversion by the army and security services (Martin 1990: 91).

There are further similarities with Peru. Guatemala is also characterized by mass poverty, guerrilla warfare, an extremely fragile democracy and a large indigenous population: more than 50 per cent of the population is of Mayan descent. Yet Guatemala has a relatively stable economy: annual price inflation averaged 'only' 16.8 per cent in 1980–93, one-twentieth of the rate of Peru during the same period (UNDP 1996: Table 20, p. 176 and Table 25, p. 186). Guatemala also has slower urbanization: the proportion living in urban areas grew slowly from 32 per cent in 1960 to 41 per cent in 1993. Nevertheless, by the early 1970s, one-third of the population lived in the capital, Guatemala City. They found very few Catholic priests to minister to their spiritual needs, just one for every 30,000 people. Then, in 1976, the city was shaken by a massive earthquake. Although aid flooded in from North America, the earthquake resulted in a major shift of the social landscape; religiously, this meant mass conversions to evangelical Protestantism. This, according to Martin (1990: 92), 'pulled people away from alcoholism, petty crime and corruption . . . The new faith encouraged savings . . . generally inculcating' new patterns of behaviour.

Conversions spread from the poorest and marginalized – the Mayan Indians – to the middle and upper classes, including the future presidents General Ríos Montt and Jorge Serrano.

The growth of evangelical Protestantism was particularly stimulated by massive social upheavals stemming from the earthquake which began in the poorest class before gradually moving upward into social strata habitually engaged in politics, the socio-economic elite. Protestantism not only became fashionable but also acquired a high degree of social respectability. Ríos Montt was elected in 1991 on a so-called 'Protestant platform' which stressed the twin virtues of individual and collective discipline and law and order (Garrard-Burnett 1996: 108). The overall point is that the growth of Protestantism in Guatemala does not seem to have had a clear impact upon politics one way or the other. Conservatives are still highly likely to vote for right-wing candidates while the poor and marginalized are probably less likely to do so, whatever their religious allegiances. However, for some scholars, Protestantism in both Peru and Guatemala is still regarded as little more than a camouflage for right-wing politics, directed from and by the USA (Pieterse 1992).

Brazil

It is very difficult to advance such an argument in relation to the growth of Protestantism in Brazil. It has grown into a mass religion whose followers span the political spectrum from right to left. In fact, the growth of the faith in Brazil has necessitated an academic reinterpretation of the phenomenon to go beyond the kind of ideologically restricted analyses once very common. Since the late 1960s Protestantism, particularly Pentecostalism, has enjoyed steady expansion in Brazil, becoming indigenous and self-reproducing to such an extent that nowadays it needs to rely less than Catholicism on religious personnel from abroad (Casanova 1994: 133–4).

Protestantism has also managed to penetrate new social spaces. No longer the domain of the marginalized only, it has also gained converts among the middle classes through targeted proselytizing (to sports people, artists, business people, prisoners, etc) and the corporate muscle the large popular sects now wield in the media and politics. While historical Protestants (Lutherans, Presbyterians, Methodists and Baptists) were elected to Congress from the 1930s, their presence was originally numerially small (never more than 12 at one time) and discreet, they played down their religious allegiances. Some congressmen and women had predominantly Protestant electorates, yet none had endorsement from any denomination. Dispersed among many different denominations, such people had a range of ideological positions from the non-Marxist left to the pro-military right.

After election of a Constituent Assembly – following the military's withdrawal from power in 1986 – the public face of Protestantism quickly changed; in effect, it deprivatized. This development was manifested in three main ways. First, there was a marked increase in the number of Protestant congressmen and women, increasing both their confidence in making political demands and in the range of demands. Second, there was a change in the ecclesiastical and social composition of the Protestant political class. Most members of Congress are now often official candidates of their denominations, particularly the Assemblies of God (the largest Protestant denomination in Brazil), the Four-Square Church and the Universal Church of the Kingdom of God. Finally, the political style of the Protestants has changed to become more openly concerned with corporate goals. The Assemblies of God has been the most politically active. In 1985, its General Convention decided to elect one member from each federal State to the Constituent Assembly: 18 State conventions chose official candidates and 14 were elected (Freston 1996: 4). On the other hand, some large Pentecostal groups – including the Christian Congregation and God is Love – have so far remained aloof from electoral politics.

The basic cause of evangelical Protestant politicization is to do with the religious field itself, while the main beneficiaries of corporate politics have been the Church leaders. Unlike the historical Churches, with their tradition, middle-class clientele and professional and bureaucratic standards, the new Protestant Church field is comparatively young, fast-growing, popular and *sectarian*. Their pastors often suffer from a status contradiction: they are leaders in the Church but marginalized by society. Going into politics, or sending in a relative or protégé, can reduce such tensions and help professionalize the Protestant terrain. Their public connection helps internal structuring by strengthening certain positions and organizations. Politics also helps access to the media (half of the Protestant congressmen and women since 1986 have had links with the media). Politics and media reinforce each other in structuring the Protestant world in Brazil (Freston 1996: 4).

Certain moral and social issues are of great importance to the socially conservative leaders of the Assemblies of God. The Church's political involvement is partially explicable by its attempt to turn back what it perceives as a threat to freedom of religion and a danger to the family. Issues like availability of abortion, homosexuality, growing numbers of divorces, and a drift away from media censorship are of great concern. The perceived threat to family values is about defending what the Church regards as a fundamental benchmark. As Bruce (1988: 7, 16) notes, such a reaction is best understood as an attempt to undo 'changes in the social milieu which threatens to undermine the group's capacity to maintain its culture'. In short, the Church's organizational resources are utilized in pursuit of a range of social goals, best achieved, it is believed, by legislation.

The second main issue – defence of 'religious freedom' – is not about a struggle for basic Protestant civil rights, which have long been granted. Rather, the issue is emblematic of something wider: a statement of intent to join battle with Catholicism for space in civil religion. Having broadly the same numbers of practising members as the Catholics – about 25 million each – the evangelical Protestant denominations now demand equal status in public life.

In summary, conservative Protestants in Brazil seeks a variety of political goals. They include a desire to strengthen internal leaderships, to protect the frontiers of sectarian reproduction, to tap resources for religious expansion and to dispute spaces in civil religion with the Catholics. Their achievements are assisted by aspects of Brazil's political system, including its federalist structure, a relatively open mass media, weak political parties and a proportional electoral system. In addition, a continuing economic crisis places strain on traditional urban political clientelism from which the new Protestant Churches are well placed to benefit (Freston 1996: 4). Finally, corporate politics *à la* Protestantism gives access to both concrete and symbolic resources which collectively serve to structure this vast popular religious field whose rapid expansion is always producing new leaders anxious to strengthen their positions.

Conclusion

As the decade of the 1990s draws to a close, the great majority of Latin America's national Catholic Churches can no longer be properly regarded as State-Churches. Nor can Catholicism claim still to be the national faith in many countries. The Catholic Church is no longer even properly perceived as the religious wing of the ruling elite; it hardly ever overtly supports one particular party or partisan option in the political societies. Equally, the widespread self-designation of the Church in the late 1960s and 1970s as the 'preferential option for the poor' has now lost much of the connotation it once had. Then its discourse was strongly informed by the traditional populist rhetoric of 'people' versus 'oligarchy' and by Marxist visions of the impending class struggle. The election of a socially conservative Pope both symbolized and galvanized a markedly rightward turn for most of the region's Catholic Churches. The overall consequence of this series of events was that the Church (perhaps temporarily) deprivatized in many countries, arguing that as democracy had now returned it was time to leave political society to others.

By the 1980s and the 1990s, many Latin Americans, particularly among the region's poor and marginalized, were showing a growing preference for evangelical Protestantism. Sectors of the middle classes became estranged from the notion of the popular Church and, for example in Guatemala, Peru and Brazil, looked around for religious alternatives; often evangelical Protestantism fitted the bill. However, given the mostly fragile democracies and continuing economic crises in the region, which is producing ever-growing numbers of economic losers, it is unlikely that the Church will withdraw permanently to the privatized sphere of the spiritual care of souls. It is plausible – though not that likely given the haemorrhaging of support to Protestant rivals – that it may again soon become the 'voice of the voiceless', the champion of those whose views and interests do not find institutional representation in the region's various national political societies.

Several political conclusions can be made about the recent growth in support for evangelical Protestantism. First, there is no clearcut, one-dimensional picture: Protestantism is not simply a right wing phenomenon but covers a range of political and social opinions. Second, the American religious right, although it may have a certain demonstration effect, functions in a religious and political context which is totally different from Latin America: there is no clear evidence that local Protestant denominations are funded or guided from the USA. In fact, quite the contrary: their members support the work of their Churches by regular payments from often meagre incomes. Despite inter-Church similarities – a concern with questions of sexuality, family values and censorship – the differences (of methods and demands, of background and of prospects) are far more important. In Peru, where the Protestant field is smaller and less Pentecostal than in many other countries of the region, the sudden entry into politics in 1990 owed a lot to a secular initiative (the Fujimori campaign) and affected above all the historical Churches. In Guatemala, the most Protestant country in Latin America, both Protestant presidents (Ríos Montt and Serrano) were already politicians before their conversions. Protestantism entered politics through its penetration of the ruling class. At the same time, in the rural areas of the country where the indigenous Indians mostly live, Protestant congregations have become a focus of community and ethnic identity. This is by no stretch of the imagination a simple manifestation of 'right wing' politics.

In Brazil, key figures in Protestant Churches are often denominational heads, leaders of popular sects growing so fast that their corporate clout enables them to begin to use the State for their own ends. The Protestant evangelical eruption into politics from 1986 followed a corporate model: the great majority of connected parliamentarians are official candidates of the new Churches. Unlike in the USA, however, such people are not leaders of agencies like the Christian Coalition whose *raison d'être* is to mobilize Protestant opinion, elaborate agendas and monitor the activity even of non-Protestant Members of Congress. Nor is there in Brazil the nostalgia for a lost past that characterizes the world view of US fundamentalist Christians. Brazilian leaders are in a different socio-economic and political setting and they have a different position not only in the religious world but also in terms of a distinct relationship to civil religion and national identity. The point is that the new Brazilian denominations have grown rapidly but have not (yet) won complete social and cultural respectability. There is still a semi-official Catholic Church and only patchy and fragmentary economic expansion. It is in this context that the Protestant Churches have launched themselves into politics.

The ironic result of regional democratization may have been to bring it home to many people that the process of electing political representatives does not necessarily lead to clear improvements to their own lives. Under such circumstances, many Protestant Churches fulfil an important community-solidarity function, increasingly filling the gap left by a retreating State unable widely to deliver much in the way of welfarist goods. Unlike Catholic priests, widely viewed as culturally different, representatives of a class which can never know the hopes, fears and aspirations of poor people, Protestant ministers normally come from the same class and culture as their congregations. The final point is that many converts to Protestantism come not from groups who participated in CEBs, but rather from the large majority of people who viewed themselves culturally as part of the Catholic Church but who, in reality, were never active in the Church's congregation. What this represents is not an 'invasion of the US sects'; rather, as Berryman (1994: 10) notes, it represents the 'Protestant coming of age', the end of regional Catholic hegemony. Yet, it is inappropriate to leave the impression that what is happening is a clear *regional* trend. Future research must examine theological, class and organizational differences *between* rival Protestant Churches – as well as those that separate them collectively from the Catholic Church – and to explain why Protestantism is growing in some countries but not all.

Chapter 4

Western Europe: secularization and the religious response

The Western European past has featured many instances of Christian religions and institutions playing a part in the running of the State. The relationships of the various Christian denominations to the State was introduced into Western Europe by the Reformation,[1] leading to a variety of forms of theology and of relationships between Church and State. However, over the last 200 years or so there has been a widespread privatization of religion and public secularization of the State.

Western liberal thought has long included the principle of separation between State and religion, even though the practice in Western democracies has not always followed the dictum. Separation is designed to ensure that those in charge of religion, the clergy, will not be able to use the State's coercive power to force any religion on the public. It is intended to safeguard the freedom of religion and of thought of the citizens. As Clark (1992: 44–50) explains, secular assumptions underlying contemporary political and civil organization in Western Europe are the result of a combination of events and developments, including the Enlightenment and the ideas of figures like Voltaire, the French and American revolutions and the secularism of Napoleon. The overall result was that during the nineteenth century the terms of the old Church–State alliances became progressively more relaxed, while liberals and radicals fought for the introduction of religious toleration, liberty and equality. The recognition of these principles involved breaking the link between citizenship and adherence to a dominant creed, accepting the rights of individuals to choose their own religious orientation (or none) and removing the barriers to equality of civil status which attached to religious differences (Madeley 1991: 36–7).

In Protestant Europe, opposition to these trends came not so much from the leaderships of the mainline Churches as from revivalist groups who objected to the dilution of faith apparently tolerated by relatively easy-going mainline Church elites. A consequence was a 'growing pluralism of religious, anti-religious and religiously indifferent belief and behaviour as the secularizing impact of modernization processes and the various countervailing movements of religious revivalism and liberal

---

1. The religious revolution of the sixteenth century which gave rise to the various Protestant organizations of Christendom.

reform undermined the religious unformity which had characterized the old monopoly system' (Madeley 1991: 37). However, over time, there emerged a widespread consensus, particularly in much of Protestant Western Europe, that it was appropriate to have a *secular* State and *private* religion.

This is not to claim that religion has no political resonance in the region at all. Many Western Europeans perceive themselves widely differentiated on a number of broadly religious criteria, at least potentially relevant to politics. They include:

1   The Catholic/Protestant divide, especially in Northern Ireland and to an extent in Germany. In the former, religious divisions are the main social basis of local political parties.
2   Religious differences – roughly along right–left political lines – internal to the main confessional traditions. In Britain, for example, there is the cross-party, socially conservative Movement for Christian Democracy, while in both France and Italy there are Christian movements.
3   The position of Muslim immigrants, especially in Britain, France and Germany; Islam retains for many an important basis of identity reflected in burgeoning socio-political movements and groups.
4   Differing patterns of Church–State relations. There has been a marked increase in the readiness of some Churches – for example, in England, Spain, and Germany – to speak out in their corporate capacity on issues of public policy in recent times.

This chapter examines these issues and strives to identify trends involving religion and politics in contemporary Western Europe.

Church–State relations

The Western European trend has, for a long period, been for privatization of religion and a diminution in the political importance of religious organizations. Therborn (1994: 105) points out that leaderships of various Christian denominations – Roman Catholicism, Anglicanism, Orthodoxy, Lutheranism and occasionally Calvinism – have historically 'been closely linked to the State', but not always in a position of equality. Three broad positions can be identified: co-option, subordination and equality. First, in many mainly Protestant societies – like England and Denmark – the relationship between State and Church has been expressed in terms of the former's *de facto* co-option by the latter. Second, after the 1789 Revolution in predominantly Catholic France the relationship was marked by hostility and partial repression. The Church lost a great deal of its power, privilege and moral authority. Third, in Catholic Spain,[2] after Franco's victory in the civil war, and since World War I in Italy, Church and State have – until recently – been firm allies. Generally, however, the Catholic Church's ability to influence its followers on moral and social issues

2. The Franco era was one of 'national Catholicism', where the Church and nationalism were widely regarded as inseparable.

– especially divorce and abortion – is declining across Western Europe (Wilson 1992: 201, Hooper 1996a, Ramet 1995: 58–9). This is because most societies in the region are highly secular.

Churches and secularization

Religion has become widely privatized in Western Europe, reflecting the fact that the region is 'marked by an extraordinarily high level of secularization' (Madeley 1991: 30). Secularization *does not* denote the idea that people are necessarily becoming less interested in spiritual matters but refers to the following measures of religious observance: most mainline Churches have increasingly serious financial crises because the numbers of believers willing to pay sufficient sums for their upkeep is falling; dropping numbers of religious professionals coming into the Churches; declining Church membership and less – and less regular – attendance; dwindling social and moral influence of spiritual leaders and of general attitudes towards the importance of religion; and State policies pursued without clear heed to specifically religious injunctions or interdictions (Wilson 1992: 198, Casanova 1994: 224, Wroe 1996; Hooper 1996a). What this amounts to is that nearly everywhere in Western Europe the political and the religious are to a considerable degree disengaging from each other, reflecting the continuing process of decline of the social significance of religion.[3] Western European states, in varying degrees, have managed to limit the range of the Churches' religious activities by promoting 'understandings of religion within evolutionary perspectives' and by controlling 'the expression and content of religious faith, especially in education and public media' (Martin 1994: 2).

A consequence of religion's declining social significance is that religious elites have generally lost a great deal of political and cultural significance (Hunter 1987: 361–2). Political rulers and their policies in the main no longer *need* the direct or indirect legitimation of religious elites, although this is not to say that the former do not prefer to have their support. In other words, comparatively and historically speaking, the opinions and interests of religious elites – whether conservative or liberal – have become marginal to the major social forces operative and determinative in Western Europe. The decline in the prestige and influence of religious elites in Western Europe corresponds to the secularization of social structure and of culture – including the diminished import of religious symbols – and the accompanying privatization of religious institutions that normally accompanies economic and political modernization.

Some maintain, however, that there are recent signs of a reversal of secularization, that throughout much of Western Europe a process of 're-Christianization' is occurring. Kepel (1994: 81) argues that 're-Christianization' is due to the destabilizing impact of social crisis in Western Europe from the mid-1970s, 'taking over as a

3. This can even be seen in countries like Spain, nominally around 90 per cent Catholic. Support for Franco's dictatorship and association with all that was right wing and repressed in the country have left the Church isolated during the two decades since Franco's death. In that time, Spain has grown to be one of the most liberal societies in Europe.

Table 4.1 The populations of selected Western European countries by religion and confession, late 1980s

Country	All Christians (%)	Membership of historically dominant confession	Membership of other main confessions	Non-religious/ Atheists	Others
British Isles	86.9	56.8 (A)	13.1 (C)	9.5	20.6
England	–	69.0	14.0 (P), 10 (C)	5.0	2.0
Scotland	–	67.0	16.0 (C), 9 (P)	5.0	3.0
Wales	–	45.0	40.0 (P), 6 (C)	4.0	5.0
N. Ireland	–	25.0	38.0 (P), 25 (C)	2.0	12.0
W. Germany	92.8	46.7 (L,CV)	43.8 (C)	4.6	4.9
Spain		86.0 (C)	2.0 (P)	7.0	3.0
France	80.1	76.4 (C)	2.0 (P)	15.6	4.3

Notes: The data refer to 1980. A = Anglican, C = Roman Catholic, CV = Calvinist, L = Lutheran, P = Protestant; Others = mostly Muslims.
Sources: Madeley (1991: Table 2.1 34–5); Casanova (1994: 89).

practical source of the inspiration and solidarity which the secular utopias of the industrial age no longer had the power to provide'. Martin (1994: 1) contends that 'we may be approaching the decomposition of two hundred years and more of statist hostility to religion . . . Ideologies and secular religions [that is, presumably, communism] promoting the State and promoted by the State may . . . fade into history', leaving secularism[4] 'as the residual smile on the face of the vanishing cat'.

Martin and Kepel are alleging that religion is deprivatizing, becoming once again an important socio-political actor in Western Europe. Certainly, despite the march of secularization, many millions of people in Western Europe still identify themselves with a religious denomination, as Table 4.1 indicates.

However, it is important to differentiate between those who are only nominally members of a religious denomination and those who are committed believers.[5] Despite the fact that 69 per cent of English people identify themselves as members of the Church of England, 'only 2 per cent are regular Church-going Anglicans' (Bunting 1996a). Fogarty (1992: 313) reports that of the 40 million adults in Britain, about 5.5 million (13.75 per cent) attend the mainline, Free or Catholic Churches on a weekly basis; a further 3.5 million (8.75) attend once a month. Thus, not much more than one in five of Britons go to Church, even once a month. It is the mainline Churches – especially the Anglican, the Methodist, the Baptist – which have seen the greatest declines in Sunday turnouts. On the other hand, the Adventists and other popular evangelical and Pentecostal denominations, are 'generally believed to have thriving numbers of devout members' (Goulborne and Joly 1989: 86).

In France, the figures for the Catholic Church are similar: one-quarter of the 80 per cent of people who call themselves Catholics attend mass once a month

4. Secularism is the belief that the State, morals and education should be independent of religion.

5. The position is made more complex when one bears in mind that even if people do not attend Church regularly they may still be affected by what religious leaders say. But this seems almost impossible to measure.

or more (Davie 1994: 62), although evangelical groups thrive (Kepel 1994). The situation in Spain is broadly the same: 86 per cent of Spaniards consider themselves Catholics in the 1990s, but only 30 per cent – down from 38 per cent a decade before – attend mass 'regularly' (Gooch 1996). Nearly 82 per cent of Germans in the eastern part of the country belonged to the main Protestant Churches in 1950; by 1970 just over 40 per cent of the population retained membership. By 1988, the Churches could count on a mere 23 per cent of people. The situation was broadly the same in the western part of Germany: Madeley (1991: 60) reports 'declining Church attendance' and general 'cultural and political secularization'. In sum, it is plausible to conclude that in Britain, France, Germany and Spain there has been a clear trend towards secularization over the last two or three decades.

However, this is *not* to claim that Britons, French, Spaniards and so on are necessarily becoming less interested in the spiritual and religious, even though adherence to traditional religious denominations is declining. In fact, it appears that the opposite may be happening: the development of what has been called a 'spiritual supermarket' (Bunting 1996b). Millions of people take part in religious rituals, but they are not necessarily those of their parents. The growth of religious pluralism in Western Europe – from Islam and Buddhism to the Hare Krishna movement and Tibetan Bon spiritualism – meets the religious and spiritual needs of many, especially, it appears, of those most dissatisfied with the materialist-oriented norms of contemporary society with which Western Christianity seems to be too much at home.

The advent of the spiritual supermarket has coincided with the era of post-modernism marked by the apparent collapse of all the great utopian projects of the last 500 years of modernity:[6] many no longer believe reason and science to be the engines of human progress, the promise of the Enlightenment project, that is, the assumption of universal progress based on reason, and the 'modern Promethean myth of humanity's mastery of its destiny and capacity for resolution of all its problems' has, for many, come to an end (Watson 1994: 150). Even the promise of Mammon – that is, the glitter of the 1980s enterprise culture – has, for many, become shoddy and tasteless. In short, there is little apparent sense of optimism or enthusiasm about the future. However, post-modern spiritual movements are the exception, but they are optimistic only on a 'very personal, individualistic, level as they seek their own self-perfection' (Bunting 1996b). The point is that post-modernism not only involves a rejection of absolute ways of speaking truth – including the dictums of the main religious traditions – but also entails, for many, the adoption of a personalist moral code. The privatization of morality is a most unwelcome development for the leaders of the mainline Christian denominations. Dr George Carey, Archbishop of Canterbury and overall head of the Anglican Church, argues that if a society loses its commitment to certain core Christian moral values it becomes one in which everyone does what is right in their own eyes: 'All we seem to be left with is a rather bleak and despairing relativism.' Because for many there

6. This includes the Marxist 'promised land' of an equal society. Does anybody believe in the communist paradise any longer?

is 'no point of reference beyond myself or beyond yourself, then reason, justice and law become exploitable by the powerful and the influential, and the weak have nothing left to appeal to . . .' (*Guardian* 1995).

It is against the background of the decline in the social importance of traditional Christian values that the recent attempts of Christian leaders to involve themselves in contemporary moral, ethical and political debates should be understood. Leaders are genuinely concerned at the direction in which society is heading. As a result, the Anglican Church in England has become increasingly concerned with societal issues, including abortion rights, housing shortages, inner city decline, the social role of the State, conservation of the natural environment, immigration, Third World aid, nuclear disarmament and peace (Fogarty 1992: 309–10). More generally, since the 1970s 'there has been a marked increase in the readiness of British Churches to speak out in their corporate capacity on issues of public policy' (Fogarty 1992: 301). Mushaben (1983: 3) has documented a similar trend in Germany. There the leadership of both the Lutheran and Catholic Churches have 'opposed rearmament . . . and have been at the forefront of the pacifist and leftist wing of the anti-nuclear movement'.

The concern of institutional religious elites to make public pronouncements on social and political issues is a growing feature in much of Western Europe. It is, in effect, an attempt to deprivatize religion from where the process of secularization seems to be sending it: to socio-political marginality. It also reflects growing disquiet at the direction which modern society seems to be taking: away from the teachings of Christianity towards an increasingly amoral, selfish conception of what is appropriate. The result is what Hunter (1987: 373) calls an 'aggressive promulgation of these ideals in the public sphere', that is, an effort to move religious elites out of the periphery and back to the centre in order to try to regain the social power that had previously been exclusively their own. Let us look next at the position of leading Churches in three countries – Britain, Spain and Germany, predominantly Protestant, Catholic and mixed Protestant/Catholic respectively – to see how the objective of rejoining the public sphere is being pursued and with what consequences.

Case studies

Britain

Britain (here used to mean the United Kingdom of England, Scotland, Wales and Northern Ireland), is a constitutional monarchy exhibiting several different types of arrangement between the State and the mainline Christian Churches. The Anglican Church is the national Church established by law. Its head – 'defender of the faith' – is the sovereign, crowned by the Archbishop of Canterbury; the Church is represented in Parliament by bishops in the House of Lords. The Queen of England is both the constitutional head of State and formal head of the Anglican Church. The monarch does not, of course, exercise the *real* authority enshrined in these offices:

the Prime Minister and the Archbishop of Canterbury, respectively, are the *effective* heads of these offices. The Church of Scotland is also an established Church although Presbyterian in its organization and free from government interference. There are no established Churches in Wales or Northern Ireland.

Formally, Britain is a Christian Protestant society with other religious denominations present. In reality, however, Protestantism has given way to secularism based on a rationalism common to most of North-west Europe. This subsequent dual character of British society – Christian but secular – is evident in the composition of several major institutions in the country. In a constitutional sense Church and State are not separated in England, although in practice State and Church are neither estranged nor very closely connected. But they are tightly bound together as a result of Britain's island history which separates the country from Continental experience.

The separation of the *formal* and the *actual* manifests itself in many aspects of British life, including education, the courts system, council meetings and marriage services. The 1988 Education Act, instigated by lay Christians of the political 'New Right', stipulated the mandatory teaching of religion and reintroduced Christian worship within State schools. In courts of law it is customary to take the oath on the Bible, while in both Parliament and city council meetings proceedings begin with a prayer, irrespective of the political party in office. Clergy officiate at marriages and these are automatically valid before the law (Goulborne and Joly 1989: 77–78).

Regarding religion and party politics in Britain, outside Northern Ireland, unlike mainland Europe, religion has not been an important aspect of party politics for most of the twentieth century. This is because the rise to prominence of the Labour Party around the time of World War I brought with it a new political agenda of class-related issues, which largely erased earlier political traces of religious antagonism (Madeley 1991: 39). In short, with the exceptions of Northern Ireland and British immigrant Muslims (both examined below), religious difference in Britain has not been a major divisive factor for a very long time.

Despite the Church of England's constitutional significance, its socio-political importance has long been in decline. A 1971 *Times* survey indicated that only 2 per cent of those questioned believed that the Church was 'very influential' in public life (Mews 1989: 286). Since then, however, there is some indication that, as issue politics have replaced class politics, the Church has become more significant in national debates. From the late 1970s until the early 1990s it was the policies of the Thatcher Conservative Governments which introduced a new element of strain in Church–State relations, leading many Church leaders to speak up in opposition to her policies. Thatcher declared that her Government was to be one of conviction rather than consensus and, in the wake of a wave of public sector strikes in 1978–9, set out to restore the authority of the State. Her Government sought to combine traditional Tory values with a new populism; yet, for many clergy, now preaching a gospel of reconciliation and social concern, these new emphases were profoundly disturbing. As Bishop Mark Santer of Birmingham said in 1989: 'The goal posts have changed . . . the things I say could be associated with old style *noblesse oblige* Conservatism and they're suddenly felt to be outrageous' (quoted in Mews 1989:

287). When the then head of the Church of England, Robert Runcie, 'criticized the visible increase in greed and the decline of Christian charity in Britain', this was taken to be a severe criticism of the Thatcher Government (Goulborne and Joly 1989: 87).

During Thatcher's first and second terms of office (1979–87) there were frequent clashes between the Government and the Anglican Church. *The Church and the Bomb* (1982) and *Faith in the City* Archbishop of Canterbury's Commission (1985) put forward radical alternatives to government policy, a government headed by a Prime Minister who declared: 'There *is* no alternative.' The appointment of David Jenkins in 1984 as Bishop of Durham also displeased the Government, not least because he called for compromise to settle the 1984–5 miner's strike and his 'exposition of a moderate liberalism in theology' (Mews 1989: 287). Governmental dissatisfaction with Dr Jenkins, coupled with the refusal of the Government to appoint the liberal Bishop James Thompson of Stepney to the vacant bishopric of Birmingham (Bunting 1996a),[7] were issues implicitly referred to by Archbishop Runcie in a speech in early 1988. He referred to the 'curious expectations' of politicians that the legal status of the established Church had to be paid for by uncritical support of the Government. It was not by any means only the Anglican Church, he argued, which supported the common Christian philosophical principles of the welfare state: it was a consensus shared in all the main Churches, he said, including the Catholic Church (Fogarty 1992: 310). Runcie's words were supported by, *inter alia*, the Methodists who, in June 1988, voted overwhelmingly to 'declare a sense of outrage' at the way government policies were increasing 'the wealth of the rich at the expense of the poor' (Mews 1989: 288–9).

After Thatcher was deposed in November 1990, her place was taken by John Major, until his electoral defeat in May 1997. But the change of prime minister did not lead to reversal of Church policy, that is, a return to the days of covert, rather uninfluential, pressure on government for or against certain policies and programmes. For example, the Catholic bishops' document, *The Common Good and the Catholic Church's Social Teaching*, published in October 1996, focused on support for a minimum wage and the end of poverty, a positive approach to trade unions, and support for a bill of rights. A further document, *Unemployment and the Future of Work*, was published the following April, and indicted the Government for a lack of apparent unconcern with high unemployment levels. Such reports did not, it is perhaps unnecessary to add, find favour with the Conservative Government which saw its initiative as tantamount to an endorsement of the opposition Labour Party. A further expression of religious principles became clear with the ideas of the Movement for Christian Democracy led by Alan Storkey, a Christian Democrat candidate in the 1997 election.[8] His programme was concerned with issues arising from 'Christian faith and values', including the end of the arms trade, an end to 'the

---

7. In an attempt to heal the breach between the Church of England and the Conservative Government, Thatcher met with eight senior bishops in late 1987 to make the point that she wanted a new emphasis on personal morality.

8. Storkey gained 289 votes on a turnout of 46,533 – that is, 0.0062 per cent – in the Enfield Southgate seat in north London.

injustices of marital and parental unfaithfulness', the need for a wealth tax and progressive taxation, and 'the abuse of procreation through abortion' (Storkey 1997).

As 'New' Labour – after the May 1997 elections the party of government – continues to steal Conservative thinking from crime to the free market, there is a growing feeling among religious leaders that everyone is speaking for the middle class and no one for the poor. As the political landscape in Britain converges, mainline Church leaders are saying things elected politicians, anxious not to irritate their middle-class electorates, dare not utter. They begin to look more radical, not because they have moved to the left, but because secular politicans have moved to the right. This does not mean that 'religious values' are becoming more central than hitherto, so much as reflecting a decline in the traditional left–right polarization of politics in Britain. No one is speaking up for the poor and marginalized; someone has to do it and the mainline Churches attract attention when they do. Whether what they say has any influence is another matter.

Germany[9]

Germany's post-reunification population of 80 million is divided between various religious denominations and non-believers. Some 28 million Germans belong to the Catholic Church and around 40 million to various Protestant Churches, including the largest, the Evangelical Church. The remaining 12 million are divided between members of the Muslim community (1.75 million) and groups of Orthodox Christians, Jews and non-believers (McEwan 1989: 84). The relationship between religion and politics is of interest for several reasons: Germany is the only part of Europe where Catholics, Lutherans and Calvinists have been represented since the Reformation, with areas of specific local dominance; the country spans large areas of both very high and very low levels of religiosity, and it is the European country where 'the political potential of the religious factor was first realized and transposed into the forms of modern party politics' (Madeley 1991: 53–4).

It is impossible to understand the present-day Church–State relationship in Germany away from the context of the collapse and legacy of the Nazi regime. After 1945, there was a completely new political beginning amid massive economic, social and political reconstruction. So far as the Churches were concerned, one of the main challenges was the need to come to terms with the recent past, especially the war guilt attributed to the whole nation by the Potsdam agreement and the even deeper sense of collective guilt provoked by the final disclosure of the Nazi regime's most barbarous atrocities against the Jews. In effect, national revulsion against Nazism created a vacuum the Churches were well-placed to fill, given that the vast majority of Germans no doubt had a strong desire to return to traditional standards such as the rule of law and personal and political freedoms. As the only important organizations to span the four occupation zones, Churches were not only entrusted with a wide variety of civil functions but were able, with some justification,

9. This chapter is mostly concerned with the former West Germany. Erstwhile communist East Germany is examined separately in Chapter 5.

to declare themselves to be the sole legitimate voice for the German nation. The point is that the Churches enjoyed a very high post-war status, reflected in the Basic Law of 1949, returning to the pre-Nazi period separation of Church and State and the guarantees of religious freedom. It also erected 'generous systems of financial support through the levying of Church taxes by the tax authorities' (Madeley 1991: 57).

The highly negative experience of World War II was also instrumental in bringing it home to the various Christian confessions how much they had in common with each other. While Catholics had been in a clear minority position before the post-1945 partition, after the war (until reunification) Catholics and Protestants enjoyed near demographic parity. Numerical equality, added to the shared experience of Nazism, meant that the religious boundaries between Catholics and Protestants largely broke down. This was especially the case among Protestants, who, Madeley (1991: 56) explains, 'provided much of the support for right-wing nationalist parties' before the war. After 1945 many discovered a commonality of Christian values with the Catholics from whom they had earlier politically separated.[10]

The end of World War II also marked a further development involving Germany's Christians. Predominantly Catholic parties were completely remodelled, signalling a shift from denominational politics to the politics of Christian democracy[11] (Glasman 1996: 41–2), involving, *inter alia* (a) a commitment to liberal democracy; (b) a political desire to promote values of Christianity – the rule of law, respect for the family and, more generally, an attempt to seize the political centre ground – rather than to represent the interests of individual Churches; (c) a shift to a lay political leadership in the main Christian Democratic Party, the CDU (*Christlich-Demokratische Union*). The CDU had roots in both Protestant and Catholic inspiration, combining social Catholicism with a commitment to political democracy, religious pluralism and human rights. It was unique among Christian Democratic parties in Western Europe because of its genuinely cross-confessional basis, differing from secular parties, such as the socialist SPD, both in the ultimately religious basis of its political programme, and in the social orientation of its philosophy and political programmes. In effect, it represented a 'middle way' between liberal individualism and collectivist socialism, stressing the importance of a pluralist welfare state democracy as the form of government most faithful to the principles of the Christian gospels (Sigmund 1993: 331).

For nearly three decades after its foundation in 1946 the CDU (and its Bavarian sister party, the CSU) enjoyed enviable electoral success, but this did not stop them from becoming the butt of criticism from the leading Churches for the alleged unconcern with a variety of crucial political and economic issues, including questions regarding the world economic order, nuclear energy, ecology and peace (McEwan 1989: 84). However, the Catholics tended to focus more upon personal morality, while the Protestants laid a greater stress on the societal context necessary for a moral life. The rise of the Green Party in the mid-1980s – with radical anti-NATO,

---

10. Furthermore, it was the political divisions between Catholics and Protestants that played an important contributing role to the weakness and collapse of the Weimar republic.

11. For a concise discussion of the main political attributes of Christian democracy in post-war Germany, see Glasman (1996: 41–3).

pro-ecology and alternative lifestyles policies – stimulated Cardinal Joseph Höffner to urge Catholics not to vote for them because of their views on NATO and abortion (they were pro-Choice). His colleague, Professor Hans Maier, President of the Central Committee of the Catholic Church in Germany and Bavarian Minister of Culture, defended the Cardinal's views, arguing that the Church was not there simply to acknowledge and follow trends in society, but to present arguments and views aiming to imbue society with the Church's values (McEwan 1989: 84).

The reunification of the two Germanies led to the Churches becoming relatively politically marginalized in the 1990s. However, as in Britain, there are some signs that they wish to enter the mainstream of political debate, given the development of post-modern ideas in Germany and the alleged decline of personal morality and the massive rise of unemployment, especially in the east of the country.

Spain

A concordat of 1753 gave the crown the right to appoint bishops, a prerogative only abandoned more than 200 years later on the death of the dictator, General Franco, in 1975. However, relations between the State and the Catholic Church – the religious denomination of nearly nine out of ten Spaniards – were periodically affected by periods of anti-clericalism, most acrimonious in the years before the Civil War in 1936. Franco's victory was followed by a long period of 'national Catholicism', whereby the country's Church and 'Spanish nationalism were regarded as inseparable' (Walsh 1989: 259–50). Reflecting the Church's pro-Franco stance, at the Second Vatican Council (1960–5) Spanish bishops constituted one of the most conservative blocs of the assembled Catholic hierarchy. However, the announcement of the encyclical *Pacem in Terris* (1963) marked a turning point within the Church: a Christian Democratic sector emerged which took the lead in demanding the end of authoritarianism, the institutionalization of the rule of law and the protection of the human, civil and political rights of the Spanish people (Casanova 1994: 83–4). Within the Church, Latin was dropped in favour of Spanish, while the training of priests underwent a fundamental overhaul. Many young priests – some of whom adopted various forms of social service and political activism – were keen to embrace the new direction, engendering a confrontational attitude with many of their own older colleagues and the Church hierarchy.

The Vatican's intervention in Spanish affairs, in changing the organizational structure and the composition of the Spanish episcopate, tipped the balance of forces decisively in favour of the new social Catholicism in the early 1970s. Reformers gained control of the newly created National Conference of Bishops, replacing the Conference of Metropolitans. The Church took the initiative in watering down links with the Franco regime in 1971, a move reflecting wider changes taking place in politics and society.

During the Franco era, the norms and values of civil society and the democratic traditions of liberal Spain were preserved and transmitted through the family, the working class and intellectual networks. Consequently, the democratic opposition movement emerged independently of the institutional Church in the early 1970s.

Unlike in Poland or South Africa or Brazil, the Spanish Church did not become 'the voice of the voiceless' or the promoter of the reconstitution of civil society (Rueschemeyer *et al.* 1992: 213). Nevertheless, as Casanova (1994: 87) explains, it did contribute to the growth of the democratic opposition in two important ways: (a) by offering religious legitimation for the democratic principles upon which the activities of the opposition were based, that is, freedom of expression, freedom of association, civil and political rights; and (b) by offering its Churches and monasteries as relatively protected sanctuaries. There, opposition activists could meet to coordinate and unite the diverse sectors of the democratic opposition into a unified movement. When Franco died in November 1975, important sections of his regime were prepared to accept the legitimacy of a series of 'pacts' which dissolved all important Francoist institutions, legalized all political parties (including the Communist Party), and permitted elections for a constituent assembly to produce a fully democratic constitution. Democracy was overwhelmingly endorsed by a referendum in December 1976; six months later a democratic government was voted into office.

The Church played a low-key, yet positive, backstage role during the transition. It now accepted both the reality and the principles of separation of Church and State, and of religious freedom, declining either to sponsor a 'Catholic' Party or to support directly any of the Christian Democratic Parties in the 1977 elections.[12] Casanova (1994: 89) identifies three main factors that probably led to the Church's decision: (a) 'a genuine desire for religious peace'; (b) the realization that the Catholic community, including clergy, had become politically pluralistic and would not, therefore, support any monolithic party; and (c) the fear that an 'official' Catholic Party would become a minority party, thus undermining the Church's claim that Catholicism was Spain's national religion. The entire process amounted to the recognition of the voluntary principle of religious allegiance in Spain. Furthermore, it was clear that the Church not only finally accepted disestablishment from the State and the reality of a pluralist society, but also understood that it was no longer a Church in the Weberian sense of being an obligatory monopolistic community of faith coextensive with the nation. Put another way, Catholicism had ceased to be the national faith, so the principles of religious faith, national identity and political citizenship could be uncoupled. By recognizing the fact and the principle of a pluralistically organized civil society, the Church became a denomination, a powerful one to be sure, but a denomination nonetheless, functioning within civil society. Given such circumstances, what are the chances that the Church could find a role as a public religion?

The restoration of a constitutional monarchy and – in the 1980s – an elected Socialist Government, led the Church in a rightward direction, straining relations with the State (McEwan 1989: 249–50). But the numbers of practising Catholics was swiftly dropping. Although 86 per cent of Spaniards regard themselves as Catholics, less than half that number – 38 per cent – attend mass regularly; among the young the decline is even steeper: no more than 30 per cent of young Spaniards attend Church 'regularly' (Gooch 1996). Practising Catholics are distributed evenly

12. None of the three competing Christian Democratic Parties were able to survive the elections.

throughout the population in terms of class. An estimated 25 per cent of those voting for the Socialist Party in 1982 were practising Catholics. What this amounts to is that 'there is currently no longer a Catholic vote susceptible of political mobilization by the Church' (Casanova 1994: 89).

The Church in Spain can no longer regulate Spaniards' public morality; many people disregard its opinions. According to a 1984 survey,[13] 65 per cent of Spaniards approve the use of contraceptives, 54 per cent would accept married priests, 47 per cent approve divorce – against 40 per cent who do not approve – while 45 per cent – against 41 per cent – accept that premarital sexual relations will occur. What these data amount to is that Spain is a quickly secularizing society. Consequently, it is hardly surprising that the Church failed to block – or even amend – through institutional corporate pressure or through Catholic mobilization, legislation introduced by the Socialist Government on issues which the Church regarded as falling within its own sphere of competence: limiting religious education and facilitating easier divorce and abortion. When it comes to the Church's political influence, public opinion frowns upon its overt involvement: 43 per cent think that the Church should not try to exert influence over government although 32 per cent believe it appropiate to function as a political force (Casanova 1994: 90).

The main conclusion that emerges from the survey is that Spain seems to have adopted the general Western European pattern of secularization; religious faith and morality are privatized. It is not clear what the Church's response will be: will it reinforce the trend by withdrawing to the spiritual care of souls or will it attempt to use its remaining institutional and moral weight to reinforce its moral and social voice? There are some indications that the Church is attempting to resist privatization. During the 1996 general election campaign, it used the pulpit in support of the narrowly victorious conservative Popular Party (PP) led by José Maria Aznar (Gooch 1996). Animated by broadly the same issues as Church leaders in Britain and Germany – abortion choice, moral decline, corruption in national life, unemployment, the importance of the family as the foundation of society – Catholic sermons to churchgoers were seen as blatant electioneering by the then Socialist Government. Yet, if the Church had hoped that a PP victory would lead to a tightening up of abortion laws, it was to be disappointed. While Aznar is a practising Catholic, he left abortion legislation alone for similar reasons to those of President Clinton: there was no wish to alienate centrist voters, especially women. In such a climate it is hard to see the Church in Spain regaining its former predominance when it comes to social and moral issues.

Resisting secularization: religion and politics in Northern Ireland and among Muslims in Western Europe

So far I have examined the impact of secularization upon the mainline Christian Churches in Britain, Germany and Spain. The main conclusion is that, as the hold

---

13. The findings are reported in some detail in Casanova (1994: 89–90).

of religion diminishes, the Churches find themselves on the defensive trying to resist or reverse the tide of secularization and to involve themselves more fully than in the recent past in issues of public concern. In the current section, I focus upon two sets of actors who utilize their religious beliefs as part of socio-political campaigns. First, I examine the theologically conservative Protestant clergy in Northern Ireland who are likely to be more politicized than the laity and are typically as conservative politically. Second, I highlight Muslim immigrant communities in Britain, France and Germany which have shown themselves – in varying degrees – willing to utilize religious beliefs as the basis of political campaigns.

Protestantism in Northern Ireland

The conflict in Northern Ireland between Catholics and Protestants has its roots in the attempts by the British State from the sixteenth century onward to use community settlement to pacify Ireland, a troublesome neighbour. Those who settled in the north-east of the island in the seventeenth and eighteenth centuries were Scots Protestants, whereas the natives were Catholics. 'These are not simply two different religions; they are antithetical and have developed identities in competition' (Bruce 1993: 51).

Following the rise of the Irish nationalist home rule movement in the nineteenth century and an ensuing anti-colonial war against British control, Northern Ireland (Ulster) was created through the partition of the predominantly Catholic island in 1921.[14] Currently, of the 1.5 million people in Northern Ireland, 28 per cent are Roman Catholic; among the remaining 72 per cent, the majority are Protestants divided into Presbyterians (22.9 per cent), Church of Ireland (19 per cent), Methodist (4 per cent) and other small sects (7.6 per cent) (Mews 1989: 294). These are by no means nominal religious adherences: some 70 per cent of Ulster people regularly go to Church, nearly four times the average figure in the rest of the UK.

While several interpretations of Unionism contend, in terms of religion, identity and loyalty they all acknowledge the importance of the religious divide between Catholics and Protestants for the playing out of politics (Aughey 1990). Bruce (1993: 50) argues that in the basic structure of the Protestants' conflict with Catholics, 'religion remains a vital part of their sense of identity'. While not all Ulster Protestants by any means are theologically conservative Christians, he argues that even those who are not find themselves turning back to conservative Protestant ideologies and language to make sense of their apparently beleaguered position and to give purpose to their political agenda. The bottom line is that they have an immense desire, for the most part, to remain part of Britain rather than join 'papist Eire'. To many Ulster Protestants, the nationalist Catholic threat is quite sufficient to give a political role to fundamentalism. Its representatives, most famously exemplified by

14. In 1921 Protestants formed 11 per cent of the population of the island; only 4 per cent of the population of the Republic of Ireland are now said to be Protestants (Bruce 1993: 51).

the Reverend Ian Paisley, a minister of the Free Presbyterian Church, expend much energy in vilification of the 'anti-Christ' (the Pope). Paisley and his like proclaim the Pope's desire is to wipe Protestantism from the face of Northern Ireland because it is the last bastion of evangelical Protestantism in Europe (McCrystal 1996).

Between 1921 and 1971, Northern Ireland was controlled by the Unionist Party, governed by a directly elected parliament at Stormont, near Belfast. Under the premierships of Captain Terence O'Neill (1963–9) and Major Chichester-Clark (1969–71) there were attempts to improve relations with the Irish Republic. However, the Civil Rights Movement protest – against anti-Catholic discrimination in employment and housing – sparked off a popular Protestant backlash in 1971 which swept figures like Paisley and the Reverend Martin Smyth, also a Presbyterian minister and Grand Master of the Orange Order, into positions of socio-political prominence. The 'troubles' had begun. Over the next two decades, several Unionist parties emerged including Paisley's Democratic Unionist Party,[15] each trying to outdo the other as most loyal to the British crown.

The prominence of religion in the politics of the Unionist parties gives weight to the hypothesis that religion in secularizing societies is likely to retain a high place in people's attentions and in their politics when it does something else than mediate between them and God. Because Catholics and Protestants are divided most obviously by religion, it has become *the* symbol of everything that divides the communities. Theologically conservative Protestants – about a third of the non-Catholic population of Northern Ireland – perceive their opposition to a united Ireland as religiously rooted; they have, as Bruce (1993: 53) puts it, a consciously religious view of the civil conflict. At the same time, he argues, religion also has a considerable influence even on those who are *not* themselves evangelicals.

In the early days, Paisley's DUP drew heavily on the membership of the Free Presbyterian Church (FPC) of Ulster; in elections in the 1970s and 1980s nearly two-thirds (64.2 per cent) of DUP candidates were from the FPC, while 'only 1 per cent of non-Roman Catholics are FPs' (Bruce 1993: 55). When they are not from the FPC, DUP activists are very often members of other conservative evangelical denominations. Yet, as noted earlier, many Northern Irish Protestants are neither conservative evangelicals nor Christian fundamentalists. But, as Bruce (1993: 55) explains, 'when given the choice between secular right-wingers and religious right-wingers, many working class *secular* voters have preferred the fundamentalists of the DUP'. The reason for this apparent anomaly becomes clear when one bears in mind the ideological foundations for ethnic identity. Ulster unionism *needs* evangelical Protestantism whereas Irish nationalism does not rely on Catholicism in the same way: the presence of the Irish Republic – over 90 per cent Catholic – encourage northern nationalists. Most Protestants, however, believe that unionism is precarious, because there is nothing more the British Government would like than

15. Winning nearly 250,000 votes (one sixth of the electorate), Paisley became the most popular Unionist politician in the 1984 elections to the European Parliament.

to wash its hands of the problem of Ulster, in the same way that is has been only too willing in many cases to relinquish its hold on other colonies elsewhere in the world when the returns from them fell away. Consequently, the requirement for unionists to assert and defend their claims to be British has compelled them to be clear about the characteristics of their identity. Because successive British Governments have shown themselves to be less than enthusiastic in embracing the unionists, the only other thing to fall back onto is evangelical Protestantism.

The point is that the main purpose of Ulster conservative Protestants, in religion and in politics, is to preserve their identity in the face of two threats: Catholics and lukewarm British Governments. Cultural defence also involves protection of a highly conservative religious world view against liberalism and ecumenism. To defend their religious perceptions, Paisley founded his own Church in the same way that American Christian fundamentalists did three-quarters of a century ago. The Free Presbyterian Church (FPC) now has 10 independent 'Christian schools' and a Bible college; their function is to produce ministerial, missionary and education students. The latter also turn outs 'periodicals and tape recordings, and organizes a round of social activities that form a distinct subculture' (Bruce 1993: 57). The point is that the FPC is not only a spiritual organization ministering to the pastoral care of believers but also conducts social and moral crusades against liberalizing the laws on homosexuality, public house licensing hours and Sunday trading laws. Ulster religious conservatives more generally are also concerned with maintaining citizenship, especially through the DUP, and the fighting of elections. The overall aim of both Church and Party campaigns is to mobilize popular support in defence of the particularistic culture of the Ulster Protestants against those who, they believe, seek to undermine it.

Muslims and politics in Britain, France and Germany

Like the political and religious activities of the Ulster Protestants, Muslim communities in Western Europe have attracted attention in recent years. Islam there is mainly associated with communities of immigrant origin, while the numbers of Muslims have grown as a consequence both of immigration and conversions. This occurred from a time – the 1970s – of widespread European economic recession and an international environment where political upheavals – including Western–Muslim friction following Iran's revolution – have been to the fore. These factors have led to explicitly political positions being taken by elements of the region's Muslim communities. At the same time, they seem to attract increasingly hostile reactions to their presence. Both developments are related to each other.

For Western Europe until the 1960s, Islam remained rather alien, notwithstanding the establishment of a few mosques in some cities. The situation began to change with the expansion of labour migration. Initially, such immigrants were principally defined by the host society vis-à-vis their economic function (as 'guest workers'), their skin colour or their nationality, and only to a lesser extent by their culture

Table 4.2 Numbers of Muslims in selected European countries

Country	Numbers (a)	Total population (b)[1]	Percentage (a of b)
France	2,450,000	57.5	4.26
Germany	1,715,000	80.9	2.12
Britain	800,000	57.9	1.38

Notes: Data refers to 1989, unless indicated otherwise. [1] 1993 figures.
Source: Etienne (1989: 30–31).

and/or religion. 'This reflected the migrants' own perception of their place in their European surroundings, and their relative lack of concern with opportunities for socio-religious expression within the context of the host society' (Nonneman 1996: 382).

Beginning in the 1970s, the religio-cultural dimension became an important social issue in relations between Muslim societies and host communities. This, Nielsen observes (1992: 2), 'was the unforeseen consequence of the drastic change in European immigration policy at the time of the 1972–4 recession'. Although governments halted further labour immigration, they allowed family unification. The result was that the Muslim presence in Western Europe changed from one of migrant workers to social communities in a fuller sense. As a result, contacts between the immigrants and the host society saw a major expansion. By the late 1980s, the number of Muslims in Britain, France and Germany – countries where the families of male 'guest workers' had been allowed to join them – totalled just under five million people.[16] The national breakdown is shown in Table 4.2.

By the 1980s, some elements in many Islamic communities were becoming increasingly politically active. This was especially the case among 'second generation' Muslims, the offspring of migrant workers and their spouses. Born in Europe, they were familiar from the start with Western assumptions about political participation. In some countries – for example, Britain and France – it was relatively easy to acquire citizenship.[17] The effect of the accompanying expectations on the part of these Muslims became apparent in their increased willingness to agitate for what they perceived as their rights.

It was in Britain and France that a backlash against Muslim residents could first be observed. This coincided with the intrusion, from the early 1980s, of international events and concerns into the domestic scenes of many Western European countries, including that of fears of 'Islamic fundamentalism'. As a result of real

16. The majority of French Muslims are from North Africa; most in Britain are either Pakistanis or Bangladeshis (mainly from North East Sylhet in the north-east). Turkish immigrants form the bulk of Germany's Muslim population.

17. In Britain, all individuals coming to the country from the Commonwealth – Pakistan and Bangladesh are both members – 'may vote after a year's residence, become members of the armed forces, the civil service and serve on juries; they may also stand for local and national elected offices' (Goulborne and Joly 1989: 82).

or perceived discrimination and insensitivity to cultural differences, some Muslims – especially of the second generation – began to identify with some of the causes of their fellow Muslims in the Middle East, for instance the Iranian revolution or the Palestinians' struggle for a homeland. Some sections of public opinion in the host societies then reacted by focusing on the perceived excesses of 'Islamic fundamentalism' outside Europe, believing Muslim communities in their own countries were a threat to stability because they adhered to the same beliefs as the 'fundamentalists'. Such a view was exacerbated by growing unemployment. The overall result was the potential for misunderstanding, and increasing friction between communities was considerable.

There were two issues – the Salman Rushdie imbroglio in Britain[18] and the 'headscarves of Creil affair' in France – which were particularly important in focusing attention on the position of Muslims in Western European societies. Both centred around the questioning of some Muslims of the secular principle in Western socio-political life. The progress of the disputes seemed to make it clear that the cultural and religious integration of all elements of Muslim communities might not happen, except in the distant future. Instead, in the short term at least, there was widely observed friction, conflict and disagreement between host societies and elements in the Muslim communities.

The main question which emerged was: is there an inherent, an inevitable, incompatibility between Islamic values and the secular organizing principles of the Western European State? The short answer is no. Scholars including Ayubi (1991) and Piscatori (1986) have argued convincingly that Islam has a history of pragmatism: separation was historically common between the essence of the religious principles and institutions, on the one hand, and those of the temporal ruler and the State, on the other; there was, in short, a large amount of compatability between Islamic precepts and, as Piscatori (1986) puts it, the 'world of nation-states'. The point is that there does not appear to be any impracticable obstacle of principle to a reasonable degree of compatibility between 'Islamic' and 'Western' practices regarding citizenship and the nature of socio-political organization. As Nonneman (1996: 384) notes, 'European Muslims' reactions (themselves varying strongly) may often be less a matter of "Islamic practice" than of a cultural minority's sense of discrimination leading to a search for rallying points'.

Muslim leaders frequently express concern for the development of Islam in Western Europe, especially the moral well-being of believers, particularly where the second generation is concerned. Western society is often portrayed as meaningless, rootless, characterized by crime, juvenile delinquency, riots, the collapse of marriages and sexual promiscuity; in short, suffering many of the deficiencies characteristic of a post-modernist society (Ahmed 1992). Islam, it is postulated, can provide an alternative lifestyle in contrast to the materialist secular society of the West, producing good citizens, a point underlined in the headscarves of Creil and Rushdie affairs.

18. While the Rushdie affair was in many ways a global issue, it was of particular resonance in Britain where the author lives.

Muslims in France: the Headscarves of Creil affair

An example where the national culture of a country has had a major impact on the interaction with Muslim elements perceived as being outside this culture is the French headscarves affair. The headscarves affair erupted in the autumn of 1989 – just after that of Rushdie – and involved the desire of several young Muslim girls to wear Islamic headscarves to school in Creil in Northern France. The affair is usually understood as an attempt to introduce communalism into the religiously neutral sphere of school. France is, of course, *the* country of the Enlightenment, with the related conviction that the common ground for the French is *rationality*, with religion taking a decidedly secondary position. A consequence is that visible signs of religious identity are perceived by many French people as highly disturbing.

The affair not only highlighted the distaste many non-Muslim French have for signs of religion in public life, but also indicated how Islamic networks have spread in France. The offensive was taken by Islamic groups largely composed of students from the Maghreb. They wanted to stage a trial of strength by confronting the French State on the sensitive ground of *laïcité* (secularism) (Kepel 1994: 40). The students' militant defence of Islamic culture seemed to strike a chord with many French Muslims who, it appears, wanted 'positive discrimination' in favour of Muslim girls in French State schools, allowing them to wear the 'Islamic' headscarf and to be excused physical training and music, thus implementing in daily life the break with the surrounding French *jahiliyya* (infidel State and society) (Stenberg 1996: 158). The student militants self-appointed themselves as representatives of 'Islam', aiming to negotiate a 'positive discrimination' which would allow practising Muslims to withdraw, in certain domains, from the laws of the Republic and obey *sharia* law. Thus, Islamic militants succeeded in bringing a religious demand relating to everyday life into the political sphere. They found powerful allies: the hierarchy of the Catholic Church and some leading rabbis supported them because they too were 'determined to seek a renewal of the Christian and Jewish faiths in the teeth of *laïcité*' (Kepel 1994: 41). The conclusion is that in the headscarf affair strong 'defence of Islam' was justified by the perceived attempt by the State forcibly to secularize Muslims by allowing behaviour many perceived as anti-religion. In other words, militant Muslims joined together to defend their religion and culture from attacks from unwelcome secularizing forces.

Muslims in Britain: the Rushdie imbroglio

Like their French counterparts, Muslim immigrants in Britain seek 'to maintain their religious practices in an alien, or at least *new* territory' (Goulborne and Joly 1989: 77). The Rushdie imbroglio is a long-running *cause célèbre,* apparently pitting 'intolerant' Muslims against the principle of free speech. The affair was triggered by a book – *The Satanic Verses*, written by Salman Rushdie, an Indian-born British novelist of Muslim origin – which allegedly insulted the Prophet Muhammad and his wives. For his pains Rushdie received a 'death sentence' from the Iranian leader,

Ayatollah Khomeini. Supported by Iran, *imams* (religious leaders) in Bradford and Dewsbury publicly burnt copies of the book.[19]

How should this incident be perceived? For many Muslims the issue was simple: the book was obscene and should be destroyed; very few seemed to be aware of the significance of book-burning in European history, in the Inquisition and during the Nazi era in Germany. For many non-Muslims, however, the book-burning simply confirmed the idea of Muslims' intolerance. As Nonneman (1996: 385) points out, this mutual incomprehension highlighted the unfortunate socio-political impact of a 'relatively sudden and large influx' of people of a religious culture – Islam – into Britain, a country where religious priorities are not pronounced. Like the contemporaneous French headscarves affair, that involving *The Satanic Verses* was actually about the overall position of Muslims in a highly secular society. When the Rushdie affair exploded at the end of 1988, there was already a growing socio-political movement among some elements of Muslims with the goal of seeking to create better conditions for Islam. Two factors combined to bring about a fertile ground for re-Islamization, or in other words, Islamic deprivatization. First, there is the poor socio-economic position of many second generation Muslims.[20] Second, reduction of State welfare provision under Conservative Governments in the 1980s encouraged Muslims to turn to self-help networks run by the more than 500 British mosques (Golbourne and Joly 1989: 92). For many Muslims, community life is structured by family networks and by the mosques. This structuring results from the characteristic of 'Islam as a *din*, governing not only religious practice and morality but social relationships, marriage, divorce, family relations, economics, politics, and the most humble actions of everyday life' (Goulborne and Joly 1989: 92).

In Britain, as in France, the field of education has led to friction between the State and some elements of the Muslim community. It is hardly surprising that education is an important issue because Muslim parents wish to safeguard Islam among their young, heavily influenced of course by their school experiences; many parents, it appears, believe that their children's school curriculum should incorporate the teachings of Islam, including celebrations for the main Muslim festivals: *Eid ul Fitr* and *Eid ul Adha*; prayer facilities in school; halal food; exemption from sex education; and modest clothing, especially for girls (Goulborne and Joly 1989: 92–4). When such conditions are not met, Muslim children may well be withdrawn from State education. Mohamed Mukadam, parent governor of Birchfield Community School, a Birmingham primary school where 500 Muslim children were withdrawn from mainstream religious education in 1996, believes segregated education is necessary to stop young Muslims drifting away from the faith: 'We have no doubt that if we don't act to preserve our traditional faith it will be diluted, as the Christian faith has

19. According to Kepel (1994: 38), they were inspired by a Pakistan-based Islamist group, the *Jama' at-i-islami*, founded by A. A. Mawdudi, a follower of Sayyid Qutb, initiator of the Muslim Brotherhood. In addition, Dewsbury is the European headquarters of the Tabligh, a transnational Islamic society. During the 1987 election campaign, some British Muslim networks were calling, *inter alia*, for a ban on 'books presenting an "unauthentic" image of Islam'.

20. 'In Bradford, 78 per cent of young Asians and blacks are still without a job one year after leaving school, compared to 60 per cent of white youths' (Mews 1989: 291).

been', he opined (Narayan 1996). There was a similar development in Batley, West Yorkshire, where 1,500 pupils had been withdrawn from religious education in 40 schools by mid-1996. Britain had 24 Muslim schools in February 1996, including a growing number of schools set up by parents (Narayan 1996).

Reflecting growing concern with the maintenance of Islamic values in a secular society, places where many Muslim immigrants live – working-class suburbs in inner city areas – are increasingly 'covered by a huge web of Islamic associations of various shades of feeling and opinion' (Kepel 1994: 37). Such re-Islamization is reflected in the formation of Islamist groups: the Young Muslims, *Al Muntada al Islami*, Muslim Welfare House, *Al-Muhajiroun*, and *Hizb ut Tahrir* (Liberation Party). Such groups reflect a range of Islamic positions; *Hizb ut Tahrir*, the most militant, is believed to have 2,000 members in Britain. Its activists preach separation from Western society, employing 'anti-Israel, anti-homosexual, anti-liberal rhetoric' (Dodd 1996). Some young Muslims are believed to be attracted to *Hizb ut* because they have 'higher expectations than their elders, and a correspondingly deeper sense of injustice' (Mews 1989: 291).

In sum, in both Britain and France, it was the encroachment of secular values upon Muslims which was at the root of growing militancy. Whereas most of Britain's and France's Muslim immigrants come from areas – the Indian subcontinent and North Africa respectively – where Islam is an integral part of local culture, the same is not true to the same extent among Muslims in Germany. Nonetheless, there has been a 'return' to Islam among a proportion of Turkish Muslims in Germany in response to the impact of secular society upon them.

Muslims in Germany: Islam and Turkish immigrants

Seventy-four per cent of the 1.7 million Muslims in Germany are of Turkish origin (Etienne 1989: 31). German sociologists choose the term 'ethnic group'[21] to describe the country's Turkish community because the term is wide enough to indicate the strong, deep-rooted specificities which bind together Turkish nationals as well as the social and political diversity within the Turkish community. Turkish immigration to Germany has been focused from within the Anatolian peasantry. It is argued that such people are often shocked by the lifestyle of the city-dwellers among whom they live; the result is that many of the Muslim immigrants return to their traditional values based on religious identity. As in Britain, this is a means of ensuring the cohesion of the community and the family, the best antidote to the perceived destructive effects of German urban life.

From the beginning of Turkish emigration in the 1950s, the conditions in which it took place helped to establish a central place for Islam – both as faith and as an expression of identity – in the daily life of many immigrants. As in France and Britain, immigration galvanized the creation of Islamic networks in the secular

---

21. As Bozarslan (1989: 115) notes 'an ethnic group is never a uniform mass; the term signifies a community characterized by various socio-economic conditions and often by varied cultural and political conditions'.

environment of Germany. They had been forbidden in Turkey since the era of the secular leader Kemal Atatürk in the 1920s; in Germany, however, they were free to re-emerge, organize, expand and express themselves. A battle for dominance grew between various Islamic movements, including the *Süleymanci* and *Milli Görüs*, with close ties to the current Prime Minister Necmeddin Erbakan and the Iran-backed Cemaleddin Kaplan group, 'which advocates nothing less than an Islamic revolution in Turkey' (Bozarslan 1989: 115–17, 120).

The main point is that there is a high level of religious and ethnic disunity among Turkish immigrants in Germany. Alignments and divisions in Turkey are replicated in Germany; they are much more important than theological differences or differing views of the place of Turks as Muslims in Europe. The break-up of religious unity has led to the politicization of Islam in Germany. Yet, contrary to the apocalyptic vision often presented in the media, the majority of Muslims in the country see Islam as a way of life, 'a sacred code of moral standards, rather than as a political programme' (Bozarslan 1989: 123). Unlike growing numbers of mostly young Muslims in France and Britain, few in Germany seem to want to fight for the transformation of Germany into a part of *dar-ul-Islam*. While wishing for a transformation of Turkish society, most Muslims – no doubt concerned about their status as the need for 'guest workers' is increasingly questioned by German politicians and society – do not seek to upset things, limiting their intervention in the public arena to the defence of religious autonomy. Islam is moderate, even conformist; it is a force for the political representation of community interests, increasingly ready to flirt with the idea of integration.

Conclusion

Western Europe is a region where religion had an important political role in the historical past. The evidence of this chapter suggests, however, that with growing secularization that role is now much diminished. On the other hand, we are witnessing a new religious lease of life in political debate. This century there have been a few basic responses to the relationship of faith and politics. Sometimes, Christian convictions have been expressed in socialist or other ideologies. Or a moral gloss, seen as vaguely Christian, has been put on a laissez-faire market approach. More often, however, Christianity has failed to engage with political issues. In other cases, faith has been a matter of private conviction and good standards, but must not be spoken in the public arena. There was a trend for the Churches to withdraw from the public realm as religion became increasingly privatized. Only in Northern Ireland have a number of Churches – collectively those ministering to the beleaguered Protestants – retained a high public profile. Similarly, for at least a significant proportion of Western Europe's Muslim immigrants, religion forms an important basis of identity, informing socio-political organization especially in the light of hostility from some elements within the host communities.

More recently, however, there has been a growing readiness of many Churches to speak out in their corporate capacity on issues of public policy. This is partly because religion and spirituality are seen as increasingly important: there is grow-ing consciousness that society's problems are no longer susceptible to mere politi-cal solutions; they also have to do with people's spiritual formation. There is also a widespread perception that, in the post-modern era, individualism and a decline of public morals have reached alarming proportions. As a result, many Church leaders are determined to take a leading role in the debate about the future of society.

But this is not to suggest that Churches and their leaders are likely to regain a high degree of political persuasiveness. The paradox is that while political leaders across Western Europe are willing enough to proclaim their adherence to 'Christian values', most people no longer attend Church regularly or even believe that Church leaders should have much – or any – political influence. So it is easy for politicians to pay lip-service to what Church leaders say, in the comfortable knowledge that they no longer represent important constituencies. An interest in religion and spiri-tuality may well be growing, but it is likely to be an individualist, self-interested thing without clear ramifications for politics. It is reflective of highly secular soci-eties which – for the most part – show little or no sign of turning back to institu-tional religion.

Chapter 5

Eastern Europe: from communism to belief

Theories of modernization have long predicted the weakening of religious faith and the consequent demise of religious institutions as societies became more 'modern', that is, more secular. Science, attacking faith unremittingly, called into question spiritual explanations of the world. Literal interpretations of religious teachings, on which traditional religious hegemonies were based, would be fatally undermined. However, things have not gone entirely as the theory expected: while industrialization and urbanization undoubtedly transform world views based on the givens of kinship relations and village culture, there is no concomitant certainty that religious believers will cease to believe.

However, in much of Western Europe the old secularization theory seems to hold. With growing modernization, key indicators of secularization have increased: on the level of expressed beliefs, on numbers of people coming into the clergy, and on the level of Church-related behaviour, such as attendance at services of worship and adherence to Church-dictated codes of personal behaviour on sexuality, reproduction and marriage. In particular, Catholics – once regarded as completely under the thumb of papal domination – now increasingly choose to follow their own conceptions of morality rather than the Church's (Hooper 1996a). In two of Western Europe's Catholic centres – Italy and Spain – there is a rapid decline in Church-related religion. The Church is now much less authoritative than it once was when pronouncing on social, moral and ethical issues. The situation in Eastern Europe[1] seems to be following a similar pattern. Where Catholicism is strong – in Poland, the Czech Republic, Slovakia and Hungary – the post-Communist era is not witnessing a continuing presence of the Church as a permanently important political actor (Michel 1994). This adds weight to the view that secularization *normally* proceeds in industrializing societies except when 'religion finds or retains work to do other than relating people to the supernatural' (Wallis and Bruce 1992: 17). In other words, *only* when religion does something more than mediating between

1. The term 'Eastern Europe' no longer covers the Czech Republic, Hungary or Poland, which believe they are joining the West. Because of this, it is now common to refer to 'Central and Eastern Europe' instead of Eastern Europe *tout court*. However, for reasons of stylistic conciseness I will use the term 'Eastern Europe' in this chapter to cover all the former communist states of the region.

the individual and God does it retain a high place in people's attentions and in their politics.

Regarding Europe, exceptions to this rule include Protestants and Catholics in Northern Ireland and Muslim emigrants to Western European cities. What these groups have in common is that they by and large retain their religious behavioural codes in order to cope with identity problems or the perceived encroachment of alien cultures. However, such counter-examples are not sufficient to falsify the theory that normally modernization leads to a general secularization. The result, Berger (1997: 35) claims, is that 'there is now a massively secular Euroculture and it is not fanciful to predict that there will be similar developments in eastern Europe'.

It was once widely believed that communist domination had greatly hastened the decline of the hold of religion in Eastern Europe. Communism attempted to absorb the religious in the political, and even the scientific within the political. Furthermore, the repressive force of the State and decades-long official atheistic campaigns were believed to have accelerated the processes of secularization, making predictions of religious demise all the more compelling. How then to explain the pivotal role of Christian Churches in the overthrow of communism in the late 1980s? How then to interpret the widely reported religious resurgence since then?

At the end of the 1980s, almost overnight, it seems, there was an extensive – and, for the most part, surprisingly peaceful – shift in power. In the USSR's erstwhile satellites, flags of precommunist territories replaced the hammer and sickle. After the mid-1980s State policy in Russia itself moved increasingly emphatically away from an anti-religion posture. President Yeltsin, in attending services for the high points of the Russian Orthodox liturgical year, clearly intends to underline the increase in the Church's status, while the country's cathedrals have now been returned to their original owners, the Orthodox Church. Religious liberalization has also been exemplified by the fact that other Churches are allowed to operate and their clergy to proselytize, although, as we shall see, this has led to a religious turf war in Russia. Nonetheless, in contrast to the communist era now they can 'own property and function as legally recognized entities' (Ramet 1991: 80). These changes amount to a huge – and hugely unexpected – reversal in the fortunes of religion not only in Russia but also in Eastern Europe more generally. At the beginning of the 1990s, Patrick Michel (1991: 125) argued that such changes could happen only 'by some miracle'. Martin (1994) claims to see evidence of a reversal of secularization, in effect, a re-Christianization of Eastern Europe.

It is important to be clear as to what has and what has not happened. Religion's right to exist does not necessarily amount to a situation where its institutions will enjoy *permanent* accretions of *political* power and of social significance; the onward march of secularization will still occur if there are no strong reasons for it not to. And it seems that, as Berger claims, secularization *is* progressing, if we mean by the term a reduction of the political importance and social significance of religious dictates and institutions.

I will argue in the current chapter that the focusing of pro-democracy demands in Christian Churches in the 1980s was not because anti-Communists necessarily believed that religious involvement was a *sine qua non* of democratization, but for an altogether more mundane reason. In communist societies there were no alternative social spaces where opposition could organize; everything else was dominated by the Party-State. However, church buildings sometimes offered a physical space, *if* their clergy were sympathetic to pro-democracy demands. Not all were: many worked for the KGB or the *Stasi* (Philps 1997). Yet, crucially, the State – watched closely in the 1980s by international human rights groups – was no longer prepared to use the strong-arm tactics of the 1950s to try to crush religion *tout entier*. Yet a shift to democracy is not necessarily sufficient for Churches' social and political prominence to be maintained if – as seems likely is occurring in much of Eastern Europe – society is no longer prepared to accept its leadership on important social and moral issues.

I will also argue that in Eastern Europe the Churches' political importance was essentially transitory (Johnston 1993, Michel 1994). It was almost wholly reflective of a fundamental shift in public opinion – that is, an increase in dissidence which of necessity focused upon the Churches as relatively open social spaces, places from where the anti-Communist struggle could be organized – *at a certain brief historical period*. However, once democracy was won, Churches' political influence quickly waned. Put another way, there was a partial religious reprivatization which, as in Latin America after democratic renewal, led to a declining voice in political society. To add weight to the argument I offer case studies of three countries: Poland, East Germany and Russia. Each has a different Christian denomination predominating.[2] In sum, the chapter focuses on three main issues: (a) Church–State relations in Eastern Europe generally before the *annus mirabilis* of 1989; (b) the association between religion and nationalism in the USSR's satellite countries; and (c) the decline in the political significance of Churches in the 1990s. The main contention is that, despite continuing adherence to religious beliefs at the level of the individual, the aggregate trend in Eastern Europe is that, under conditions of democratic pluralism, secular materialism turns attention away from traditional forms of religiosity.

The Catholic Church is the leading religious institution in several Eastern European countries. As in Latin America, the impact of the *aggiornamento* ('updating') and of Vatican II encouraged national Churches in the region to adopt a higher political profile. However, under the influence of Pope John Paul II, the Church later withdrew from overt engagement in politics to concentrate upon pastoral concerns. The result was that Eastern European Catholic Churches found themselves in a situation comparable to that of their Spanish and Latin American counterparts after their countries' return to democracy: despite being leading voices in pro-democracy movements, they swiftly became politically marginalized (Michel 1994: 40, Casanova 1994). In Spain, this was because the reintroduction of institutionalized political competition gave at least partial vent to nationalist aspirations, channeling communal conflict away from potentially virulent combinations of God and Nation. As late as 1974 – a year before the death of General Franco and the

---

2. In Poland the dominant Church is the Catholic Church, in East Germany it is the Evangelical-Lutheran Protestant Church, while in Russia the Russian Orthodox Church is spiritually hegemonic.

subsequent collapse of his regime – both Basque and Catalan nationalists had very strong religious components helping the expression of opposition. However, by the 1990s, the linkage between nationalism and religion had almost disappeared under democracy and prosperity (Johnston 1992: 68). The same pattern seems to be occurring in Eastern Europe: as we shall see, Churches were nearly always emblematic of anti-Soviet nationalism in the USSR's satellites. But once communist regimes were removed and competitive party systems introduced, most people quickly transferred political allegiances to secular parties.

Church and State during the communist era

Before the overthrow of communist governments, the countries of Eastern Europe were characterized by Church–State relations where the latter dominated the former. Following the example of the Soviet Union,[3] after World War II the new communist regimes made serious attempts drastically to reduce the social status and significance of religion. In Medhurst's (1981) terminology, such regimes were 'anti-religious polities', making serious attempts to 'throttle' religion. No religious organizations had the right to be actively engaged with matters of public concern or to play a role in public life. Churches were to be confined to liturgical institutions alone, that is, their only permitted role was the holding of divine services. The point is that the communist regimes saw that it was impossible to get rid of religion completely so they grudgingly allowed people to retain their religious beliefs, but only as a *private* concern. On the one hand, this constituted a kind of promise that the authorities would respect the privacy of people's religious faith and practice. On the other, it was normally no more than a camouflage for a policy of aggressive religious privatization.

Before the democratic revolutions of 1989–90, Church–State relations fell into two broad categories: 'accommodative' and 'confrontational'.[4] Church and State were in *confrontational* mode when they argued over the premise for their mutual relations and operated in the absence of a *modus vivendi*; neither side felt able to make serious compromises. In this situation, State hostility towards religion was overt and scarcely disguised. Consequently, Churches would often be thrown into postures of defensive defiance. Czechoslovakia and Poland offer perhaps the best examples of *prolonged* confrontation between State and Church. In Czechoslovakia after the communist-led coup d'état of 1948 there was bitter confrontation between the State and the Catholic Church.[5] In Poland, the authorities had to proceed with considerable caution against the Church because it enjoyed a great deal of popular support; over 90 per cent of Poles are Catholic (Ramet 1991: 78, 80).

The *accommodative* style, on the other hand, involved compromise on both sides; in other words, there were rules of the game to which each side adhered. One

3. In the USSR the number of permitted places of worship was greatly reduced after the 1917 revolution.

4. This section simplifies a complicated picture. For a full discussion of the issues, see Ramet (1991).

5. Catholics outnumbered Protestants by more than 10–1 in Czechoslovakia.

important factor on the part of the Church was that religious officials would strive to avoid criticizing government policies in order to be left in peace. Another aspect was that the majority of priests and high-ranking Church officials – with the exception of Poland and to a degree Hungary – consistently failed to confront the State on a variety of issues. Some religious officials actively collaborated with State security forces (Slater and Engelbrekt 1993: 49, Martin 1994: 8).

More frequently, however, State–Church relations oscillated between confrontation and accommodation. For example, in East Germany they were confrontational from 1948 until 1971; after that there was more accommodation noticeable. In the USSR, the Russian Orthodox Church also experienced periods of both accommodation and confrontation: State policies of repression were apparent in 1917–43, 1958–64 and 1975–85. They were interspersed with periods of relative harmony between Church and State (Hackel 1989: 272).

However, the overall effect of trying to remove God from public discourse only resulted in religion being driven underground. By 'merely' surviving, religion nevertheless constituted an often intolerable dissidence to Marxist states' desire for totalitarian control. The extent to which they failed to expunge religion from people's minds was made clear by the anti-Communist revolutions of 1989–90, almost everywhere in the region led or coordinated by Christian Churches (Huntington 1991). By this time, communism had not only taken on the negative associations of power once borne by many Churches, it had also gone further, seeking to deny *any* transcendental point of reference beyond itself. When the all-embracing world view started to decompose, the victim turned out to be both communism as ideology and the Communist State as institution. The removal of the totalitarian ideology left a gaping hole; for many people religion filled it.

Grinding governmental authoritarianism, a lack of economic growth and the inhibition of personal and political freedoms – including freedom of worship – were important factors in the collapse of Eastern Europe's communist regimes. Churches, in the absence of alternatives, increasingly found themselves the focus of popular demands for democracy as opposition activists gravitated to the – often tenuous – open spaces many managed to maintain. Encouraged by this and by growing perceptions of regime weakness, some Church figures began openly to criticize their governments. However, as in Latin America at the same time, there were both dissident and quiescent figures within the Churches; the former attacked the latter for their willingness to acquiesce to religious privatization and grinding State control. Attempting to undermine the position of religious dissidents, the authorities sought to exploit intra-Church tensions for their own ends, in effect, to divide in order to facilitate dominance. Such tactics were not new: in the early years after 1945 there had been active State encouragement of priests' associations independent of hierarchical control. Political regimes hoped they would weaken religious leaders' authority by creating the social conditions in which both ordinary religious believers and priests would be as little dependent on the hierarchy as possible. Yet, in the long run, divide and rule tactics failed: instead, in the USSR's satellite states, religion became strongly associated with nationalist goals of independence from Soviet rule.

Religion and nationalism in the USSR's satellites

Domination by the USSR – a multi-national, imperial State – became increasingly onerous for many in its satellite states as time went on. Despite the attempts of the authorities to suppress religion, nationalist sentiments were kept alive, passing into people's world views 'through primary socialization in . . . religious-nationalist value system[s]' (Johnston 1992: 68). Frequently nationhood was legitimated in terms of a community of the faithful. The Church and nation were merged, with nationalist demands giving rise to calls for religious freedom. Nationalism, deprived of the right to express its sentiments openly, began to coalesce around the only possible symbols of dissidence: the Churches. The latter became in many cases the epitome of the desire for freedom from Soviet domination. Over time, religion and nationalism became closely entwined, together forming ideologies of resistance to communist rule, 'from Czechoslovakia to Georgia' (Martin 1994: 10).

The close association between national oppositions and national Churches led to the development of religio-nationalist subcultures which fed off mergers of nationhood, language and national Church. Catholic Poland and Czechoslovakia offer useful examples in this regard. Despite years of governmental repression and anti-religious campaigning, anti-Soviet and anti-State linking of Church and nation were highly consequential for the demise of their communist systems. In both countries, the identification of the nation with Catholicism was so strong during the communist era that loyalty to the Church was viewed as a question of patriotism. The Church was a great deal more popular than the official international proletariat line pumped out by the local communist parties. As Martin (1994: 11) points out, 'whatever their internationalist pretensions, and all the talk about the international working class, [the parties] often promoted the crudest chauvinism'. In Poland in particular, where the Church was never cowed by the authorities, dissidents openly used it as a focal point for opposition. In Czechoslovakia, there were numerous Catholic affiliates of the human rights group, Charter 77.

Throughout the region the close association of Church and nationalists led to the emergence of what has been called 'Christian undergrounds', even when there was a less close relationship between Church and nation than in Poland. For example, because the East German 'nation' was a post-war concoction, opposition figures had nothing like the same relationship with the leading Evangelical Church as their counterparts in Catholic Poland. Nonetheless, a Church-focused underground covertly grew. Yet because religious privatization and secularization had proceeded far, the religious underground was compelled to take up various non-religious issues – for example, environmental pollution, which the authorities had declared an exclusively capitalist phenomenon – so as to defray the accusation that they were only religious groups. In Hungary, on the other hand, grassroots organizations with a strong Christian-pacifist tinge, analogous to Latin America's base communities, were formed in the 1970s and 1980s. In sum, religious dissidence in the Soviet satellites fed off two main grievances: (a) the desire for personal ethical autonomy free of grinding State control and (b) the corporate pursuit of nationalist autonomy. The important point is that local nationalisms were unwilling to be compliant vehicles of domination from Moscow and joined up with Churches to produce potent ideologies of opposition.

The power elites of communism were able to *harness* nationalism in only two situations. The first was when Soviet authorities used the compliant Russian Orthodox Church as a vehicle of national sentiment against the autocephalous Churches of the Ukraine, especially the proscribed Uniate Church (also known as the Greek Catholic Church), a focal point of Ukrainian nationalism. Second, where there were competing nationalisms – especially at the peripheries of the empire – the Soviet authorities would back one group over others, in effect, using divide and rule tactics to ensure its continuing dominance. Mingling religion and ethnicity, various nations at the periphery – Armenian Christians confronting Azeri Muslims over the Nagorny Karabakh territory or disputes in Tatarstan between local Muslim Tatars and Christian Russians – were in conflict throughout much of the 1980s (Martin 1994: 11–12). Yet, as Soviet power began palpably to decline, the Government made ultimately unsuccessful attempts to buy off discontent at the margins of the empire by backing certain religio-ethnic groups in their nationalist struggles.

This section has sought to illustrate how cultural and political subordination to the Russian centre accentuated the merger of religion and nationalist oppositions in the satellites. Pursuing autonomy or independence, religious-nationalist opposition subcultures – exalting cultural traditions and national Churches and languages – strongly emphasized historical periods of political freedom to rally support against Soviet domination. National Churches were highly important symbols of the nation and of regime illegitimacy in many areas, including Poland, Czechoslovakia, Georgia, Armenia, Ukraine and the Baltic states of Latvia, Estonia and Lithuania. In Russia itself, however, the national Church, the Russian Orthodox Church, was supportive of the communist regime, sometimes deployed under strict State control as a vehicle of national sentiment against rival Churches in, for example, the Ukraine.

Churches and opposition in Poland, East Germany and Russia

In this section I turn to an examination of the role of Churches in the emergence of anti-Communist opposition in Poland, East Germany and the USSR in the 1980s. Each has a different national Church – respectively Catholic, Lutheran Protestant and Russian Orthodox – while their positions in relation to their specific communist regimes ranged on one extreme from more or less outright confrontation in Poland, to a more emollient line in East Germany, to periods of strong support for the State in the USSR at the other.

Economic failure, massive pollution, denial of basic human rights and political rights prevailed in each of the three countries by the 1980s. Encouraged by the ripple effects of *perestroika* and of the Soviet leader, Gorbachev's, refusal to send in the tanks to crush revolt, opposition forces grew in strength, with Churches in both Poland and East Germany playing important roles in the structuring of pro-democracy groups.

Poland

Poland's anti-Communist resistance was a crucial factor in the emergence of similar movements elsewhere in the region in the 1980s. The role of the Polish Catholic Church went far beyond the purely symbolic. Because its organization was public, and its resources considerable, it was able to play a substantial role in the early mobilization and coordination of the opposition. Unlike any other Church in Eastern Europe at the time, the Church in Poland had schools and universities, while its organization was freed from the demands of mere survival. These factors allowed the application of resources to more expansive goals, while control of educational facilities gave it a ready audience for its goals of fundamental change. In short, its considerable resources were put to use, directly and indirectly, in propagating the illegitimacy of the regime and galvanizing opposition to it.

As already noted, after the founding of the communist State in 1948, the Catholic Church had engaged in long periods of confrontation with the regime. However, by the early 1970s it was being criticized by secular opponents of the Government for its caution in this regard. Catholic dissidents from the official strategy of critical dialogue with the regime were given encouragement by the decision of the Church hierarchy in the Vatican to offer a clear lead on issues like democracy and human rights. The result was that the institutional Church in Poland became greatly encouraged to throw its considerable weight into openly opposing the regime. The shift in emphasis became even more noticeable with the accession of a Polish pope, John Paul II, in 1978. He began immediately to speak out eloquently for human rights and against authoritarian government. A papal visit to Poland in 1979 lent powerful symbolic support to the anti-Communist opposition forces (Diamond 1993: 57).

Buttressed by the Pope's personal commitment to human rights and democracy, the Church became especially prominent in the pro-democracy movement in the early 1980s, playing a pivotal role in the initial organization of opposition (Chrypinski 1989, Casanova 1994, Chilton 1995). This was not only because of the popular perception of the Church as the *national* Church but also because of the absence of viable alternatives: the Church was a *relatively* open space in an otherwise authoritarian society, so it was appropriate that it would emerge as a principal vehicle for protest, if Church leaders were supportive. Following the Pope's visit, most were. Initially in tandem with the secular trade union movement, Solidarity, the Church opposed, denounced, frustrated and – eventually – was pivotal in removing the Communist Government in 1989 (Huntington 1991: 73–85). The formation of Solidarity was strongly influenced by the papal visit of 1979. The relationship of Polish Catholicism to Solidarity changed over time. Solidarity became both politicized and secularized, and, with a changing context of political opportunities, it left its roots in the Church behind.

We need to understand the Church's *political* opposition in part as stemming from the difficulty of fulfilling its *spiritual* objectives under the communist regime. Any Church's mission is of course primarily spiritual; but if the conditions for ministering to souls are highly unfavourable it is not surprising that a Church will harbour the desire for a more favourable religious terrain. Due to the repression and totalitarian tactics of the communist regime in Poland which, like its counterpart in the Soviet Union, sought to crush religion, there developed a theology of resistance that amounted to a *de facto* grassroots politicization of the Catholic Church. Initially, senior figures in the Church – such as Cardinal Josef Glemp – played a cautious role of mediator between government and opposition, rather than throwing full weight behind the reformists (Huntington 1991: 82). However, a cadre of mostly youthful, junior priests – who collectively identified with society's aspirations towards the achievement of basic political and social freedoms – took leading roles in the creation and consolidation of representative social movements, even before the Pope's visit (Chrypinski 1989: 222). Such activists received a great fillip from the papal visit in 1979 in their efforts towards fundamental social and political reforms. Some – like the celebrated priest and social activist, Father Popieluszko – were murdered by the State for their efforts.

The Communist Government finally collapsed in late 1989. Flushed with success in helping to overthrow the hated regime, some Polish Catholics, most of them lay, began to press for the 'reinstatement of ecclesiastical norms in public law' (Martin 1994: 4). But they met with no success, because the majority of Poles did not want it. As Michel (1994: 34) notes, the problem for the Church was how to define its place within the post-Communist world. 'Everything seems to indicate that it will be a challenge much more difficult than that posed by the Soviet system.' Why should this be the case? The paradox is that while many Poles looked to the Church as a nationalist focal point of anti-Communism, once democracy was won most shifted their attentions to conventional – that is, secular – political parties to try to achieve socio-political aspirations and objectives. The diminishing socio-political power of the Church was clearly illustrated when it became obvious that its opposition to abortion, divorce and the suitability of a former communist for the post of national president in the 1995 election were not endorsed by most Poles. In short, there was a swift – and clear – 'distancing of Polish political culture from the Church' on such issues (Johnston 1992: 71–2). No doubt aware of its declining influence, the Church did not dare sponsor or even overtly support one particular political party. This was probably because of fear that its position would be undermined further if its favoured party did poorly in elections.

The saga of the role of the Catholic Church in undermining and then bringing down the Communist Government suggests that in a certain historical period – the 1970s and 1980s – its political and social influence among ordinary Poles reached its apogee.[6] The swift decline in influence in the 1990s – with the views of the Church unable to prevail on a range of political, social and moral questions – adds weight to the view that Poland, in many ways a rather secular society, was happy to see the Church fulfil a leading opposition role when there was no other viable alternative, but less willing to afford it a principal voice during a period of democracy and pluralist politics. Put another way, religion was partially reprivatized after the communist era. Such an outcome is in line with the argument that *under normal circumstances* modernization leads to growing secularization.

---

6. The public approval rating of Catholic clergy reportedly fell by 10 per cent between 1989 and 1997. I am indebted to my colleague, Dr Stephen Carter, for this information.

The German Democratic Republic (GDR)

Whereas the Polish Catholic Church became the leading voice of the opposition in the 1980s, it is more difficult to assess the role of the main Protestant Churches in the GDR in the same period.[7] This was because in the GDR the influence of the Churches was greatly curtailed during the communist era; they did not function as a focal point of opposition in anything like the same way as they did in Poland (Martin 1994: 9). Instead, they were reduced, partly by the onward march of secularization, partly by State pressure, to the status of voluntary associations. However, unlike in Poland, the subordination of Church to State in (East) Germany was actually the historical norm. This traditional relationship helps to explain why the East German secret service (the *Stasi*) was able to infiltrate the country's Churches and to recruit among the clergy (Lease 1993). By the 1980s, Churches in East Germany were often perceived as fatally compromised by their association with the State. Consequently, it was impossible for them to function easily as conduits of secular opposition. Unlike in Poland, the Churches had no real claim to be emblems and symbols of popular aspirations for political change.

Secularization in East Germany was not only due to the considerable – and considerably successful – propagandistic efforts of the authorities, but also to the 'natural' trend towards a more secular society in *most* industrializing countries. Two points are worth emphasizing in this regard. First, between 1950 and the late 1980s membership of the main Protestant Churches fell by 70 per cent. Whereas nearly 82 per cent of the population described themselves as belonging to the main Protestant Churches in 1950, by 1964 a quarter of those had died or left; by 1970 just over 40 per cent of the population retained their membership in the Churches. Ten years after that only 29 per cent of East Germans professed adhesion to them. By 1988, a year before the upheavals, the Churches could count on the allegiance of a mere 23 per cent of East Germans. This rate of people leaving the Churches parallels – or even exceeds – that of many Western European countries during the same period.

Second, the steep decline in the numbers of religious believers made it quite easy for the authorities to proclaim Churches as increasingly marginal to society. The decline in their social position, regime spokesmen maintained, amounted to a situation where they should only play a 'necessary' role under socialism, they could 'never be fully integrated in . . . society as a social force' (quoted in Ramet 1991: 78). But what *was* a 'necessary' role'? What it *seemed* to amount to was that the Churches would function as some kind of interlocutor between the State and society without, however, enjoying a correspondingly important social position. The Churches as a result found it necessary to walk a tightrope between, on the one hand, opportunistic appeasement of the government and the ruling SED party and, on the other, to various interest groups within society. Such an ambiguous position nevertheless permitted the Churches to exercise whatever effectiveness remained to them: as a

---

7. About one million of East Germany's 7–10 million Christians were Catholics. Most of the remainder were Protestants of the Evangelical-Lutheran Church. I concentrate on the latter in this section.

kind of social safety valve they helped relieve some pressure by providing protected space for those who sought economic and political change (Lease 1993: 167). Since open opposition was not possible, 'private' and unofficial protests – via the Churches – were the only, albeit limited, avenues available to political nonconformists. The Churches were only able to *survive* by *not* taking an official stance in relation to dissidence, and above all by not identifying, or helping to formulate opposition. East Germany, it must not be forgotten, was a completely closed-off society. One went along with the demands of the government because there was simply no other choice: until the end of the 1980s one could not leave the country except by express permission of the authorities.

The result was that the socio-political influence of the Churches steadily declined. By the 1980s, they were reduced to the level of being a potential venue for pluralistic political thought, but not in themselves a source of such thought. What this amounts to is that the Churches, despite their role as 'official' State–society intermediary, lost the power struggle with the ruling Communist Party. At the same time, they *did* manage to preserve a significant function as a kind of collective social pressure release valve. The main point, however, is that the Churches *had* to fit into the system, while simultaneously providing a quasi-alternative to the very structure of communist domination of which they were forced to be an integral part (Lease 1993: 168).

There is controversy over just *what* was the Church's role in the overthrow of the communist regime in November 1989. On the one hand, some argue that the leading Protestant Churches were collectively the main force in the overthrow of communism (Prins 1990, James 1991). However, others maintain that their role in this regard has been unwarrantedly exaggerated (Lease 1993). This is because after four decades of subordination to communist rule it is inconceivable that the Churches were in an organizational position to be in the vanguard of demands for fundamental change. However, because the State authorities were unwilling to use violence to maintain their position, the Churches – still *relatively* open social spaces in the absence of alternatives – *were* able to take up an important position in chairing discussions between the regime and the opposition. Ramet (1991: 92) claims that Churches made a considerable contribution to the political changes 'by providing organizational support to an otherwise relatively inchoate opposition'.

If the Churches were not the main catalyst galvanizing the social upheavals of 1989, what was? The impetus, Lease (1993: 168) argues, came from two main sources: first, there was a lack of legitimation from Moscow for the use of military force so the regime was at a loss as to how to proceed to deal with the situation; as a result, the situation was allowed to drift, which only encouraged the opposition. Second, the opening of the Austrian–Hungarian border in late 1989 – allowing East Germans to leave the country – became the focal point for a mass exodus from the country. This encouraged the opposition to redouble their efforts to force the regime to stand down. Yet, somewhat paradoxically, despite the steep decline in the Churches' authority, they still managed to play a major organizational role in the massive changes that occurred in 1989. How can this be explained? Generally, 'autonomous groups played a very uneven role in the sudden changes that occurred in 1989' in the GDR (Sadowski 1993: 187). The Churches had a leading role by virtue of the fact that there were no extant alternatives: few secular activists – much less organizations – were left to coordinate the transition from communist rule: most had either emigrated or been expelled to the West by the regime by this time. The result was a severe diminution of the ability of the secular opposition to establish a network of autonomous groups. Because they still had a national – albeit weakened – organizational network, the leading Protestant Churches were able to play a crucial mobilizational role, almost by default. Their influence was, however, especially pronounced in the vast demonstrations in mid-1989 around the Nikolaikirche in Leipzig. During this initial period of mobilization and of mass public demonstrations preceding the downfall of the communist leader, Erich Honecker, Churches in Leipzig, already renowned for being champions of human rights and of peace concerns, were actively involved in the organization of public protests. As the opposition momentum built up, Churches throughout the country gradually became the main forums for opposition meetings, with Christians often acting as ushers for crowds at demonstrations. Christian leaders urged 'the avoidance of all acts which might excuse recourse to the tanks visibly available in the side streets. They even offered refuge to Honecker after his fall from power' (Martin 1994: 10).

By the time of the overthrow of the communist regime, the Churches had established themselves as a leading socio-political player. Their influence was illustrated in the first post-Communist parliamentary elections of March 1990: 14 clergymen were elected to the 400-strong legislature. In addition, four serving or former priests were appointed as members of the transitory Lothar de Maiziere Government in the same year. However, as in Poland, the political influence of the Churches soon waned once a democratic regime was in place. While gaining a great deal of public trust during the political upheavals of 1989, they were still in a position to lose that trust quickly. Resentment towards them emerged when it became clear that they wanted new privileges in the post-Communist era. In particular, they demanded the same tax breaks already enjoyed by their counterparts in West Germany. For this they were widely criticized. By the early 1990s there was an 'ebbing level of sympathy for the Churches in eastern Germany; it will never be a *Volkskirche* again. There is certainly not a rush to the Churches' (Lease 1993: 170). In other words, if the Churches in the fomer GDR thought that their post-Communist mission was to proclaim and proselytize an ideology of Christianization they were to be disappointed. East Germans were simply too secular and distrustful of the motivations of Christian clergy to follow them in this regard.

As in Poland, the Churches played an emphatic role in helping the birth of democracy at *a brief historical juncture*; they were both symbolic and catalytic of immense political changes, but this role did not endure once the authoritarian regime was overthrown and democracy introduced. The point is that, as Peter Berger (cited in Lease 1993: 170) noted as early as 1954, ideologies are exchangeable. As in Poland, the East German Churches quickly lost their essentially transitory socio-political position once pluralist political parties were available. And this is a trend which we have also noted in relation to Latin America, Spain and Poland: once normal democratic politics is in place Churches seem to lose their leading political positions; instead, they are forced partially to privatize, because people in secular societies expect them to do so.

The USSR/Russia

When we turn to the Soviet Union, the repressive force of the State and official atheistic campaigns over seven decades from 1917 would seem likely to compound processes of secularization, making predictions of religious demise all the more compelling. Yet, following the dissolution of the Soviet Union, religious institutions – especially the national Church, the Russian Orthodox Church – managed to regain an unanticipated position of influence among the mass of the people. In short, Russia is experiencing a religious revival and the Russian Orthodox Church has been resurrected as a national symbol. However, this is not reflected in the Church's involvement in political discourse: there is no Church party, Church-endorsed parliamentary candidates or clear preference for one presidential candidate over others. The Church appears to be most interested in fighting to retain its hegemonic position vis-à-vis other denominations in the face of what it regards as aggressive proselytization campaigns from foreign – mostly Western – Churches. The religious challenge to the Orthodox Church in Russia parallels the fight which the national Catholic Churches are having in Latin America against the ecclesiastical challenge posed by the new Protestant Churches.

The Russian Orthodox Church is the largest Church in the country, with a reported 50 million followers in 1986 (Ramet 1991: 69).[8] Because of its historical dominance, I will concentrate in this section on the relationship between the Church and the State during and after communist rule. It was not a particularly willing or important participant in the events which led to the overthrow of the Soviet regime. This was due to historical reasons: the Church has traditionally been dominated by the State, while most senior figures in the Church are very conservative; they almost certainly regarded the prospect of fundamental change with extreme apprehension.

Long before Communist Government in the country, the Church was effectively subordinated to State power. While at various periods in Russian history either the Church or the state has played the dominant role, they have never been truly separate since the acceptance of Eastern Christianity as the State religion nearly a thousand years ago. By the eighteenth century the Church was firmly under secular control. Under successive tsarist regimes before the 1917 revolution, religious officials had been compelled 'to collaborate with the State security services' (Slater and Engelbrekt 1993: 53). During the communist era many individual priests and bishops collaborated with the KGB, the communist era equivalent.

---

8. There are several important religious traditions in the former Soviet Union beside Orthodox Christianity, including Roman Catholicism, various Protestant Churches, Islam and Judaism. In 1986, there were some 5–10 million Catholics, about 1 million Protestants, 1.5 million Jews and 14–50 million (often nominal) Muslims in the country (Ramet 1991: Table 3.1. p. 69). I will examine the role of Islam in (Soviet) Central Asia in Chapter 8.

The Church experienced a steady decline in political and social importance after 1917. No doubt fearing the likely consequences if it crossed swords with the likes of Lenin, Stalin and the Bolsheviks, it learned not to draw attention to itself by involvement in political controversies. Separation of Church and State, although a Western concept of the Enlightenment, was adopted by the communists who used it as the pretext to embark upon attempts to destroy the Orthodox Church (Slater and Engelbrekt 1993: 54). Yet there were periods of relative harmony between the Communist State and the Church, for example during World War II when the Government was anxious to build a nationalist coalition of interest groups to fight Nazi Germany. However, the regime never really waivered from its anti-religion policy and managed to restrict considerably overt expressions of religious belief. By the early 1980s there were 'only about 6,500 functioning Russian Orthodox Churches in the entire Soviet Union', that is, one church building for every 7692 (sometimes nominal) members of the Church (Slater and Engelbrekt 1993: 49). In the late 1980s, however, reflecting Gorbachev's more liberal outlook, the Church's fortunes revived: hundreds of church buildings were returned by the State (Ramet 1991: 87). The Church's waxing star was also illustrated by the State's willingness to draw up liberal religious legislation. In sum, by the late 1980s it seemed that the long era of Church repression at the hands of the State was drawing to an end.

But, unlike the Catholic Church in Poland and, to a lesser degree, the main Protestant Churches in East Germany, the Orthodox Church showed little inclination to use its growing influence to involve itself in political issues. There were two main reasons for this. First, unlike the Catholic Church in Poland, the Russian Orthodox Church is not part of a transnational institution with hundreds of millions of followers around the world. Unlike in the Catholic Church, there was no *aggiornamento* or Vatican II to help mould, change and radicalize the perspectives of the Church's senior officials. Most seemed content to carry on as before in a largely supportive role vis-à-vis the State. In other words, while Church leaders in Poland and other Catholic countries were no doubt encouraged by developments in the Church to press for political changes in their own countries, senior officials in the Russian Orthodox Church had no such inspiration and encouragement from overseas. Second, the Russian Orthodox Church is traditionally a strongly liturgical Church, that is, it is concerned primarily with religious rituals rather than proselytization. Its priests are not in the habit of going out among the population in order to get their message across because of competition from other Churches. As a result, there was little effort made to link up with the kind of secular dissidents who had used Churches elsewhere in the region as a platform for political campaigns.

Although somewhat uninterested in politics the Church is supremely interested in maintaining its religious dominance in the face of an unprecedented challenge from foreign Christian Churches, especially evangelical Protestant Churches from the USA. And the leading politicians are equally concerned with being associated with the Church. No Russian politician (and that includes leading figures like President Yeltsin and Victor Chernomyrdin as well as the neo-fascist Zhirinovsky and the communist head, Zyuganov) can afford *not* to be seen in Church. Reflecting this, the Church's historical subservience has now been replaced by a relationship of much greater equality. Under Yeltsin, the State has begun to cooperate in reopening and rebuilding neglected churches and has restored to the Church control over its internal and financial affairs. But this warming to the Church is not a product of democracy: in fact, it began in the twilight years of communist rule. A fundamental change in Soviet religious policy came in 1988, symbolized by President Gorbachev's meeting with members of the Russian Orthodox Church's Holy Synod in April. Over the next 24 months, two important laws were promulgated: *the Law on Freedom of Conscience and Religious Associations in the USSR* was passed in 1989, later replaced, after the demise of the Soviet State in 1990, by *the Law of the Russian Federation on Freedom of Religious Beliefs*. These liberal laws served to create much more favourable conditions for the general practice of religion in the country than before.

The changing, more tolerant, climate for religion was also reflected in the appearance of new religious periodicals, including *Tserkovnyi Vestnik* ('Church Herald') and *Protestant*; more and greater educational activities undertaken by religious organizations, including the Orthodox Church; and in the founding of new theological educational institutions (Zotz 1993: 84–5). Finally, the Russian Orthodox Church was alone not only able to publish or import some 250,000 Bibles, but also to receive back from the State hundreds of churches and seven monasteries. In short, the Church's star was once again in the ascendant. At the time, the generally more liberal climate also resulted in a notable 'politicization of religion, with some religious leaders involved in politically minded public movements and in newly formed parties', such as the Christian Democratic and the Muslim parties (Zotz 1993: 86, see also Meek 1995).

The mid- to late-1980s was of course the period of Gorbachev's *perestroika*, a time of growing dissent both *within* the Church and between some Church figures and the regime. Both secular and religious dissidents looked to the Church as an open social space to give a lead as the struggle against the communists reached its climax. Crucially, President Gorbachev allowed the Church greater freedom, not only encouraging its hierarchs to speak out, but just as importantly also giving weight to the demands of the growing ranks of the radical younger clergy. The result was that certain figures within the Church were able to 'engage in a variety of activities and movements which, *inter alia* . . . [called] for greater freedom both *for* the Church and *within* the Church (Ellis 1990: 307). The Church's deprivatization at this time was also manifested by growing influence in social and cultural spheres, with charitable activities and educational work among children especially important (Slater and Engelbrekt 1993: 52–3).

A less welcome development was that the Church also become a focal point of both nationalist and religious extremism and a participant in inter-ethnic and inter-confessional conflicts. Zotz (1993: 84) reports that certain senior Church figures wrote a number of 'extremely right-wing, usually anti-Semitic articles' at the time of the collapse of the Soviet regime. The conservatism and occasional xenophobia of some leading Church figures was also manifested in other ways. Under the Soviet regime a few privileged Church leaders had been permitted to participate in meetings of international Christian organizations. Yet, because of the regime's strong hold on State and society, it had not been possible – even if regarded as desirable, which was by no means certain – for such leaders to seek to implement more liberal policies championed by other Churches in areas like gender relations, poverty and social inequality, and racism. In signalling a change in the State's attitude to religion, Gorbachev had, in effect, granted it a new lease of life. But nothing was done to tackle the endemic problems of Church life resulting from the captivity of its leadership in the past. In other words, as the Soviet regime imploded, 'the Church [was] set on a new course but without the internal *perestroika* which many would regard as a prerequisite' (Ellis 1990: 316).

The new focus on the socio-political role of religion not only served to highlight divisions within the Orthodox Church but also the institutional problems it faced after decades of close control by the State. Perhaps most problematic was the question of what the Church's future public role should be. While religious freedom was now enshrined in the country's constitution, many Church leaders felt that this was a decidedly mixed blessing because it allowed other religious organizations to challenge their predominance. As a result, the Church pressurized Yeltsin to recognize it as the State Church in order to use its position to limit the proselytyization of its challengers (Hearst 1996, Philps 1997). Deeply conservative by nature, the Russian Orthodox Church has changed little in structure or outward appearance since the eighteenth century, a position widely seen by many believers as an anachronism in the late twentieth century. Religious opposition was novel for the Church because there has been no threat to its leadership for centuries; Russian Orthodoxy is a faith to which people are born rather than converted. Consequently, it never needed to develop a tradition of proselytizing. As an Orthodox priest, Father Vladimir Rigin, put it, 'changing your faith is treachery' (Philps 1997). Recently, however, in the face of new religious challenges, the Church has been virtually impelled to strive to boost its influence, that is, to assume a higher socio-political profile, in effect to deprivatize itself.

Newly gained religious freedom, along with the freedom of speech, is, some suspect, the perfect formula for forcing Russian Orthodoxy out of business. Orthodox leaders and clergy complain vociferously that religious rights are being 'abused' by representatives of foreign-based religious groups.[9] The problem for the Church is that its strong emphasis on ritual, tradition and symbolism – typically led by an ageing, often politically compromised priesthood – does not seem particularly attractive to many Russians, 'particularly the young and the middle-aged' (Slater and Engelbrekt 1993: 52). Many such people are attracted to foreign-style evangelical Protestantism. Fear of losing its traditional influence to such Churches was no doubt an important factor in the Church's active support for a new law restricting the activities of foreign missionaries and religious groups, announced in 1993. The Church argued that Russians were being put under 'crude psychological pressure' from foreign religious bodies. Beyond this specific issue, the 1993 law raises

---

9. Slater and Engelbrekt (1993: 52) report that an estimated one thousand foreign missionaries and 50 foreign religious organizations came to Russia during 1991–3. Such foreign religious groups tended to concentrate on the Russian Orthodox Church's collaboration with the regime under Soviet rule, ignoring the opposition of some of its members to that regime.

'fundamental questions about the role of the [Church] and its links with the State as well as . . . about limits on freedom of speech' (Slater and Engelbrekt 1993: 50). In other words, it is possible to see the 1993 law as a backward step with the State and the Orthodox Church trying to recreate the days of their political-religious dominance.

In July 1993, the then prime minister, Victor Chernomydin, was reported to have told the leader of the Church, Patriach Bartholomew, 'that the government would do everything it could to preserve Orthodox traditions in society' (Slater and Engelbrekt 1993: 53). But what was not made clear was *which* Orthodox traditions were worth preserving. Which needed overhauling? Such issues were at the core of a dispute between conservatives and reformers as to the future of the Church which became a *cause célèbre* at this time.

The Russian Orthodox Church found itself in a paradoxical situation. The problem, claimed Archbishop Kirill of Smolensk, head of its Department of External Church Relations, was this: 'the Russian people are looking to the Church for answers but they forget that the Church has been tremendously weakened. The Church must have time to be renewed, and the people do not want to wait. There is no time' (quoted in Ellis 1990: 307). Father Gleb Yakunin, a noted dissident who had been calling for greater freedom in and for the Church since the mid-1960s and who spent long periods in prison before being released in 1987, expressed the same sentiments in an interview with a Russian newspaper in June 1990. For Yakunin, the predicament was that a paradoxical situation had arisen with the fall of the Communist State: 'our society, seeking a way out of its spiritual crisis, has turned to the Church, but the Church itself is not far from the situation of society' (quoted in Ellis 1990: 308).

Yakunin is one of a group of dissidents who have consistently criticized the subservient policy of Church hierarchs vis-à-vis the State, even during the communist era. From the late 1960s to the early 1980s, the struggle for greater freedom for and in the Church was waged almost entirely by such dissidents. These activists and thinkers, many of whom, like Yakunin, paid for their efforts with long periods of imprisonment, felt themselves to be struggling not only against the Soviet State and Communist Party, but also against the hierarchs of their own Church. The latter, they felt, had become 'the captives of the State and, in part, its instrument for holding the Church in thrall' (Ellis 1990: 307). When the USSR ceased to exist, however, divisions within the Church between conservatives and dissidents exploded into the open. Thus, on the one hand, in the 1990s the Church has an almost unprecedented opportunity to expand its influence as the statist ideology of communism has now disintegrated. On the other, not only intra-Church conflicts but also foreign religious competition make that development increasingly unlikely. In sum, there is an unparalleled opportunity for the Church to deprivatize and to play a much fuller part in social and public life than at any time during the previous 70 years, but it appears that it is not in a position to exploit the situation fully because of internal schisms and the challenge posed by foreign religious competition.

The difficult position the Church finds itself in is also exemplified in a further way. Schisms *within* the Church are paralleled in a conflict between the Church and rival Churches. For example, it is involved in a dispute with a sister Church in Turkey, the Constantinople Patriarchy. Meek (1996) reports that the main issues dividing the two Churches include the charges that the Constantinople Patriarchy is 'trespassing on a brother Church's canonical territory' – that is, it has taken over from the Russian Church the jurisdiction of the tiny Orthodox Church in Estonia following the collapse of the Soviet Union – and 'forcing a schism by supporting defrocked priests'. In effect, the sweeping away of the communist regime paved the way for a turf war between the Russian Orthodox Church and other branches of Orthodoxy. This was also manifested in a dispute between the Russian Orthodox Church *in* Russia and a parallel Church, the New York-based Russian Orthodox Church Abroad, founded in the 1920s by émigrés. In the 1990s it began to proclaim itself as the true standard bearer of Orthodoxy. Reports suggest that the Russian Orthodox Church Abroad has begun to receive declarations of allegiance from parishes in Russia itself. Its attraction lies largely in its claim to be untainted by collaboration with the Soviet State. Finally, events in Ukraine seem likely to cause an even greater uproar: Russian Orthodox Church property is being seized by the Greek Catholic Church[10] (Slater and Engelbrekt 1993: 54).

The conclusion is that the Russian Orthodox Church has been much too concerned in dealing with religious challenges both within Russia and outside to bother about taking a leading political role now there is religious freedom. At the same time, more Russians than at any time during the last three-quarters of a century are interested in religion. Thus, the period of aggressive secularization in Russia has delivered two, contrasting results: on the one hand, the Russian Orthodox Church seems unable to regain political influence while, on the other, many millions of ordinary people have returned to religion, probably at least in part as a way of dealing with the unprecedented changes to their lives over the last decade.

Conclusion

Some argue that Eastern Europe has been permanently affected by the removal of the negative association between political power and faith, Church and government. Unlike in Western Europe, it is claimed, religion has returned in the Eastern part of the region as a socio-political actor of vigour, effectiveness and permanence. The argument of this chapter does not bear out this assessment. While a large proportion of people in Eastern Europe are no doubt religious believers, this does not seem greatly to affect their political choices. Nowhere in Eastern Europe in the 1990s are there important political parties with aims ostensibly moulded by religious concerns.

A central argument of this chapter was that in Eastern Europe during the communist era, Church–State relations were, rather obviously, moulded by the nature of the ruling Marxist regimes. The result was that, for the most part, Churches were resigned to privatization; they may not have liked it but the consequences of doing

---

10. Sometimes known as the Uniate Church, the Greek Catholic Church is subordinate to the Holy See but uses Orthodox rites. It was banned between 1946 and 1989 by the Soviet authorities.

otherwise were not pleasant to contemplate. The upsurge of anti-Communist dissidence in the 1980s served to change the nature of the Church–State relationships
because the Churches found themselves to be the centres to which opposition forces
gravitated. For a while, it seemed that it was the Churches themselves which were
destined to become the leading political actors. Some even argued that this amounted
to a spectacular reversal of years of aggressive secularization. Yet the point is that
Churches did not enjoy *permanent* accretions of political power and social status
in the post-Communist era. As in Spain and Latin America, a shift to democracy
per se was not sufficient on its own to place Churches as socio-political actors of
continuing prominence. Eastern Europe is a region where religious organizations
frequently have an important bedrock of support in society but this does not normally translate into a significant political role. In this respect, Eastern Europe is –
apparently inexorably – secularizing; there is no place for a permanent religious
presence in political society.

The evidence of the chapter suggests that in the final analyisis Churches' socio-
political importance was rather ephemeral in Eastern Europe. It was the result
of a specific set of circumstances connected to the slow collapse of communist
regimes in the 1980s. While reflective of a fundamental shift in public opinion –
that is, a massive growth in dissidence – their prominence in this regard did not
endure in the democratic era. This was illustrated in the three case studies: Poland,
East Germany and Russia. Put differently, there was a gradual reprivatization of the
Churches with a declining voice in political society, although at the *individual* level
people remain intensely religious.

Chapter 6

Africa: religious competition and State power

Africa[1] is home to more than 500 million people. Christianity and Islam[2] are the leading religions; each has in excess of 200 million adherents. There are declining numbers of followers of traditional indigenous religions and very few atheists or agnostics. Both Islam and Christianity were imported into Africa in the historical past. Islam was gradually spead over the last thousand years while Christianity was imported by and intimately associated with European colonialism from the late nineteenth century.

Religion and politics during the colonial era

The roots of the contemporary relationship between mainstream religious organizations and the State in Africa are to be found in the period of European colonialism, that is, from the 1880s to the 1960s. (Note that mainstream religious organizations are those which establish a regularized, systematic form of interaction with the State over time, and are regarded by the latter as 'official' representative of large numbers of people. Examples include the Roman Catholic Church, the main Protestant Churches, and the 'orthodox' versions of Islam.) During the colonial period there was, by and large, a close affinity between Christian missionaries and colonial administrators which did not rest solely on their shared Christianity but was also bolstered by the fact that both were Europeans. That is to say, even though Christian officials and missionaries may, on occasion, have been unhappy with certain aspects of colonial policy – such as European settlers' confiscation of Africans' land in Kenya's 'White Highlands' without compensation – there were many points of agreement between them and secular administrators. Both parties, religious and secular, were, after all, pursuing the same broad aims as they saw it: to bring the benefits of European civilization, including the Christian God, to Africa.

---

1. 'Africa' in this chapter refers to Sub-Saharan Africa, that is, the region that excludes the five northern Arab-dominated countries of Morocco, Algeria, Tunisia, Libya and Egypt.
2. Nearly all Muslims living below the Saharan desert are followers of Sunni Islam.

A second factor to unite them, at least initially, was the challenge of Islam. By the late nineteenth century, Islam was a highly significant religion in west, east and, to an extent, central Africa. At the outset, there was widespread conflict between Muslims and Europeans. By the early twentieth century, however, Muslim leaders and colonial administrators had by and large arrived at ways of working together. The normal arrangement was that the former would guarantee their communities' acquiescence to European rule in exchange for personal financial rewards and for a large measure of religious and social autonomy. Christian missionaries had no choice but to accept the *fait accompli*; in some places, for example, in Muslim-dominated northern Nigeria, they were not even allowed to proselytize.

Of course Europeans did not only bring Christianity but also many other aspects of Western-style modernization, including the money economy, urbanization, Western education and governmental centralization. Collectively they helped to mould Africans' changing responses to European colonialism. From an initial welcome, a groundswell of demands for autonomy and then independence gathered pace. By the early 1950s, African nationalist leaders, encouraged by the success of India in achieving independence from colonial rule in 1947, were demanding the same for themselves and their followers. Many leading nationalists were Christians educated in mission schools and colleges, but they perceived European-dominated Christian Churches to be strongly associated with colonial rule and, as a consequence, viewed them with distrust. With regard to Muslims, the absence of an institutional Church within Islam and the perceived 'backwardness' of many Muslims, led nationalist leaders either to ignore them or to coopt them into the nationalist project as and when necessary.

How could Church leaders deal with a situation where, by the early 1960s, power was moving inexorably, and swiftly, from Europeans to Africans? The answer is that the Churches changed their positions in the face of political changes on the ground. Churches were initially opposed, then sceptical, and finally won round to the idea of African independence. As for the African nationalists, they were highly suspicious of the Churches for reasons already mentioned, even though the Churches themselves sought to Africanize their personnel as soon as possible once freedom from colonial rule was won, typically by the mid-1960s. However, the ambivalence with which the nationalists viewed the mainstream Churches – on the one hand, they were welcome purveyors of education, health care and other welfare benefits while, on the other, they were perceived as agents of colonialism – was carried into the post-colonial era. And, of course, the nationalist agitators became the first rulers of independent Africa.

Because changes from colonial to post-colonial rule were accomplished via a relatively systematic handover of power there were few overt changes in the relationship between the mainstream religious organizations and the State. Of course Europeans were replaced by Africans in leadership positions in the Churches, but this did not alter the nature of the relationship between State and Church. As in the colonial period, Churches strove, often successfully, to act as intermediaries between society and the State. Partly because of the colonial tradition of support for the State and partly because of the normative desire of religious leaders to seek stability and consensus, mainstream religious organizations – both Christian and Muslim – were very often supportive of government, irrespective of the form (one-party, personalist, military) or content (dictatorial, authoritarian, totalitarian) of rule.

There were three main reasons for the generally strong support of the State by mainstream religious organizations in the two decades after independence. First, both religious and secular leaders shared an interest in the maintenance of the status quo; second, mainstream religious organizations obviously had a strong desire to maintain their religious influence, best assured in a climate of good relations with the State; third, many had a normative concern with political stability as a good thing in itself. As far as government was concerned, the role of mainstream Christian Churches, both Catholic and Protestant, in providing public goods, especially education and welfare, was especially welcome. In some cases – for example, Zaire and Tanzania – it was an absolutely crucial addition to their own increasingly feeble efforts.

The relationship of Christian Churches to government in Africa, as elsewhere, is in theory a simple and clear one, and is well expressed in the following:

> The limits of the State's sphere of action are set by the definition of 'temporal',
> that is, those activities of civilization that arise in the 'earthly' city ... The Church
> in no way limits the State's rights: Church and State complement one another, each
> by working in its proper realm.
>
> (*Documents pour l'action 8*, March–April 1962, pp. 99–100,
> translated and quoted in Boyle 1992: 52)

Yet, as cordial relations between Catholic Church leaders and the now departed Mobutu regime in Zaire made plain, it was in the former's interests as much as Mobutu's for there to be stability, even if that was a stability arrived at through authoritarian means. As Joseph Malula, Archbishop of Kinshasa, observed in 1965, in a message addressed to Mobutu: 'Mr President, the Church recognizes your authority, because authority comes from God. We will loyally apply the laws you establish. You can count on us in your work of restoring the peace toward which all so ardently aspire' (quoted in Boyle 1992: 49). Until 1992, the Catholic hierarchy was consistently hesitant to engage the regime in direct public confrontation; that is, until an unprecedented show of public displeasure – significantly involving young priests and nuns – galvanized the Catholic hierarchy into voice in the early 1990s. The point is that senior figures in the Catholic Church were often bought off by material inducements, while the institutional role of the Church was seen as one which ought to be supportive of the temporal regime for, as Malula's quote indicates, God is thought to give governments authority. Understandably, Malula was anxious to re-establish a good working relationship with the State authorities, to resume the mutually supportive arrangement which had typified the colonial period. Then, as Schatzberg (1988: 117–18) notes, occasional differences between the Catholic and colonial authorities were 'minimal in comparison to the numerous isues on which Church and State worked in concert'. Between 1965 and 1970, 'relations between Church and State were generally good', and from then only intermittently rocky.

For Church leaders more generally in Africa, silence in the face of poor and corrupt government following independence reflected a number of concerns: many benefited materially from the status quo; they were inherently conservative; they believed that governments, however bad, were exercising authority ordained by God; and, finally, they recognized that their Church's corporate position in a country was in part dependent upon State support. In Zaire, as Boyle (1992: 51) illustrates, the value of cooperation with civil authorities for Church leaders led them 'to employ . . . indirect modes of communication and influence in their relationship with society and the political regime'. This is the idea of the 'two realms' of Church and State, where the former may attempt to influence the latter by persuasion but has no other means at its disposal if it wishes to retain its privileged position. In other words, Church hierarchies often felt able to be no more than an intermediary between State and society; many did not, until recently, openly proclaim political preferences or try to change the political trajectory of regimes.

A further factor explaining Churches' unwillingness openly to challenge regimes – apart from concerns with stability and the fears of repercussions of openly challenging regimes – is that some Christian leaders were personally closely associated with ruling regimes, to the extent of holding political appointments. In Lesotho in the early 1970s, for example, 'the post-independence government of Chief Leabua Jonathan and the National Party was predominantly Catholic in support and conservative in policy', and as such was favoured by South Africa's Government (Hastings 1979: 189). In Zaire, where political activists of the ruling party, Le Mouvement Populaire de la Révolution (MPR), and the ubiquitous secret police together dominate society, the Catholic Church (with around 19 million followers in a population of about 37 million) had only a very limited desire to challenge Mobutu for many years. This may be attributed in part to the fact that senior Church figures were well treated personally by Mobutu's regime: 'Cardinal Malula lived in a mansion that the President gave him . . . the President gave a Mercedes to every bishop, Protestant or Catholic' in the early 1970s (MacGaffey 1991: 261–2). The result is that Catholicism, in partnership with the independent, but powerful, Kimbanguist Church, 'assumed some of the functions of an ideology in the service of the dominant class' in the 1970s (MacGaffey 1991: 261–2). The position was similar in Togo: there the ruling party, Le Rassemblement du Peuple Togolais, had – and in some respects retains – a dominant position in society analagous to that of the MPR in Zaire, while the Catholic Church is the leading Church. A further example is provided by the situation in Rwanda. Until 1985, the Catholic Archbishop of Kigali was on the central committee of the single party, the Mouvement Révolutionnaire National pour le Développement. Finally, Bishop Mutale's membership of the commission for instituting a one-party State in the 1970s in Zambia was a concrete manifestation of the empathy between State and Church at the time (Hastings 1979: 188).

Before the current era of democracy, when Christian leaders *did* criticize governments they tended to accuse them of violating fundamental moral values. Church leaders regarded themselves as the principal guardians of morality, whereas (in pursuance of the 'two realms' idea noted in Boyle's quote above) government's job was concerned fundamentally with political issues. The discussion of the role of the

Catholic Church in recent democratization initiatives has highlighted how ambivalent some of its senior figures were on the issue of fundamental political change. Apart from a tendency towards conservatism, which is of course a characteristic of the leaders of many large, powerful institutions, both religious and secular, there were also more material concerns at stake, not least their control of their Church's followers.

Church–State relations: 1960s to 1980s

I noted in the introductory chapter, five common categories of relationships between Church and State at the current time. In Africa, before the recent demands for fundamental political change, three were of note. First, the *Marxist secular*, for example, Ethiopia between 1974 and 1991, where secular power held sway over religion, forcing it to validate its rule and, when necessary, 'to sanctify economic oppression and the given system of stratification' (Casanova 1994: 49). Second, *the confessional*, where ecclesiastical authority is pre-eminent over secular power, enabling religion to shape the world according to God's ways. An example of an African 'theocratic'[3] regime is provided by Sudan, where the regime of General al-Bashir has ruled in partnership with the National Islamic Front since 1988. However, the more religion wants to transform the world in a religious direction – as the case of Sudan shows – the 'more religion becomes entangled in "wordly" affairs and is transformed by the world' (Casanova 1944: 49). In fact, theocracies are rare at the current time in Africa – as elsewhere – but I thought it useful to describe the situation in Sudan as it seems to be little understood. The third – the *liberal secular* polity – involves distance, detachment and separation between religion and the State. Officially, no religion is given official predominance or preference by secular power: the State claims to be even-handed in its approach to all. An example of religious neutrality, albeit with a clear bias toward one Church, is provided by the apartheid era in South Africa (1948–94).

Each of these examples illustrates a common factor in relationships between religious organizations and the State before the late 1980s: the proclaimed ideology of the regime was relatively unimportant in understanding the nature of the relationship between State and leading religious institutions. Commonly, religious leaders seemed as concerned with their personal positions as with the corporate status and prosperity of their religious organizations. Supportive of the status quo, religious leaders often sought to defuse serious political challenges to the status quo. However, the situation changed quite remarkably following the eruption of democracy demands. From then, the political climate underwent rapid change with leading Christians in the forefront of demands for fundamental change.

---

3. The idea of theocratic government usually refers to an absence of division between secular and religious power. I use quotation marks around the word 'theocratic' in relation to Sudan's Government because it is not clear that there is no separation between secular and religious power-holders. Nevertheless, it is unquestionable that some Muslims have an important voice in government.

Ethiopia

Ethiopia's population of more than 50 million people is divided fairly equally between Christians and Muslims. About 40–45 per cent are Sunni Muslim; many of them live in Eritrea, now an independent country. About 45 per cent of the population belongs to the Ethiopian Orthodox Church, an indigenous African Church, which was founded nearly two thousand years ago, and which has historical links with the Egyptian Coptic Church. Less than 5 per cent of Ethiopians are Protestants or Catholics, while about 12 per cent are followers of traditional African religions (Clapham 1989: 73).

Although Ethiopia was not really a colonial country its ruler, Ras Tafari, Haile Selassie, judged by radicals a stooge of the United States, ruled his country dictatorially. After the 1974 revolution, the Derg (Provisional Military Administrative Council) lacked a coherent policy relating either to individual religious freedoms or to Christianity and Islam more generally. During the fervour of revolution in the late 1970s, the Government stripped the Ethiopian Orthodox Church of most of its landholdings. The Derg leaders were, however, astute enough to realize that religious traditions formed an important, even integral, facet of Ethiopian life and that it was somewhat counter-productive to attempt to crush religion completely. By the early 1980s, as problems with the revolution became apparent, the Government courted the two most senior religious figures in the country, the Orthodox patriarch and the chief Muslim mullah of Addis Ababa, seating them both close to the Marxist rulers at important State events.

The Orthodox Church's reaction to Ethiopia's revolution had initially been marked by apparent passivity and resignation. Its great disadvantage, in common with former mission Churches in Africa, was that in the revolutionaries' eyes it was heavily inculcated with symbols of the past, especially the feudal system based on oppression and exploitation of ordinary people. During Haile Selassie's rule the Orthodox Church was the established Church, supported by the State, with its organization and administration governed by law (Barrett 1982: 284–5). The Catholic Church, with some half a million members, and the Protestant Churches with perhaps four or five times as many, on the other hand, had not hitherto been politically influential in the country, and had no close links with the *ancien régime*. Leaders of the Catholic Church were, however, cautious in denouncing the revolutionary regime. There was no serious confrontation between the Catholic hierarchy and the State, while the Church's welfare activities continued as before.

In sum, Ethiopia's Marxist rulers sought as far as possible to reach a *modus vivendi* with national Christian and Muslim leaders alike. Obviously, it is one thing to proclaim a revolution from the top down, yet it is quite another to infuse a set of radical political changes throughout society, that is, to gain widespread acceptance for the validity, comprehensiveness and practicality of such ideas. The unexpected characteristic of Ethiopia's revolution in a religious sense was the ability to retain the personal support of both Christian and Muslim leaders. Neither mainstream religious institutions nor the State had the ability to thrive without the sanction of each other: the State could make life difficult for religious institutions, although the latter, because of their social and cultural importance, were also crucial for the State in gaining and maintaining popular acceptance.

South Africa

During the era of apartheid (1948–94), the State looked to its main religious ally, the Dutch Reformed Church, for religious justification for the State policy of 'separate development'. Because the struggle to end apartheid was for many a religious struggle it was of great importance for the State to continue its historically close links with the Church because of its social and religious significance for many Afrikaners.

South Africa's population of more than 38 million comprises about four-and-a-half million whites of European origin, nearly three million 'coloureds' of mixed race, about one million 'Asians' (mostly of Indian subcontinent and East Asian origin), and about 30 million black Africans. About two-thirds of black South Africans, and four-fifths of whites, are Christians. The traditional English-speaking denominations are predominantly black, and consistently opposed apartheid. There are over two million Roman Catholics, slightly fewer Anglicans and less than one million Lutherans. Some 12 million black Christians belong to African independent Churches. It is claimed that South Africa has the greatest proliferation of independent Churches in the world, more than 3,250 in 1980 (Oosthuizen 1985: 71).

Muslims comprise around 1.5 per cent of the population, some 500,000 people. They are roughly equally divided between Asians of Indian subcontinent extraction (20 per cent of the total, predominantly Sunni) and Cape coloureds (Afrikaans-speaking ethnic Malays). Until recently, few black South Africans were followers of Islam (Harris *et al.* 1992: 466–7). The Call of Islam was formed in Cape Town in 1984 to inform non-Muslims about the beliefs of Islam; it achieved some success in recruiting black South Africans by projecting Islam as an anti-colonial, anti-white religion, and in seeking to relate the way that the *tauhid* (way) of Allah was violated in South Africa during the apartheid era. It aimed to bring Muslims back on to the path of righteousness by making them more conscious of their religious duties to build a 'just' society. What this implied, in effect, was that Muslims in South Africa were involved in political struggle against an 'unjust' secular State, rather than opposing spiritual leaders for religious laxity, which is much more common generally in Africa.

The largest Christian Church, to which about two-and-a-half million Afrikaner-speakers of Dutch ethnic origin belong, is the Dutch Reformed Church (Nederduitse Gereformeerde Kerk or NGK). The Dutch Reformed Church is the denomination of most members of the former apartheid government. There are two ultra-conservative whites-only breakaway Churches from the Church: the Nederduitsch Kerk, established in 1858; and the Gereformeerde Kerk (the 'Doppers') established in 1859, to which former State president de Klerk belongs. Until 1986 the Dutch Reformed Church sought to produce theological justifications for apartheid.

Non-white members of the Church had to belong to one of three sister Churches established by mission: the Nederduitse Geregormeerde Sendingkerk (NG Mission Church) for 'coloureds'; the (Asian) Reformed Church in Africa for 'Indians'; and the Nederduitse Gereformeerde Kerk in Afrika (NG Church in Africa) for blacks. After 1990, the four Churches attempted to overcome the racial divisions between them, without success. A February 1993 summit meeting between them failed to agree on conditions for unity. On this occasion, the Dutch Reformed Church leaders refused to recognize the errors of the past, failing to declare apartheid to have been a heresy, or to repudiate the members of the Broederbond – former prime ministers, D. F. Malan, Hans Strijdom and Hendrik Verwoerd – responsible for introducing the racial system in 1948. Instead, President de Klerk described these three as 'men of great personal integrity, sincere in their belief that separate development could bring justice to black South Africans' (Sparks 1993).

The Dutch Reformed Church has a historic role in South Africa analagous to that of the Orthodox Church in Ethiopia. It is regarded by many as the Church of the colonizers, a conservative force acting to reinforce the political dominance of a white, Afrikaner elite. The role of the other main Christian denominations – Roman Catholic, Anglican and Evangelical Lutheran – was, on the other hand, to lead public critiques of apartheid. What this points to is that the struggle against racial discrimination in South Africa was regarded by many as being as much theological as it was political. Even though the great majority of South Africans are Christians, their commitment to their faith is heavily conditioned, as elsewhere in Africa, by class interests and religious interpretations (Fine 1992). The Dutch Reformed Church was, in effect, an element in the structure of apartheid which reinforced its relationship with government right until the end of white minority rule in 1994.

Sudan

An Islamic Government has been in power in Sudan since 1988. Sudan is unique among African countries, because it is only there that Islam has achieved the status of State ideology. Its institutionalization manifests itself in a society where human rights and political freedoms appear generally to have been quite seriously downgraded and where certain ethnic groups – including the Dinka, Nuer and Nuba – have been victimized in the name of the ruling Islamic-military dictatorship and State homogeneity.

The process towards islamicization in Sudan began in the early 1980s. The then State president, Ja'far al-Numeri, began to adopt Islamic dress in public: the *jellabiya* (robe) and *anima* (turban) were worn for many public appearances, thus jettisoning the military uniform that Numeri had hitherto appeared to favour. He also issued new currency which showed him resplendent in his new Islamic persona. *Sharia* law was imposed in 1983 (although never made to stick in the largely Christian/animist south of the country). Such acts, as Bernal (1994: 48) notes, served to assert 'Sudan's Muslim and Arab identity while associating Islam with power and nationalism'.

Foreign and domestic pressures coalesced to convince Numeri of the appropriateness of his policy of Islamization: Sudan's chief aid provider of the time, Saudi Arabia, as well as the most important domestic Islamic actor, the Muslim Brotherhood, joined forces to demand a more trenchant imposition of Islamic norms. Political discourse in the country became increasingly phrased in Islamic terminology; Numeri's political opposition also adopted the language of Islam to press their case. Since the early 1980s, successive regimes have attempted to emphasize their power by underlining Sudan's proclaimed Muslim–Arabic identity. Following the rupture of Sudan's relations with Saudi Arabia during the Gulf War of 1991, Iran emerged as an important new patron of the now Islamic regime.

The current military-Islamic regime of Omar Hassan al-Bashir, which achieved power following a military coup d'état in June 1989, sought to combine an Islamic social control with the organizational skills of the military. It attempted to use the *sharia* in a way which was reminiscent of communist states' use of Marxist–Leninist dogma to justify policy. The attempt at hegemony by the Muslims of the north over the mostly Christians and animists of the south has consistently been portrayed as that rare phenomenon in Africa, a religious war. Nevertheless, the true conflict is about Arab domination over non-Arabs, rather than religion as such: ethnic competition is the context. The Muslim Nuba, non-Arab Sudanese, living in the area of the Nuba Mountains in the north of the country, have been consistently victimized by Arabs as not being 'real' Muslims, when the really significant issue was actually that they were not Arabs (Flint 1993).

The main manifestations of traditional Sunni Islam in Sudan – the Khatmiyya (a Sufi order) and the various Ansar Sunna sects – found themselves in conflict with the military government of President al-Bashir and the regime's Islamic allies, the National Islamic Front of Hassan Turabi (Flint 1993). Sufi Islam has traditionally been strong in Sudan, where in addition to the Khatmiyya are to be found their arch-rivals, the Sammaniyya, along with the Sanusiyya, Qadiriyya, Shadhiliyya and Tijaniyya sects. There has never been a strong *ulama* class (i.e. Islamic scholars and theological leaders) in Sudan, in marked contrast to neighbouring Egypt, because of the central role of Sufism in the spread of Islam in Sudan.

A millenarian Mahdist movement, the Mahdiyya (whose members are known as the Ansar which is itself split into several factions) also exists as a significant religious force. Its political extension, the Umma Party (*Hizb al-Umma*) has been one of the main forces in Sudanese politics since independence in 1956, as has the Khatmiyya Sufi order which has worked through various political parties. Founded in 1954, Sudan's Muslim Brotherhood (*Ikhwan al-Muslimin*) soon emerged as a powerful new religio-political force. Working with the military regime of General Omar al-Bashir through its political party, the National Islamic Front (*Jabhat al-Mithaq* or NIF), the Muslim Brotherhood stepped up its campaign for increased Islamization, and especially the introduction of *sharia* law. The Ansar, for its part, issued a call in early 1993 to the army and the NIF to revive democracy or, if not, to face a campaign of civil opposition. In reply, the regime briefly detained Sadiq al-Mahdi (great grandson of the Mahdi who defeated General Gordon), leader of the Ansar and an outspoken critic of the regime, as well as dozens of his supporters.

At the same time the Khatmiyya headquarters were taken over. In May 1993 the Ansar headquarters in Omdurman were confiscated by the army.

Sudan's army rulers formed an alliance with the reformers of the NIF to build an Islamic State in Sudan along the lines of that existing in its closest ally, Iran. Even though the *sharia* gives no clear or workable outline for such a State, especially in the context of the technological, political and economic changes of the last 1,500 years, Sudan's modern version is notable for its repression, lack of human rights, political intolerance, policies of 'ethnic cleansing' and the creation of a regime which appears to negate the toleration with which Islam has traditionally been associated (Bernal 1994). Civil war in the south, which had already endured for 20 years by the mid-1990s, was probably the biggest stumbling block to the Arab north's bid for control of the polity. In the south, Islam has no more than a token presence, while armed resistance, in two wings led by Colonel John Garang de Mabior and Riek Machar Teny-Dhurgon, aimed to prevent northern hegemony but not realistically defeat it. The result is stalemate, and a proxy war between Iran (sponsors of al-Bashir's Government) and the United States which, covertly, backs Garang.

In this section I examined the role played by leading religious organizations vis-à-vis the State in Ethiopia, South Africa and Sudan, from the 1970s. I explained why it was normal for leading religious organizations to support the Government. Regimes, for their part, and sometimes despite considerable misgivings as in Ethiopia, sometimes sought the support of religious authorities only because of their educational and welfare potential. Because of the shortages of resources in all African countries and the ever-present possibility that State authorities would use force as a means of gaining compliance, it was rational for religious leaders to seek to strike a working relationship with government both for personal and corporate reasons. It made much less sense to set themselves up as leaders of the opposition. In Sudan the al-Bashir Government and its religious allies each had particular reasons for their *de facto* coalition: for the former their power was greatly bolstered by the inclusion of powerful religious figures in government who could attract financial aid from, first, Saudi Arabia, and then Iran which was crucial to the prosecution of the long-running, resources-draining civil war; for the religious figures partnership with State power was a convenient way of instilling and installing their version of Islamic orthodoxy. In South Africa, on the other hand, de Klerk's regime found it highly advantageous to have the support of the NGK as a means of communicating with its main support base: conservative Afrikaners.

I suggested that pragmatism dominated State–Church relations in Africa for two decades after independence. Both religious and secular leaders sought to manipulate political situations for personal and corporate advantage. Most of the time they were linked by shared class concerns. But why did some religious leaders – very often Christian, usually Catholic – put themselves at the forefront of pro-democracy movements in the late 1980s and early 1990s? In the next two sections, I examine the role of religious leaders – first Catholic, then Muslim – in the 1990s, a period that saw Africa's most sustained political upheavals and change for 30 years.

Religion and democratic change

> Africa has begun the final decade of the twentieth century with a wave of
> democratic movements that is sweeping away authoritarian regimes that had
> seemed firmly entrenched. At the center of most of these transformations and
> upheavals are religious leaders from a variety of Christian denominations.
>
> (Joseph 1993: 231)

Joseph's claim is that Christian leaders have often assumed central leadership roles
in democratization movements in Africa, helping to focus popular attention on
pervasive conditions of injustice and misery, often becoming, as Fatton (1992: 78)
puts it, the only 'legitimate interlocutors capable of mediating conflicts between
government and citizens'. Yet while Christian leaders, especially in mostly Catholic countries of Francophone West Africa, were clearly instrumental in helping
to negotiate democratic transformations, they were not by any means always successful; when they were, it was due more to the prestige of the Catholic Church in
certain countries, where it was strong enough institutionally to remain outside state
control and where it was part of an international and transnational religio-political
network, than to the democratic credentials of Christian leaders *per se*, or to the
power of Christian Churches more generally to force democratic change.

But perhaps the most startling development is that senior Christian figures in
Africa now routinely voice criticisms of their governments; in effect, they have
re-entered the public sphere after decades keeping out of it. Formerly, mainstream
religious leaders and regimes normally worked together to maintain a conservative
hegemony stressing the desirability of stability rather than change. Put another way,
fear of fundamental change provided a durable framework of norms and values
legitimizing State policies almost regardless of what they comprised. But in order
to maintain their positions as intermediaries between State and society it was of
course necessary for religious leaders to retain the loyalty of their followers. As
time went on and other regions, such as Latin America and Eastern Europe, democ-
ratized, there was growing pressure on African Christian leaders – from both foreign and local sources – to come out in support of democratic change at home.

As in Latin America and Eastern Europe, demands for political change in Africa
have long been expressed by a few courageous figures, mostly junior figures. Ordinary priests, as in Eastern Europe and Latin America, tended to be more strongly
opposed to a government (and perhaps to their ecclesiastic superiors who lived in
comparative luxury), because they were closer to the people who were suffering
from poor governmental policies (Luneau 1987: 164). Sometimes priests supported
human rights campaigns by allowing their churches to be used as meeting places
by opposition movements. As church buildings are commonly regarded as sacro-
sanct, they may well have been the only places outside of government or party
control where people could gather legally in large numbers. This gave priests a
potentially central role, especially in the early stages of mobilizing opposition.
Moreover, opposition movements would be based in capital cities, thus facilitating
links both internally and with external allies, including foreign allied Churches and
non-governmental organizations.

But states, backed during the Cold War by Western powers, were normally able to ignore such low-level protests. However, during the 1980s Africa's economic, social and political fabric underwent swift decline and towards the end of the decade foreign support declined. States came under vociferous attack from pro-democracy and human rights campaigners. Such initiatives normally matured from scattered innovations in civil society coupled with international pressure (Bratton 1994). In both Kenya and Ghana, for example, a combination of both international and domestic pressure did much to undermine one-party States and to compel regimes to allow multi-party elections in 1992 (Gifford 1994).

Many senior religious figures were accused of failing to confront governments over human rights abuses, the nonobservation of civil rights and the lack of democracy (Gitari 1988, Okullu 1978). Christian leaders, it was argued, were failing to come up with 'an answer to the question of how best to relate to political, social and economic structures' in an era of almost unprecedented changes (Gitari 1988: 12). Why were religious leaders silent when it came to criticizing secular administrators and politicans? Often those 'with the greatest organizational resources to place at the disposal of a political perspective rarely fulfilled their political potential' (Demerath 1991: 37). This is because if they wished to retain their independence, it was advisable not to make statements about political issues, both for fear of losing the material benefits which went with their favoured positions and also because of the potential consequences if the State took exception to their criticisms. From the late 1980s, however, many Christian leaders – especially Catholics – added their personal voices to attacks against government, especially once a groundswell of criticism was building. If religious leaders failed to join in attacks against a clearly unpopular government – once they reach a certain stage of intensity – it would no doubt suggest to ordinary people that they and the regime were as one.

Pressure by Christian leaders on government for wideranging reforms was particularly significant in Kenya. Fifteen Catholic bishops and six leading officials from the National Council of Churches told President Moi to his face in 1992 that the people had lost confidence in his regime, and that changes to the one-party system should be made immediately (Gifford 1992). Given that the leading Christian Churches in Kenya were once renowned for their fulsome support of the very same one-party system, the volte-face needs to be explained. Two main sources of pressure should be mentioned. Ordinary Kenyans – interacting with international organizations expressing disquiet about human rights abuses – were vociferous in their criticism of the Moi Government. To this the Kenyan bishops added their voices (Gifford 1994). In effect, the country's Christian leaders were faced with two choices: take a leading role in the ranks of the reformers or be tarred with the same brush as unpopular secular leaders.

Opposition to one-party rule became a focus for rank-and-file discontent. Churchmen including Reverends David Gitari of Mount Kenya East, the late Alexander Kipsang Muge of Eldoret, Henry Okullu of Maseno South (all of the Anglican Church of the Province of Kenya) and Timothy Njoya of the Presbyterian Church of East Africa, helped to focus popular concern on the erosion of civil liberties, human-rights violations, the stifling of opposition and the drift towards totalitarianism.

They were all leading lights in the early 1990s campaign, by the Churches' umbrella National Christian Council of Kenya (NCCK), for political reforms. Conservative Church leaders, such as the Anglican Archbishop Manasses Kuria, and the country's 18-strong Catholic episcopate, added their voices to the campaign (Africa Watch 1991: 226–7, 232–3). Moi's Government used classical tactics of divide-and-rule to attempt to blunt the NCCK's opposition.

But the NCCK was able to highlight the country's abysmal human rights situation in a report published shortly before the first multi-party parliamentary and presidential elections for 26 years in 1992. It reported that more than 50,000 Kenyans were in badly maintained internment camps, while more than 1,000 individuals had been executed by the State extrajuridicially during 1992 (Simmons 1992). One of the Government's critics, Reverend Muge, was killed in a crash in August 1990, when his car was hit by a lorry about 40 miles (65 kilometres) from the town of Eldoret in Busia province (Africa Watch 1991: 222). Many Kenyans thought that Muge had been assassinated by the Government. Such fears were not necessarily fantasy: in neighbouring Malawi leaders of the then ruling Congress Party hatched a plot to kill the country's Catholic bishops in late 1992 because of their alleged involvement in a democracy campaign (*Africa Confidential* 6 November 1992).

Yet, this is not to suggest that *all* Christian leaders joined the attacks against the Moi regime. For example, the leader of the independent African Gospel Redeemed Church (AGRC) claimed in 1992 that, 'in Heaven it is like Kenya has been for many years. There is only one party – and God never makes a mistake' (quoted in Ranger and Vaughan 1993: 261). The leader of the independent Maria Legio Church, Moi's minister of employment, also supported the status quo. What this suggests is that independent Churches like the AGRC or the Maria Legio, theologically towards the conservative end of the religious spectrum, regard government as divinely sanctioned, that they rule because God allows them to. The mainstream Christian Churches in Kenya, on the other hand, were part of an international constituency which increasingly regarded the Moi regime as illegitimate. Further, the fact that the Maria Legio Church leader benefited materially from the status quo made it natural for him to support the pre-existing one-party State system. But in the case of the Catholic leaders in Kenya they were taking a leaf out of the book of their counterparts in both Latin America and Eastern Europe.

African Catholic Churches and democracy

The Catholic Church is by far the largest in Africa, with around 100 million baptized followers. In other words, nearly one-fifth of Africans claim to be Catholics, about one-eighth of the global total. The Church's well-developed institutional structure under the leadership of the Pope makes it, in effect, a transnational edifice with strong centralized control. As we saw earlier, the Church was in the forefront of recent democratic transitions in several parts of the world before Africa. Witte (1993: 11) notes that 'twenty-four of the thirty-two new democracies born since 1973 are predominantly Roman Catholic in confession'. Examples in this regard include Brazil, Chile, a number of countries in Central America, the Philippines, South Korea, Poland, Hungary and Lithuania. All of these countries received a great deal of diplomatic and sometimes material support from the United States for their democratization processes. The Catholic Church in Africa received much less international support for its own pro-democracy endeavours. In South Africa, for example, Ryall (1994) notes how neither Christianity as a faith nor the Churches as 'faith communities' were able on their own to break down apartheid. While some dedicated Christians were involved, the process was essentially and effectively dominated by secular rather than Church activists. In some African countries – for example, Zaire, Togo and Rwanda – senior Church figures were not closely associated with democratization campaigns, neither did they receive support from the United States nor other Western countries for democratic change. In short, Africa did not experience prolonged American pressure for democratization in the early 1990s; stability was the USA's predominant concern because it was keen to protect Western commercial interests.

The absence of the West's support for democracy makes the Catholic Church's efforts all the more remarkable. Senior Roman Catholic figures were centrally involved in national conferences on democratic change in Benin, the Congo, Togo, Gabon and Zaire in the early 1990s (Gifford 1994). Furthermore, Monrovia's Catholic Archbishop Francis made a number of highly publicized comments on the political composition of Liberia's (abortive) transitional government in late 1993. African Catholic figures' pro-democracy statements coincided with the Pope's encyclical of January 1991 (*Redemptoris Missio*), centrally concerned with the Catholic Church's duty to help 'relieve poverty, counter political oppression and defend human rights' (Jenkins 1991: 6). Coming in the wake of the liberation of Eastern Europe from communist rule and in the context of an apparently global move towards democracy, the thrust of such papal sentiments, coupled with the pre-existing social and religious standing of the Catholic Church in Benin and the other above-mentioned states, made its local leaders obvious choices to chair national conferences. The aim of the latter was to reach consensus between government and opposition over the democratic way forward.

Leading figures in Catholic Churches in Benin, Congo, Gabon, Zaire and Togo – respectively, Monsignors Isidore de Souza, Basile Mvé, Ernest Nkombo, Laurent Monsengwo and Philippe Fanoko Kpodzro – were chosen to chair their country's national democracy conferences. However, unlike in Benin, Congo and Gabon, in Togo, Mgr Kpodzro was unable to lead his national conference to a democratic conclusion: President Eyadema was able to remain in power following a controversial election. Similarly, in Zaire, President Mobutu made it only too plain that he believed that he alone had the ability to keep the country together.

Why were leaders of the national Catholic Churches chosen to head democratization conferences? The short answer seems to be that, despite their often close personal relations with government, in popular perceptions they were neither overtly supportive of one ethnic group or another nor in obvious thrall to government. Rather, because of the Churches' control of welfare provision, they often enjoyed a high degree of economic independence. In addition, provision of welfare functions

– educational, health and developmental programmes – made the Churches popular with many ordinary people (Luneau 1987).

In conclusion, over time, the Catholic Church – like other former mission Churches – found itself on the horns of a dilemma: to what extent dare it criticize government – even if it abused its power in ways that Christian morality found unacceptable? There were two distinct, mutually exclusive options: to speak out whenever necessary and be damned in consequence by governments or to keep publicly quiet and seek to change government policy by behind-the-scenes persuasion alone. As time went on, most Catholic leaders, encouraged by growing popular opposition to poor and arbitary government, chose the former option.

National Muslim organizations and political change

In this section I want to look at the role of national Muslim organizations in the recent period of democratization in Sub-Saharan Africa, with case studies from Côte d'Ivoire, Mali, Niger, Uganda, Tanzania and Malawi. In each of these states Islam is an important majority or minority religion.

Since independence, African governments – like their counterparts in other parts of the Muslim world – have been in partnership with leading Muslim individuals to perpetuate an ideology of domination based on a desire to reform traditional, popular modes of Islam. As Bromley (1994: 42) notes, popular Islam is normally the religion of the majority of Muslims in most African countries. It is independent of the State and, for this reason, Islamic reformers in the national Muslim organizations seek to repress popular Islam, seeing it as a threat to their position. In other words, Islamic reformers aim to bolster their standing by systematizing their group values. The function of such an Islamic ideology is to concentrate belief in the values which are necessary for the domination of one group over others. Popular Islam – anti-orthodox Islam – is the ordinary people's response. I want to examine how regimes adopt 'Islamization': how they seek to force non- or nominal Muslims either to convert to Islam or to adopt the reformers' version of the faith to enhance their religious 'purity'. The real aim, of course, is to bolster the hegemonial positions both of the reformers and of their secular allies in the State by manipulating national Muslim organizations for their objectives.

National Muslim organizations, in the same way as many mainstream Christian Churches, aim to fill the role of intermediary and interlocutor between State and *umma* (the Islamic community). Senior Muslim figures thus claim to serve a dual role: to channel the State's orders and wishes downwards, while officially passing social concerns the other way. These organizations are not only found in Sub-Saharan African states where there are majorities of Muslims – such as Niger, Mali and Guinea – but also in others, including Tanzania, Malawi, Côte d'Ivoire and Uganda, where Muslims form substantial minorities. In these latter states, government, through its alliance with the national organization, seeks to achieve control of Muslims, a potentially subversive group, they believe. Such organizations, then, function primarily as control and surveillance bodies, as 'a means of protection against the . . . development of a militant Islam, uncontrolled and subversive' (Triaud 1982: 38). This recalls the way that colonial administrations where possible chose the 'big' marabouts (Muslim holy men) as their interlocutors with Muslim society. The various national Christian Church councils today fill something of a similar role to that of the State-level Muslim bodies. Because of international links with their former 'parent' Churches they are able to maintain a degree of financial independence; Muslim national associations may also receive funds from abroad – perhaps Iran or Saudi Arabia – although these foreign governments are just as likely to fund non-State Muslim organizations, especially in states where Muslims are in a minority, such as Kenya, Tanzania and Uganda. National Muslim organizations tend to be more quiescent politically than mainstream Christian Churches, subservient in their relationship with the political rulers and highly dependent on the latter's patronage.

The State, in partnership with senior Muslim figures possessing interests in the national organization, seeks to create hegemonic rule by exploiting the religious and moral prestige, cultural leadership and ideological persuasiveness of the latter. As hegemony relates to the cultural leadership of a class in relation to society, so, in religious terms, does it refer to the significance of a leading religious institution (Islam) vis-à-vis ordinary believers.

Islamic members of the ruling establishment may well have themselves been challengers to colonial elites in the 1950s; the aim then was to counter Western (Christian) colonial supremacy and to install themselves in positions of power. They often formed the leadership of Islamic renewal and reform movements which aimed to give a new impulse to Islam by defining new modalities of both social organization and education, and to reform the Sufi brotherhoods (Coulon 1983: 153). Such reformers usually looked to Saudi Arabia or Egypt for their inspiration. Radical and reform movements spread their ideas to Africa, deriving inspiration from the works of, *inter alia*, Jamal Ad Din Al Afghani (1838–1897), Muhammad Abduh (1849–1905) and Rashid Ridha (1865–1935) (Kane 1990).

Reformers were also influenced by the Salafiyya, the Egyptian intellectual movement led by Muhammad Abdu (d. 1955), whose programme was concerned with a return to the fundamentals of Islam. This involved renovation of Arabic as a religious language, of Islamic education and of the development of modern Islamic scientific knowledge and technology in order not to be dependent on the West. In the 1950s and 1960s, schools with curricula based on such ideals were founded by members of the Salafiyya in Guinea, Chad and Senegal (Coulon 1983: 153).

Governments were anxious to find common cause with Islamic reformers for two reasons: the first and obvious one is that regimes always wish to control any potential force of dissent or opposition; the second was that Islamic revival was deemed by black African leaders 30 years ago as little more than an Arab plot for control of Africa. Europeans were decolonizing; Arabs, it was thought, were seeking to step into the vacuum. African governments were determined to ensure that the Arabic roots of Muslim renewal were not utilized by Arab States as a means to gain undue influence with local reforming groups. While African regimes are naturally suspicious of their Muslim nationals' ties with the governments of foreign Muslim states, they are happy to use national Muslim organizations to help regularize cultural and religious contacts with the Arab world, and to entice Arab development capital. It is not unusual for their leaders to be included in diplomatic missions or to be named as ambassadors to Muslim countries outside of Africa.

What this suggests is that black African governments are often ambivalent about Islam, especially when it is not the religion of the majority: whereas its value as social cement is welcomed, historical ties between Muslims in North Africa and elsewhere in the continent predate the drawing of modern State boundaries, which obviously threatens the modern masters of the post-colonial State. For example, the Libyan Sanusiyya has widespread links with Muslims in West Africa. This helped to facilitate Colonel Qaddafi's ultimately futile expansionist dreams in the region in the 1970s and 1980s. Followers of Sanusiyya in Chad, a State dominated by southern Sara Christians, for a time appeared to have more in common with their co-religionists over the country's northern border than with 'Christian' State leaders. Yet eventually Qaddafi's expansionist foreign policies served to unite Chad's competing factions (albeit temporarily) from the mid-1980s (Kelley 1987).

Islamic reformers are closely linked to modernizing secular power holders, are part of the elite and target traditionalists. Formally and ostensibly they seek a return to the original principles of Islam, as related by God to the Prophet Muhammad. By treating the *sharia* as an ideological reference book, reformers seek to use it as a blueprint for reorganizing society to solve extant social, moral, economic and political dislocations.

Muslim reformers, despite their predeliction for the revival of a 'pure' (or purist) version of Islam, nevertheless find it expedient to borrow from the West's organizational models, including the formation of bureaucracies and management systems (Cruise O'Brien 1986: 78). Using modern methods, they collect and collate useful political information through networks of appointees and confer upon their State's Muslims the feeling that they have a national body working for their interests. Members of the Muslim national organizations receive salaries from the State, have the ear of governments and are important in the maintenance of political order. They aid the creation of a Muslim political allegiance to the State in a way which is far more complete and systematic than that achieved by the mainstream Christian religious bodies. Even though ulama may sometimes lead popular protests when religious concerns are at issue, they must play a shrewd and skilful game to appear to be all things to all people: oppositionist enough to lead discontented Muslims when necessary, quiescent enough to maintain their relationship with State rulers.

Côte d'Ivoire, Mali and Niger

The influence and political significance of Muslim reformers appear generally to have grown over the three decades of African independence. They have been notably successful in Côte d'Ivoire, where Muslim reformers are integral facets of the State itself. Their position among the country's Muslims was facilitated by the patchy presence of Islam in the country. Around one-quarter of Côte d'Ivoire's 13 million people are Sunni Muslims of the Maliki school, concentrated in the north-west of the country among the Mandinka, Dyula and Kono. Conversion to Islam has been swift since the first decade of the twentieth century, at which time only about 7 per cent of those living within present-day Côte d'Ivoire were Muslims.

In neighbouring Mali, reformist ideas began to circulate from the 1920s, spread by local Muslim traders returning from the *hajj* to Mecca. Reformers came into conflict both with the marabouts and with the French colonial administrators, who had made political allegiances with the marabouts. As in Côte d'Ivoire, reformers gave their political support to nationalist politicians. They built their own mosques and schools, and challenged the marabouts to religious disputation. Support for the refomers grew steadily from 1945. Following Mali's independence in 1960, the reformers, 'in political terms . . . constituted an indispensable element in the support base of the military rulers of Mali' (Cruise O'Brien 1986: 79). Support was institutionalized by the formation of the Association Malien pour l'Unité et la Progrès de l'Islam (AMUPI) in 1981. AMUPI was formed, at least in part, in response to a perceived threat from an Islam newly radicalized at the time by the Iranian revolution and by Libya's activist foreign policy in West Africa (Haynes 1993: 129–32). The national leader, General Moussa Traoré and the ruling Mali People's Democratic Union Government were overthrown 10 years later in March, 1991, after a military coup. His successor, Alpha Oumar Konare, was as concerned as his predecessor to keep opposition Islamic groups under close supervision by AMUPI.

In neighbouring Niger a similar kind of neotraditional corporatism, with Islam as an ideological referent, was also created after independence. Seyni Kountché's military-dominated regime founded the Association Islamique du Niger (AIN) in 1974 for six interrelated purposes: to unite Niger's ethnic groups politically within their common Islamic culture; to serve as a focus of Islam in Niger in order to attract foreign aid from wealthy Arab states, such as Saudi Arabia; to apply Islamic ideology to all areas of national life; to help spread Arabic as a lingua franca; to serve as a means of combating Libyan-inspired radicalism; and finally, to form a focal point for Niger in international Islamic bodies (Triaud 1982: 37). AIN sought to perform the task of intermediary between State and society, and to serve as an insurance against Qadaffi-inspired subversive Islamism. Marabouts were attacked by AIN's zealots. In sum, AIN represented the religious side of the alliance between State power and the reformist cadres who were united against the alleged obscurantism and self-serving tactics of both traditional Islam (marabouts and the Sufi orders), as well as the threat of radical Islamism (Lapidus 1988: 851). What this amounted to was that Islamic reformers had official sanction for their campaign for religious purification and restoration, which was aimed at their competitors for popular allegiance, the 'petits marabouts charlatans' (Clévenot 1987: 215–16).

Uganda, Tanzania and Malawi

National Muslim organizations are not necessarily under the control of members of the ulama, especially where a State contains only a minority of Muslims among the population. When the latter is the case, the organizations will be dominated by

Muslims who hold powerful secular positions in the State apparatus; their objective is to facilitate control of Muslims and obtain their loyalty to the State, rather than to reform Muslims' spiritual behaviour. For example, in the Uganda Muslim Supreme Council, created by Idi Amin Dada in the early 1970s, five of the thirteen members (38 per cent) were senior figures in the police or armed forces (Coulon 1983: 163). In Tanzania – approximately one-third Muslim concentrated in coastal groups – the single party, Chama Cha Mapinduzi, recognized the fact that the traditional power structure was too strongly entrenched to be pre-empted by its *arriviste* socialist ideology. Traditional leaders, including where appropriate Islamic authorities, were inducted into its official leadership structure. A National Muslim Council of Tanzania was formed to supervise Islamic affairs on the mainland; its leading figures comprised Muslims with stature in society. The Mosque Council of Zanzibar, founded in 1981 and led by Shaikh Ameir Tajo Ameir, fulfilled a similar role in Zanzibar. In Malawi, in areas where Islam predominates, officials of the former dominant party, the Malawi Congress Party, were nearly always Muslims. Malawi's State Muslim body, the National Muslim Association (NMA), was actively involved in provision of mosques and *madrassahs* (Islamic schools) to enable State appointees to control religious education and worship. It was also useful in providing sinecures to State employees of the NMA (Bone 1982: 134). These examples suggest that national organizations will contain a variety of Muslims, whose common characteristic is that they are all allies of the ruling regime.

What these accounts of various national Muslim organizations have underlined is that one of their chief purposes, in addition to seeking to purify Muslim practices, is also to aim to control local Muslims for the benefit of the State. They 'accomplish this work of encadrement with all the more zeal as they are themselves much more dependent on the State than the "traditional" Muslim leaders' (Coulon 1983: 164). African regimes, when possible, seek to utilize Islam as a facet of national identity and State power, and to bolster autonomy and influence in the international Muslim community. The State aims to dominate all international Muslim transactions; it strives to be the interlocutor, the negotiator and the beneficiary of all relations and communications that its national Muslim community maintains with the wider Islamic world. The State seeks to make use of Islam as an ideology of national unity. National Muslim organizations channel the faith of the Prophet into specific organizations, offering material rewards in order to integrate any putative Islamic counter-elite into the State-controlled Muslim framework (Bayart 1993: 190).

Conclusion

In this chapter I have examined the role of the leaders of the Catholic Church, as well as that of national Muslim organizations and other important Muslim factors, in the context of recent moves towards democratization in Africa. A feature shared by the two groups was that, until recently, senior religious figures from both religious traditions forged close relationships with the State; this often made them rather ambivalent towards the concept of fundamental political change. Senior Islamic figures had a religious agenda: the aim was to seek to undermine and belittle the traditional expositors of Islam – the Sufi brotherhoods – in order to replace their rather eclectic variant of Muslim beliefs by an 'Arabized' version which sought, literally, to do things Islamic 'by the book'. The goal of religious reform coexisted with a more material concern of Muslim elites to enjoy the political and economic advantages of leadership positions in national Muslim organizations. Secular leaders found it advantageous to endorse the climate of reform which national Muslim organizations sought to perpetuate because it enabled the latter to gain control over local Muslims, to make them feel that someone was looking out for their interests. In recent times, however, in the context of economic downturn and democratic aspirations, the partnership between national Muslim organization and State entered a period of strain. Whereas liberal democracy *per se* was not necessarily of major concern to Muslims – believing as many do in a continuity of religion and politics which makes strictly secular goals of deeper democratization somewhat irrelevant – it was the case that reform of Islamic practice and of the forms of control which it represented were increasingly questioned.

I argued in the case of the Catholic Church that their leaders were generally formerly involved in a similar kind of relationship to their Muslim counterparts: they sought to prosper, both religiously and materially, within the context of their relationship with the State. The peculiarities of Africa's economic downturn, coupled with authoritarian rule, acted together to push popular demands for political reform to the top of the agenda. Roman Catholic leaders tended to be ambivalent about the concept of fundamental political reform because they feared emphatic change every bit as much as did the entrenched political elites. Although on occasions they headed conferences, it was not at all clear that they wished personally to endorse the demands for change until the groundswell of public opinion was such that not to do so would emphatically link them with the secular political elites at a time when demands for change focused on the latter's role.

Chapter 7

The Middle East: religions in collision

The Middle East[1] is one of the first regions that many would think of when the issue of religion in politics arises. This is partly because of the decades-long struggle between Jews and (mostly Muslim) Arabs, especially since the founding of the State of Israel. Given their history of mutual antipathy, it might be assumed that there is something fundamental dividing the two religions, driving them inexorably towards conflict and confrontation. Yet both religions actually come from the same roots and have many theological similarities. The main issue dividing the Jews and the Arabs is not religious, but is a question of who is permanently to control Palestine with its holy places. But religion has become the main *symbol* of the division between the two peoples, exemplified by the rise of religious radicals posing serious challenges to modernizing governments. Such regimes share a desire to privatize religion, to reduce significantly its political importance.[2] But tensions between rulers and ruled over the public role of religion in the region are by no means novel. As Vatikiotis (1987: 56) points out, 'rulers of Middle Eastern states have for over a century now relentlessly eroded the religious character of the State. The expansion of State functions has been purely at the expense of the role of certain religious leaders and institutions.'

This chapter focuses on four countries: Israel, Turkey, Egypt and Algeria; the first is predominantly Jewish, the remainder preponderantly Muslim. In each, religion has emerged – or re-emerged – as an important political actor since the 1970s. What all four countries have in common is that despite long periods of modernization – involving State attempts to privatize religion – religion has great political importance. There is continuing civil war in Algeria, during which an estimated 60,000 people have died since 1991, between the State and Islamists. Something similar is occurring in Egypt where Islamists seek the Islamic State,

1. In this chapter the term 'Middle East' refers to the Arab countries plus Turkey and Iran. Despite its importance in the context of religion and politics in the region, I do not focus upon the latter. This is because there are many existing sources of information for those interested. See, for example, Owen (1992), Haynes (1993), Bill and Springborg (1994) and Keddie (1995).

2. This is a debatable contention in the case of Israel where, since the Likud victory of 1977, regimes of both right and left have been obliged to accept the presence of religious parties in government due to the vagaries of the electoral system.

often by violent means. In Turkey politics was dominated in 1997 by a stand-off between the Government and the military over the public role of Islam; evidently the military triumphed and Islamist-orientated regime fell. Finally, in Israel, the Prime Minister, Yitzhak Rabin, was assassinated by a religious Jew in November 1995, focusing attention on the growing polarization between non-religious and religious Jews, often called Jewish 'fundamentalists' (Silberstein 1993). The emergence of Jewish fundamentalism – represented by organizations such as *Gush Emunim* – is often explained by the impact of Israel's victory over the Arabs in their 1967 war. Jewish fundamentalism is considered by Lustick (1993) and Sprinzak (1993), among others, as a product of the victory. For many religious Jews this was a particular triumph: it led to the regaining of the holiest sites in Judaism from the Arabs: Jerusalem, the Temple Mount, the Western Wall and Hebron and was, they believed, a sign of divine deliverance, an indication of impending redemption. Even some secular Jews spoke of it in theological terms.

For Arabs, on the other hand, Israel's victory exemplified the social and political crises enveloping their countries. For Piscatori (1986), the emergence of Islamist movements can only be understood against the background of Arab military defeats, especially that of 1967. The political and cultural crises they engendered created a situation of political instability and religious turmoil. Loss of control of holy Muslim sites, such as Jerusalem, the Temple Mount, the Dome of the Rock and the El Aksa mosque, generated a religious crisis. This loss, Silberstein (1993: 15) suggests, coupled with 'the ensuing political vacuum, opened the way for the growth of [Islamic] fundamentalist movements . . . fueled by the ongoing sense of shame, frustration, and victimization fostered by the continued occupation by Israel of an Arab population of 1.5 million in Jerusalem, the West Bank, and Gaza'. As I will explain, however, this is only part of the *raison d'être* for Islamist groups. As their rise in once strongly secular, non-Arab Turkey shows, they are also reactive against secularization, enforced modernization and a corresponding decline in Islam's social importance. Like their counterparts in Egypt and Algeria, Turkey's Islamists have profited from a declining economic situation, growing unemployment and serious State-level corruption presided over by self-proclaimed modernizing governments.

A number of factors – history, culture, religion, colonial experiences, constraints of underdevelopment and the ideologies and self-interest of political elites – were important in modelling the characteristics of the region's post-colonial States. Governments relied on centralist and centralizing development strategies and modes of rule. However, while importing doctrines of nationalism with its structure of the nation-state, many failed to provide acceptable alternative bases for the legitimacy of the State and its patterns of authority. The point is that the narrow political issue of 'nation' and nationalism have particular complexities in the Middle East. In the post-colonial period the view of the 'nation' that was given primacy in efforts at 'nation-building' was the citizenry occupying the territory of the new states. Subsidiary identities – especially those pertaining to shared religious and cultural identities – were dismissed as atavistic by modernizing regimes. Because of the cultural importance of both Jewish and Muslim identities, however, there were other possible bases for identity; particularly for the latter, whether in locally focused Islamist world views or in transnational ideologies such as pan-Islam.

The pursuit of modernity resulted in sharp divergences from Islamic or Judaic sources of authority, without integration on an alternative consensual basis. The result was an impasse regarding society's future direction. Currently, throughout the region the main challenges to political stability came from religious activists intent on changing the status quo. In the next two sections, I want to examine the religious and political characteristics of Islam and Judaism in order to put the following case studies into their proper contexts.

Islam and Judaism in political perspective

Islam and politics

From its inception in the seventh century CE from a particularist religio-political community in present-day Saudi Arabia, Islam has developed into a world religion, albeit with different and rival, Shia and Sunni interpretations.[3] Islam is the unique historical case of a religion founded simultaneously as both a religious charismatic community of salvation and as a political community. This was expressed in the dual religious and political charisma of its founder, Muhammad, who was both God's messenger and a political and military leader. It is even more literally expressed by the fact that the Islamic era begins not with the birth or death of a founder or with the date of revelation but, rather, with the *hijra*, or migration, which marks the foundation of the Islamic political community in Medina ('the City'). There Muhammad established a political community, the *umma*, the importance of whose founding is commemorated in the Islamic calendar which begins from its inception in 622 CE rather than 610 CE, the year of God's first revelation to the Prophet. Under his leadership, the Muslims established their dominance over much of the Arabian peninsular, resulting in the welding of the disparate Arab tribes into a single polity with common institutions and a common ideology, a unity which endured until Muhammad's death in 632 CE.

Muhammad's passing was the prelude to the establishment of the caliphate period (632–1258), during which Islamic ideology and institutions as they are understood by Muslims today were formed and developed. This period is of special importance in the context of the rule of the first caliph (*kalifa* or 'successor'), since it is the period to which contemporary Islamic radicals turn to for guidance in attempting to define the preferred character of their putative Islamic states.

The process of creating a Middle Eastern Islamic civilization took 600 years, from the beginning of the seventh to the thirteenth century CE. The consolidation of Muslim rule was followed by its spreading to other regions. By the end of the fifteenth century Islam had established itself as the dominant religion in North Africa, and was of growing importance in sub-Saharan Africa and in many parts of Asia. The spread of Muslim power and the mass conversions with which it was

3. There is inadequate space in the present work to examine the theological and other differences between the two rival interpretations of Islam. Those interested are directed to Haynes (1993).

accompanied brought into the faith a wide range of beliefs, superstitions, religious practices and social customs. The result was that Islam was no longer a simple, rational anti-idolatrous faith, characteristics with which it had initially been marked. The several types of Islamic societies – in the Middle East, Africa and Asia – can therefore be analysed in terms of various patterns of institutional arrangements involving State, parochial and Muslim religious institutions. In each case the pattern of relations describes a variant form of Muslim society. Although inherited patterns would be a powerful force in the shaping of Muslim societies in the post-colonial era, as they entered the modern era they were to be drastically changed. This was the result of three main developments: internal reorganization, European imperialism and the growth of the global economy.

There are two important themes in Islam that traditionally impact upon politics. First, it is often suggested that religion and politics are inseparable in Islam. It is said that the *umma*, the Islamic community, has traditionally seen itself as simultaneously both religious *and* political community, that is, the community of believers and the nation of Islam. The result is that it is completely 'natural' for religious actors to seek to gain political goals. Such a suggestion does not, however, go unchallenged; others believe that it is quite inaccurate to argue that Islam has no differentiated religious and political spheres. Indeed, it is suggested, the history of Islam is best viewed as the history of the various institutionalizations of the dual religious and political charisma of Muhammad into bilateral and differentiated religious and political institutions.

Certainly Islam's holy book, the Quran, depicts the faith as a belief system encompassing both religion and politics. The Quran, divine revelation received by Muhammad, and the *hadith*, prescriptions laid down by him on the basis of his own reflections, are sacred texts for Muslims. *Sharia* law, at least theoretically and in many cases practically, also helps regulate Muslims' conduct. Partly as a result, it is widely assumed, especially by non-Muslims, that politics and religion cannot logically be separated in Islam. However, at the very least the all-encompassing nature of this assumption can be strongly challenged. As respected scholars like Ayubi (1991), Piscatori (1986) and Owen (1992) have convincingly argued, Islam has a history above all of pragmatism. And, as Asad (1986) points out, there has never been a Muslim society in which *sharia* law has governed more than a fragment of social life. In practice, there is, on the one hand, very often separation between the essence of the religious principles and institutions and those of the temporal ruler and State. On the other, there has frequently developed a pragmatic compatability between Islam's precepts and the very different imperatives of a world of secularizing states. The important point is that Islamic history contains innumerable examples of thought and action where *din* (religion) and *dawla* (State) have been sharply distinguished. What this amounts to is that the most spectacular recent example of Islam's political involvement – Iran's Islamic revolution of 1978–9 – is not the norm: actually it is historically novel. Further, there would appear to be no insurmountable obstacle of principle to a fair degree of compatability between 'Islamic' precepts and pragmatically modernizing State practice as regards citizenship and the nature of socio-political organization.

The second main theme is that most *ulama* (learned clergy) have historically been close to those who wield political power. So close has this relationship been that in some countries such religious figures are known as the 'ulama of the establishment' (Gaffney 1994), denoting their close identification with the politico-religious status quo. Numerous ulama – normally proponents of establishment Islam adhering closely to the ideal as described in texts and interpreted by religious scholars – have connived with State authorities in the name of perpetuation of their interpretation of Islam. 'In return for material favours and recognition of their status' many ulama have sought to use their positions to underline the importance of obedience to authority, in the process closely identifying themselves with government (Bill and Springborg 1994: 59). In short, 'establishment' Islam is in many instances the State religion and as such is formally bound up in the legitimacy of government. The establishment ulama are often in conflict with two tendencies: (a) 'popular' Islam, that is, the Sufi *tariqas* (orders)[4] and (b) Islamists. Popular Islam comprises those religious beliefs and practices which prevail among the ordinary people. Due to a variety of factors, many Muslims – especially the poorly educated and those residing away from Islamic centres – may not have access to religious scholars and written texts. Because of this it is natural for them to adhere to their own unorthodox interpretations of Islam.

While the Sufi orders have often incurred the suspicion of both religious and secular authorities over time, a more recent development has been the emergence of the Islamists with their overt threat to the political and religious status quo. They are often regarded by governments and analysts alike as representing the very epitome of the religiously negative, because they are regarded as both defensive and backward-looking. Islamists are said to champion a 'set of strategies by which beleaguered believers attempt to preserve their distinctive identity as a people or group' in response to real or imagined attacks from those who wish to draw them into a 'syncretistic, areligious or irreligious cultural milieu' (Marty and Scott Appleby 1993: 3). Some portray them as appealing exclusively to poor, simple people, especially those disoriented by the stresses and strains of modernization. Such people are judged to be easy prey for the Islamists, allegedly cynical, manipulative champions of a vision of religious dogma which promises spectacular improvements in the lives of ordinary people once the Islamic State – where life is governed according to religious laws – is a reality. In fact, the character and impact of Islamist doctrines are located within a nexus of moral, social and political issues revolving around State–society interactions. Islamist groups pose a challenge to State power because of their sharp critiques of existing religious and political elites. Their ideas amount to a 'manifesto' – a programme of political action – for social change and reform of the status quo. Apart from the perceived attack on religion by their modernizing governments, the rise of the Islamists has also been in response to the military

---

4. The *tariqas* are brotherhoods of Islamic mystics who search for divine knowledge through the emotions rather than purely through the intellect. The Sufi orders emerged from the ninth century as an antidote to the austere, scripturalist, rational nature of Islam. Sufism has always met with, at best, ambivalence, at worst, outright condemnation, from most ulama. Periodically, brotherhoods have been outlawed by the authorities.

defeats of the Arabs by Israel and as a result of the stimulus provided by the Iranian revolution.

The point is that the Islamists are counter-elites who perceive establishment ulama, the unorthodox *tariqas* and the State collectively as the 'enemies of Islam'. The expansion and contraction of Western colonialism, the dissolution of the Ottoman Empire, and the emergence of Muslim nation-states after World War II all undermined the traditional forms of institutionalization of the *umma* as a dual religious and political community. It opened up the way for all kinds of religious-political experiments in the name of returning to the original *umma*. It is misleading, therefore, to view the emergence of the Islamists as primarily an anti-modern traditionalist reaction. It is more appropriate to view them in their various manifestations as experiments in Islamic 'reformation' and 'revolution'. Below I examine Islamist groups in Algeria, Egypt and Turkey. First, however, I examine Jewish fundamentalism, in some ways a parallel to its Islamist counterpart.

Judaism and politics

Islam is, more perhaps than any other religion, a *blueprint* of a social order. It is in the *totality* in which Islam is a social movement which sets it apart from Judaism. However, like Islam, Jewish identity has been understood, traditionally, as an overlapping combination of religion and nation. Put another way, the people of Israel think of themselves as a nation inhabiting a *Jewish* State created by their covenant with God. The interpretation of the covenant and its implications gives rise to the characteristic beliefs and practices of the Jewish people. Vital to this covenant is the promise of the land of Israel. Following their historical dispersions under first the Babylonians and then the Romans, Jews had prayed for centuries for the end of their exile and a return to Israel. However, except for small numbers, Jews lived in exile, in separate communities, for centuries. During the diaspora while awaiting divine redemption to return them to their homeland, Jews' lives were defined by *halacha* (religious law), which largely maintained the national component of Jewish identity. The Jews' historical suffering during the diaspora was understood as a necessary continuation of the special dedication of the community to God.

While monotheistic, Judaism lacks the universalist and proselytizing tendencies of Islam and Christianity. As former Chief Rabbi Epstein put it: 'when paganism gave place to Christianity and later also to Islam, Judaism withdrew from the missionary field and was satisfied to leave the task of spreading the religion of humanity to daughter faiths' (quoted in Parrinder 1977: 67). Jews have a different view of revelation from Christians. For the latter, the proclaimed messiah – Jesus Christ – has already come; Jews, however, look forward to the arrival of their *Mashiach* at some future date.

There are two main strands of the Jewish faith, Orthodox and Reform Judaism. The division between them is ostensibly on the question of whether tradition can be changed in the face of new situations. In other words, is the Torah, the Jewish holy book (essentially the first five books of the Hebrew Bible), totally immutable in theory? Over time, the hegemony of Orthodoxy has declined. In medieval times Jewish ritual life had been highly elaborated as a result of the dominance of the rabbis, both spiritual counsellors and teachers of the traditions of the Torah. Various injunctions of the Torah controlled nearly all acts of everyday life in both the home and the synagogue, serving constantly to remind Jews that they were God's chosen people (Smart 1989: 265). Ethically, Jews were expected to keep to the high standard of the Ten Commandments and other injunctions promulgated by the rabbis, such as monogamy. Regarding doctrine, the insistence on strict monotheism has always been vital.

The traditional view of Judaism as a revealed religion governing every aspect of life began to face severe challenges at the end of the eighteenth century following the French and American Revolutions. Henceforward, many Jews began to participate fully in the life of Western society, increasingly to share in its values, 'in contradiction to traditional Jewish life and values' (Jacobs 1992: 31). A consequence was the emergence of the *Haskalah* (Enlightenment) movement, led by a German Jew, Moses Mendelssohn. The *Haskalah* aimed to influence Jewish intellectuals towards a greater appreciation of the need to adapt to the new order. They did not seek to reject tradition, but to promote a new approach whereby it could live side by side with new learning and social forms. Essentially, the *Haskalah* was a Jewish Renaissance whereby the Jewish Middle Ages came to an end. It spread to Eastern Europe where it met with considerable hostility on the part of traditional rabbis but its impact was such that no Jew could be impervious to its claims (Jacobs 1992: 31).

During the second half of the nineteenth century, Zionism – the political endeavour to create a national home for Jews – emerged. Fundamental to Zionism is the recognition of the national identity of the Jews, the rejection of the exile and a belief in the impossibility of assimilation. While the Bible is central to secular Zionists as a 'historical' document, many seem to be unclear concerning the centrality of religious elements in Jewish cultural history and the rejection of orthodox practice. The 'political' Zionism of Theodor Herzl's[5] World Zionist Organization (WZO), founded 1897, was condemned as 'idolatry' by many of the orthodox, who felt it replaced reverence for God and the Torah (law) by secular nationalism and the 'worship' of the land. Some orthodox Jews, instrumental in founding the *Mizrahi* party (*Merkaz Ruhani* or Spiritual Centre) in 1902 and *Agudat Israel* (Association of Israel, founded 1912), did, however, support Zionist efforts to establish a Jewish State. By the 1930s there was growing support for the idea of Israel from many orthodox Jews, although the Holocaust in Nazi-controlled Germany – some six million Jews were killed – was pivotal in the founding of the State of Israel in 1948.

---

5. Theodor Herzl (1860–1904) was a Hungarian journalist living in Vienna. He was persuaded by the Russian pogroms and the Dreyfus trial in France to conclude in his pamphlet *Der Judenstaat* (1896) that the only way Jewish people could live was to have their own nation-state. In 1897, at the first WZO congress in Basle, Switzerland, the leading Jewish intellectual and organizer, Chaim Weizmann (1874–1952), called for a Jewish homeland to be created in Palestine.

In the next section I want to examine the interaction of religion and politics in Israel, where historically religious Jews and more recently a fundamentalist group – *Gush Emunim* – have been significant political actors. After that, I survey the situation in mainly Muslim Egypt, Algeria and Turkey where Islamist groups have risen to prominence in recent times.

Religion and politics in Israel

Since the establishment of the State of Israel as a homeland for the Jews, there has been intense controversy in the country over whether the State should be a modern, Western-style country – where normally religion would be privatized – or a *Jewish* State with Judaist law and customs paramount. At the end of the 1960s, Luckmann (1969: 147) noted that Israel was characterized by a bureaucratization along rational business lines, reflecting accommodation to an increasingly 'secular' way of life for many Jewish Israelis. Moreover, according to Weber's (1978: 56) classificatory schema, Israel is a 'modern' State, with a powerful legislative body (the Knesset) enacting the law; an executive authority – government – conducting the affairs of the State; a judiciary branch enforcing the law and protecting the rights of individuals; an extensive bureaucracy regulating and organizing educational, social and cultural matters; and security services – the police and the armed forces – protecting the State from both internal and external attack.

Yet, to many, Israel is not 'just' another Western State. This is largely because religion has gained an increasingly central public role over the last few decades. Religious Jews warn of the social catastrophes that they believe invariably occur in secular, 'godless', societies, while many non-religious Jews see such people as intolerant religious fanatics. The assassination of Prime Minister Yitzhak Rabin in November 1995 by Yigal Amir, a 25-year-old religious Jew, led some Israelis to fear that violence would henceforth characterize the already tense relationship between religious and secular Jews. Yet what appeared initially to be the onset of a religious war among the Jews may actually have little long-term impact in a setting where, despite much intense political and social conflict, religious interests have never been able to determine major issues of public policy.

Exploiting the divisions between the two groups, governmental policy has traditionally favoured the political centre ground; consequently, neither religious nor anti-religious extremes have been able to dominate the political agenda. Increasingly, however, religious Jews have become an important political voice, although like Christian fundamentalists in the USA, they are not strong enough normally to determine outcomes. They are particularly vocal on the issue of conceding parts of biblical Israel for the sake of peace with the Palestinians, a subject of intense controversy profoundly dividing the country. Further, the issue of the State's role in determining what are traditionally religious concerns – Sabbath observance, kosher food, secular marriage, divorce, burial, abortion and other medical matters, the definition of who is a Jew, and the rights of non-Orthodox congregations and their rabbis – is of growing public concern.

The public face of religion is expressed through a number of religious parties. Traditionally, the National Religious Party (NRP) and *Agudat Israel* were the most important, although later others emerged. Normally in elections religious parties achieve about 15 per cent of the vote – about 20 per cent of the Jewish population of Israel is strictly religious-observant – and 15–18 seats in the 120-seat Knesset.[6] However, in the most recent election in 1996 they gained an unprecedented 23 seats, just under 20 per cent. This meant they were a crucial element in the new Likud Government headed by Binyamin Netanyahu.

The predecessor of the NRP, *Mizrahi*, won 16 seats in the first general election in 1949, before becoming the NRP in 1956 after a merger of several parties. Its success in 1949 meant that it was able to force a series of compromises from the then Head of State, David Ben-Gurion, despite the fact that he regarded the new Israeli State – rather than religion – as the sole centre of allegiance for the citizenry. Nonetheless, he agreed both to set up a ministry of religious affairs with formal authorization over many aspects of Jewish life, and not to draw up a permanent constitution because NRP leaders feared that the status of *Halacha* (religious law) would be diminished.

From the 1950s to the 1970s the NRP held at least two cabinet posts under successive Labour Governments. Through control of the Ministry of Religious Affairs, it had wide-ranging control over the rabbinic establishment and the religious councils operating in both the urban and rural areas, providing religious services to the citizenry. It also periodically had authority over the Ministries of the Interior and Social Welfare giving it, by control of the latter, patronage abilities in relation to the social-welfare allowances of the underprivileged. This power enabled it 'generally' to get such people's electoral support 'as a token of gratitude' (Dieckhoff 1991: 10–11). In the 1980s, however, the NRP saw its electoral support fall away dramatically as many erstwhile supporters perceived it as not radical enough (Morris 1989: 129).

Agudat Israel, with four or five seats, was the second largest religious party until the late 1980s, when it was overtaken by *Shas*. *Agudat* traditionally represented a section of the ultra-orthodox community but only rarely sought cabinet posts in the Labour Governments. In 1977, however, when Likud ousted Labour, it became a regular feature in government. In 1977–84, *Agudat* had the chair of the important Finance Commission as well as the vice-speakership of the Knesset. It was able to introduce and strengthen religious legislation in various areas, including abortion, autopsy and national airline flights on the Sabbath. In the national unity governments between 1984 and 1988, its role diminished as the Labour–Likud coalition could function without it. However, it returned to prominence following the Likud election victory of 1990, gaining several cabinet seats. It was behind several pieces of religious legislation in the early 1990s, such as the banning of 'offensive' advertisements (displaying parts of the body of a man or a woman), the sale of pork, the closing of businesses on the Sabbath and further restrictions on abortion rights. The party's political influence in the early 1990s reflected the fact that many religious

6. Religious parties gained 18 seats in the 1988 general election, 16 seats in that of 1992.

Jews were coming to the conclusion, like Christian fundamentalists in the USA, that the defence of their interests was best pursued via involvement in the decision-making process rather than by a holy separatism.

Also understanding the importance of political involvement rather than standing aside, *Shas* (Sephardi Torah Observance) – an orthodox party, representing the interests of the Sephardi constituency[7] – was founded in 1984. It gained six seats in both the 1988 and 1992 general elections, rising to 10 in 1996. Like the NRP and *Agudat*, it held various ministerial posts – Absorption, Communications and the Interior. Closely linked to *Shas* is yet another religious party, *Degel Torah* (Torah Flag) an ultra-orthodox party which gained two seats in the 1988 election. In the 1996 election – as United Torah Judaism – it increased its representation to four seats.

The presence of religious parties in government since 1949 was both to protect the interests of the religious community and to increase its influence in a variety of social areas. Until 1967, they remained a subordinate trend in the society. But Israel's decisive victory – to religious Jews, ushering in the messianic age and the recreation of the kingdom of Israel – provided an important incentive for new religious movements such as *Edah Haredit* (God Fearful Community), *Neturei Karta* (Guardians of the City) and *Gush Emunim* (Bloc of the Faithful). The most important, *Gush Emunim*, was from its founding in 1974 committed to establishing Jewish settlements in the West Bank and, until its handing over to the Palestinians, the Gaza Strip, judged to be integral parts of the biblical land of Israel (Sprinzak 1993: 347). The general point is that such groups – mouthpieces of the strictly Orthodox settlers – had a major and direct influence on Israeli politics in addition to that wielded by the traditional religious parties.

Gush Emunim was formed in early 1974 in the West Bank settlement of Kfar Etzion. Its main concern was the conquest and settlement of the whole land of Israel. Between the mid-1970s and mid-1980s, *Gush* was able to grow rapidly, especially afer the 1978 Camp David agreement led to the return of the Sinai desert – grabbed by Israel in the 1967 war – to Egypt. *Gush Emunim* and other fundamentalist groups, such as the late Rabbi Meir Kahane's organization, *Kach* (Thus), argued against giving back territory to Egypt on religious grounds. The biblical entity, *Eretz Israel*, they argued was significantly larger than today's Israeli State. To hand back any territory to Arabs, non-Jews, was tantamount to going against God's will. Simmering religious opposition to the peace plan with the Palestine Liberation Organization, involving giving autonomy to the Gaza Strip and to an area around Jericho, reached tragic levels in February 1994 when a religious zealot, Baruch Goldstein, who had links with militants of both *Kach* and *Kahane Chai* (Kahane Lives), murdered at least 30 people in a dawn attack on a mosque in the West Bank town of Hebron. After the massacre both *Kach* and *Kahane Chai* were banned by the Israeli Government, a sign of its commitment to crush religious extremist groups systematically using violence to gain their ends.

But this was not to be the end of political murders in Israel. Less than two years after the Hebron massacre, Israel suffered another destabilizing blow when Prime

---

7. Mainly Jewish immigrants from Muslim countries.

Minister Rabin was assassinated. After the killing, the 1996 general election was widely assumed to be a likely win, because of the expected huge 'sympathy vote', for Labour, then the governing party. As the election campaign progressed, however, it began to dawn on many Israelis that the Labour Government's undeclared aim was to assist in the creation of an independent Palestinian State in the West Bank and Gaza Strip. 'Labour's coalition partner, Meretz, was open about these objectives; Labour was more cautious' (Bhatia 1996). As far as the Israeli secular right wing and the ultra-orthodox were concerned this meant the slow dismemberment of the Jewish State. Their leaders were not prepared to accept Yasser Arafat's assertion that his people finally recognized Israel's right to exist within its pre-1967 borders. When the Labour Government began to discuss the issue of Palestinian refugees returning home, the religious and right wing disquiet grew. 'They were not only worried about the fate of 150,000 Jewish settlers in the West Bank and the Gaza Strip, but they were also concerned at the prospect of hundreds of thousands of Arab refugees converging on the [Israeli] homeland' (Bhatia 1996).

Such concerns were important in the Likud (Unity) Party's victory, achieved under the flamboyant leadership of Binyamin 'Bibi' Netanyahu. Likud and its secular allies won 45 seats, while religious parties gained 23 seats in the 120 seat parliament, giving the Netanyahu Government a clear majority. The religious parties' 23 seats meant that they could hope to occupy some very important ministries, including Education, Housing and the Interior. Control of the Ministry of Education would allow a new stress on the importance of Jewish religious traditions and culture in the country's schools, while management of Housing would almost certainly lead to increases in funding for Jewish settlements in Palestinian areas. Domination of the Interior would allow them to 'reward' those municipalities – like Jerusalem – controlled by like-minded politicians, and allow the religious new influence to impose edicts such as that all shops, pubs, restaurants and night clubs would have to close on the Sabbath (Saturday).

There was speculation that the rise in the religious parties' share of the vote heralded a crisis in Israel's politics. As in 1988, when the religious parties' share of seats increased to 18, the outcome of the 1996 election prompted commentators to write of impending 'war' between the religious and non-religious. Many secular Jews appeared to fear that the religious constituency would attempt to create a theocratic State by using their new strength to lever substantial religious concessions as the price for their support of Netanyahu's Government (Black 1996, Bhatia 1996, Oz 1996). While almost certainly not heralding a theocratic State, the rise in the share of the vote of the religious parties does reflect the period of intense self-questioning as to Israel's identity as a nation in the late 1990s. The self-scrutiny takes many forms – from the meaning of 'Jewish' in the phrase 'the Jewish State', as formulated in Israel's Declaration of Independence (1948), to the adherence to the democratic values, which are also enshrined in the same Declaration, in the light of an anticipated Arab majority.

There are several reasons why the political impact of religious parties and movements in Israel is unlikely to diminish significantly in the near future. First, the basis of both nationality and the creation of the State of Israel is religious identity.

This makes it highly vulnerable to the claims of the religiously observant militants. Second, there has been a spectacular growth of orthodox Jewry since the early 1970s. In the late 1990s, one in three Jews in Israel 'respects the religious commands' and one in ten belongs to the *haredi* (ultra-orthodox) community. Sixty per cent of the *haredi* population is under 25 years, so the proportion of the orthodox is likely to grow: they have big families (Bhatia 1996). Such people are highly likely to be impressed by the arguments of the religious movements and parties. Third, the latter will continue to have major political influence because of the nature of the country's political system. As in the past, they have a capacity to gain numerous benefits in return for support of either Likud or Labour. Finally, a dovetailing of secular right wing concerns (security) and religious interests (fear of secularization) produced a powerful coalition likely to endure until – or if – the issue of the Palestinians is finally settled.

Islamist movements in Egypt, Algeria and Turkey

Israel's decisive victory against the Arabs in 1967 and its capture of vast portions of Arab land, including East Jerusalem and the West Bank, provided an incentive for Jewish religious movements. It was also a catalyst for Islamist groups, but from a negative perspective. As Silberstein (1993: 15) notes, the view that Islamist 'movements emerge in a situation of social and political crises is clearly supported' by the history and political engagement of Islamist movements in the region, and in particular those in Egypt, Algeria and Turkey.

Egypt.

Over 90 per cent of Egypt's more than 60 million people are Muslim. Reportedly, a growing number are sympathetic to Islamist goals, including rejecting Western values and influence – such as 'women's liberation' – and reintroduction of Islamic norms and morals, necessary because of the perceived lack of piety among many Muslims. A drop in faith is believed by many to be the main cause of the decline of Egypt's position in the Arab world (Auda 1993). The principal target of the Islamists is the modernizing State which has neither striven to eradicate Western influences, nor to deliver on promises of material improvements for the mass of people, nor truly to democratize.

The process of division between an increasingly secular, Western-oriented elite and Islamist opposition is well advanced, stimulated by government's diminished legitimacy and authority. The main support base of the Islamists is the growing body of young, frequently unemployed, often alienated people, victims of Egypt's economic travails. Urban unemployment is a serious problem: there are currently more than three million unemployed graduates of universities and high schools, believed to be the main source of recruits for the Islamist movements (Auda 1993: 385). Voll (1991: 346) notes that while many Islamist cadres 'have had the greatest exposure to modern technologies, educational systems, political processes, cultural values and lifestyles' they can also relate to the experiences of 'ordinary' Egyptians. Many share the experience of unemployment: economic restructuring, involving privatization of State industries, throws tens of thousands of people out of work. Hardships are probably more difficult to bear for many ordinary people because of the obvious corruption of the Government, the bureaucracy, and the military elite, and the ostentatious wealth of the *arriviste* middle classes (Gaffney 1994). Islamists are also thought to be inspired by the success of the Afghan mojahideen who managed to rid their country of the 'godless' Russians. Many Egyptian returnees from the Afghan War are said to play leading roles in the Islamist opposition (Salame 1993: 27).

According to Voll (1991: 345), the Islamists' popularity is reflected in the fact that hundreds of thousands of Egyptians are involved 'in some way in the Islamic resurgence', in some respects representing 'the majority of society'. Large numbers listen to radical preachers, such as Shaykh Muhammad Sha'rawi and Shaykh 'Abd al-Hamid Kishk, either in person or via audio cassettes and video tapes (Gaffney 1994). The Islamist movement has not only prospered by pointing out what is wrong in society, they also provide a variety of welfare measures, including medical facilities and schools, especially for the urban poor. In effect, they are gradually replacing the State in many urban areas in the provision of a variety of goods which the latter cannot – or will not – provide (Gaffney 1994).

The most important Islamic movement in Egypt is the Muslim Brotherhood, founded by a teacher, Hasan al-Banna, in 1928. Over the years it grew to become a mass movement with tens of thousands of followers (Deeb 1989a: 64). Initially, however, it was just one of a number of small Islamic associations engaged in charity work among the poor of the country's fast growing cities. Mosques, schools and clinics were built by the Brotherhood, providing an Islamic welfare framework by which Muslims could live 'without reference to the western and secular influences around' them (Ayubi 1991: 131).

Following al-Banna's assassination in 1949, the Brotherhood became close to the revolutionary government of Gamal Abdul Nasser after it took power in 1952. By the mid-1950s, however, relations had soured: following an unsuccessful attempt on Nasser's life, the Brotherhood was proscribed and its leader, Sayyid Qutb, arrested and executed in 1966. During his captivity, he produced a comprehensive commentary on Islamic history, arguing that Egypt was not an Islamic country, but in a State of *jahilya* (religious ignorance). Muslims could not live a proper religious life in such circumstances; it was necessary to overthrow the existing political order (Zubaida 1989: 51–3).

Following President Anwar Sadat's accession to power in 1970, the Brotherhood enjoyed a period of improved relations with the Government because it was anxious to cultivate their aid in the fight against leftists. Taking advantage of Sadat's overtures, the Brotherhood built mosques, schools and clinics. Its financial position improved following the founding of a range of profitable companies and financial institutions. Such entrepreneurial flair was not, however, appreciated by all Brotherhood members, as the movement split into two sections, 'radicals' and 'moderates'. The latter believed in a gradualist approach, slowly to Islamize society by increasing the Brotherhood's influence over time. Later, after Sadat's assassination in 1981 at the hands of Islamists, the moderate Brotherhood entered the electoral arena, consistently winning a few seats in the national legislature under President Mubarak's 'limited democracy'.

The radicals were too impatient for change, too opposed to what they perceived as a sham democracy, to join in such a programme. Breaking away from the moderates, several new organizations – including *Takfir wal-Hijra* and *al-Jihad* – were founded. Together they were the core of a shifting set of religio-political organizations under the general title of *al-Gama'at al-Islamiyya* (the Islamic Groups). Stimulated by the writings of Qutb, they were characterized not only by a denial of conventional electoral politics but also by a resort to terrorist tactics to achieve the Islamic State (Owen 1992: 180). Members of *Takfir wal-Hijra* were responsible for a number of political assassinations, while the *al-Jihad* group not only killed Sadat, but also tried to kill two government ministers and the Parliamentary Speaker at the same time (Deeb 1989a: 63–4). Consequently, the authorities decided to crack down on the radicals. More than 300 members of *al-Jihad* were arrested and some executed, specifically for their alleged involvement in the murder of members of State security forces in the town of Asyut in the early 1980s.

From the mid-1980s, *al-Gama'at al-Islamiyya* were involved in a *de facto* civil war with the authorities while also turning their attentions to the Coptic Christian minority, murdering several. Foreign tourists were also killed (Bromley 1994: 134–5, Pugh 1994). The aim was threefold: (a) to curtail foreign investment and the influx of foreign tourists to put the authorities under pressure, leading, it was hoped, to (b) conditions ripe for overthrow of the Government, to be followed by (c) the Islamic State. In pursuit of this aim, over 900 people are thought to have died in the conflict between 1992 and 1996 (*Guardian* 1996).

In conclusion, the division in world views between secularists and Islamists in Egypt developed in the 1980s into a conflict between two different conceptions of society and the direction of desirable social change. It spilled over from the religious sphere into the fields of politics, economy and social affairs; in the process it split Egypt's society vertically between the haves and the have nots. Islamist political activism aims – whether by the ballot box or by violent methods – for the reinstitution of Islamic law, to change the language of politics, to build as broad as possible opposition forces and to deliver welfare benefits to the urban poor. Islamists, irrespective of the extent to which they differ in terms of tactics and precise visions of the Islamic society, want to reverse what they see as the cataclysmic slide into modernization and a secular society. The aim, in short, is to introduce *sharia* law to recreate the Islamic society, a project with the ancillary objective of removing secularizing elites from power. So far, however, the Islamists have been unable to shift the Government from its view that modernization is the best strategy for achieving progress.

Algeria

Ayubi (1991: 118) argues that Islamist movements are more vigorous in countries like Egypt that have 'openly discarded some of the symbols of "traditionalism"'.

But this surely misses the point: Ayubi's argument suggests that countries like Egypt should have stronger Islamist lobbies than, for example, Saudi Arabia, whose constitution is an Islamic one. Yet while Saudi Arabia's stability is challenged to a limited degree by an *Islamist* opposition, modernizing governments like those of Tunisia and Morocco have managed to keep the lid on Islamist dissent. This is explicable in the case of Morocco by the fact that King Hussain is able to trace his ancestry back to the Prophet; hence he has a high degree of *religious* legitimacy. In Tunisia, on the other hand, the Islamist opposition – led by the *al-Nahda* group – has been very moderate in its tactics and aims. But State policies have helped to keep its importance limited. This suggests that rather than it being a question of 'tradition' versus 'modernization', it is more an issue of government skill in dealing with Islamist demands in a variety of ways. Partial democratization – as in both Tunisia and Morocco – seems to help; so does real – if limited – increases in living standards. In 1980–93, Tunisia's per capita GNP grew by 1.2 per cent a year, as did Morocco's, while Algeria's declined swiftly by 0.8 annually (World Bank 1995: Table 1, pp. 161–2).

Precipitous economic decline – coupled with governmental illegitimacy – helped stimulate the growth of Islamist opposition in Algeria. Islamists were able to link religious and cultural issues with the country's economic predicament. Following independence from France in 1962, Algeria was governed by the secular National Liberation Front (FLN) for nearly three decades. An Islamist movement emerged in the 1970s advocating a reversal of modernization and the application of *Sharia* law to replace Algeria's – French-influenced – civil code. Islamists pushed for reforms based on 'Islamic principles': a stricter dress code for women, more religious broadcasts on radio and television, and the banning of consumption of alcohol in public places. Initially ignored by the Government, they began to seek their objectives by taking over State-controlled mosques and installing their own preachers; sometimes bloody clashes resulted. Conflict also erupted on several university campuses between Islamists and secular students; in addition, 'inappropriately' dressed women were harassed (Deeb 1989b: 7). Although the State soon began a systematic clampdown on the Islamists – arresting leaders and controlling activists' movements – an Islamist movement, *Ahl al-Da'wa* (the People of the Call), grew underground (Kepel 1994: 45). By the mid-1980s, a thriving Islamist network had developed pursuing the goals of anti-Westernization, anti-unemployment, anti-poverty, anti-corruption and pro-Arabization. The latter goal was manifested in a campaign against French, the language of the elite, when nearly everyone else spoke Arabic.

In the early 1980s, economic problems followed a collapse in the price of oil, a commodity providing 98 per cent of Algeria's export proceeds. By the mid-1980s, the country could not feed itself: only 25 per cent of the country's food came from local sources, down from 90 per cent in 1969. In order to qualify for desperately needed aid from the West, Algeria's rulers were persuaded to allow multi-party elections, apparently not realizing how unpopular they had become.

The Islamist movement grew swiftly, especially after the constitution was liberalized in February 1989, following food riots the previous October. Before this, it had been both fluid and nebulous; after the riots, it managed to concretize into a variety of distinct organizations, including both political parties and Islamic movements with combined religious, social, cultural and political objectives. The largest party was the Islamic Salvation Front (FIS), followed by Hamas (*al-Haraka li-Mujtama' Islami*; Movement for an Islamic Society) and the MNI (*La Mouvement de la Nahda Islamique*; the Movement for Islamic Renewal). Smaller groups included *Rabitat al-Da'wa al-Islamiyya* (League of the Islamic Call) and the Party of Algerian Renewal (Roberts 1991: 133). While differing in their tactics to achieve the Islamic State, they agreed that Algeria's problems were caused by the public downgrading of Islam during decades of modernization.

Following local elections in June 1990, the FIS emerged as the main political rival to the ruling FLN. It took control of more than 50 per cent of municipalities, with over 54 per cent of the vote. The FIS platform was that Algeria should move at once to the Islamic State on the basis of *sharia* law and *shura* (consultation) to replace Western-style pluralism and representative democracy. The FIS – along with *Hamas*, MNI, and the Party for Algerian Renewal – then took part in elections for the National Assembly in December 1991, winning 188 of the 430 seats in the first round of voting (3.26 million of the 6.8 million votes cast, or 47.9 per cent) (Tahi 1992: 407). This impressive result was achieved despite – or because of – the fact that its leaders, Abassi Madani and Ali Belhadj, were in prison. The other Islamic parties did much less well in the election.

Tahi (1992) argues that the FIS success reflected popular dislike of the incumbent regime as much as – if not more than – a desire to see an Islamic State in the country. He has a point. Although the FIS victory was both comprehensive and unexpected, the party's more than 3.25 million votes needs to be contextualized by reference to the fact that the electorate was 13.25 million people. In other words, just 24.5 per cent of eligible Algerians chose the FIS in the December elections, compared to the 1.6 million (12 per cent) who chose the ruling FLN. In all, recognizably Islamist parties gained about 50 per cent of the vote in the poll, with the FIS taking the lion's share. This indicates there was not an overhelming popular preference for the FIS: only one in four eligible Algerians chose to vote for it.

Most independent observers characterized the elections as among the most free ever held in the Arab world. The result, however equivocal in terms of popular preferences, *did* come up with an FIS victory. It was virtually certain that it would have gained enough seats in the second round of voting in January 1992 to secure an overall majority in the National Assembly. Instead, the army stepped in, cancelled the elections and then ruled the country behind various frontmen. The overturning of an election result which would have been the democratic will (however unpalatable that might have been to certain constituencies) was defended on the ground that an FIS victory would have been a recipe for Algeria's fragmentation, because it would have probably led to demands for secession by the anti-FIS province of Kabylia and to the withdrawal of crucial international loans. In addition, with an emphatic electoral victory, it was feared that the FIS leaders would have been unable to restrain the party's radicals who wished to abolish the pluralist constitution. But it is difficult to separate self-interest from national interest concerns in the army's coup. On the one hand, its cessation of the electoral process was a clear sign of its hesitancy at letting Algerians choose their government; on the other, the fact that the FIS gained only a quarter of the electorate's votes, while its chief rival, the FLN, achieved only one eighth, gives some credence to the army's claims that its actions represented the implicit will of many voters: a plague on the houses of both the FLN and the FIS.

The army forced the FLN's leader, Chadli Benjedid, to resign, replacing him with a five-man collective presidency, the High Committee of State (Haut Comité d'Etat, HCE), chaired by Mohamed Boudiaf. Boudiaf was assassinated in June 1992, probably not by the FIS, but almost certainly by or at the behest of certain senior army figures. They were allegedly alarmed that Boudiaf was setting in train corruption investigations which threatened to implicate them and their associates, a shadowy group popularly known as 'the mafia' (Roberts 1992: 454).

The FIS was banned and thousands of its activists and supporters incarcerated, while an estimated 60,000 people died in the civil war by late 1997. However, presidential elections in November 1995, attracting a large turnout despite threats by Islamic militants to kill voters, gave a clear victory to the government's candidate for the presidency, Liamine Zeroual. For the regime to hope realistically to crush the Islamists it would, at the very least, be necessary to induce strong economic growth over a sufficiently long period of time to improve the quality of life for the mass of Algerians. But the problem is that every four years a million more Algerians enter the job market, while over two million urban unemployed struggle for non-existent jobs. The FIS was able to capitalize on the economic and social crisis of the country with millions of people voting for the party partly in protest against high unemployment, housing shortages, State-level corruption and steep price rises of consumer goods. Unless the Government can somehow deal with such issues it is highly unlikely that the Islamists will fade away.

Turkey

As in Egypt and Algeria, the re-emergence of political Islam in Turkey puts into serious question the goal of Western-style modernization. Turkey has seen a long period – nearly three-quarters of a century – of aggressive modernization since the suppression of public Islam by Mustafa Kemal 'Atatürk' ('Father of the Turks') after World War I. Atatürk was a military hero who imposed Western civil law and in effect created Turkey as a nation-state from the ruins of the Ottoman empire. Like his contemporary, Lenin, he perceived the indigenous traditions of his own country as expressions of backwardness, and saw progress in emulating the institutions and absorbing the values of the European powers. This ideology was firmly enforced over time by the State with the assistance of the powerful armed forces.

The emergence of the Islamist *Refah Partisi* (Welfare Party) to become the senior partner in the ruling coalition which took power in 1996 firmly placed the issue of the role of Islam in Turkey back on the agenda. As in Egypt and Algeria, the rise of *Refah* is principally the result of two developments: (a) disappointment, especially among large sections of the urban poor of the sprawling cities of Istanbul and Ankara, that Western-style modernization has not led to sustained increases in well-being and (b) widespread disquiet that governmental inadequacies are making progress less rather than more likely. On the other hand, it is not clear that most Turks want an Islamic State *per se*; it seems likely that *Refah* has achieved electoral support because neither main alternative – secular parties of the right and left – are widely judged to have the solutions to the country's problems.

Turkey stands at the crossroads between Europe and Asia. Ninety-eight per cent of Turks are Muslims; most of them are Sunnis. The post-Ottoman Republic of Turkey was declared a secular State after the abolition of the (Muslim) Caliphate in 1924 and the official banning – although not in practice the disappearance – of Sufi orders a year later. Other secularization measures included scrapping the use of Arabic script, banning religious schools and introducing a Western dress code which removed the veil and fez (traditional conical head gear for men). Atatürk attacked institutionalized Islam, reducing its power and status and placing it firmly under State control: in effect, removing Islam from politics and limiting it to the private, individual sphere.

Yet, despite aggressive secularization, interest in Islam was sustained over the years by the underground survival of Sufism. Following relaxation of the rules banning public expressions of Islam in the 1960s, the National Salvation Party (NSP) was founded. The NSP advocated the restoration of Islamic law and practice and closer ties with the Muslim world. Its popular appeal was probably enhanced during the 1970s when the country was affected by terrorism from both secular right and left. Indeed, one of the claimed reasons for the 1980s military coup d'état was that the army feared the activities of the NSP were inflammatory and socially disruptive, or too popular. As a result, the party was banned (Özbudun 1993: 262).

Following the end of military rule and the unbanning of religious parties at the end of the 1980s, *Refah*, the NSP's successor, began to pose a growing challenge to the Westernizing, Enlightenment-oriented ideology inherited from Atatürk. By the 1990s, *Refah* had succeeded in supplanting the secular left as the 'natural' representative of the rural and urban poor. Using this electoral base to contest the modernizing and secularizing policies of the secular parties, *Refah* managed increasingly to challenge the assumption that Turkey was an emergent 'Western European' country. A former prime minister, Tansu Ciller, had managed to persuade the European Union to enter into a customs union with Turkey in the early 1990s, arguing that it would raise prosperity and, she hoped, stem the rise of Islamism (Gray 1996). However, *Refah* stressed Turkey's Muslim cultural heritage and argued that the country's natural allies were neighbouring Islamic countries rather than Europe.

The rise of *Refah* was facilitated by the triumph of the Islamic revolution in neighbouring Iran, providing a concrete example of a Muslim alternative (Shaikh 1989: 270). Yet the rise of political Islam also led to an exacerbation of traditional societal conflict, for example, between the Sunni majority and the minority Alawi Shias. Some Turks feared that the resurgence of Shia revivalism in neighbouring Iran could only worsen the situation. However, the Khomeini line did not command much support in Turkey despite the fact that one Cemalettin Kaplan, a former *mufti* (Islamic legal expert) known as the 'Local Khomeini', strove to emulate the late

Iranian leader. Kaplan tried to use fiery sermons – smuggled into Turkey on audio- and videocassettes from Germany where he lived – to gain support for an Islamic revolution, but without success (Harris *et al.* 1992: 476). Opinion polls in the early 1990s – coinciding with a wave of terrorist killings by a group calling itself *Islami Hareket* (Islamic Movement) – showed very little support for the Islamic State in Turkey (Harris *et al.* 1992). But there was support for a relaxation of strictures against Islam. Following a *Refah*-led campaign, the State softened its anti-Islam policy, not only allowing Sufi orders to function openly for the first time in decades but also permitting the re-establishment of faculties of divinity in universities and the building of new mosques and *imam-hatip* (schools for the training of prayer leaders and preachers).

Whether any of this necessarily represents unequivocal signs of aggressive Islamic reassertion is, of course, a matter of interpretation. On the one hand, it could be argued that the State's willingness to tolerate religion in politics is a symptom of its liberalism. On the other, it could equally be contended that it is the very strength of religion which forced the State to revise policies. Whatever the true picture, secular Turks express concern at what they see as religious renewal, exemplified in the campaign led by some female students, reminiscent of similar developments in France, for them to be allowed to wear the traditional headscarf. A number of small Islamist movements organize, including the *Nurcus,* the *Süleymancis,* the *Isikcilar* and the *Fethullahcilar*. Such groups organize mass demonstrations and education and electoral campaigns, rather than revolutionary activities (Keddie 1995: 125).

One useful way of assessing the strength of a religious political party is to ascertain how well they do in the polls. By this reckoning, *Refah*'s progress has been steady, rather than spectacular. Advocating restoration of Islamic law and practice and closer ties with the Muslim world, *Refah* managed 8.5 per cent of the vote in 1987, 16.4 per cent in 1991 (during a period of alliance with the ultra-nationalist right), and 19 per cent on its own in local elections in 1994, winning the mayorships of Istanbul and Ankara (Rugman 1995c). In the next national-level elections in December 1995, *Refah* won 22 per cent of the vote, making it the largest party – with 158 seats, up from 40 in 1991 – in the 450-seat legislature. Thus, in a decade support for the party tripled from a twelfth to nearly a quarter of the popular vote. The fact is that *Refah* has managed to gain electoral advantage from a system designed to produce government by a single party ruling alone. In 1987, for example, the Motherland Party gained 292 (65 per cent) of the 450 parliamentary seats, with only 35 per cent of the vote. It is not inconceivable that a rise in *Refah*'s share of the vote to about 30 per cent could give it power alone.

Refah's strongest support, according to Ersin Kalaycioglu, professor of political science at Bosphorus University, is found among those 'opposed to the establish- ment: the Kurds in the south-east, the very poor and the lower-middle-class crafts- men threatened by the advance of neo-liberal capitalism' (quoted in Rugman 1994c). Such people are thought to have four main grievances against secular politicians: the slow pace of material improvements; the failure to help protect the Bosnian Muslims during the Civil War in former Yugoslavia; widespread corruption in local and national government; and a number of morality issues – including a growth in prostitution in the cities and the selling of alcohol in restaurants (Rugman 1994b). In addition, as Ali Nabi Kocak, mayor of the *Refah* stronghold of Sultanbeyli, a shanty town of around 200,000 people on Istanbul's Asian shore, put it: 'The only party Turks haven't tried is *Refah*' (Rugman 1994c). In Sultanbeyli, the *Refah* administration has used State money to build roads and pipe water to illegally built houses, while streets are cleaned thoroughly and rubbish collected frequently; in consequence, the party is held in acclaim by many among the nearly 400,000 poor, mostly largely uneducated migrants who pour into Istanbul every year. The influx has created vast illegal suburbs – like Sultanbeyli – where the party recruits well (Rugman 1994a).

It may well be that *Refah* is the principal beneficiary of the cultural contradictions which have plagued Turkey since Atatürk's day. It is often forgotten that the average urbanized Turk is only a generation away from his or her Muslim village roots (Günes-Ayata 1994: 54). It may well be that for such people in particular, Islam provides a moral refuge and a sense of continuity during often traumatic modernization. In addition, Islam may help solve the dilemma that a once great empire – like Turkey's – faces: how to arrive at a position on the world stage once the days of imperial splendour are over. In the early 1990s the Government trumpeted the country's growing influence in the former Soviet republics of the Caucasus and Central Asia; it was, it argued, natural to seek influence among fellow Muslims. In government, *Refah* has moved further in this direction: it recalled the golden memory of the Ottoman–Islamic past, the capture of Constantinople (Istanbul) by Muslims in 1453 and an empire once stretching from Poland to Egypt. Such unashamedly nostalgic sentiments find favour among many nationalist Turks, not only Islamists.

But *Refah*'s appeal is not only couched in foreign policy and nostalgia terms: its manifesto for the 1995 general election was both radical and Islamic. It announced that it wanted to create Islamic-style interest-free banking (with banks supervised by 'moral bureaux'), to end Turkey's dependence on International Monetary Fund loans, to start an Islamic common market and to renegotiate the customs agreement with Europe, dubbed by the party's leader, Necmetin Erbakan, 'the poison of Frankenstein'. Erbakan blamed a trio of malign interests – the CIA, the Freemasons, and Zionism – for many of Turkey's social ills. Nevertheless, despite such rhetoric, it should be emphasized that *Refah* is a broad Church, including technocrats like Erol Yarar, the head of a pro-Islamic business association representing 6,000 Turkish companies. As Yarar points out, 'when theory comes to application, many things have to change. Structural change can be evolutionary rather than revolutionary' (quoted in Rugman 1995c). In short, *Refah* is an umbrella group – containing both moderates and conservatives – like the FIS was in Algeria before the civil war radicalized the party *tout court*. Moderates may well believe in regular elections, a multi-party system and a liberal, free market economy, but it is not clear that all shades of opinion in *Refah* adhere to such values. As Dr Narli of Marmova University puts it: 'Are *Refah*'s members ready for an "historic compromise" with the system, like the one the Italian Communists aspired to [in the 1970s], or are they practising *taqiya* – the concealment of one's true aims for the welfare of Islam?' (quoted in Hooper 1996b).

Following a short-lived attempt at governing by the two main centre-right secular parties – True Path and the Motherland Party – *Refah* took power, in a coalition with True Path, in mid-1996. *Refah* ministers implemented a number of populist measures – such as tax breaks for the lowest paid, and a tax amnesty for debtors – while giving civil servants a 50 per cent salary increase and doubling the minimum wage. While the last two measures need to be seen in the context of a more than 80 per cent annual inflation rate, they were almost certain to increase *Refah's* popularity among the low paid. Even though the financial impact of the measures would add £5–7 ($8–11) billion to the country's already huge budget deficit, their popularity among some sections of the society might well ensure *Refah's* re-election next time. Yet, if the aim is cheap popularity, an early poll and an outright majority, then there is a serious risk that the country could be pitched into economic chaos before 2000. If this were to happen it is highly likely that the armed forces would step in, and democracy would be snuffed out. And, in mid-1997, they did.

However, not wishing to speculate too far, *Refah* is not on its own sufficient to oust the secular parties or to mount a realistic challenge to the Turkish State. Turkey is not, in the late 1990s – unlike Algeria or Egypt – a radically divided and unstable State in which Westernized elites are fighting an increasingly militarized rearguard action against Islamist insurrection. At the same time, developments in Turkey do fit into the pattern of Islamist progress being made in many Muslim countries by Islamist parties and movements. As Gray (1996) argues, the powerful global political renaissance of Islam is a devastating blow to the theories of government which have guided the policies of modernizing Muslim countries for years. Yet, *Refah's* accession to government did not signal swift Islamization but a welcome willingness to be pragmatic. In fact, it made a remarkable series of u-turns from its manifesto position: first, it renewed the mandate of the United States-led air force operating out of southern Turkey to protect Iraq's Kurds; formerly, *Refah* had called it an 'occupying force'. Second, it decreed another period of emergency rule in the south-eastern part of the country where security forces were fighting Kurdish guerrillas; in opposition, *Refah* had demanded that emergency rule be ended. Third, despite years of anti-Zionist rhetoric, *Refah* deputies voted for an investment protection agreement with Israel. Fourth, after bitterly criticizing the use of arbitrary measures by previous administrations, *Refah* employed the self-same 'authoritarian laws', with a decree having the force of an act of parliament (Hooper 1996b).

Whether the pragmatic approach was a strategy which would lead to a much more serious attempt at Islamization later was hotly debated. Mehmet Ali Birkand, one of the country's most respected columnists, reckoned that *Refah* was turning out in government to be just like its secular rivals: say one thing in opposition, do another in government. He believed that it 'was highly encouraging for the future' (quoted in Hooper 1996b). Mirkand's views reflect one of two main arguments regarding the 'true' aims of *Refah*. The first claims that the party is only a 'paper tiger' when it comes to Islamization. *Refah*, it is said, has been playing by the rules of Turkish democracy since its founding in 1983. Moreover, *Refah* is not deemed to be 'fundamentalist' – like Iran's Islamic regime – but, instead, to be rather like Christian Democratic parties in Europe, that is, seeking pragmatically to apply religious values to otherwise secular policies. The alternative view – that *Refah* is a religious wolf in sheep's clothing – is held by sceptics like Dr Nilufer Narli of Marmara University. He believes that the parallel with Europe's Christian Democrats is misplaced, suggesting that *Refah*'s tentative attempts to introduce Islamic principles and practices in Turkey is indicative of a gradualist approach, but no less serious for all that. For Dr Narli, *Refah* is simply biding its time.

In March 1997 the military-dominated National Security Council announced that the *Refah*-led Government would sign a list of measures designed to stamp out Islamism, including the closure of Quranic schools. By mid-1997, however, the crisis had not been resolved. There was great pressure from the military – which staged three coups since 1960 – to oust *Refah* by parliamentary means, that is, by getting its coalition partner, True Path, to withdraw its support (Nuttall 1997). This was because the Prime Minister, Necmettin Erbakan, despite intense pressure, had failed to implement measures, including banning the Muslim Brotherhood, restricting gun sales and reducing the influence of religious schools. If the stand off continued there was a high probability that the military – seeing itself as the last bastion of the secular republic – would step in again to prevent what it saw as the inexorable slide into the Islamic State.

Conclusion

The growth of Islamist parties and movements in Egypt, Algeria and Turkey, on the one hand, and the parallel development of Jewish fundamentalist groups in Israel, on the other, reflects growing challenges to post-war modernizing State policies in the Middle East. Their popularity suggests that several regimes have failed to increase people's feelings of well-being, while the pursuit of Western-style modernization offends the growing constituencies of the religious. Further, both Islamist and Jewish fundamentalist groups, especially in Israel and Egypt, received a fillip – for differing reasons – from the outcome of the 1967 war. In the former, the victory was widely perceived as a sign of God's approval for the State of Israel, while the feeling among many Muslims was of despair at how poorly their countries armies had performed in the war.

A second fillip to the rise, respectively, of Islamist and Jewish fundamentalist groups was the Iranian revolution and the Camp David accord. Iran's revolution suggested to many Islamists that the Islamic State was achievable, necessary to redress the failures presided over by 'anti-Islamic' governments. However, Islamist attempts to gain political power both attracted and repelled different sections of the population. Western-oriented elites and intellectuals seem horrified by them, while the unemployed and the alienated youth see them as beacons of hope for meaningful change. But both constituencies in effect cancel each other out and the result is impasse: neither the religious nor the secular forces are able to triumph.

Among the Islamist groups, however, it is possible to discern a variety of strategies to achieve the Islamic State, from gradualist policies via the ballot box, as in Turkey, to armed insurrection, as in Egypt and Algeria. In Israel, on the other hand, the continued electoral importance of religious parties – and the rise of Jewish fundamentalist movements – collectively ensured that they retain an important political position. However, the assassination of Prime Minister Rabin in late 1995 and the unprecedented electoral success of the religious parties in the following election may mean that there will be an even sharper polarization between secular and religious Jews in the future. If that happens, it bodes ill for the country's political health.

Chapter 8

Central Asia: The return of Islam to politics after communism

Following its break-up, it was widely believed that the new Central Asian countries of Kazakstan, Kyrgyzstan, Tajikistan, Turkmenistan and Uzbekistan[1] – all former republics of the Soviet Union – were seriously threatened by Islamist takeovers. Huntington (1993) and Fukuyama (1992) have pointed out the unwelcome strategic and security implications for the West of such a development. An alternative view was put forward by Husain (1995: 250). He posited that Islamic revival in Central Asia was neither 'exclusively fundamentalist', 'predominantly political', nor 'remotely anti-American or anti-Western in character'. In fact, he averred, what was happening in Central Asia in the early 1990s merely paralleled the trend in the rest of the former Soviet Union: people were now free to 'embark on a journey of open cultural and spiritual rediscovery' (1995: 250). Thus, the revitalization of Islam in Central Asia was, to him, primarily cultural and not political.

While having its merits, Husain's argument neglects certain important issues. First, Islamist organizations – that is, *religious* organizations with *political* goals – exist in all the countries focused upon in this chapter. They are strongest in Tajikistan and Uzbekistan, although as Juergensmeyer (1993: 132) puts it, 'more subdued' elsewhere. Second, in several Central Asian countries, radical Islam offers an alternative development model to that presented by the 'reformed' governments who, unable to provide sufficient material improvements to the mass of the population, want to deny Islam a political voice.

Third, we need to be aware that, *inter alia*, anti-Western Afghanistan and Iran have been supplying material support to Islamists for years; sometimes, as in Tajikistan, a country of Farsi speakers, there are strong cultural and linguistic ties facilitating religious links. Huntington (1993) argues that Iran is the 'true' inspiration behind the rise of Islamism, while Olcott (1990: 205) claims that revivalist religious influences from Iran were actually minimal during the Soviet years. She argues this is because the 1979 Shia revolution was a rather distant event for the average Central Asian Sunni Muslim, particularly under the watchful eye of Soviet administrations. However, there is plenty of evidence of Iran's recent interest in

1. This chapter focuses on these countries, all located between the Caspian Sea and China.

aiding the struggles of Central Asian Islamists for two principle reasons: (a) to pursue Iran's foreign policy goal of having friendly neighbouring governments; (b) to help deliver Islamist governments to rule in line with God's will.

The Islamist regime in Afghanistan also supports the spread of radical Islam in Central Asia. Islamists, especially in Tajikistan and Uzbekistan, are reportedly inspired by the success of the Afghan mojahideen (Steele 1992, Hiro 1993: 20). It is widely believed that the latter's triumph hastened the demise of the USSR. Leaving Afghanistan in disgrace in February 1989, the last Soviet troops crossed the bridge into the Soviet Union at Termez, Uzbekistan. As Barylski (1994: 394) points out, the memories of Afghanistan followed the army home, contributing to a general perception in Soviet Central Asia that something important was happening at the apex of the empire. Three years later, in 1992, the overthrow of the then communist Kabul Government by the Afghan–Tajik Islamist, Ahmed Shah Massoud, also encouraged the Islamists. It is not yet clear what effect the latest development in Afghanistan – the triumph of the fearsome Taliban in 1997 – will have upon the political situation in Central Asia. It needs to be understood, however, that in no cases is foreign influence the *pivotal* factor in the growth of Islamism in Central Asia: it cannot *create* the conditions where Muslim radicals can thrive, but it can fan the flames of discontent upon which Islamism thrives.

Husain (1995: 250–1) argues that to forestall the advance of radical Islam in the region, the West should 'cultivate Islamic revivalists and prevent popular expressions of Islam from degenerating into anti-Western hatred'. Further, he proclaims, the 'United States and its allies must learn to accept Islam as a legitimate socio-political force and not work to defame or discredit'. If not, he warns, 'Western hostility towards the Islamic revival in Central Asia may make dire predictions of Central Asian fundamentalism sadly self-fulfilling'. While admirably sensible it is not clear whether such a prescription would, in fact, be followed by such governments. It is rather difficult to imagine that the United States and other Western governments would be deft enough to discern the differences between 'good' and 'bad' Islam; to date, the track record vis-à-vis, for example, Iran, Somalia and Afghanistan does not suggest optimism.

But the likelihood of radical Islam emerging in Central Asia seemed remote before the demise of the USSR in August 1991. Until then, aggressively secular Soviet control of its Central Asian republics seemed well ensconced. Given that one of the main goals of the Soviet State was to eliminate the public face of religion, 'to reduce Islam to a "private affair"', as Benningsen (1981: 120–1) puts it, then the re-emergence of Islam as a public actor in Central Asia is unexpected. This chapter has several objectives. First, it describes the historical background to the contemporary emergence of Islamism in Central Asia so as to put recent developments in context. I explain that although Islam was rigorously – sometimes brutally – privatized it never lost popular appeal. Consequently, once communism collapsed, Islam was well placed to serve as cultural 'anchor' and, in some cases, vehicle of popular discontent among certain groups. Second, I explicate the local roots of the Islamic revival, arguing that the relative political importance of Islam in Central Asia is linked to several factors: where there are both 'strong' – that is, authoritative

Table 8.1 Selected indicators of the Central Asian republics

COUNTRY	Size (million hectares)	Popn. (mns.)	Urban popn. (%)	Real GDP per capita ($)	Human D'ment Index[a]	Percentage of Indigenes	Percentage of Muslims (approx.)	Literacy rate (%)	Adult life expectancy at birth (yrs)
Tajikistan	14.30	5.8	33	1,380	0.616	70	85	96.7	70.4
Kyrgyzstan	19.85	4.6	39	2,320	0.663	52	65	97.0	69.2
Uzbekistan	44.74	21.9	41	2,510	0.679	71	70	97.2	69.4
Turkmenistan	48.81	3.9	45	3,120	0.695	72	80	97.7	65.1
Kazakstan	271.73	17.0	59	3,710	0.740	40	65	97.5	69.7

Notes: All statistics relate to 1993. [a] = The Human Development Index is a measure developed by the United Nations Development Programme. The nearer the score is to 1, the higher the level of human development.
Source: UNDP (1996), Olcott (1992: 257).

– governments and ethnically and religiously fragmented populations, then Islam seems unable to express itself as a coherent political actor. But it seems to help the Islamic cause if there is material and/or diplomatic support from foreign Muslims, as in the cases of Tajikistan and Uzbekistan.

Before proceding with the chapter, it is necessary to point out that we are concerned with rather diverse countries, despite the shared Islamic cultural background and seven decades of Soviet rule, as Table 8.1 shows.

Because of mass immigration during the Soviet era, Muslims amount to half – or less – of the populations of Kazakstan and Turkmenistan. Consequently, they have complex mixes of cultures, nationalities and religions, and political Islam is of less significance than in Tajikistan or Uzbekistan. Political tensions in the post-Communist era have principally revolved around ethnic frictions in the former countries. There are also important size differentials: Kazakstan is by far the largest country in Central Asia, more than five times bigger than the second, Turkmenistan. It is also the most urbanized and materially richest, with the largest per capita income. Kazakstan's Government, under the strong leadership of Nursultan Nazarbaev, looks to the aggressive modernization of Yeltsin's Russia as its role model. Neither Kazakstan nor Turkmenistan has seen an important political role for Islam in the post-Communist era. Gharabaghi (1994: 105) explains this by reference to their ethnic and religious diversity, facilitating the government's ability to crush opposition.

However, the governments of two of the materially poorest countries – Tajikistan and Uzbekistan – have been strongly challenged by Islamist groups. It is plausible to suggest that this is – at least in part – because radical Islam offers an attractive political ideology to many, especially the powerless, particularly the poor and the young. Such people have been relatively neglected by governments over the years, whether communist or post-Communist. As already noted, the impact of neighbouring countries and cultures – especially the triumph of Islamism in Afghanistan – has also been of importance in encouraging Islamism. But such factors need to be closely assessed to explain the *variable* impact of political Islam in the region. Consequently, case studies will examine regional diversity in this regard in the second half of the chapter. First, however, it is necessary to examine the historical background.

Islam in Central Asia: the impact of the 1917 Revolution

On conquering Central Asia after the 1917 Revolution, an important Soviet aim was to eliminate public expressions of Muslim belief. Consequently, traditional leaders – including religious ones – were removed from power 'in favour of a new peasant elite' (Benningsen and Lemercier-Quelquejay 1967: 38). In pursuit of secularization and communist-style modernization, the Bolsheviks believed it of primary importance to reduce in size and authority Central Asia's religious establishment. Henceforward, Islamic teachers (*ulama*) suffered persecution: thousands were executed, others fled abroad or went into hiding. Actions incumbent on every Muslim were either prohibited – for example, the pilgrimage (*hajj*) to Mecca – or so discouraged that it became dangerous to be seen to observe them. In 1927, Quranic courts and *madrassahs* (religious schools) were abolished and *waqf* lands (charitable endowments) confiscated to the State. Whereas there had been some 26,000 mosques in 1912, after the Revolution, very many – including the most historic and holy in the cities of Bukhara and Samarkand – were closed; others were destroyed or turned over to secular use. By 1968, there were fewer than 500 in the whole of Soviet Central Asia (Juergensmeyer 1993: 128). Then, in the pursuit of Russification, there was a change of scripts, first from Arabic to Latin in 1930, then from Latin to Cyrillic in 1940 (Akiner 1989: 282–3). Taken together, the State's anti-Islam policy greatly weakened the traditional religious way of life. Virtually all public manifestations of Islam were expunged from the national life of the Central Asian republics for decades after 1917.

However, despite the persecution of religious professionals and the religious way of life, Islamic traditions and culture still managed to survive, especially in the more remote rural areas where many village communities, among the most isolated and unmodernized in the communists' empire, were left largely undisturbed (Benningsen 1981: 132). Helping to keep religion alive were various kinds of 'unofficial mullahs', including wandering 'irregular' adepts or *divana* ('possessed ones'), claiming both spiritual and magical powers. Their popular – that is, unofficial – brand of Islam was the faith of many peasants who were least integrated into the State's modernization policies (Naumkin 1992: 133). In short, State efforts did not lead to the eradication of Islam from the popular consciousness, but they did aggressively privatize it. However, a tolerant and flexible popular form of Islam – Sufism or 'folk' Islam[2] – survived.

Several Sufi groups – including the *Khadjies*, the *Ishans,* the *Toras*, the *Naqshabandiyas* and the *Qadiriya* – played an important role in the organization of Muslims during Soviet rule. The *Qadiriya* were a particularly large and important group; their founder's tomb – in Bukhara, Uzbekistan – was an important traditional centre of pilgrimage. The *Qadiriya*, represented in many Islamic countries from West Africa to South East Asia – were particularly strong in the Ferghana valley, cutting across Uzbekistan, Tajikistan and Kyrgyzstan and now a centre of radical Islam. In addition, there was the *Yasawiya* order, traditionally centred on the town of Turkistan but active throughout much of southern Kazakstan, with two further offshoots, the Laachi and the Hairy Ishans (Harris *et al.* 1992: 460). The overall point is that Sufi groups were crucial for the survival of the faith during a time of aggressive religious repression.

Culturally and socially, expressions of popular Islamist belief were 'integral elements in the major life-cycle rituals (circumcision, marriage, death), in popular festivals and in dietary laws' (Akiner 1989: 284). While there were a variety of beliefs and practices within popular Islam, it was emphatically not elite nor clerical Islam nor the religion of cultivated intellectuals. Rather, it reflected the living practice of the religion among ordinary people, evolving over time. The fact that its

---

2. Popular Islam was referred to as 'ishanism' in the Soviet-era literature; Ishan' is an alternative title for the Sufi leaders.

roots were in the customs of ordinary people, rather than the formal urban centres of Islamic learning controlled by the Islamic scholarly elite, 'made it well suited to survive when the Soviet regime persecuted, and reorganized to its own taste, the urban Islamic establishment' (Atkin 1989: 608). In fact, as Johnston (1993: 238) points out, popular Islam operated as a network of highly trustworthy but covert social relations standing in opposition to the public life and official values of the State. While differences between the urban Islamic establishment and popular Islam is neither new nor unique to the former Soviet Union, its ability to 'stay put' during an era of aggressive modernization facilitated the re-emergence of Islamic beliefs when the USSR collapsed.

Because there was a great shortfall of trained religious leaders, practitioners of popular Islam – with varying levels of sincerity and of religious learning – officiated at important family events, contributing to the general maintenance of Islamic identity. Yet such people, for the most part, had little inclination to assume a wider religious teaching role (Akiner 1989: 284). It is important to emphasize that this was not a form of political Islam *per se*; rather, it was a matter, not necessarily of reasoned conviction with a clear understanding of Quranic law, but of sentiment, augmented with superstition, concerning a variety of popular practices. This was scarcely surprising, given the virtual absence of religious literature and professionals; because of communist policy, there was hardly anyone to explain the basic tenets and practices of Islam for many years after 1917.

The heyday of the 'unofficial' mullahs was the 1920s and the 1930s when State anti-religion policy was at its height. In the 1940s, once the initial intense period of the Revolution had run its course and the policy of enforced religious privatization had largely triumphed, the State began to allow a small number of State-supported mosques to function. They were run by prayer leaders (*imams*) often managing to establish themselves in positions of power and influence, intermediaries between State and society, especially in urban areas. Imams were, however, State employees: they no doubt understood that, in order to retain their positions, they must sublimate many religious traditions and manifestations of Islamic culture under a façade of Soviet-secular mores.

The 1940s – a period of relative liberalization in relation to religion – followed Stalin's years of terror, during which tens of millions were killed by the State for alleged 'anti-revolutionary activities'. Satisfied that Islam had lost the power to challenge communism ideologically, small – yet symbolically important – concessions were granted to Muslims. Notably, four Muslim Spiritual Directorates were created; one in Tashkent (Uzbekistan), established in 1946, was responsible for the whole of Central Asia. There are two ways of seeing the introduction of the Directorates. The first is to see in them an exemplification of the State's growing tolerance of *privatized* religion at this time. The other is to view them as an attempt to impose State power on Muslims via domination by religious professionals who were totally dependent on the State for their positions. While both interpretations have their merits, perhaps the most important point is that the State understood that it could not completely crush religion, but must seek to *control* it. State sponsorship of religious professionals meant not only that Islam had formal recognition from an officially atheistic State but also that it retained an administrative structure which was later to help such Muslim figures take advantage of the opportunities provided by *glasnost* and *perestroika* in the 1980s.

Apart from the brief, if intense, anti-religion campaign of 1958–64, further concessions were granted to Muslims from the 1950s. Two *madrassahs* were reopened, the first in Bukhara in 1956, the second in Tashkent (both in Uzbekistan), in 1971. The best graduates were allowed to travel to Muslim universities in Egypt, Libya and Morocco to complete their training. This not only offered opportunities to learn Arabic but also to make personal contacts with foreign Islamic scholars. On their return, such people were often appointed to positions in the official mosques. Yet by the early 1980s, the number of such mosques in the entire Soviet Union was still only about 500; most were in Central Asia. However, taking advantage of wider liberalizations, religious publications – sometimes informed by the ideas of Ayatollah Khomeini and Sayyad Qutb – began to circulate. Six separate editions of the Quran, a collection of the *hadith*[3] and a new, quarterly journal, *Muslims of the Soviet East*, appeared. The State also allowed the pilgrimage to Mecca to recommence, although initially only for about 20 carefully selected believers each year (Akiner 1989: 283–4).

To summarize events between 1917 and the 1980s: Islam was, in turn, savagely repressed, warily tolerated, repressed again, and then, finally from the late 1960s, grudgingly accepted. The Soviet State managed for a time to quell the official teaching and propagation of Islamic doctrine, yet much of the traditional Islamic culture of Central Asia managed to survive. Kept alive by unofficial practitioners, popular Islam remained a crucial component of culture, central to important life-cycle rituals in the rural areas. It was the survival of popular Islam which helped to lay the foundations for the re-emergence of political Islam in the 1970s and 1980s. Finally, we have seen that the contemporary reinvigoration of Islam in Central Asia has deep roots. Underground for years, it re-emerged once political circumstances were favourable.

Political Islam in Central Asia after the USSR

But how best to explain contemporary manifestations of political Islam in Central Asia? There are, in fact, a combination of reasons which I will describe below. The orientations and sentiments people have towards political arrangements are formulated within the context of the views they have of themselves and their identity. As Kamrava (1993: 164) notes, 'it is their sense of identity which largely determines how people behave politically and in turn view their own political environment'. Throughout Central Asia in the post-Soviet era, the search for cultural and historical roots, including the repressed Islamic heritage, is a striking feature (Abdurazakova 1992). After the demise of the communist State, the absence of widely accepted,

---

3. The *hadith* is a collection of the sayings and reports of the actions of Prophet Muhammad and his closest companions. It is second in importance only to the Quran for most Muslims.

enduring norms and social values made it difficult for all people in Central Asia to form opinions with certainty about what exactly their identity *was*. Just as important, certain characteristics of many Central Asian countries – political uncertainty, economic crisis, widespread ecological damage and swift urbanization – fostered widespread despair and pessimism about the future, especially among certain groups, such as the unemployed, the young, and migrants from rural areas who often found it hard to put down firm roots in the urban milieu. Such categories of people form the backbone of Islamist movements in Central Asia (Juergensmeyer 1993: 130).

But it would be a mistake to suggest that radical Islam appeared in the region only *after* communism fell. During the 1980s, the Soviet State began to realize that radical Islam was making inroads among the Central Asian Muslim population (Abdurazakova 1992: 85). In response, the State strove to bolster the position and credentials of a new generation of Islamic leaders, placing them in positions of religious authority at relatively young ages. One such was 36-year-old Mamay-usupov Muhammadsaddyk, appointed the head of the Tashkent Directorate in 1989, replacing the aged – and rather anonymous – Mufti Babakhanov. Muhammadsaddyk obtained permisson to open fifteen new mosques, ten in Uzbekistan, five in Tajikistan. He also received consent not only for new buildings for *madrassahs* in both Bukhara and Tashkent to accommodate planned increases in student numbers but also to reintroduce the teaching of Arabic in religious schools (Akiner 1989: 184–5). He was furthermore behind the decision to increase greatly the numbers allowed to take part in the *hajj*. The overall point is that President Gorbachev saw fit to introduce religious reforms in Central Asia in part because of radical Islamist ideas, especially in the light of the embarrassing reversal in Afghanistan. However, the policy was too little, too late: by this time, Mickulsky (1993: 146) reports, 'Islamic fundamentalists' were not only already occupying empty former mosques but also taking over those controlled by the official Spiritual Administrative body, driving away the official imams and electing their own. Thus, as the State fell apart, Islamic radicals strengthened their hold upon many mosques.

Official Soviet accounts long took it as self-evidently true that a developed socialist, industrialized, secular society had been built in Central Asia (Abdurazakova 1992: 85). Three distinct classes were said to have emerged: the working class, the peasantry and the intelligentsia. However, with closer observation, it might have been clear to Soviet social scientists that such a society existed – and then only partially – in parts of Russia, Ukraine and Byelorussia. Soviet Central Asia, on the other hand, remained by and large traditional. According to Mickulsky (1993: 141), 'the social order [was] a kind of Asian way of production . . . characterized by . . . land divided into two parts – communal and personal', with a social structure in the rural areas largely unchanged from before the Revolution. By the time of its termination, communist rule had only succeeded in *deforming* – not *transforming* – traditional society in Central Asia. As noted earlier, popular Islam retained the cultural allegiance of many ordinary people, especially in rural areas. As the Soviet State fell apart, and widespread changes occurred, many people looked to Islam. Islamists gained the support of many disaffected people, especially the young, people without jobs and rural dwellers affected by economic and ecological problems (Gharabaghi 1994).

For many such people, the answer to contemporary travails – unemployment, social turmoil and the breakdown of cultural traditions – was the Islamic State.

Several examples will illustrate this contention. First, it is no coincidence that the Ferghana valley (cutting through Kyrgyzstan, Uzbekistan and Tajikistan) is a hotbed of Islamic radicalism; members of Islamist groups there 'consist mainly of rural people' (Naumkin 1992: 135). Local culture, identities and many people's sense of worth had long been challenged by a negatively valued rampant secularism emanating from the Soviet State. The area has been badly affected by both economic downturn and ecological degradation. For many people, Islamist programmes offer an alternative to failed Soviet-style modernization, serving as a central facet of group solidarity, expressing community responses to unwelcome changes perceived as the result of modernization policies. Second, Bushkov (cited in Mickulsky 1993: 144) gives the example of the city of Khunjent (formerly Leninabad) in the Matchi area of Uzbekistan where Islamist groups also prosper. Many residents were forcibly removed to Khunjent from a nearby *kishlak* (rural community), Staraya Matcha, to grow cotton during the Soviet era. Many found it very difficult to adapt to the new conditions of life due to a variety of reasons, including the new ecological conditions and the severing of traditions and community ties. The result, according to Bushkov, was that such people tended to form a marginal group, providing the core of the Islamist movement.

The overall point is that many rural migrants found it difficult to establish themselves in the towns and cities. Because population growth rates in Central Asia are very high – in not atypical Tajikistan, 52 per cent are under 18 years of age and three-quarters of local people live in traditional villages where unemployment is sky high – the rural young in particular look to the urban areas for (often non-existent) jobs.[4] The Russian ethnologist, Valentin Bushkov (cited in Mickulsky 1993: 142), argues that many from *kishlaks* find it exceedingly challenging to become accustomed to the individualistic conditions of city life, since their inner world had been fundamentally conditioned by 'community forms of living regulated by custom and tradition'. Many quickly lose their traditional cultures, becoming 'socially marginalized', turning to crime, drugs or 'Muslim fundamentalist groups' (Mickulsky 1993: 142). Such groups are strongest in 'socially and ecologically disturbed areas, such as large cities and their suburbs, and in the so-called industrialized zones which bear a mixture of rural and township features' (Mickulsky 1993: 144).

Apart from alienated rural–urban migrants, who else looks to the Islamist movements? While little detailed research has been done, it appears that several urban groups are attracted, including some intellectuals, technocrats and elements among both unqualified and qualified workers. It is also reported that some opportunistic politicians have adopted Islamist terminology for the purpose of winning votes rather than necessarily from conviction. Juergensmeyer (1993: 111) claims that some former communist leaders in Central Asia have even become mullahs.

---

4. Overall, approximately 600,000 of the 2.5 million adults – about 24 per cent – were reported to be without work in Tajikistan in the early 1990s (Frankland 1992). Under such circumstances it is not altogether surprising that Islam is seen by many in impoverished Tajikistan to be the way forward.

Leaders of Islamist groups are often people aged 35–45 years, some are intellectuals, others 'unqualified workers and janitors . . . engineers and technicians' (Mickulsky 1993: 144). Such people have normally acquired knowledge of Islam via self-study, hardly surprising in the virtual absence, until recently, of *madrassahs*. However, it is reported that they are often much better educated than the official *mullahs*. Both Naumkin (1992) and Mickulsky (1993) claim that the middle and lower stratum in the Islamist hierarchy comprises young people, often between 20 and 30 years. Generally, Mickulsky (1993: 145) claims, Islamist (male) cadres 'can easily be recognized by their beards and semi-traditional, semi-European clothes'. He notes that 'the younger sons of the poor and the non-noble families that comprise the most deprived part of the population' feature prominently among the Islamist membership. Furthermore, 'there is some information that the fundamentalist group [sic] is connected with rich non-traditional traders who, in spite of their wealth, are not admitted to traditional market corporations and therefore feel themselves deprived and marginal' (1993: 145). In general, Islamists often proclaim their religious credentials by widely practising charity (*zakat*), taking an oath to help the poor and the deprived (Naumkin 1992: 135). The result, Mickulsky (1993: 147) claims, is that they are widely respected for their piety – not, as is traditional, for their 'age, or nobility'. He also notes that 'fundamentalist' structures and views may one day 'radically change the whole of Central Asian traditional society'.

Regrading the social make-up of the Islamist groups, it is now possible to make some tentative conclusions. First, Islamist cadres tend to be young, while their leaders are often middle-aged. Second, both often come from groups without traditional sources of status. By giving *religious* status to young and middle-aged people, there is a clear reversal of traditional Central Asian social norms, where age is traditionally respected. Finally, the Islamists are strongly opposed not only to the official Muslim spiritual leaders, working in the government-controlled Spiritual Administrative bodies, but also to the non-official local *mullahs*, accusing them of corruption, ignorance and servility before political rulers.

Having analysed the social make-up of the Islamists, it is necessary to say a little about what they want. As Juergensmeyer (1993: 132) points out, Islamists have a range of positions. At one extreme, there are groups like the Islamic Renaissance Parties of Tajikistan and Uzbekistan and the *Alash* party in Kazakstan, demanding the Islamic State, run by the clergy along the lines of Iran, via revolutionary methods. They discount the benefits of the traditional Islamic *mazhabs* (law schools), arguing that every Muslim should appeal directly to the Quran and the Sunna, because in the ideal Islamic community there is no need for a special caste of priests. They also oppose many of the 'customs and traditions that have spread in contemporary Central Asia', including 'expensive funerals, weddings and other rituals from which immense profits accrue to traditional [i.e. State appointed] religious leaders' (Mickulsky 1993: 145–6). A second group calls for the Islamic State via 'Islamic democracy', that is, the goal will be won through the ballot box in competition with other political parties. A third group calls for 'Islamic social mores and Islamic nationalism in a non-theocratic State'; the Islamic State *per se* is seen as a distant goal unless being preceded by much greater levels of piety among the mass of

citizens (Juergensmeyer 1993: 133). What all three groups have in common, however, is a shared rejection of the post-Communist, secularist and secularizing socio-
political reality and a desire to reform and remould Islam by returning to the
primary values of the religion and the Islamic community. In sum, Islamists in
Central Asia – while differing on tactics and to an extent on goals – see themselves
as proponents of a purer, more uplifting, more spiritual Islam. They are both political and religious rebels, believing that the end of communist states in Central
Asia was not an end in itself but the beginning of the struggle for the superiority
of Islam over godless secularist values and policies.

In the next section, I want to examine the contemporary relationship between the
State and Islamic radicals in the five Central Asian republics. I start with Tajikistan,
then go on to Uzbekistan: they are countries where political Islam is an important
socio-political actor. Then I examine the remaining three countries – Turkmenistan,
Kazakstan and Kyrgyzstan – where political Islam is less conspicuous, and explain
why this is so.

Case studies: political Islam in Central Asia

Tajikistan

Before Soviet rule much of Tajik territory was ruled by the unenlightened Emir of
Bukhara. The Red Army invaded the area in 1920 and the Tajik Soviet Socialist
Republic (SSR) was formed in 1924. Tajikistan became a constituent republic of
the USSR in 1929. Of the current population of more than five million, more than
65 per cent are ethnic Tajiks hailing from Farsi-speaking Iranian stock; the remainder are predominantly Uzbeks (23 per cent) and Russians (7 per cent).

Tajikistan is the most impoverished country in Central Asia, with high unemployment and deprivation. The withdrawal of Moscow's food subsidies after 1991
meant serious hardships for many people. In the post-Soviet era, the renamed
Communist Party – now called the Democratic Party – regime of Rahmon Nabiev
has struggled to wield its authority. Nabiev – a 'reformed communist' – promised
swift economic improvements which did not materialize. Instead, the fragile economy
unravelled, making social problems worse and helping to stimulate an Islamist
challenge. The socio-political situation was not helped by the lack of a Tajik State
tradition. Regional and clan rivalries undermine the pursuit of a feeling of nationhood. When Tajiks organize today they have little to inspire them but their religion,
region and/or clan.

Tajikistan – where Islam arrived over 500 years ago – is the most 'Islamized'
country in Central Asia. Religious factors have played a major part in the recent political upheavals of the country. Even prior to the formal declaration of independence
from the USSR in 1991, the role of Islam in Tajikistan was 'much more pronounced
with respect to social organization than in the other republics' of former Soviet
Central Asia (Gharabaghi 1994: 110). While there were officially only 17 mosques
in Tajikistan in 1989, by the mid-1990s there were 'thousands' (Rugman 1995b).

Mosques and madrassahs opened in great numbers during the 1990s, supported by public donations and by funds from Egypt, Saudi Arabia and Iran, often channelled through the Muslim World League. This climate of Islamic reinvigoration was an important dimension of the nationalist euphoria which followed Tajikistan's announcement of independence from Moscow. But it did not aid the development of post-Communist stability. From 1992 the country was engulfed by an anti-Communist, Islamist-led insurrection, proving that 'Islam can provide an influential idiom of protest in Central Asia' (Husain 1995: 255). Russia and the West viewed the development of events in Tajikistan with apprehension. 'People in Tajikistan want to be free, but Russia fears we will join up with Afghanistan or Iran,' argued Jan Bek Akabirov, a Tajik poet (Rugman 1995a).

The trigger for civil war was the controversial presidential elections of November 1991. Khudonazarov, the opposition candidate of a cross-party alliance, took 34 per cent of the vote, while the winner, Nabiev, gained 58 per cent. Believing that the ballot was rigged in favour of the latter, anti-government demonstrations erupted in the capital, Dushanbe. At this stage there were three main opposition parties, ranging from the secular–nationalist Democratic Movement (DM) to the radical Islamic Renaissance Party (IRP). The DM mostly comprised intellectuals from both the Tajik majority and the Russian minority. The aim was a fully democratic, secular Tajikistan. Then there was a 'moderate' Muslim group, *Rastokhev* (Renaissance), arguing for Islamic principles in public life, but stopping short of a demand for the Islamic State. *Rastokhev* first came to prominence in 1990 when its members tried (and failed) to secure the then communist government's resignation. Following this the party's leaders were persecuted and imprisoned, even though they claimed they would pursue their goals only through democracy and that after 70 years of official atheism the advent of the Islamic State in Tajikistan was remote.

The IRP, like *Rastokhev*, mostly comprises ethnic Tajiks, but unlike it seeks the Islamic State – by any means necessary – as the only solution to the country's economic, social and political ills. Its leaders reportedly have close links with the Muslim Brotherhood in Egypt and the *Jama'at -i Islami* in Pakistan, ties built up during years of working underground. The IRP became a legal political party in 1991, only to be banned again two years later. At the time of the 1991 elections, young bearded men and veiled women took to the streets of Dushanbe, calling for an Islamic State. The IRP was regarded as especially dangerous by the Nabiev regime for two reasons: first, because it drew much of its support and financial muscle from Afghan Tajiks. The Islamic Party of Afghanistan provided combat training camps for Tajiks, 'giving rise to speculation that there may be plans for some type of Islamic Afghan–Tajik territorial union' (Gharabaghi 1994: 110). The second reason was that its stated aim was to build the Islamic State.

An attempt at power sharing between regional clans, religious leaders and former communists proved impossible: civil war followed in 1992. Nabiev's pro-Moscow Government fought a coalition of forces led by IRP militants. The conflict led the Russian Federation to intervene on the side of the Government to attempt to restore peace (Barylski 1994: 389). Tajik Islamists fled to Afghanistan, Pakistan or Iran. Some received military training. The Islamists' 'government-in-exile' was established in Taloqan, Afghanistan, where Rezvon, a famed opposition military commander and 'defence minister', and Abdullo Nuri, an important religious leader, established their headquarters. By 1994, there was stalemate: some 50,000–100,000 people had died; more than 500,000 others were refugees (Rugman 1995b). However, Shadovlat Yusmon, Chairman of the IRP, proclaimed that, 'we will continue resistance until we gain real independence. We have enough strength to do that' (Korolov 1994).

The Government, now led by Imomali Rakhmanov, held further presidential elections in 1994 and parliamentary polls in 1995. Neither Islamist nor secular politicians were permitted to participate – both *Rastokhez* and the IRP were banned – and many among the opposition were in jail or exile. Press freedoms were curtailed (Rugman 1995b). Yet, despite its authoritarianism, Rakhmanov's Government received considerable diplomatic and financial support from the governments of Russia, Uzbekistan and the USA. They believed that Tajikistan was being targeted by Islamists from Afghanistan, Pakistan and Iran as the first step in an Islamic conquest of Central Asia. A Western diplomat in Dushanbe warned that if the IRP returned it would be under pressure from Afghan warlords to pursue a more radical agenda. 'The IRP is a clandestine political movement with an Islamic agenda throughout the region,' the diplomat claimed (Rugman 1995b). The Chinese were also 'concerned about the potential spread of Islamic activism' from Tajikistan over the border into the Xinjian region (Earnshaw 1996).

It seems unlikely, however, that the IRP would find it easy to retain power – even if it managed to displace the incumbent regime which seems unlikely in the short term – in part because it does not have enough support throughout the country. The northern part of the republic around Khujand is industrialized and heavily Russified; Islamists have very little support. Sixty per cent of Badakhshan in the south is Shi'ite – but of the moderate Ismaili[5] kind – and, as as result, suspicious both of the Sunni IRP and Iran's revolutionary brand of Shi'ism. But the IRP is supported by an important religious figure, the spiritual leader of the country's Muslims, Akbar Turajon-zoda (Steele 1992). Further, the IRP is highly regarded among rural dwellers who regard it as their champion which, in power, would hopefully improve their material position and solve the country's social problems (Frankland 1992).

After more than five years of civil war there was a serious attempt to end the political stalemate in early 1997. In February ruling and opposition politicians agreed to the creation of a coalition government pending elections and the integration of the armed Tajik opposition into the country's armed forces. But the two sides failed to agree on a list of *which* opposition parties would be allowed to compete the elections; the IRP was not permitted to participate. The issue was to be reopened in further negotiations in Tehran in May but the meeting was cancelled following an attempt on the life of President Imomali Rakhmanov, killing two people and wounding 60, in the northern city of Khudjand. The alleged perpetrator was an Islamist, Firdavs Dustboboyev (Hearst 1997).

---

5. A politically quietist branch of Shi'ism following the religio-political leadership of Ismail, a son of Ja'far al-Sadiq and his descendants. The spiritual leader is the Aga Khan.

The incident highlighted how relations between the State and some sections of society are characterized by extreme suspicion; for some, the regime fundamentally lacks legitimacy. Yet, while the Islamists have failed to triumph, the Rakhmanov Government has not managed to crush them. While the country's short-term future seems clear – more civil unrest – the longer term outlook is less so. In short, Tajikistan's future is highly uncertain. Religious and ethnic conflicts will no doubt destabilize and fragment the country for a long time. The situation is not helped by the clash of international interests: the Uzbek, Russian and American Governments remain determined to prevent an Islamist takeover; Iran and Afghanistan continue to support the IRP in its bid to win the Islamic State. Support for the Islamists is unlikely to wither among the deprived sections of the Tajik majority; with the support of Iran and Afghanistan there is a chance that the Islamists will eventually achieve power.

Uzbekistan

Like neighbouring Tajikistan, the Bolsheviks established Soviet power in Uzbekistan soon after the 1917 revolution. The Uzbek SSR was formed in October 1924 (from lands formerly part of Turkestan), becoming a constituent republic of the Soviet Union in May 1925. With a rapidly growing population of over 20 million, Uzbekistan is now the most populous of the former Soviet Central Asian republics. Uzbeks – from a number of Turkic tribes – comprise around 70 per cent of the population, while Russians amount to some 8 per cent; the remainder are from a variety of groups, including Kyrgyz, Ukranians and Germans (Olcott 1992: 257).

After the demise of the USSR, the only chance the leading Communist Party ideologist, Khatan Abdurahimov, felt the party had of retaining power was 'to play the nationalist card', that is, to mix religious and (Uzbek) nationalist themes hoping to capture the popular imagination (Olcott 1992: 256). To this end, the Government sought to control *political* manifestations of Islam, while making much of the country's Islamic *cultural* heritage. It also stressed the attractiveness of its ally, Turkey's, secular and nationalist development path. But, like Tajikistan, Uzbekistan has serious societal tensions. Principal among these is the issue of Tajik loyalty. There are an estimated one million ethnic Tajiks in Uzbekistan. Most live along the border with Tajikistan in the Samarkand–Bukhara area and in the Ferghana valley. Tajik nationalists claim both Samarkand and Bukhara, historically Tajik cities, and denounce their Uzbek 'takeover' (Frankland 1992). President Rakhmanov has pursued a hardline anti-Islamist strategy partly out of fear that Islamic radicalism would cross the border from Tajikistan to envelop ethnic Tajiks living in Uzbekistan. Fearing Tajik–Islamist aggression, an Uzbek 'warlord', Abdul Rashid Dostam, has prevented Islamist training and recruitment on the Uzbek–Afghan border territory that he controls (Rugman 1995b).

Following the demise of the USSR, Uzbekistan's Communist Party changed its name to the People's Democratic Party (PDP). By a policy of divide and rule, the Government and party were able to keep the opposition parties – the moderate

Islamic Party, *Birlik* (Unity), the radical Islamic Renaissance Party (IRP) and the secular ERK (Freedom) Party – from uniting on a common anti-government platform. Like its counterpart in Tajikistan, the PDP Government also used a policy of repression and strict censorship to hinder the progress of the opposition parties (Hyman 1993: 293).

The ERK represents a secular strand of moderate reformism. It was permitted to field a candidate in the presidential elections of 1991, but failed to make serious inroads into the PDP's share of the vote. *Birlik* styles itself an Islamic democratic movement. *Birlik* activists regularly work with the IRP at grassroots level. *Birlik* aims to create a pluralistic government in Uzbekistan that respects Islamic culture and values. But the movement was handicapped from the start when President Karimov refused to allow it to be registered as a legal organization. Although the ban was lifted in October 1991, *Birlik* was not permitted to register as a political party. Its leader, Abdurahim Pulatov, was unable to run for election as president in 1991. In June 1992, he was seriously assaulted by unknown assailants (Olcott 1992: 262, Hyman 1993: 293).

The IRP, like its counterpart in Tajikistan, wants the Islamic State; Iran is the role model. Its leaders are mostly 'fundamentalist-style clerics . . . trained outside of the official establishment' (Olcott 1992: 255). The roots of the Party are to be found not only in a concern for a higher public profile for Islam but also in the declining economic situation. From the early 1980s, the then wealthy Ferghana valley – the spiritual centre of Uzbekistan – was hit hard when the price paid for the region's main crop – cotton – plummeted (Poliakov 1992). Islamic militancy in Uzbekistan is focused in the towns of the valley, south-east of Tashkent, where ethnic Tajiks are found in large numbers. Ferghana is the most densely populated region of Central Asia, large families predominate, while Islam is the traditional way of life for many and has been for centuries. But support for the IRP is said to be spreading among young people in the valley; many of them are unemployed. In a development which must worry the Government, Islamic fervour is also said to be spreading among the youth of both sexes in many parts of the country, not just the Ferghana valley itself (Husain 1995: 260). This is potentially politically explosive because half the population is under 20 years of age. Support for political Islam is not only reflected in membership of the banned IRP but also in the spread of Islamic-oriented *Adalat* (Justice) groups. Islamists are also to be found in provincial centres such as Namangan, Andijan and Kokand (Mickulsky 1993), while Olcott (1992: 262), reports that Islamist groups are 'having a perceptible influence on young people' in the capital, Tashkent. In short, although illegal, the IRP has a considerable following, especially in the major towns and in the Ferghana valley.

But the Government is so far meeting the Islamic challenge. Its representatives in the Ferghana towns do not seek confrontation with Islamic activists; instead, concessions are made, for example, buildings which used to be mosques or madrassahs are returned to their previous use. Further, the old communist names of streets have been changed to traditional Muslim forms. Finally, party secretaries have been renamed *hakims*, the traditional name for a judge in an Islamic religious court, and their offices entitled *hakimiat* (Hyman 1993: 293–4).

But, as in Tajikistan, the long-term outlook for political Islam in Uzbekistan is not clear. Gharabaghi (1994: 107) discounts the possibility of any form of Islamic government in the foreseeable future, because of the apparent strength of the Karimov Government and the divided nature of the opposition. However, Migranyan suggests that it is quite possible that Uzbekistan may eventually have an Islamic government, if the present regime weakens sufficiently to allow in the Islamic opposition and the latter manages to work together. He argues that because 'Uzbekistan has great Islamic traditions, religious figures are influential, and there is no [coordinated] Islamic opposition only because there is no acknowledged Muslim leader. As time goes on, Uzbekistan will be drawn deeper into the Muslim world' (Migranyan 1992: 13). While such comments underline the richness of Uzbekistan's Islamic past, it is also important to bear in mind the importance – especially to ethnic Tajiks – of the historic Islamic centres of Samarkand and Bukhara and the Ferghana valley, where Islam traditionally has constituted the predominant belief and value system. It is conceivable that – sooner or later – the IRP and *Birlik* will find sufficient common cause to mobilize opposition against the Karimov regime. To help counter such a move, the Government strengthened its ties with Turkey.[6]

But apart from the threat of Islamic radicalism, Uzbekistan is also afflicted by serious ethnic tensions. In 1994 Uzbek nationalists used violence against minority groups, including fellow-Muslim Kyrgyz and Meshkhetian Turks, to underline their claim that Uzbekistan belonged to the Uzbeks (Husain 1995: 255).[7] Such incidents served to underline how both ethnic diversity and the unclear public role for Islam in the post-Communist society are proving to be a significant obstacle in the development of a cohesive nationalism. Issues of religion and ethnicity are made more complex by the cross-cutting appeal of 'regional as opposed to national or ethnic identification' (Gharabaghi 1994: 106).

Turkmenistan

After the Red Army captured the main city, Ashkhabad, in 1920, the Turkmen SSR was formed four years later. Turkmenistan was made a constituent republic of the USSR in 1929. Turkmens, who comprise over 70 per cent of the population of about four million, are from a mix of Turkic tribes and an ancient non-Turkic population. Uzbeks and Russians, together about 20 per cent of the population, with a smattering of Urkainains, make up the remainder.

Turkmenistan is often judged the most stable country in the region. Post-Communist opposition to the Government of the President, the popular and charismatic Sapurmarad Niazov, has been insubstantial. As Gharabaghi (1994: 104)

6. It is not clear at the time of writing (mid-1997) if Turkey's *Refah*-led Coalition Government will fundamentally alter its policies towards Uzbekistan.

7. A mooted Pan-Turkic confederation attracts many Uzbek nationalists because, they claim, 'it is impossible to live separately – we need such a grouping' (Rugman 1995b). However, they contend, unity must be based not on Islam but on a shared Turkic identity. Islam is seen as a brake on progress. Intellectuals among Uzbekistan's smaller non-Turkic nationalities – Kyrgyz and Tajiks – may well regard such sentiments a cover for Uzbek chauvinism.

comments, 'it is difficult . . . to determine any coherent expression of ideology, either at the level of the State or at the societal level, in Turkmenistan'. One of the most backward of the Central Asian republics, Turkmenistan is more of a tribal confederation than a modern nation-State. Yet, because of its abundant natural gas and oil reserves, it has considerable economic potential, with a 'successful economic transformation quite conceivable' (Hyman 1993: 291).

There is little in the way of organized Islamist challenge to the regime, although Islam has a strong traditional position in the countryside. However, Niazov – another 'reformed communist' – has managed to divide and rule what little opposition there is. His Government is widely believed to be the one with the greatest staying power in Central Asia, both because of the lack of an organized opposition, whether religious or secular, and Turkmenistan's potential for aggregate economic growth as a result of its oil and gas resources. The Government has emphasized its preparedness to accommodate both ethnic diversity and an Islamic belief system, although the constitution declares Turkmenistan to be a secular State. Niazov (quoted in Gharabaghi 1994: 105) explains that 'the Muslim clergy is firmly committed' to the principle of secularity as State policy, while, he believes, the 'concrete influence of Islam on the life of society' is 'a favourable one'. To Niazov, Islam preaches 'purity and nobility of thought, it preaches mercy, and it criticizes greed, avarice and cruelty . . . secularism is tempered by the practice of folk Islam'. President Niazov has embraced Islam himself while increasing the 'public role of religious elders in setting up and supervising the social mores of the Turkmen people' (Olcott 1992: 264). Aiding the Government's pursuit of social and political stability, Turkmenistan's religious establishment is relatively unified, willing to cooperate with the Government, and largely unchallenged, unlike in Tajikistan and Uzbekistan, by Islamist radicals from outside the religious establishment. The Government is, however, sensitive to what it perceives as Islam's potential political influence, especially from neighbouring Iran which beams religious and political radio programmes to Turkmenistan. In some parts of the country the only radio broadcasts that can be heard are from Iran (Akiner 1989: 282).

It is clear that the apparently popular government of Turkmenistan, aided by considerable natural resources, has, with only limited apparent effort, managed to keep the lid on even incipient Islamist militancy. This State of affairs is no doubt aided by the fact that the country's population is organized along tribal lines where the potential for forming ideologically oriented political groupings is limited. It is not clear what impact Iran's propaganda is having on the country, although at the current time the achievement of power by Islamists is unthinkable. Assiduous use of material resources by the Government is likely to keep things like this.

Kazakstan

The Red Army defeated nationalist forces in 1920, leading to the formation of the Kakaz SSR the same year. Kazakstan was made a constituent republic of the USSR in 1936. Kazaks, who comprise only 40 per cent of the population, are from a mix of indigenous Turkic tribes and nomadic Mongols. Non-Muslim Russians make up a further 40 per cent of the population; Germans, Ukrainians, and Uzbeks, the remainder.

One of the last republics to break away from the former USSR and the stranglehold of Soviet central planning, Kazakstan has emerged as one of the most stable countries in Central Asia. Like Turkmenistan, it has large reserves of oil and natural gas and, in addition, coal. By far the largest of the Central Asian countries – roughly the size of Western Europe – Kazakstan extends over 2.7 million kilometres from the Caspian Sea to China. It is, however, very sparsely populated with 17 million people. The principle political issues are, on the one hand, the speed and extent of democratization and, on the other, the jockeying for position among ethnic groups. To counter potential ethnic instability, Kazakstan's president, Nursultan Nazarbaev, elected in December 1991 with nearly 99 per cent of the votes, has tried to build a Kazak 'national consolidation' party. The Party dominated by secular-minded intellectuals, aims to defuse the appeal of its main challenger, also a secularist party, the *Azat* (Freedom) Party.

Islam has little political voice in Kazakstan, except for the unregistered *Alash* Party, named after a legendary ancestor-hero of the Kazaks. Unlike Islamist parties in Ukbekistan and Tajikistan, *Alash* has a goal of a *regional* Islamic State of Turkestan (Olcott 1992: 264, Gharabaghi 1994: 108). However, the fact is that religion has not assumed a major part in Kazakstan's political development since independence, nor is it likely to in the future, largely because of the high degree of ethnic fragmentation in the country and the large numbers of non-Muslims. Although the Kazaks themselves are Sunni Muslims, Islamic values are much less embedded in Kazak society than in the societies of other Central Asian states.

Kyrgyzstan

The Red Army defeated opposition forces in 1919 and the Kyrgyz SSR was formed in 1926, becoming a constituent republic of the USSR 10 years' later. The Kirgiz, about 52 per cent of the population, are from the tribes near the Yenisei river in northern Mongolia. Russians make up about 22 per cent of the population, Uzbeks 13 per cent, and Ukrainians and Germans most of the remainder.

A variety of opposition parties – including a moderate Muslim group – banded together under the organization of the Kyrgyz Democratic Movement (KDM) after communist rule ended in 1991. One branch, the Kyrgyz Democratic Wing, expressed plans to build mosques and madrassahs throughout the country. However, as in Turkmenistan, religion is regarded by the Government as an appropriate – even integral – facet of cultural, but not political, life. There is, however, a small Islamist movement – a branch of the outlawed Sufi order, the Hairy Ishans – whose members in Kyrgyzstan mostly live in the country's portion of the Ferghana valley. The Hairy Ishans are, however, not a new force, having been opposed to secular government since the 1917 Revolution (Juergensmeyer 1993: 132).

Kyrgyzstan is often reckoned to have a bright future as an emerging democratic country (Gharabaghi 1994: 109). But as in Kazakstan, the largest source of political friction comes from ethnic tensions. There were riots in the city of Osh in mid-1990, with their roots in inter-ethnic tensions between Kyrgyzians and Uzbeks, yet the new country managed to weather the storm. However, problems between Kyrgyzians and Uzbeks, both belonging to the Sunnite branch of Islam, manifest themselves in cultural, ethnic and linguistic differences. Mongolian and Kazak cultural elements are predominant in the case of the Kyrgyzians, while the Uzbeks are more influenced by Iranian–Islamic culture; yet neither has retained a high degree of allegiance to Islamic traditions (Gharabaghi 1994: 109). But some credit must go to the Government of Askar Akaev which has managed – by skilful and flexible rule – to keep ethnic conflict at a reasonably low level since 1990. Hyman (1993: 290) reports that Akaev's aim is to 'create a Central Asian Switzerland where prosperity and democracy can flourish, enjoying the stability which Tajikistan lacks'. What this suggests is that if the Government can preside over democratic consolidation and deliver clear-cut economic gains for the majority of people, then ethnic – and incipient religious – tensions will remain within the Government's control.

Conclusion

This chapter has sought to explain that the variegated re-emergence of political Islam in post-Soviet Central Asia has its roots in a variety of domestic circumstances, encouraged or hindered in several cases by foreign actors. The collapse of communism, economic crisis, environmental degradation, democratic shortfalls and widespread, often virulent, ethno-nationalism form common backgrounds to recent political developments. After 70 years of Soviet rule, many Central Asians – especially the disaffected and disadvantaged – are questioning their identity to a degree unimaginable a decade before. Identity crises, exacerbating religious and ethnic cleavages, have become a common facet of politics in Central Asia. This represents, in several cases, a variable threat to national integration and to political and economic development. Islam, traditionally fulfilling the role of cultural anchor for many people during the communist era, now increasingly serves as a political symbol and emblem of opposition to regimes – such as those in Tajikistan and Uzbekistan – lacking a high degree of popular legitimacy. But while Islamists are clear what they do not want – the continuation of the 'reformer communist' regimes – they are less clear what should replace them. Some, like the IRP in Tajikistan and Uzbekistan, call for the Islamic State *tout court*, others – like *Birlik* – seem to prefer a political arrangement involving a form of popular democracy with the Islamic State an *eventual* outcome. However, whether radical or moderate, the Islamists are commonly calling for a higher public profile for Islam.

Events in the former Soviet republics of Central Asia confirm the validity of Islam as a vehicle for political action. In a region isolated for decades from the rest of the Muslim world, an Islamic revival is clearly – albeit patchily – in evidence. Regional governments would like to keep it at the level of a cultural renaissance, although knee-jerk reaction to manifestations of political Islam – often to ban it – is likely only to lead to an action–reaction syndrome serving to radicalize Islamic renewal. Not permitted to operate legitimately, Islamists will perhaps become increasingly radical in their methods to hammer home the issue of 'Islamic justice' and the need for greater socio-economic fairness to transform the Central Asian republics into countries living by Islamic principles.

The main causes of the politicization of Islam can be seen in the crises of development and democracy. It may be that Islamists are gradually emerging as the greatest power for change in the region – as is happening in much of the Middle East and North Africa contemporaneously – ultimately to overshadow the efforts of secular democrats. To be sure, many former communists are playing the Islamic card to bolster popular support. It is a dangerous game: by encouraging Islam as a *cultural* referent there is a strong probability that it will also develop into a popular *political* option. In sum, the patchy but growing Islamic revival in Central Asia is being radicalized by the failure of those in power to tackle the overwhelming problems of the region. The West, in the name of stability, is funding oppressive regimes whose legitimacy is low. This policy may backfire, fuelling an Islamic radicalism which is strongly anti-Western.

Chapter 9

Politics and religion in India: Hindu and Sikh nationalism

In the 1980s, Casanova (1994: 6) contends, and the chapters of this book have so far confirmed, there was 'a widespread . . . refusal to be restricted to the private sphere of religious traditions' in a number of religions, including Judaism, Islam, Hinduism and Buddhism. In particular, the public resurgence of Islam has been one of the main developments thrusting religion back into public view. While Iran's Islamic revolution captured world attention, the pattern of religious revolt found in Egypt – examined in Chapter 7 – more accurately represents the great majority of current religious involvement in politics. That is, as in Egypt, religious activists in many parts of the Third World are reacting against leaders who often appear, to many Western observers at least, to be both moderate and sympathetic towards religion. Such leaders are men – rarely women – who adhere at least nominally to the main religion of their country, but who do not wish to pronounce the country a religious State. Often, there will be two main reasons for their reticence: first, because strong minority religious communities inhibit them; second, because they are often strong believers in a secular nationalism that, to them, defines a modern nation-state.

This chapter focuses principally upon two groups of religious actors in India, Sikh and Hindu nationalists. Each has reacted intensely against the secular visions of modern nationalism, using a number of strategies for change, including targeting the traditional secular parties, the political process and even the political culture underpinning the whole process. What is striking about these Indian cases is how consistently they aim at political targets in order to solve religious problems or to bring about a consolidation of religious identities and values. The level of violence in the movements has become intense in recent years; political assassinations are frequently enacted. The Indian cases are also useful for understanding the variety of ways in which religious militants seek to achieve their objectives: from guerrilla movements to involvement in electoral politics. Both strategies have at their heart a total rejection of India's secular State.

India's secular State emerged out of the trauma of a communal holocaust, leading – in 1947 – to partition along communal lines, with (East and West) Pakistan as the designated homeland for Muslims. Since then, it has been impossible in India to replicate a Western version of secularism through a strict institutional separation between Church and State. This is partly because Hinduism, the religion of most of the population, does not have an institutionalized hierarchy – hence, no 'Church' – and partly because of the historically short time since the founding of India. Comparable attempts at building secular states in Western Europe, it should be remembered, took at least four centuries.

The rise of the politics of religious identity underlines a central problem: how can religiously plural India survive the creation of a powerful sense of identity based upon religion? Eighty-two per cent of the one billion Indians are Hindus,[1] 11 per cent are Muslim, 2.5 per cent are Christians, 1.6 per cent are Sikhs. There are also small numbers of Buddhists, Parsis, Jains and followers of traditional religions. Because of such diversity it was central to the concept of the Indian State at independence that its leaders would pursue a development path firmly located within a secular socio-political and cultural milieu. The core of Indian secularism is tolerance towards religious plurality, denoted in the Sanskrit phrase *sarva dharma sambhava* ('equal treatment for all religions'). Perhaps the most significant implication of the recent electoral success of Hindu nationalism is not a formal Hindu State, which may never come about, but the general stimulation it provides for extremists from other cultural groups: the secular features of the existing State are becoming weakened, giving fuel to political campaigns by extremists from regional Muslim, Christian and Sikh communities. However, this is not Hindu *fundamentalism* – which would in common understanding be linked to the revealed words of God as a set of socio-political aspirations and goals – but instead a *nationalist* project with Hindu identity at its centre.[2]

Various theories have been offered to explain the resurgence of political religion in India. Like Casanova, most see the 1980s as the crucial period. But why the 1980s? It was not a decade when India's Government overtly sought to privatize religion, but it was a period of pronounced economic instability and of 'new distortions of the homogenised Western menu of modernity and its consumerist culture peddled through its multi-nationals' (Ray 1996: 10). This coincided with the re-emergence of the question of both Hindu and Sikh national identity, issues which quickly became central in Indian politics.

Explanations for the religio-political resurgence can be roughly divided into the following theories: political, psychological, socio-economic and cultural and in terms of the impact of modernization. It is important to note that they are not mutually exclusive – none can claim to be exclusively 'correct' – but taken together they may explain reasonably well the rather unexpected resurgence of religion in politics in India in recent times.

1. Hinduism has spread beyond the shores of India; the island of Bali in Indonesia is principally Hindu, while forms of Hinduism are of growing interest in many Western countries.
2. Ram-Prasad (1993) argues that the Hindu nationalist parties cannot be 'fundamentalist' because Hinduism does not have a single holy book on which to draw. Hindu nationalism is synonymous with cultural chauvinism, based on the selective adaptation of tradition, rather than a close adherence to religious texts as in Christian fundamentalism and Islamism. Contemporary Hindu nationalism is not *sui generis*: Mahatma Gandhi, the great Indian nationalist, a committed Hindu, was assassinated by a Hindu extremist in 1948 for the 'crime' of appearing to condone the creation of East and West Pakistan.

Arguing for a political explanation, Juergensmeyer (1989: 100) asserts that the secular Congress Government became a target for the wrath of Hindu national- ists because it was perceived to be favouring Muslims, Sikhs, Christians and other religious minorities. In particular, 'the rise of Sikh fundamentalism in the Punjab especially played on Hindu nerves' (Copley 1993: 57), while increased Muslim assertiveness – following the Iranian revolution – seemed to many Hindus to threaten them.

Psychological theories, on the other hand, frequently stress apparent high- caste alarm at the conversion to Islam of *dalits* (erstwhile 'untouchables') in various parts of India, especially the well-publicized case of the Tamil Nadu village of Meenakshipuram in 1984 (Copley 1993: 57). This incident is thought to have led many Hindus to vote for the leading Hindu Nationalist Party, the Bharatiya Janata Party (the BJP, or Indian People's Party). More generally, Chiriyankandath (1996b) notes that many conservative Hindus were incensed over the Government's protec- tion of mosques built over Hindu sacred sites during the Mughal period. In 1984 the Vishwa Hindu Parishad (VHP) called for a reassertion of Hindu control over a dozen such sites. Both Sisson (1993: 58–9) and Talbot (1991: 149–51) point out that many Muslims would consequently see themselves as the focus of Hindu attacks, perhaps encouraging Islamic radicalism.

Also encouraging communal friction was political instability caused by econ- omic uncertainty, the third factor. In the 1980s, Callaghy (1993: 194–5) notes, the Indian economy was suffering serious problems: 'the balance of payments and inflation moved beyond control; foreign exchange reserves dropped; a debt crisis loomed; and pervasive statism and bureacratic controls were having increasingly negative consequences . . .' The Government attempted (timidly) to liberalize the economy; the main impact, however, was unintended: the creation of a tiny group of super rich and a growing class of extremely poor people. Many urban middle- class Hindus were unsettled by the economic reforms and, like many poor Hindus, looked to a party – notably the BJP – which promised that Hindus would be privil- eged over other groups. In sum, economic changes were probably an important factor in the growing appeal of Hindu nationalism among both the poor and the rapidly expanding sector of urban middle-class producers and consumers.

Fourth, Hindu nationalism also received a cultural boost: the immensely pop- ular Hindi serializations of the *Ramayana* and *Mahabharata* appeared on State television, no doubt helping to foster an all-India Hindu self-consciousness. It is in the context of cultural change that the final set of theories – those linked to the impact of modernization – are located. As Chiriyankandath (1994: 36–7) notes, 'much of the recent electoral success of the neo-religious parties can be ascribed to their endeavour to provide those uprooted from their traditional environment with a bridging ideology'. What he is referring to is the Hindu nationalist appeal which not only offered an intensely needed emotional tie with the past, but also claimed to provide a 'philosophical and practical framework for coping with, and regulating, change'. The BJP aim, according to K. R. Malkani, a vice-president of the Party and its chief theoretician, was to 'remain anchored to our roots as we modernise so we don't lose ourselves in a tidal wave of modernisation' (quoted in

Chiriyankandath 1994: 36–7). In sum, the BJP and other Hindu nationalist parties expressed their political programmes in the form of reinterpretive responses to the impact of Western expansion and accompanying technological modernization within the historically well-established Hindu religious traditions.

These five factors helped to facilitate the rise of the Hindu nationalists while leading to an increase in minorities' self-awareness. In the 1980s, movements such as the VHP attempted to contrive a 'fundamentalist' version of Hinduism, while Hindu nationalist political parties – notably the BJP – fought for political power through the ballot box. Unlike Sikh nationalists who, because of their small numbers and intra-group schisms, cannot plausibly achieve their objective – independent Khalistan – through the electoral process, Hindu nationalists have progressed electorally. From the late 1980s, the BJP made an increasingly effective showing in the electoral battle against what its leader, Lal Krishna Advani, called the 'pseudosecularism' of secular politicians (Juergensmeyer 1993: 81). From two seats in 1984, rising to 85 in 1989, the BJP won 119 seats in 1991, making it the largest opposition party in the Lok Sabha, India's national parliament[3] (Hellman 1996: 237). Five years later, the Party secured 188 seats, making it the largest single party.[4]

Juergensmeyer (1993: 81) notes that 'one of the reasons why India has been vulnerable to the influence of Hindu nationalists is that Hinduism can mean so many things'. Before continuing it may be useful to describe briefly, first, the essential characteristics of Hinduism and, second, the traditional relationship between Hinduism and politics in India. After that I will explain the success of the Hindu nationalists in Maharashtra State and their lack of it in Kerala. Finally, I will examine the rise (and partial fall) of militant Sikhism as a response to Hindu nationalism.

What is Hinduism?

The term 'Hindu' has been used to refer to what has been believed and practised religiously for around 5,000 years by many people living in present-day India. Taken as a whole, the Hindu tradition is one of the oldest religious traditions in the world. But it is exceedingly difficult to take as a whole, for it is also one of the most diversified extant religious traditions. There is no single teacher acknowledged by all nor any one creed recited by all. As Lewis and Slater (1969: 31) put it, Hinduism 'is a great Ganges River of religious beliefs and practices fed by many streams'. Chiriyankandath (1996b: 45) asserts that the 'plural religious culture of Hinduism . . . renders it meaningless to try to discern any singular religion or "faith"'.

Perhaps all that can be stated with confidence when referring to this great tradition is that we are dealing with a cluster of practices arising on Indian soil and largely, but by no means entirely, confined to India. Religiously, the Hindu tradition

3. In 1991, the BJP also gained control of several State governments, including Uttar Pradesh, the largest State.
4. For an analysis of the 1996 general election, see Chiriyankandath (1996a).

is notable for the following: it has no central Church; it has no historical basis and stands in contrast to the West Asian Judaic tradition; it has a cyclical vision of universal evolution: creation, maintenance and destruction are the processes that recur over macro time spans called *yugas* or epochs; its beliefs and practices are a compendium of animistic, polytheistic and monotheistic principles; the caste system; the concept of Absolute Brahminism (Venugopal 1990: 78). A basic idea is shared with Buddhism: that of *karma*, denoting the conception of moral causation, that is, the idea that what people are and where they are today is largely determined by what they have done in past lives (moral responsibility). *Moksha* is the notion of salvation, signifying emancipation from the bonds of present existence. To attain this it is necessary to transcend *avidya* (ignorance) or *maya* (illusion) (Lewis and Slater 1969: 32).

Hinduism caters to a variety of groups. In general, most ordinary people follow a mixture of animistic and polytheistic beliefs, while those belonging to the reformed sects have a monotheistic base. A notable dimension of Hinduism is its immanentism, that is, the belief that gods are pervasive and easily accessible to the people. The Hindu notion of *avataras* implies that gods take birth in animal or human form to redeem humankind. Hindu soteriology – that is, the way to achieve salvation – rests on the renunciation of worldly ties and the attainment of *moksha*, wherein the cycle of births and deaths no longer operates.

Hinduism rests on a stable social organization: the caste system. In this ascriptive stratification system some castes are placed higher than others in order of ranking. The higher castes are believed to be purer in ritual terms than the lower ones. People are expected to follow the traditional practices and rites prescribed by their caste. For most ordinary Hindus the final goal is not *moksha* but simply a scrupulous observance of rites prescribed by the sacred texts. Two widely used Indian terms may be mentioned in this connection. These are the *varnas* (originally meaning colour), the four basic caste divisions, which are notional rather than empirical. There are four varnas – *Brahmin*, *Kshatriya*, *Vaishya* and *Sudra* – arranged hierarchically. Empirically, however, there are numerous castes, high or low, which are concrete constituents of varnas. They are called *jatis*. No one is born into a *varna*, but everyone is born into a *jati* (Venugopal 1990: 79).

The Hindu sacred literature, written in the ancient language of Sanskrit, consists of four *Vedas*, collections of hymns, prescriptive rites and procedures for five sacrifices, believed to bring prosperity or victory to the performers. Today, however, Vedas are read almost solely as sacred verses. The Vedas reflect changes of thought over time. Many of the gods mentioned in one of the early Vedas, the *Rig Veda*, disappear from view by the end of the Vedic period. In the later Vedic texts the main trend of thought is neither polytheistic nor theistic but in the direction of a pantheistic monism. In the epic scriptures, however, the trend is theistic. References abound to the high gods, Vishnu and Shiva. They, together with the god Bramah, later constitute what is sometimes called the Hindu trinity (Lewis and Slater 1969: 33). Second, there are the *Upanishads*, philosophical, speculative discourses usually held between master (*guru*) and pupil. Third, there are the *Puranas* (myths), held in high popular esteem. Immanentism is central to the Puranas because gods and goddesses arrive on earth to redeem humans from their tormentors. Fourth, there is the *Bhagavad Gita* ('the Song of the Lord'). The *Bhagavad Gita* is part of the epic *Mahabharata*, which, along with the *Ramayana*, discusses the dynastic struggles of antiquity. Both were writen down in their present literary forms around the first century BCE. It is generally agreed that the *Bhagavad Gita*, more than any other sacred text, informs contemporary Hindu thought and conduct. Many scholarly Hindus believe that the *Bhagavad Gita* brings together all that is the most significant in the Hindu tradition. For many Hindu nationalists it is the most sacred text (Jaffrelot 1995).

Hindus and politics in pre-modern India

Like other traditional societies, in pre-modern India there was no clear distinction between the spheres of religion and politics. Hindu culture traditionally embraced all people and aspects of life. In classical Hindu social theory, each role in society, including kingship, had its own *dharma*, that is, the necessary path for individuals to follow in order to escape the chain of human existence. The prime duty of the King, as enunciated by the fourth century BCE Hindu political theorist Kautilya in the *Arthashastra*, was to maintain power and uphold the *dharma* of the social whole. The religious importance of kingship is indicated by the fact that gods are portrayed as playing regal roles in the Hindu epics, the *Ramayana* and the *Mahabharata* (Juergensmeyer 1989: 98).

During most of India's history, however, there was not a single, centralized monarchy. Rather, there were hundreds of small princedoms, with a system of local governance based on representative committees, the *panchayats* ('councils of five'). The absence of centralized government probably facilitated invasion by Muslim invaders from Central Asia and Persia, allowing them to establish the Mughal dynasties that dominated the country from the sixteenth century until the arrival of Europeans in the nineteenth century. The Mughals were Muslims, yet the political system they established pragmatically did not interfere to any great extent with the Hindu religion. Instead, like their British successors, they formed alliances with local rulers. The result was that traditional Hinduism was largely untouched despite this influx of foreign influences.

Over time, however, there were attempts to reform Hinduism from within. Devotional reform movements, from the fifteenth century led by *gurus* (authoritative spiritual personages), emerged. During the nineteenth century, organizations like the *Brahmo Samaj* and the *Arya Samaj* sought to promote mass education, women's rights and improvements in conditions for *dalits* (formerly 'untouchables'), those at the bottom of the social pile. Seeking to avoid overt political involvement, they were the forerunners of more recent Hindu movements for spiritual and social reform. Regionally – rather than nationally – organized and disruptive of Muslim–Hindu harmony, Hindu reformist groups prepared the way for expressions of national self-consciousness in the 1920s.

Hinduism and nationalism

Although officially secular, emergent nationalist leaders drew much of their '...
inspiration from religious faith. Religious appeals and symbolism popularized the
nationalist message' (Talbot 1991: 134). India's independence movement couched
its message in recognizably Hindu terms, referring not only to the notion of dharmic
obligation, but also to the idea of Mother India with the characteristics of a Hindu
goddess. Breaking with what they saw as the Hinduized nationalist movement,
Mohammad Ali Jinnah and the Muslim League demanded a separate State for Muslims. After bloody civil conflict, the goal was achieved in 1947. Although 'Mahatma'
Mohandas Ghandi, the leader of India's nationalists, strongly protested against the
partition of India and the communal hatred it involved, militant Hindus considered
that he had capitulated to Muslim pressure. He paid the ultimate price: a member
of the extremist Rashtriya Swayamsevak Sangh assassinated him in 1948.

In the first years after independence, with the murder of Gandhi no doubt fresh
in many people's minds, religion as a source of political tensions appeared to
be a spent force (Parrinder 1977: 69–70, 105–7). India's first post-colonial prime
minister, Jawaharlal Nehru, stressed the themes of economic modernization and
secularism, which were enshrined in the 1950 constitution. The Preamble to the Constitution states: 'We the people of India, having solemnly resolved to constitute
India into a sovereign socialist, secular democratic republic . . . in our constituent
assembly . . . do hereby adopt, enact, and give to ourselves this constitution.' The
constitution itself sought to remove the threat of the disruptive potential of religion
in two ways. First, it employed an intentionally unclear concept of secularism that
was, however, widely interpreted as according equal respect to all religions, while
protecting religious minorities. Second, the 25-state, linguistically based federal structure would, it was hoped, prove to be sufficiently flexible to allow for the cognizance
of ethnic plurality.

However, it seems very likely that the absence of an accepted role for religion
in politics made for an unworkable situation in post-colonial India: 'as a generally
shared credo of life [secularism in India] is impossible, as a basis for State action
impracticable, and as a blueprint for the foreseeable future impotent' (Madan 1987:
748). Democratization and secularization would, it was feared, work at cross purposes. Increasing participation in the political arena drew in new social and religious
forces whose demands for greater formal recognition of Sikhism, Islam, Christianity
and Hinduism were partly 'responsible for making religion the dominant issue in
Indian politics today' (Mitra 1991: 759).

There was a relative – albeit short-lived – religious calm in the first decade and
a half after independence. However, the year of Nehru's death, 1964, saw a sharp
increase in communal incidents. Two thousand lives were lost that year to fighting
between Muslims and Hindus (Sisson 1993: 58). In the 1970s and 1980s communal
violence continued. The average annual number of deaths during the former decade
was 111, while in the latter it was four times higher, 454. At the heart of the matter
lay the question of the role that religion should play in a modernizing society.
Nehru and his fellow secularists believed that the only way forward was steady

reduction of religion's influence and creation of a more secular culture, to be achieved primarily via a progressively more prosperous society. To this end, Nehru sought to promote the existence of an inclusive political community within which groups were differentiated by economic and social interests rather than by ties based on religion, language ethnicity or locality. However, this glossed over the glaring paradox at the core of the State: India's secular constitution gave no role for religion in public affairs; this situation was to be superimposed on a society where religion was a vital interpersonal bond for hundreds of millions of people. It would have been miraculous if religion did not at some stage become central to politics. In the 1980s, it did.

Hindu nationalism and politics in the 1980s and 1990s

The selective adaptation of tradition is indispensable to Hindu nationalism. The long campaign to construct a temple upon the site of a mosque at the supposed birthplace of the deity Rama (or Ram), the Hindu god of war, in Ayodhya, had a dramatic influence upon the pattern of politics of some Indian states (for example, Uttar Pradesh, Gujarat) but not others. Reference to popular regional religious and cultural traditions may help explain the differential response to the contemporary Hindu nationalist evocation of tradition. However, because of the potential repercussions for the country's 110 million Muslims and other minority groups, Hindu nationalism – focused by the violence surrounding the destruction of an historic mosque at Ayodhya in December 1992 – is widely thought to threaten seriously India's survival as a pluralist democracy (Chiriyankandath 1994: 32). This event conclusively destroyed the democratic, secular consensus envisaged by the architects of the Indian Constitution (Copley 1993: 47).

What religious edifice would take pride of place at Ayodhya had long been a contentious issue. In 1949, following riots, the mosque was closed down by the Government. Forty years later, *The Times of India* claimed presciently that the 'laying of the foundation stone of the Rama temple in Ayodhya can be seen to be a dangerous turning point in the history of independent India' (quoted in Copley 1993: 47). However, the wider significance of the Ayodhya incident was that it threw into the open an issue ignored for a long time, that is, 'the relationship between religion and politics, and, more darkly, its seemingly inevitable concomitant relationship with communalism' (Copley 1993: 47).

But Ayodhya did not come out of the blue. Anti-Muslim rhetoric informed the ideology of the Bharatiya Jana Sangh (BJS),[5] the BJP's predecessor, 30 years

---

5. Leaders of the BJS eschewed the adjective 'Hindu' for *Bharitiya*, a Sanskrit word meaning a member of the Indian nation. In doing so, they turned the State definition of secularism on its head. To quote a 1980s manifesto: 'Secularism as currently interpreted in this country . . . is only a euphemism for the policy of Muslim appeasement. The so-called secular composite nationalism is neither nationalism nor secularism but only a compromise with communalism of those who demand price even for their lip loyalty to this country' (quoted in Juergensmeyer 1989: 100). While this did not exclude the minorities, it insisted that they be Indian *on the terms of* the Hindu majority. The leader of the BJS, Vajpayee, put it thus: 'the Muslims or the Christians did not come from outside India. Their ancestors were Hindu. By changing religion one does not change one's nationality or culture' (quoted in Copley 1993: 55–6).

before (Chiriyankandath 1996b: 53). But the BJS did not enjoy anything like the same electoral success as the BJP. Part of the reason was historical. Because overt Hindu communalism was discredited in the backlash following Gandhi's assassination, the BJS had to narrow its sights. It had to be content with sniping at the Muslim way of life shored up by the Urdu language and loyalty to *sharia* law. But this was not electorally successful. In addition, in Uttar Pradesh, the focus of the BJS's linguistic anti-Urdu campaign in the 1960s, the Congress Government was itself staunchly pro-Hindu, and the BJS made little headway. Nationally at this time, the BJS was only able to identify itself as a 'narrow, northern, regional, Hindi, imperialist Party', without wider appeal (Copley 1993: 56).

The picture changed in the 1980s. From being just one of the diverse currents in the ebb and flow of Indian politics in the 1960s and 1970s, the Hindu nationalists, by now focused in the BJP, began to project themselves as the Party of the future. Between 1989 and 1991 its share of the vote tripled to 20 per cent. By 1991, it had become 'the strongest official parliamentary opposition to the Congress Party since independence' (Chiriyankandath 1994: 31). Between 1990 and 1995 the BJP won power in the National Capital Territory of Delhi and in six of India's 25 states, four in the Hindi-speaking belt of north India and two on the west coast. Of the 119 BJP members in the 545-seat Lok Sabha in 1995, 106 came from these areas, while only eight of the 220 seats in the eastern and southern regions of India were held by the Party. Yet, in the 1996 general election the BJP's share of the vote did not increase much above the 1991 figure, only to 23.5 per cent. But this was enough to give it and its allies 188 seats, that is, more than a third of seats on less than a quarter of the vote. The geographical unevenness of the Hindu nationalist support reflects the plural character of the Indian political scene. The challenge for Hindu nationalism is 'to overcome the centrifugal trends that arise from this heterogeneity, based both on vertical (caste and class) and horizontal (language and region) distinctions' (Chiriyankandath 1995: 1).

However, the 1996 result also confirms the steady polarization of Indian society. Congress lost seats heavily in the north, west and south, although it managed to maintain its position in the east of the country, hanging on to 36 seats. The share of the vote for Congress declined from 48 per cent in 1984 to just over 28 per cent in 1996. The fading of Congress in the first three regions was hastened because of the failure of India's Muslims to do what they traditionally have done: vote for the Congress Party. In the 1995 round of State elections, it is reckoned that most Muslims voted against both the BJP and Congress in favour of candidates or parties with secular credentials (Bhatia 1995). This helps explain the rout of the ruling Congress Party in 1996: many Muslims identified the Party with pro-Hindu sentiments, particularly because of the demolition of the mosque in Ayodhya four years earlier. More widely, the Ayodhya incident also had a dramatic influence upon the pattern of politics of several states – Uttar Pradesh, Gujarat, Maharashtra, where the BJP or its allies made huge gains – but not in others – Kerala, Tamil Nadu – where the Hindu nationalist message was received with coolness.

However, partial scepticism was not enough to prevent the BJP's relentless electoral progress. But, like Christian fundamentalists in the USA or Islamists in Turkey, the BJP was not able to achieve power on its own. The BJP's chief difficulty lay in persuading those unimpressed by its nationalistic agenda that its political aims had a wider applicability in India's pluralist society. The BJP did not manage to convince non-nationalist politicians: following its failure to stitch together a government, the second largest party – Congress (I) – was able to help put together a ruling coalition that managed to survive into 1997. (Congress split in 1975 into two parties. Congress (I) was led by Mrs Indira Gandhi until her assassination in 1984.)

The BJP now dominates the political landscape of north and west India; however, it has found the south and west of the country a tougher nut to crack: this is because it is regarded as a northern-dominated party, intent on imposing its narrow version of the Hindu tradition, at the expense of alternative regional traditions. In the 1996 elections the BJP and its allies only managed to acquire a handful of seats in the south and east. Compare this to the 180 it gained – of the 323 on offer – in the north and west. In these regions, its communalistic programme, perceived by many Indian secular intellectuals as the expression of primordial sentiments indicative of the underdeveloped nature of the people concerned, was obviously highly appealing to millions of Indians. Why does the BJP – and Hindu nationalism more generally – appeal? Why in some regions and not others?

The genesis and appeal of Hindu nationalism

Hindu nationalism grew in the 1980s, exerting a spectacular influence on Indian politics. Partly in response to a perceived increase in Muslim militancy, there was a remarkable rise in Hindu activism. Cultural organizations such as the Rashtriya Swayamsevak Sangh (the National Volunteer Organization, or RSS) grew in size (Talbot 1991: 142). New Hindu cultural–political movements, such as the Vishwa Hindu Parishad (the All Hindu Conference, or VHP) and the Bombay-based Shiv Sena (Shivaji's Army), expanded (Juergensmeyer 1989: 100, Talbot 1991: 143).

As already noted, however, the main political expression of resurgent Hindu nationalism was the BJP. An Indian secularist, Praful Bidwas (1991), has described Hindu nationalism in general, and the BJP in particular, as a 'forced attempt to forge a Semitic, monolithic chosen people, identity for Hindus based on a perverted, sexist, and iniquitous version of the great tradition (promoted at the expense of folk or little traditions) . . .' Chiriyankandath (1996a: 4) notes that a large proportion of the BJP and its allies' support in 1996 came from middle-class, upper caste, well-educated Indians, people who may perhaps be less impressed by the Party's pro-Hindu stance than by its new-broom status after nearly 50 years of Congress rule. Yet such people are believed to have a 'modern and secular outlook' (Copley 1993: 48). Why should they vote for an avowedly sectarian party?

The answer in part is that the BJP seeks to 'weave together . . . religion, culture and language to underpin a singular, assertive conception of the State' (Chiriyankandath 1994: 42). Its appeal is expressly *civilizational* in scope, deriving strength from its identification with Hinduism. The BJP's ideologues and chief political votaries of 'Hindu-ness' (*Hindutva*) have tended to try to ignore or gloss over caste, sect, linguistic and regional distinctions. As indicated earlier, this was central to the failure of the BJP to increase its share of the vote in the south and east in 1996. Regional suspicion of the nationalists' project is probably their main Achilles' heel, a large threat to the creation of overarching solidarity among all India's Hindus (Ram-Prasad 1993).

Yet, if the BJP relied upon the assertive promotion of *Hindutva* alone it is unlikely that it could have achieved the numbers of seats it did. What it *did* manage to do was to get erstwhile Congress voters to abandon Congress. It is thought that in north India the growing confidence of the lower castes and Muslims spurred many upper-caste voters in response to these 'threats' to abandon the Congress Party and transfer their allegiance to the BJP. According to Chiriyankandath (1996b: 4) in Uttar Pradesh and Bihar in 1996 the BJP gained two-thirds of the upper caste vote, while enjoying 'disproportionate representation of young people, urbanites, middle-class professionals and business people'. In short, in such areas the BJP appears to have succeeded in shedding the image of being a party of the Hindi-speaking north Indian *baniya* (small trader) for one representing the interests of forward caste, and middle-class, northern Hindus as a whole. In the north – and the west where it also gained major success in 1996 – the BJP managed to forge a Hindu political identity transcending caste and, to an extent, class divisions.

Shiv Sena and Hindu nationalism in Maharashtra

In the west, Bombay and Maharashtra State stand out as a focus of support for the Hindu nationalists. In the 1995 State elections, the BJP and its ally, Shiv Sena, won 33 of the 48 seats that were up for grabs. Bombay is a prosperous, fast-growing city with a large Muslim minority. Shiv Sena took most of the seats in the city, increasing its representation from 4 to 15. Its success is thought in part to have been due to a fear of Muslim militancy, encouraged by the growth of Islamic radicalism not only in Bombay itself but also further afield, in Iran, Pakistan and the Middle East (Talbot 1991: 154, Hansen 1995: 16–17).

Shiv Sena is a Hindu nationalist movement with a reputation for thuggishness: it concentrates on recruiting young men who are inducted into the movement through bonding practices. Its members embrace a lifestyle that takes in the totality of their social being. Amid the confusion and anomie induced by modernization, membership in Shiv Sena is thought to provide 'spiritual balm, emotional succour and a secure intellectual framework', in short, 'a sense of belonging' (Chiriyankandath 1994: 36–7, 39, Talbot 1991: 142–3, 154–6). Shiv Sena was founded by Bal Thackeray, a political cartoonist, in Bombay in 1966. Initially, the movement's targets were affluent fellow Hindus from southern India and other outsiders who then dominated the job market. This strategy won Thackeray local support but alienated most non-native Bombayites (Joshi 1970). Later, Thackeray 'changed to Muslim-bashing because it appealed to the rising tide of Hindu' nationalism (Bhatia 1995). After winning the 1985 Bombay municipal elections, Shiv Sena began to establish branches throughout the Maharashtran countryside. It raised support in the villages by making use of religious slogans and by taking advantage of the anti-*dalit* sentiment among many high-caste Hindu landowners (Talbot 1991: 142). By the mid-1990s Shiv Sena had a reported '40,000 dedicated followers called *Sainiks*, most of them thugs who do Mr Thackeray's bidding' (Thomas 1995). Bal Thackeray's brand of anti-Muslim demagoguery invites comparisons with Europe's neo-fascists:

> let the Muslims of India do a favour to the nation. Let them find the Bangla [Desh] and Pakistan Muslims who have come here and taken the right to vote . . . India's Muslims have to prove their credibility. If India loses a cricket match to Islamic Pakistan, they should not celebrate by letting off crackers. I want to see tears in their eyes because their country has lost.
>
> (Thackeray quoted in Bhatia 1995)

Hindu enmity towards Bombay's Muslims came to a head in sectarian riots in the city in January 1993 when 'an estimated 2,000 Muslims were killed and more than 10,000 homes destroyed', by Hindu mobs, including Shiv Sena supporters (Bhatia 1995). 'It has been a popular myth,' explained a Muslim community leader at the time, 'that British colonial rule succeeded in India only by fostering divisions between Hindus and Muslims. But long after the British have gone, the two communities maintain an uneasy coexistence and do not mix.' According to this man, 'the city is irrevocably divided' (Bhatia 1995). It is somewhat paradoxical, then, that reports after the State elections of 1995 suggested that the Hindu nationalists won a significant share of the *Muslim* vote, in some areas up to 15 per cent. The reason, according to *India Today* (31 March 1995), was that many Muslims were thoroughly disillusioned with the Congress Party who they felt had let down India's minorities. 'At least we know who these people [i.e. the Hindu nationalists] are – it is better to be attacked by an enemy than by a friend,' a Muslim resident of Bombay declared (Bhatia 1995).

There was a similar result in Maharashtra's State elections in February 1995: Shiv Sena won 30 out of 34 parliamentary seats in the metropolitan region of Bombay, gaining up to 15 per cent of the vote from local Muslims. According to Hansen (1995: 2), this surprising outcome was essentially an anti-Congress – rather than pro-Shiv Sena – vote: the former was widely seen as corrupt, dependent on fine-spun clientelist networks to acquire votes. What Shiv Sena offered was a viable alternative to Congress: an anti-corruption Party which was also against Muslim 'extremism'. The Hindu nationalists employed religious metaphors and narratives of the historical and contemporary antagonisms between Hindus and Muslims. This served to undermine the erstwhile secular idiom of the country's centrist and leftist forces, portraying the Hindu nationalists as the only viable alternative to Congress. The march of the Hindu nationalists in Maharashtra did not, however, merely reflect the overall trend in India since the 1980s, when religious symbols and communal sentiments came to the fore; it also underlined the strong local standing of the Shiv Sena in Bombay itself (Hansen 1995: 1).

A further factor is that the demographic make-up of Bombay is swiftly changing. The Hinduization of Bombay is a contingent effect of a broader democratic revolution in the city. It involves a popularization of the political culture by which a new breed of political leaders and activists from the Marathi-speaking intermediate Hindu castes and lower classes have displaced the older city elite, mainly Parsees and Gujaratis. As already noted, this more effective enfranchisement of Hindus in Bombay provoked a corresponding assertiveness among other linguistic and religious groups – especially Muslims – and a 'concomitant escalation of symbolic competition between cultural communities' (Hansen 1995: 16–17). Shiv Sena played a very ambiguous role in the popularization of political culture in Bombay. On the one hand, it was a major vehicle and focus of collective identification, enabling hitherto passive or marginal groups to come to the fore, articulate grievances and hope for recognition in the public sphere. On the other hand, its growing position was facilitated by the galvanization of youth into a violent xenophobic campaign against the local Muslims. This dualistic nature of the Hindu nationalist appeal was also clear in the 1995 State election campaign, premised both on communal rhetoric and on direct anti-Congress themes. Shiv Sena employed open anti-Muslim rhetoric, supporting campaigns around shrines in Kashi and Mathura in Uttar Pradesh where the VHP was demanding the removal of mosques. Anti-Muslim rhetoric was juxtaposed with anti-corruption drives and a free-housing-for-the-poor campaign. No doubt Shiv Sena appreciated that its electoral and political future was inextricably tied to the continued militant assertion of *Hindutva* and to an unequivocal representation of itself as the ultimate defender of the Hindus, especially the disadvantaged. In so doing, the Party made itself dependent on the process of communalization and polarization which it had been instrumental in creating. It used anti-Muslim discourse combined with aggressive anti-Establishment rhetoric successfully to expand its electoral appeal.

But this does not explain the appeal of the Hindu nationalists to the urban middle classes. As Chiriyankandath (1996a: 4) notes, Hindu nationalist voters are often upper caste, well-educated and urban: 'a third or more in each of these categories' voted for the BJP in 1996. These are the people – if secularization theses are to be believed – who would increasingly put religion behind them when it came to making political choices. Why, then, do they vote Hindu nationalist in large numbers? One factor, no doubt, is fear of militant Islam, but this is surely not enough on its own to explain the shift in support to the Hindu nationalists. Another reason for the increased electoral appeal of the Hindu nationalists may be that the BJP has sometimes tried *not* to portray itself as a communal party, but as a *civilizational* party: thus, it is OK to vote for the BJP, these are not extremists, but patriots. The BJP strives to define Hinduism in cultural rather than religious terms: all Indians are, by this definition, Hindus. The Indian minorities have no separate identity: they are Hindu Muslims, Hindu Christians, Hindu Buddhists, Hindu Sikhs and so on. The BJP claims that Indian-Hindu nationalism can transcend sect and caste divisions and fashion a Hindu unity. How successful was this strategy away from the north and west of the country? Why was support for Hindu nationalists low in the south and east?

The lack of electoral appeal of Hindu nationalism in Kerala

The nationalist project of the BJP and Shiv Sena is about striving to create a Hindu national identity based, however, upon a highly pluralistic religious tradition. So far they have not been entirely successful, failing to build an electoral base in the south and east of the country. Of the 220 seats up for grabs in 1996, Hindu neo-religious parties managed to win just eight, less than 4 per cent of the total. In the southern State of Kerala, secular-leftist parties took over the running of the State in 1996, ousting a Congress-led alliance. It was noted above that one of the reasons for the voters' desertion of Congress was the party's alleged corruption; partly for this reason, it appears, many – including even some Muslims – voted Hindu nationalist in the north and west. In the south-western State of Kerala, however, it was the secular left that reaped the benefit of widespread disillusionment with Congress; Hindu nationalists failed to win *any* seats there in 1996. To understand why, it is necessary to know a little about Kerala's socio-political background.

Kerala has a population of 30 million living in 41,000 square kilometres, the size of Switzerland (whose own population was seven million in 1993). Successive State governments have been impelled by voters' preferences to put the poor first. The latter are both well-organized and vocal; the result is that governments are, of necessity, committed to help them. Over time, a political culture has emerged in Kerala which is geared towards the improvement of the lot of the have-nots in society. Most of Kerala's villages have access to basic health provision, clean water, education, transport services and family planning provision at a level rare in India. Schools and clinics are spread throughout the State, while ubiquitous 'fair price shops' sell basic goods at low cost. A comprehensive – and successfully implemented – land reform programme redistributed land to 1.5 million tenants and labourers. Such policies had the desired effects: Durning (1989: 63) reports that, in the late 1980s, Kerala ranked first of India's states in provision of basic services in 15 of the 20 categories. This is also reflected in an array of statistics: Kerala's adult literacy rate, over 90 per cent of adults, is nearly twice that of India's generally (52 per cent); its people live on average to 72 years, compared to the national figure of 61 years; the birth rate is a third lower than India's generally; the death rate of infants – 27 per 1,000 – is one third of the average in India (World Bank 1995: Table 1, pp. 162–3).

The picture of Kerala's population that emerges is of relatively healthy, educated citizens with a concern for social justice. It may not be coincidental that Kerala is one of only two states with populations of more than five million (the other is neighbouring Tamil Nadu) where Hindu nationalists have never won a parliamentary or State assembly seat. This is not because they have not tried. Hindu nationalist groups, including the Rashtriya Swayamsewak Sangh (RSS), have been organizing in the State for more than 50 years. The lack of success is explained by two main factors: first, the Hindu nationalists are widely regarded as a northern-dominated movement, unable or unwilling to cope with the 'diversity of political cultures/subcultures found in India's regions' (Chiriyankandath 1996b: 45); second, the people of Kerala – a State of remarkably plural cultural and religious character

– simply seem to be unimpressed by communalist arguments. Apart from Punjab (Sikh), Kashmir (Muslim) and the small north-eastern states (Christian/traditional religions), it is the least 'Hindu' of Indian states. Christians and Muslims each constitute a fifth or more of the population, while Hindus are sharply differentiated along caste lines. While the RSS tries to play down caste distinctions its leaders are overwhelmingly upper-caste Hindus; most ordinary members also come from the upper castes.

Reflecting its cultural diversity, Kerala's religious festivals tend to be 'ambiguously Hindu in character, allowing space for the participation of local Christians and Muslims' (Chiriyankandath 1996b: 47). Their pan-religious significance obviously poses problems for Hindu nationalists because they represent an alternative mythic past of religious coexistence. It is not easy to reconcile this with attempts to promote hegemonic all-India myths as in the focus upon Ram in the Ayodhya campaign. While the television serializations of the *Ramayana* and *Mahabharata* epics in the late 1980s are widely held to have contributed to a 'nationalization' of Hindu culture, there were significant regional variations in their popularity. In Kerala, for example, viewing figures for the *Mahabharata* were exceeded by those for the weekly local language feature film (Chiriyankandath 1996b: 49).

Religious tolerance and coexistence do not imply that there has been no communalization of politics in Kerala. In fact, 'all but one of Kerala's governments since 1967 have relied upon the support of parties either avowedly communally based or identified closely with a particular community – such parties have usually claimed at least a fifth of the Assembly seats' (Chiriyankandath 1996b: 51). Three sets of circumstances have been important in the development of a distinctive style of politics in Kerala. First, as already noted, regional traditions emphasize coexistence and a shared identity. The second factor is the approximate balance in numbers between the main communal groupings, reinforced by the electorally significant focus of Muslims in northern – and Christians in central – Kerala. There is also a reasonable spread of material influence, with different groups achieving significance in, for example, administration, the liberal professions, commerce, industry, education and so on. This has made intercommunal business and professional relationships commonplace, helping the development of tolerance and consensus. Finally, there is a high degree of public political awareness, the result of a combination of near-universal education, radical social reform movements and class- and gender-based socio-political organizations. Overall, the result of these factors is that politicians have been impelled towards developing patterns of communal accommodation that are also sensitive to social and class factors; significantly, there has been much less communalization of politics than, for example, in Maharashtra, Uttar Pradesh or Gujarat.

On the other hand, it would be naive to suggest that Kerala has some kind of near-utopian tolerance and societal consensus which sets it apart from other parts of India. Despite factors facilitating communal harmony, Hindu nationalists managed to increase their share of the vote in district council elections fourfold – to more than a million votes – between 1982 and 1991 (Chiriyankandath 1996b: 58). But such support was rather thinly spread; its main importance was that it sometimes split the vote between the main secular-leftist parties. However, the BJP consist-ently wins over one-tenth of the vote in only one of Kerala's 14 districts, Kasaragod on the northern border with Karnataka, while doing relatively well in Malappuram and Kokhikode districts; each has high proportions of Muslims: the former about two-thirds, the latter one-third of their populations. These figures, it will be recalled, are significantly higher than the State average of around 22 per cent (Chiriyankandath 1996b: 57). The point seems to be that when Hindu nationalism does reasonably well in elections, it is the result of particular local factors emphasizing subregional cultural differences. Yet it should once again be noted that, in spite of the RSS's long record of activity, Kerala's Hindu nationalists remain peripheral actors. Their aim to reduce diversity to produce one India-wide political Hinduism has not found success in Kerala, a State of particular cultural and religious diversity.

In conclusion, perhaps the pivotal aspect of Kerala's politics is the accent on mediation and reconciliation of demands expressed in terms of both class and community. Hindu nationalism expresses political issues in alternative terms, seek-ing to emphasize a pan-Hindu identity which not only tries to gloss over regional and caste differences, but also seeks to stress differences between 'Indian' (Hindu) and 'non-Indian' (mainly Muslim and Christian) religious traditions, which in Kerala have been downplayed. Kerala's failure to adopt the ideology of *Hindutva* does not imply, however, that the State is immune to the centripetal influences at work in modern India. Rather it implies that the Hindu nationalists have serious problems with coming to terms with regional political cultures different from their own. The lack of success which the Hindu nationalists have also experienced in Tamil Nadu and West Bengal, like Kerala states with a strong sense of regional identity, adds weight to this conclusion.

Sikhs and politics

Muslims in Kerala have organized themselves in a political party – the Indian Union Muslim League – which has been a part of the State Government for much of the last 25 years. This factor has facilitated the achievement of political and social progress for Kerala's Muslims which has probably served to reduce the significance of potential communal tensions in the State. Elsewhere in the country, however, significant minority groups have found it much less easy to achieve their objective of community progress. One of the most serious, and long-running, chal-lenges to the Indian State has come from the Sikh minority, about 2 per cent of the population, some 13 millon people at the time of the 1981 census. Sikhism (the Hindi word for 'discipline') is generally recognized as an offshoot from the Hindu tradition; present-day Sikhs trace their origins to a North Indian monotheistic sect founded by Guru Nanak (1469–1539), which later developed into a military and political confederacy.

As Ahmed (1996: 260) notes, traditionally separatist nationalism, 'such as that displayed by sections of the Sikh community, is an anomaly in Indian politics'. Recently, however, the dominant trend in Indian politics – religious and communal revivalism – has been manifested not only among Hindus, but also *inter alia* among Sikhs and the Muslims of Kashmir. Hindu nationalists often believe that they are the only group loyal to India, while minorities, like the Sikhs, want to break up India and achieve their own State.

Clause 2 of Article 25 of the Indian Constitution declares the Sikhs to be part of Hindu society. The aim was that low-caste Sikhs would then benefit from the system of reservation of seats in both local and national assemblies, as well as reserved government jobs. Over time low-caste Sikhs did indeed benefit from the policy, yet communal-minded Sikhs were opposed to being categorized as Hindus. When separatist nationalism developed among sections of the Sikh community, demands were made to classify Sikhs as a distinct religious community. Adding fuel to communalistic sentiments was the fact that many Sikhs felt disappointed with the outcome of the independence struggle against the British. They did not even control their own portion of India – Punjab – because there they formed less than half the electorate. During the 1950s a movement emerged calling for the redrawing of the State's boundaries to include only those who could speak the Punjabi language, a demand that was synonymous with calling for a Sikh-majority State. After a hunger strike by the Sikh leader, Sant Fateh Singh, the Government capitulated: the Punjab State was carved into three, producing not only a new, smaller Punjab with a population the greater part Sikh, but also two new states, Haryana and Himachal Pradesh, with Hindu majorities.

The violent movement for a Sikh State that erupted in the 1980s had some ties with the earlier movement for a Sikh Punjab, but it was more fanatical and more religious (Tully and Jacob 1985). It began in 1978 with a conflict between a group of radical Sikhs, led by a preacher, Jernail Singh Bhindranwale, and a Sikh splinter group, the Nirankaris. Although encouraged by sections within the Congress regime, the Bhindranwale group turned against the Government when accused of killing a Hindu publishing magnate in the Punjab. Groups of young Sikhs began killing Hindus, apparently randomly, while in 1981 an Indian Airlines plane was hijacked (Juergensmeyer 1993: 94).

Bhindranwale preached that Sikhs were in imminent danger of losing their identity in the climate of growing secularism or, even worse, as a result of resurgent Hindu nationalism. His most common theme was the survival of the Sikh community or *quam*, a term that carries overtones of nationalism. As for the notion of a Sikh State (Khalistan), Bhindranwale initially said that he was neither for or against it (Juergensmeyer 1993: 95). What he did support was the Sikh concept of *miri-piri*, the idea that temporal and spiritual power are linked; he implored his mainly youthful followers to rise up, speaking of a coming great war between good and evil, 'a struggle . . . for our faith, for the Sikh nation, for the oppressed' (Bhindranwale quoted in Juergensmeyer 1993: 95).

Various militant Sikh groups began to establish their bases, bringing in supplies of modern weapons, in the Golden Temple at Amritsar in Punjab. In June 1982 Bhindranwale and several hundred of his well-armed followers entered the temple in pursuit of sanctuary and proceeded to create what was in effect an alternative government (Ahmed 1996: 275). By the following year, his power had grown to the extent that the Government of Indira Gandhi felt it necessary to rule Punjab directly from Delhi. Consequently, Bhindranwale intensified his anti-government campaign and, along with Sikh leaders resident in North America and Britain, began propagating the idea of a separate Sikh homeland (Helweg 1989: 313–19). However, although a serious situation was developing, for nearly two years the Government, despite sometimes strenuous efforts, was unable to do anything decisive to contain it.

The situation came to a head in June 1984. Mrs Gandhi ordered troops into the Golden Temple to oust Bhindranwale and his supporters in an action code-named Operation Bluestar. Following a prolonged battle, Bhindranwale and hundreds of his followers were killed, as were dozens of innocent Sikh pilgrims who had been inside the temple at the time of the armies' assault (Juergensmeyer 1993: 94). The assault on the Golden Temple, the Sikhs' holiest shrine, provoked outrage even among moderate Sikhs. Horrified at the spectre of the Indian Army rampaging through the holy place, dozens of Sikh troops mutinied and Sikh officers resigned their commissions in protest (Tully and Jacob 1985: 192–217). Seeking to avenge the desecration of the Golden Temple, two of Mrs Gandhi's Sikh bodyguards assassinated her on 31 October 1984. On the following day, more than 2,000 Sikhs were killed in Delhi alone by angry mobs, while in the rest of India, outside Punjab, Sikhs were also brutally treated.

These catastrophic events focused great attention on Sikh designs for Khalistan. Erstwhile Sikh unity fractured, with a struggle for dominance between the followers of Bhindranwale, who were using terrorism in pursuit of their aims, and the 'moderates', led by Punjab's chief minister, Surjit Singh Barnala, whose chief tactic to achieve Sikh autonomy was negotiation. By 1987, the hardliners had (temporarily) triumphed. Radical organizations, such as the Khalistan Commando Force, the Khalistan Liberation Force and extremist factions of the All-India Sikh Students Federation, were in control of the official Sikh leadership. More than a hundred people a month were being killed by extremists in the villages of Punjab (Juergensmeyer 1993: 96). The Punjab conflict dragged on over the next few years: some 35,000 people were killed between 1984 and 1991, while there was a general collapse in law and order in the State (Ahmed 1996: 277). The Indian Government accused Pakistan of aiding the Sikh militants, which Islamabad denied. However, in 1993 the situation dramatically improved. The police used their powers to eradicate the radicals' network, killing several thousand in the process. For the first time in years there was a State of calm in Punjab, although the tensions between the Sikh community and the Government were not really resolved (Sarin 1990). The Government had won against the militants, not necessarily because it was able to persuade the mass of ordinary Sikhs that it was right, but because the public was weary of the conflict; what people wanted above all was a return to normality, the absence of conflict and violence (Juergensmeyer 1993: 99). However, there remains among many Sikhs a residual desire for a greater recognition of the authority of the Sikh religious community, a demand galvanized by the electoral successes of the Hindu nationalists. It would be premature to say that the militants have been finally crushed; isolated terrorist incidents, notably, in September 1993, a car bomb that exploded in Delhi killing eight people, is a reminder that the goal of Khalistan is not dead. There is no certainty that the movement will not re-emerge if the conditions are propitious.

Conclusion

> When religion becomes a code for a total system . . . When it involves identification with the State, it becomes a yardstick for what position you occupy in that State, a basis for participation, for a sense of legitimacy . . . as long as you identify one culture, one race, one religion as your key concept for defining the public agenda, you may be magnanimous, you may be humane, you may be tolerant, but those who are outside that faith can never feel that they are fully equal.
>
> (former Sudanese government minister, Francis Deng, interviewed in *Middle East Report*, no. 172, September/October 1991, p. 32)

Deng points to a serious problem that India encounters: the difficulty of reconciliation between India's distinctive religious traditions. If you are not one of *us*, you must be one of *them*; as a result, your loyalty to the common good is suspect. While the BJP prospers, Sikh militancy à la Bhindranawale seem dormant. However, what Hindu nationalists, Sikh militants and Muslim separatists of Kashmir have in common is that they fear that India is irrevocably secularizing; consequently, their own distinctive cultures and way of life are under serious threat. As Berger (1997: 33) notes, each of these neo-religious movements are upsurges of essentially conservative religion which shun – and wish to reverse – the trend towards modernization and secularization; instead, they want to defend their religio-cultures from degeneration or even disappearance. Militant religious activists perceive India's political structure as illegitimate because secular politics does not encourage candidates to be based in a religious community or claim credibility through cultural ties. Although the politics of religion is thought by many of India's secular leaders to be a step backwards to the worst of its divisive history, some concession to religion may be necessary to assure that India's future is more peaceful than its recent violent past.

But what are the chances of this? Great skill would be required of politicians of all stripes to exercise their authority in a manner which would placate the fears and apprehensions of minority groups like the Sikhs of the Punjab or the Muslims of Kashmir. Since India is a multi-religious and multi-ethnic State, secularism, democratic rule, and a more radical distribution of power between the centre and the provinces seem to be crucial preconditions for maintaining the unity of the country by peaceful means. However, not just Hindu nationalist parties like the BJP, but also avowedly secular ones like Congress, increasingly indulge in communal politics. In the absence of a strong secular political movement cutting across communal and caste divisions – and the current trend seems to be towards regional and low-caste parties – the problem of divided loyalties to the Indian State and to religious, ethnic and social particularities seem destined to plague the course of Indian politics for a long time to come. In a State such as India, based on constitutionalism and democratic values, the viable establishment of a secular political framework will ultimately depend on three arrangements. These are (a) that between the individual and religion: people are free to follow their choice of religion, or none; (b) between the State and the individual: people are not discriminated against because of their religious beliefs; and (c) between religion and the State: the latter should not privilege one religion over others. Constitutionally, India fulfils these criteria, yet recent Indian politics increasingly focuses upon communal issues. In particular, a Hindu urban class, more middle or lower-middle class than the elite, out of a sense of economic insecurity and a threat to their social status, has exploited Hindu communalism. If the politics of such a group lies in the manipulation of the sentiments of an impoverished mass, then the utopian solution lies in the conquest of poverty. However, until then it is beholden upon responsible political leaders to try to prevent the country's politics degenerating further along communal lines. The problem is that it is a moot point whether they have the political will to turn away from a project which, as the BJP's recent electoral successess indicates, wins impressive numbers of votes from increasing fearful people.

Finally, it is very difficult to argue that in a religious society like India's, religion should – or can – be kept apart from politics. But how can a country that encompasses such a religiously plural society endure the creation of a powerful – and fragmentary – sense of identity based upon religion? In India the tension between the formation and substance of a stable State, and the demands made by neo-religious politics, is almost certainly to be unresolved through the creation of a national identity that seeks to privilege Hindu identity. Such would be very difficult to sustain in the face of the complex patterns of, often cross-cutting, divisions of caste, tribe, language and region, not to mention sizeable religious minorities, especially the Sikhs, Muslims and Christians.

Chapter 10

Buddhism and politics in South-east Asia

This chapter has several objectives. First, it presents a brief survey of the essentials of Theravada Buddhism[1] in South-east Asia[2] for those who are not familiar with them. Second, it focuses on the relatively poorly documented relationship between politics and Buddhism in Burma,[3] Thailand and Cambodia.[4] The three countries have a considerable variety of historical, political and cultural contexts within which Buddhism has developed. They also exhibit politically consequential differences in the trends within Buddhism in the 1990s. In the course of the chapter, two conventional assumptions are challenged: (a) Buddhists – laypeople and religious professionals – are inherently politically passive and uninterested in political change; (b) the State and the Buddhist religious professionals are united in a shared aim, that of hegemony over the mass of ordinary people.

It is often assumed that the Buddhist countries of South-east Asia are essentially stable, self-regulating societies based upon shared religious–social values and consensus, with little concern for modern conceptions of political democracy. Buddhists are understood to perceive themselves as passive victims of an unavoidable karmic fate (Phillips 1979). The result, Fukuyama (1992: 216) claims, is that Buddhism is 'confined to a domain of private worship centring around the family', a privatized religious tradition. Huntington (1991: 73–4) explains the lack of democracy in South-east Asia as a consequence of what he calls 'Buddhist passivity'.

1. Theravada Buddhism is the oldest of the three main schools of Hinayana Buddhism. It is the form of Buddhist culture traditionally dominating religious, political and social life in Burma, Thailand, Laos and Cambodia. 'Buddhism' in this chapter means Theravada Buddhism unless otherwise stated.

2. South-east Asia comprises the seven countries of the Association of South-east Asian Nations, that is, Burma, Brunei, Indonesia, Malaysia, Philippines, Singapore, and Thailand; and the three countries of Indochina, Cambodia, Laos, Vietnam. Not all countries in the region are Buddhist.

3. Burma was renamed 'Myanmar' in 1988 by the Military Government. It is still common, however, to refer to the country by the traditional name; I shall continue with this convention.

4. While having Buddhism as the leading faith, the countries examined are different politically: Thailand is a constitutional monarchy with a relatively robust democracy, Burma is an entrenched military dictatorship and Cambodia is a post-Communist polity aspiring to a democratic future. Burma is about 80 per cent Buddhist, with Muslim and Christian minorities; Thailand is over 90 per cent Buddhist, with an important Muslim minority; Cambodia was 95 per cent Buddhist before the Khmer Rouge takeover in 1975. I have not come across recent statistics of percentages of practising Buddhists in the country. My guess is that most Cambodians would call themselves Buddhists.

However, from the earliest period of Buddhism's history, that is, from the days of the Buddha nearly 2,500 years ago, a certain tension has existed traditionally between Buddhist practitioners and political rulers: relations have varied from 'fairly cordial to positively hostile' (Ling 1993: 4). Governments in contemporary South-east Asia also vary in their attitudes and policies towards Buddhists, and this is reflected in the nature and constitution of the Buddhism found there. The political factor is not, of course, the only one that has to be taken into account when considering the varieties of Buddhist practice and institutions in South-east Asia; but, it is a factor that cannot be ignored when accounting for such variety as is found. Apart from political there are also historical, linguistic, geographical, environmental, economic and developmental factors differentiating the Buddhist communities of the region.

The starting point of this book was the assumption of an upsurge in the 1980s in the political involvement of the world religions, a 'widespread and simultaneous ... refusal to be restricted to the private sphere' (Casanova 1994: 6). Referring to Buddhism in Burma (Casanova 1994: 10) contends that the root cause of its political involvement was the State's attempts to privatize it. But, as I shall show, it was not an attempt to privatize Buddhism *per se* which led to an increase in its political profile so much as the State's attempt to deprive traditionally politically vocal monks of the right to express an opinion on public issues. This is, in fact, a more general point relating to Buddhism's political voice in the South-east Asian region: post-colonial regimes have realized that it is futile to attempt to privatize Buddhism, as most people actively desire a public role for it. Consequently, states have been compelled to seek the acquiescence of religious professionals for their policies; increasingly, such consent is not forthcoming, especially from younger, more radical elements among the body of the *sangha* (monks). It is this issue which provides the framework of Buddhism's political involvement since the late 1970s in South-east Asia. But as we shall see, this is not a new development; it was also common in the colonial era. But before discussing these issues I will set out the essentials of Buddhism for those unfamiliar with them.

The essentials of Buddhism

While sharing many features of Hinduism, Buddhism broke away more than two thousand years ago owing to dissatisfaction with the former's ritualism and the dominance of the priestly class. It developed as a separate religious tradition, both rationalistic and atheistic: there is no belief in God or gods presiding over people's destiny. However, Buddhism is a thoroughgoing *ethical* system; its followers believe that people prosper or not according to the Buddhist law of *karma*, that is, what has been enacted in some distant past affects what is possible in the present. Every individual goes through a series of births, with salvation eventually attained through cessation of the cycle of births and deaths.

For lay people to define themselves as 'Buddhist', it is often sufficient for them to declare that they go to the Three Refuges: the Buddha, the *Dharma* (the Buddha's doctrine) and the body of monks and nuns (the *sangha*),[5] and that they will abide by the Five Precepts (not to kill, steal, be unchaste, lie, or take intoxicants). There are days in the lunar month of intensified observance (*uposatha* days) when, ideally, a lay person follows the Eight Precepts, that is, the basic five, plus prohibition on all sexual activity, on watching entertainments or using adornments, and on the use of luxurious beds. This is close to lower ordination (*pabbajja*) entailing following the Ten Precepts. This is like the Eight, except the strictures against adornments and entertainments are separated, and the use of money is forbidden.

Theoretically, the single aim of Buddhist practice is to achieve *nirvana*, the extinction of desire and the end to rebirth and suffering. Traditionally, the way to attain the goal is to progress via moral purity, self-restraint and the practice of meditation to the acquirement of wisdom, a path which only a monk or nun can hope to tread successfully. Practically, however, the religious goal of nirvana is either too remote or too difficult to understand to be attractive to the vast majority of ordinary people. In addition, the Buddhist teaching that existence is 'unsatisfactory' or 'suffering' (*dukkha*) is probably only partially accepted by many people. This is because they can see or imagine states of wealth and power where suffering is outweighed by happiness and pleasure. These states, even if impermanent, still seem desirable. Thus, the ideal goal for many becomes, practically, not nirvana but a better rebirth, probably as a wealthy person.

To achieve the diminished goal of a better rebirth it is necessary to acquire merit. As a result, virtually all Buddhist religious practice, whether by monks or laity, has merit as its aim. Merit-making is compatible with doctrine, since it all contributes – ultimately – to nirvana. To attain merit, which in turn will help achieve a better rebirth, it is essential not to do bad actions. The latter produces karmic retribution in the form of a worse rebirth. Merit is perceived by many Buddhists as a kind of intangible spiritual 'currency' which can be reckoned and 'transferrred', increasing in proportion to the amount 'invested' (Johnson 1988: 734). There are 10 ways of earning merit: the most rewarding activity of generosity, especially giving food and other goods to monks in exchange for various religious services, plus observing the precepts, meditation, transferring merit, empathizing with merit, serving one's elders, showing respect, preaching, listening to preaching and holding right beliefs. For the layperson, the most important function of the *sangha* is to provide the individual with the opportunity to make merit by giving to the monks. As a result, most monks spend much of their time performing merit-making rituals – especially sermons and readings from the texts – for laypeople. Since few monks consider nirvana to be a realistic goal, such activity is in fact beneficial for them as well as for laypeople. This is because preaching and propagating the *Dharma* is one of the ways in which they require merit and thus the chance of a better rebirth. Thus, there is a symbiotic relationship between laypeople and monks: each benefits from merit-making, while overall the store of merit goes on increasing (Johnson 1988: 735).

---

5. The *sangha* is a salient feature of Theravada Buddhism, a religious tradition based to a large degree on the notion of mendicancy as the principal way to salvation. Most of the male population in the Theravada countries of South-east Asia spend at least a short time of their lives as novice monks.

Theravada Buddhism and politics in South-east Asia

Theravada Buddhism is the Buddhist tradition of South-east Asia, quite different from the Mahayana Buddhism of Mongolia, Tibet and East Asia or the Tantric Buddhism of some parts of Central Asia. The use of the Pali term 'Theravada' (Doctrine of the Elders) to define the particular school reflects the fact that the Theravadins of South-east Asia present themselves as belonging to the branch of Buddhism which they believe preserves the 'orthodox' or 'original' teaching of the Buddha, Prince Siddhartha Gautama, born 2,500 years ago in what is now northern India. Theravada Buddhism is the form of Buddhist culture which has dominated for centuries the religious, political and social life of Sri Lanka, Burma and Thailand, and, until recently, Laos and Cambodia.

Buddhism has acted as an integrative force in assuring the survival of Buddhist societies in South-east Asia. It has also permeated the life of the nations of Buddhist countries in South-east Asia, leaving its distinctive mark on social, cultural and individual activity. Buddhism has long served as one of the main socializing, acculturating, and unifying forces in certain South-east Asian societies. It has profoundly influenced the cultural, economic and political development of Buddhist nations, and continues to mould the social and political values of a great majority of the people. In other words, Buddhism may be seen in many cases as the root from which national identity and the political and social heritage grow.

Theravada Buddhism probably travelled to Sri Lanka and South-east Asia via missionaries sent out by the Indian emperor Asoka from the middle of the third century BCE. Later, during the first century BCE, the Theravada Canon was committed to writing. The monastic community, the *sangha*, was the sole repository of the Buddha's doctrine, and it was through the monks alone that the laity had access to it. This gave the monks a high degree of religious and societal importance which generally endured, except during the 1970s and 1980s in communist Cambodia and Laos, a period of ruthless religious persecution.

In South-east Asia, it is widely believed that 'religious values rank high, possibly highest, among the primary values of the masses' (Somboon 1993: 109). Thus, in a Buddhist country the close association of Buddhism with the political system would appear to constitute an invaluable means for rulers to maximize their popular legitimacy. This has periodically been the case in Thailand, Laos and Cambodia where, before the intrusion of Western ideas and power in the nineteenth century, absolute monarchy was the accepted form of rule.

It follows that the *sangha* has traditionally been an important intermediary caste between rulers and ruled, often supported by the rich and influential. In South-east Asia this often developed into a symbiotic relationship between the *sangha* and the King, that is, the chief layman. This is a way of saying that, from its inception, Buddhism has been closely associated with politics in South-east Asia. Buddhist chronicles are filled with stories of historic rulers who supported the monastic order, in turn helping greatly to legitimate their rule (Lewis and Slater 1969: 62–96). While traditionally Buddhist kings derived authority from righteous behaviour, Buddhist scriptures stress the need for rulers to maintain order in the face of human imperfections; when they do not the *sangha* often have something to say about it. The prosperity of the society was believed to depend upon the king's success in exercising political authority in a moral fashion. As a result, he had a duty to observe the Ten Royal Virtues[6] and to act as a moral exemplar, a *Dharma raja* (righteous ruler).

Historically, the Theravada Buddhist kings of South-east Asia sponsored and supervised the *sangha* as a means of promoting Buddhism and thereby securing their own legitimacy. Once Buddhism became established as the State religion, the significance of the Discipline underwent a substantial change. The preservation of the Discipline, that is, the moral purity of the *sangha*, was the essential component in the preservation and proper functioning of the nation. Thus, the monk, the embodiment of moral purity, became a figure with *public* responsibility. The King, for his part, was not only the embodiment of the State, but also had the duty of preserving the institutions of society, especially the *sangha*. Much of Theravada history is patterned by recurrent efforts of rulers to preserve or re-establish the purity of the *sangha*, since the prosperity of the nation is ultimately seen to depend upon its moral example.

The issue of the public position of the *sangha* became of increased importance when Theravada Buddhism spread to South-east Asia from Sri Lanka. Probably in the thirteenth century, Theravada Buddhism reached Thailand via Burma, gradually overcoming competitor religions, especially Mahayana Buddhism and Hinduism. Theravadin orthodoxy was established in Laos and Cambodia in the fourteenth century, while a little later a reforming king of Burma, Dharmaceti, imported the ordination tradition from Sri Lanka, unifying the *sangha* and establishing a monastic hierarchy (Johnson 1988: 730). Following Dharmaceti's reforms, a single authority structure for the national religious framework – in effect, the 'Church' – headed by a monk with two deputies, was gradually established in the Buddhist countries of South-east Asia (Eisenstadt 1993: 18). In Thailand especially, such a religious structure developed into the institutionalized hierarchy of offices still evident today (Johnson 1988: 731).

While Thailand was able to keep colonialism at bay in the nineteenth century, other Buddhist countries in South-east Asia did not, undergoing European penetration and control. The intrusion of Western powers served decisively to weaken traditional modes of government (Somboon 1993: 126). Nowhere was this more evident than in Burma where royal patronage of the *sangha* ceased abruptly following the British takeover in 1885. One result was that the sacral nature of government was challenged and the ideological basis of the State, formerly provided by religious beliefs and values, was openly questioned. Colonial administrators employed Western-educated indigenes whose horizons embraced Western models of government. The disruption of the traditional integrating systems caused by the intrusion of Western power and ideas had, as a consequence, the effect of separating the religious and political components of those systems. Eventually, however, nationalist movements

6. The Ten Royal Virtues (*dasaraja Dharma*) are: generosity, morality, liberality, uprightness, gentleness, self-restraint, non-anger, non-hurtfulness, forbearance and non-opposition.

emerged whose leaders were drawn from the ranks of both Western-educated patriots and Buddhist figures. By this stage, however, the traditional institutional position of Buddhism had been permanently downgraded. While Buddhism did not collapse, it did mean that the *sangha* lost much of its organizational structure.

There were several consequences of the European intrusion. First, during the late colonial period – from the 1920s and 1930s – monks as individuals as well as the *sangha* collectively were involved in independence and nationalist movements (Smith 1990). Second, the impact of Western 'rationalist' interpretations fed into Theravada cultures, leading to 'modernist' movements which rejected many traditional Buddhist beliefs and practices. Third, the introduction of Western education and the spread of literacy caused the *sangha* to lose its monopoly of educational authority. From this the idea developed that each person was responsible for his or her own salvation, and thus for the welfare of the religion in general.

More extreme religious privatization occurred in the countries of Laos and Cambodia. In 1975, the communist Lao Patriotic Front (*Pathet Lao*) took over the government of Laos, while in neighbouring Cambodia the Khmer Rouge – under the leadership of the infamous Pol Pot – achieved power. Consequently, in Laos, the *sangha* lost a great deal of its traditional influence, although later there was a gradual watering down of the anti-religion position by the increasingly pragmatic communist regime. While the role of the monastries (*vat*) diminished as a result of modern education and governmental promotion of a secular culture, religion was able to retain some status via the national Lao Unified Buddhist Association (Hunter 1989: 160). In Cambodia, Buddhism was temporarily destroyed during Khmer Rouge rule. However, following the overthrow of the Pol Pot regime by the Vietnamese there was a strong Buddhist revival (Harris *et al.* 1992: 400).

Whatever the specific national circumstances, it is clear that Buddhism contributed greatly to the development of the new South-east Asian nation states as colonialism gave way to independence. Since independence, however, it has found it necessary to strive to resist the pressures put on it by post-colonial governments and their policies. In some cases, the State sought to restrict or repress Buddhism and the cultural values it represented. Furthermore, especially since the end of World War II, Buddhism has had to contend with, and adapt to, the pervasive cultural, economic and political influences of both the West and communism.

In response to the twin assault from Western influences and communism, Buddhism had to show both tenacity and adaptability. But like all traditional religious world views it found itself increasingly subject to the eroding influences of foreign secular ideas. In particular, there was the notion of *secularism*, that is, the idea that the State, morals, education and so on should be independent of religion, and *secularization*, that is, a decline in the prestige and influences of religious institutions, personnel and activities and a change in the overall character of human thought and action, such that it becomes less governed by mystical or transcendental criteria. Both have undermined the traditional Buddhist world view in South-east Asia. In response, Buddhism had to make major efforts to shore up its traditions, institutions, scriptural integrity, monastic discipline and moral values. Both renewal and reform have, of necessity, taken place, involving new activism on the part of the

Buddhist laity. Monks, too, have found it necessary to reinterpret the religious tradition to appeal to increasingly modernized, urbanized and educated people.

This train of events began when colonialism was overthrown in the years after World War II. In the struggle for independence, Western notions of equality, liberty, self-determination and so forth had been employed by nationalist leaders to seek to legitimize the quest for national freedom. While notions of representative government were an important part of external attacks on traditional religious–political modes of government in South-east Asia in the early nineteenth century, as Somboon (1993: 127) notes, by the time of independence after World War II only a small group of Western-educated elites had 'developed a real comprehension of, and commitment to, new secular values'. Their attempts to impose secularization on the traditional culture of society escalated conflicts and tensions leading to a legitimacy crisis for the ruling elite and their policies of political and administrative modernization. Many ordinary people, imbued with traditional religious modes of thought, became rather alienated from the political process.

Post-colonial State policies toward Buddhism in South-east Asia were shaped not only by the new rulers' goals of Western-style modernization but also by their need to legitimate their rule and to unify often ethnically and, in some cases, religiously divided peoples. The main problem for rulers was that the two goals – modernization and building nation-states – often seemed to be mutually exclusive. As Keyes *et al.* (1994: 5) explain, while striving for 'modernization entails rejection of those aspects of a society's past deemed impediments to a rationalized bureaucratic order, nation-building depends on the very opposite move. The nation is always imagined as a community of those who share a common history.'

Thus, modernization and nation-building were mutually exclusive. Under the prevailing circumstances of conflict and tension, the leaders of countries in South-east Asia were compelled to turn once again to religion and society's religion-based values for assistance. The concept of national religion was invoked to initiate, explain and legitimize the actions, political institutions and programmes of the ruling elite. As a result, religious interest groups became prominently active in politics in a number of South-east Asian countries, including Burma, Cambodia and Thailand (Somboon 1993: 127).

In contradistinction to the view of Buddhist 'passivity' and consensus, one can point to a number of high profile political struggles involving Buddhists in South-east Asia, both during the colonial and post-colonial periods. Especially since the 1970s, political developments in the region – ranging from popular protest against authoritarian rule in Thailand and Burma, to the rise and fall of the murderous Khmer Rouge regime in Cambodia – have increasingly called assumptions of social consensus and Buddhist 'passivity' into question. This is especially clear when we look, as we shall shortly, at the political actions of the emergent middle class in Thailand. There, several interest groups, including radical students, Western-educated elites, and unionized workers, have all been in the forefront of political agitation for fundamental changes (Juree and Vicharat 1979: 419–35).

When we turn to the rural dwellers it is by no means certain that their Buddhist culture impels them towards political passivity. Several studies have emphasized how so-called Buddhist 'passivity' may merely reflect the rather general lack of political power of most ordinary people vis-à-vis the State in the region (Tambiah 1976, Smith 1978). Such people may collectively decide that it would be foolhardy openly to confront the State when they know they have no chance of success. This is hardly a trait of Buddhist peoples alone. Rather than Buddhist culture *per se* producing political passivity, the point is that powerful states are sometimes able to *create* high levels of passivity through the manipulation of ordinary people by showing them that under normal circumstances popular resistance to the power of the State is not only futile but also highly dangerous (Scott 1985). It is relatively unimportant which religion such people adhere to, yet we never read of *Muslim* or *Christian* passivity in, for example, the Middle East or Africa, even though power-less rural people are just as likely to be as politically 'passive' as their counterparts in Buddhist countries.

But whereas South-east Asian states may normally have relatively little trouble in controlling their rural populations, the same cannot always be said for Bud-dhist monks. The notion of a symbiotic relationship between secular and religious power does not always reflect reality. South-east Asian Buddhist states tend to face periodic dilemmas in their relationship with the *sangha*. The life of a Buddhist monk is austere, tightly regulated by over 200 rules of conduct, the *vinaya*. To ensure the maintenance of high standards of behaviour from monks necessitates a highly effective – but difficult to achieve – disciplinary regime. If regular, effective inter-vention by secular political authorities is not forthcoming, monastic discipline tends to degenerate. The result is a decline in the morale and status of the Buddhist order. Yet secular political authorities often have their own agendas for intervening in *sangha* affairs: they are often predominantly concerned with neutralizing potential or actual sources of disaffection. In relation to this goal, that of promoting or uphold-ing Buddhism *per se* is secondary.

It is appropriate to see the contemporary high profile for Buddhism in politics in South-east Asia as the most recent expression of religious changes which have been of significance for at least three-quarters of a century, that is, since the institution-alization of Western influences in the region. As noted above, the ending of col-onialism and the advent of independence brought extensive changes in political ideology and increasing access to modernized lifestyles for many people. A conse-quence was that the social, cultural and religious landscapes of the predominantly Buddhist countries of South-east Asia were radically altered (Schober 1995: 308). One manifestation of such changes was the emergence and development of new Buddhist movements in swiftly modernizing Thailand, involving both lay people and religious professionals; there is now an uncontrolled religious market. Religion has a new clientele: a middle class with different tastes and with the money to indulge them. They are sophisticated consumers of religion, expecting results. There is no evidence, however, that Thailand's modernization is leading to a greater pro-portion of atheists. The result is actually greater – albeit more diversified – religious enthusiasm, not estrangement. As O'Connor (1993: 330) notes, the new middle class has caused 'religious ferment while a crisis in legitimacy explains a new Buddhist movement as well as the fervour for amulets and forest monks'. In short, 'the new Buddhist movements redefine the role of religious community within society, helping to promote further laicization – that is, religious issues are opened up to lay people – in religious matters' (Schober 1995: 315).

The overall point is that Buddhism in South-east Asia is an evolving, politically engaged religion which by no means necessarily evinces passivity vis-à-vis secular authorities. This is not a particularistic development of the 1980s in response to attempts to privatize it; but reflects a long-standing tradition whereby religious professionals do not passively accept dictates from temporal power but instead question and challenge it when necessary. Next I present case studies of Thailand, Burma and Cambodia. In each, the impact of political, economic and social changes has had profound effects upon the relationship between Buddhist religious professionals, society and the State.

Case studies: Thailand, Burma and Cambodia

In Thailand, uncolonized but nonetheless strongly affected by Western influences, Buddhism has for many years fulfilled the role of State ideology. In recent times, however, the emergence and growth of new Buddhist movements – some with overtly political goals and aspirations – suggests that when religion develops in response to changing temporal conditions it will reflect the aspirations for change of its followers. In Burma, materially the poorest of South-east Asian countries, there is a different position. Buddhist monks there contributed greatly to the attainment of freedom from colonial rule, in many cases having leading roles in the nationalist movement. However, the post-colonial period has been one of intermittent conflict between *sangha* and State. In the virtual absence of an emergent middle class the *sangha* has retained the colonial role of chief political opposition. The third case study focuses upon Cambodia. There, Buddhism had to contend with more than five years of government by the murderous Khmer Rouge which not only tried assiduously to exterminate religion but also killed millions of Cambodians. Following the Khmer Rouge's overthrow in 1979 by a Vietnamese invasion, an initially hesitant State gradually recognized the continuing popular appeal of Buddhism and allowed it a resurgent voice in national affairs.

Thailand

It is often thought that Buddhism in South-east Asia both provides the State with an ideological basis and political legitimacy, and is widely used to facilitate government policies and to maximize its legitimacy. Thailand, where over 90 per cent of the people are Buddhists, traditionally provided a good example of such a political connection between Buddhism and political rulers. The present monarch, King Bhumipol Adulyadej, must profess and defend both the Buddhist *dharma* and the *sangha*. However, reflecting the prevailing power arrangements, he must also reach a modus vivendi with the most powerful social group – the military – because of its role as power broker (Chai-Anan 1993).

The interaction between Buddhism and political rulers in Thailand is taken as a case of reference because, first, since the formation of the Thai State, Buddhism has uninterruptedly been the dominant religion of a great majority of its people. Second, unlike Laos, Burma or Cambodia, Thailand did not experience the effects of colonial rule. Third, as a result, its traditional mode of government has recognizably continued for many centuries (Somboon 1993: 109–10). The general point is that the mobilization of traditional institutions, notably Buddhism and the monarchy, in aid of political stability in Thailand, has been remarkable. In other words, Buddhism and the monarchy have together functioned traditionally as the most visible symbol of national unity.

Yet, as Swearer (1987: 64) notes, while 'the national monastic order strongly supports the State, there have been instances of charismatic monks . . . who have resisted pressures by the State towards standardization of monastic education and practice'. This points to what Somboon (1982: 7) describes as a 'continuous dialogue' between the country's Buddhist order and the State. At the heart of the interlocution is the question of whether Buddhism is, or is not, the State religion. Buddhism is known in Thailand as the *sasana pracham chat*, that is, the 'inherent' national religion. However, no Thai constitution has ever specified that Buddhism is actually the State religion, although all have stated that the King must profess the Buddhist faith. Thus, the constitutional position of Buddhism is open to interpretation and its public role open to debate.

Historically, a number of measures have highlighted attempts by the secular authorities to bring Buddhism under firm control. This was well expressed in the 1962 *Sangha* Act which sought to make direct use of Buddhist monks in the service of the State. Henceforward, monks were enlisted in various programmes combining Buddhist proselytizing with combating communism and spreading State ideology to Thailand's minority (non-Buddhist) tribal peoples with the goal of assimilating them into mainstream society. Since the early 1970s, however, not all interaction between monks and the State has been mutually supportive. The catalyst for change was the so-called 'October Revolution' of 1973 when student- and monk-led demonstrations succeeded in toppling the military dictatorship of Field Marshals Thanom Kittikachorn and Praphat Charusathien. The result of the monks taking the side of the opposition in 1973 was that henceforward the traditional pattern of a subservient *sangha* legitimating an authoritarian government was emphatically broken. From this time, monks openly and regularly took political sides: some on the side of political liberalization and reform, others against it: the latter expressed the view that the post-1973 regime was dangerously liberal, seriously undermining traditional State–*sangha* relations.

The most radical monks looked beyond the confines of State–*sangha* concerns: some openly supported a reformist student movement campaigning for a modern democratic system while others canvassed for the avowedly secular Socialist Party in the 1975 elections. Both professed to see a clear parallel between the inequality and authoritarianism of the *sangha* hierarchy, and wider socio-economic injustices in Thailand. However, monks whose politics challenged the power of the State were not easily tolerated. Many were severely disciplined (Somboon 1982: 56–61, 84–90, 103–5). At the other end of the political spectrum, an outspoken right wing monk, Kittiwuttho, founded an extreme nationalist movement, Nawaphon, declaring a 'holy war' on communism, proclaiming that 'killing communists is no sin' (McCargo in preparation). Despite such inflammatory statements, his organization was permitted to pursue its activities unhindered, while Kittiwuttho himself established close ties with a group of right wing military officers. This seeming double standard serves to underline the sometimes rather ambiguous nature of the 'dialogue' between religious and political authorities in Thailand. The general point is that the 1962 *Sangha* Act was the product of a period of Thailand's political history characterized by a rather crude authoritarianism. As a result of the Act, a handful of elderly and extremely conservative monks were able to rule the *sangha* with a dictatorial hand. Yet they conspicuously failed to address such urgent problems as poor internal discipline and declining numbers of long-term ordinations. It is scarcely surprising that, by the very nature of the system which selected them, such senior monks tended to be strongly supportive of the political status quo.

As already noted, however, since the 1970s challenges emerged from within the collectivity of monks which not only focused upon the nature of the State policies but increasingly upon the nature of the *sangha* regime itself. Since that time, a new generation of monks has emerged: individuals who often aim to teach a contemporary Buddhism relevant to a rapidly changing society. In some ways they resemble Latin America's Catholic priests animated by the concerns of liberation theology that were such an important feature of the religio-political scene in the 1960s and 1970s. In Thailand, such 'progressive' monks were similarly engaged in development work, including environmental, conservation and community projects and moral education, largely for the same reasons as their Catholic counterparts. The monks believed that the pre-eminent place and relevance of Buddhism in Thai society – like that of Catholicism in Latin America – must be ensured by its evolution in the context of changing circumstances. They must achieve an *active* engagement with society, rather than being satisfied with a ritual legitimation of the State alone. However, most were no more or less 'political' than their official superiors; the point is that the former worked for socially progressive goals while the latter were, for the most part, strongly conservative. It is this schism that led McCargo (in preparation) to contend that the 'existing edifice of the Thai Buddhist *sangha*, for all its traditional centrality in the rituals of the State, contains dangerous cracks'.

The division within the *sangha* is not, however, the only recent development within Thai Buddhism with political resonance. Another is the emergence of a number of 'new Buddhist movements', including Phuttathat Bhikku's Suan Moke, Wat Phra Dharmakaya, and Photirak's Santi Asoke. All have been beneficiaries of the mainstream *sangha*'s high-level paralysis and indirection. In their different ways, each movement is concerned with Buddhism's quest for modern relevance; broadly, they are society-oriented. Santi Asoke, uniquely, has openly entered the political arena. In sum, their emergence may well reflect a general shift in Thailand's political power, that is, away from traditional – and conservative – State institutions such as the military and the orthodox *sangha*, and towards a stronger and more diverse civil society (Hewison 1993: 180–1).

New Buddhist movements and politics

Since the 1930s, Thai politics has been characterized as a situation where the interests of civilian and military elites have been privileged, enjoying a monopoly of real political power. While procedural elements of democracy (political parties and elections, more or less democratic constitutions) have been present, truly representative democracy has not. There has been little room for countervailing forces of civil society – socially progressive monks, reformist business groups, trade unions, environmental protection groups, pro-democracy organizations, new political parties, the mass media and so on – to pursue essentially reformist goals. In short, until recently politics has been understood primarily as the domain of elite interests, while those challenging the status quo have been marginalized (Chai-Anan 1993: 282–7, Hewison 1993: 167–84).

The emphases and directions of new Buddhist movements in Thailand are basically reformist and should be understood in relation to the foregoing: they are attempts to make the religion meaningful to modern life, both as critique and affirmation (Suwanna 1990: 405). Put another way, they should be understood in the context of Thailand's changing political system. Recently, however, scholars including Swearer (1987), Hewison (1993) and Somboon (1993) have all argued that the rise of new social forces in civil society has invalidated the conventional elite-centred conception of Thai politics. This has occurred because, whereas in the past the elites were normally able to co-opt any challengers to the status quo, recent rapid socio-economic change has shifted power especially towards a new business class. Such business interests have worked with some of the emerging civil society groups to wrest a degree of economic power from the hands of State officials and the military. But the impact has not only been felt in the economic sphere, but also in those of religion and politics. For example, according to temple statistics, most members of one of the new Buddhist movements – the Wat Phra Dharmakaya – are from the middle class. Forty-one per cent are university students and 22 per cent private business owners. They 'seem to represent a segment of the emerging middle class that is keen on achieving both wordly pleasure and peace of mind in religious form' (Suwanna 1990: 407). In short, an area of democratic 'space' has opened up where new political and religious forces operate with greater freedom and effectiveness, challenging not just the religious, but also the wider socio-political, status quo.

The rise of the new Buddhist movements is an important part of this process of political change because they offer emergent social groups the ability to develop religious practices – broadly within the Buddhist tradition – which, crucially, are not subject to the direct day-to-control of senior monks or the Thai State. As McCargo (in preparation) notes, 'orthodox Thai Buddhism amounts to an extension of bureaucratic dominance into the religious and personal life of ordinary citizens'. There is also a widening social gulf between most ordinary monks – over 90 per cent hail from the rural uneducated populace – and the emerging middle class of Bangkok and other population centres (Suwanna 1990: 407). While many orthodox monks offer ritualistic services and give occasional sermons to the urban middle class, a widening gap exists between the two groups which the new Buddhist movements help to fill. By adopting new modes of Buddhist practice and belief, members of key civil society groups are able to define for themselves a distinct identity which is no longer subservient to State concerns. Yet changing class structure and an emerging civil society is not the only explanation for the rise of the new Buddhist movements: they are also, it is argued, a fundamental part of what has been called Thailand's 'individualistic revolution' (Keyes 1989, Taylor 1990).

However, new Buddhist movements in Thailand are difficult to account for definitively because, so far, they have not been fully quantified, nor adequately classified. It is nonetheless fairly clear that they are evidence of social change, of urbanization and of resulting spiritual dislocations. Reflecting such aspects of modernization, Thailand's new Buddhist movements are part of the global phenomenon of religious revivalism, a development which cannot wholly be correlated with country-specific patterns of socio-economic change. However, the increased pluralism of Buddhist teaching and practice offered by the new movements testifies to the emergence of a less homogeneous society, and a reduction of the capacity of the State to impose religious, social and political values upon all Thais.

Burma

When we shift focus to Thailand's neighbour, Burma, we find a quite different political and economic profile to the former. Unlike Thailand, a democratizing monarchical system, Burma, colonized by the British, has had unelected military governments for more than 30 years. Further, it is much less materially wealthy than Thailand: real GDP per capita per annum in Burma is a mere $650, one-tenth of Thailand's $6,350 (UNDP 1996: Table 17, pp. 170–1). However, despite such differences, traditionally elements in the *sangha* have challenged the political status quo in both countries.

As von der Mehden (1989: 32) points out, Buddhism – the religion of 80 per cent of Burmese[7] – 'has been a focal point in Burmese politics throughout the twentieth century'. In a tradition dating back to the 1920s, monks' organizations, such as *Sangha Parahita Aphwegyok* (Sangha Social Service Group, or SSSG) help define the place of the monastic order in society and the polity. The SSSG was a trail blazer; stimulated by the iniquities of colonial rule, it was well ahead of similar efforts elsewhere in the Theravada Buddhist world. Like Thailand's contemporary socially concerned monks, the SSSG challenged 'the traditional passive "receiving" role of the sangha and instead urged an outreach to the poor and marginalized elements of society' Matthews (1993: 412).

---

7. Muslims comprise 5–10 per cent, Christians about 5 per cent, and Hindus around 3 per cent.

During the course of the Burmese nationalist movement, monks – especially leading figures like U Ottama[8] and U Wisara – and politics became virtually synonymous (Smith 1965). Such people exemplify the tradition of some members of the *sangha* working against governments perceived as anti-Buddhist and/or illegitimate. The point is that in the absence of other national ideologies of opposition, Buddhism has frequently represented the only widely accepted symbol to focus popular grievances.

U Nu, Ne Win and Aung San[9] were leaders of the main nationalist group, the Anti-Fascist People's Freedom League, which led Burma to independence in 1948. When Aung San, the greatest hero of the anti-colonial struggle, was assassinated on the eve of independence, U Nu was called upon to form the new government. Devoutly Buddhist, U Nu sought to re-establish the traditional connection between the *sangha* and State, partly in order to legitimate his own government during a turbulent political period. U Nu's aim was to create a Buddhist socialist State where a 'true' Buddhism would be possible. The Government would provide sufficient material needs for everyone, class and property distinctions would be minimized, and government policy would inspire all to strive for moral and mental perfection. The State would, in short, meet the material needs of the people, while Buddhism would supply the spiritual needs of the vast majority of the people.

However, U Nu's commitment to make Buddhism the State religion proved unpopular with some ethnic minorities, such as the mainly Christian Karens.[10] For them and other minorities, revitalizing Buddhism was linked with increasing the cultural and political dominance of lowland ethnic Burmans, at their expense. While Buddhism was traditionally a link between ethnic minority communities, some of whom were partially Buddhist, and the Burmese, by the time of the premiership of U Nu (1948–58, 1960–2) ethnic secessionist aims had served to undermine the relationship. The promulgation of Buddhism as the *de facto* State religion and the disquiet with which this policy was received by many of the country's ethnic and religious minorities was one of the reasons given by General Ne Win for deposing U Nu as Prime Minister in 1962 (Tin Maung Maung Than 1988: 27).

Although Ne Win declared Burma a secular State, his policies in fact reflected the central and pervasive importance of Buddhism in the country. When he seized control of the polity, he inherited a relationship between 'Church' and State that, for various reasons, had become increasingly close during the premiership of U Nu. Ne Win hoped to preside over a regime that 'albeit authoritarian . . . would . . . somehow more authentically represent the traditional Burmese of the precolonial era' (Matthews 1993: 408). However, following the demise of democracy, Buddhism became involved in a long-term ideological struggle against the Ne Win regime.

Tin Maung Maung Than (1988: 28) divides the policies of the post-1970s regimes towards Buddhism into two principal phases, to which I will add a third: first, the period from 1972–74 was marked by a 'marginalization of the politicized monks

8. U Ottama spent 15 years in jail between 1921 and 1939, eventually dying in prison.
9. Aung San was the father of the leader of the current pro-democracy movement, Aung San Suu Kyi.
10. The Karens have fought for independence since 1947 when the Karen National Union was formed prior to independence one year later.

amidst eclectic secularism'; the second era, that of 1975–88, was characterized by a more interventionist strategy – with the State actively seeking to control the *sangha* – following the declaration of the 1974 socialist constitution. Since 1988, as in the colonial period, monks have taken an active role in the pro-democracy struggle.

During 1972–74, Ne Win aimed to abrogate Buddhism from the formal structures of the State by two main strategies: first, by depriving the *sangha* of government subsidies and, second, by implementing a rapid secularization programme. After a period of apparent – if wary – acceptance, military rule was increasingly resented by the *sangha*. The situation came to a head in December 1974 when thousands of monks 'joined in protesting the low-profile funeral arranged by the State for U Thant, the former UN Secretary-General. Some monks were killed and hundreds arrested' (Matthews 1993: 414). This event was pivotal in persuading Ne Win henceforward to try a different strategy towards Buddhism.

Between 1975 and 1988 the State demonstrated an increased willingness to re-integrate senior members of the *sangha* into positions of influence. This policy had two, mutually supporting, aims. First, and most obviously, the aim was to control the *sangha*'s activities so as to keep an eye on them. Second, the policy of reward-ing senior monks was intended to give them a stake in the regime, to separate older members of the *sangha* from youthful firebrands. From 1979, the Government began issuing honorific titles to senior monks for the first time since the coup of 1962, a move welcomed by the *Kyaungtaik Sayadaw Aphwe* (Presiding Abbots Association, or PAA) which sought the advancement of Buddhism with government support and assistance. It considered that the position of senior Buddhist monks had been undervalued for too long. But the military regime was suspicious of the PAA's loyalty: after 1980 its position was undercut by a new, government-controlled Supreme Sangha Council (*Sangha Maha Nayaka*) (Matthews 1993: 413).

By the early 1980s, two decades of military rule had enabled the State's control of the *sangha* to tighten; the monks found themselves closely regulated, circum-scribed by the Government in matters of administration. The power of the State was made particularly clear at a country-wide, four-day congregation of the *sangha* attended by over 1,000 monkly representatives in 1980. The gathering approved documents not only laying down basic rules for the organization of the *sangha* but also establishing procedures for settling disputes and dealing with disciplinary issues. Official *sangha* membership cards were presented to all ordained monks. A follow-up gathering in 1985 sought to deepen State control of the monks. In sum, the regime's aim was to make monks easier to oversee and to manipulate, to prevent a potential rival source of power emerging.

Not all members of the *sangha* were acquiescent to the government's aims. Many monks, especially young ones, were involved in demonstrations in 1988–90 calling for democracy. However, if judged supporters of the pro-democracy leader, Aung San Suu Kyi, they were likely to be imprisoned or even killed: between 30 and 40 monks were executed in August 1988 alone (Smith 1991: 8). At this time, when popular discontent with the Military Government was coming to a head, monks helped set up popular committees which briefly ran a number of towns. Smith (1991: 7) claims that the dissident monks' chief grievance was that the authorities had been forcing many dissenting members of the *sangha* to leave the monkhood from the late 1970s. But this can be taken further: in fact, there was a clear division in the *sangha* itself with some monks declaring support for the Government. This was likely to be the case, as Matthews (1993: 417) points out, if they were 'liberally favored with special donations to their temples or outright personal gifts such as television sets and automobiles'. On the other hand, many abbots allowed their monastries to be used by student protestors for political meetings. It is worth pointing out that in Burma, unlike Thailand where the militancy of Buddhist monks scandalized many people, Burmese regard political activity by the *sangha* as entirely normal and natural. This is a result of the tradition not only of monks' opposition to colonial rule but also of the failure of post-independence regimes to replace the traditional Burmese kings 'as effective and legitimate patrons of the *sangha*' (McCargo in preparation).

Several *sangha* political organizations came to the fore in the late 1980s. In Burma's second city, Mandalay, the Young Monks' Association (*Yahanpyo Aphwe*, or YMA), forced underground in the 1970s, resurfaced. The YMA, originally established in 1938, was originally galvanized by perceived threats to Buddhism from two sources, colonialism and communism (Gravers 1996: 304). Over the next few years, the YMA's 'quasi-militaristic fervour' gave it a 'fundamentalist and politicized approach' to socio-political and religious issues (Matthews 1993: 412). Close to the Government during the U Nu years, after the coup of 1962, the YMA moved away from the regime, believing that it fundamentally threatened not only their aims and organization but even Buddhism as a whole.

Another monks' association, the All Burma Young Monks' Union (ABYMU), also came to political prominence at this time. Following the disturbances of August–September 1988, a rival government was briefly proclaimed in Karen-held territory by former premier U Nu. Although U Nu's proclamation was somewhat vainglorious – he had little support from the military or other influential State institutions – this did not prevent ABYMU from greeting the announcement sympathetically. Perhaps ABYMU believed that a government led by U Nu would be more in accord with the aims and aspirations of the *sangha* than that of Ne Win. In the event, however, following a brutal crackdown by the Government, many ABYMU sympathizers and activists were forced to flee the cities of lowland Burma, along with students and pro-democracy agitators, for the relative sanctuary of the hills.

Following unprecedented international pressure, the Military Government – known as the State Law and Order Restoration Council (SLORC) – allowed general elections in 1990. However, after a clear victory for opposition forces led by Aung San Suu Kyi was disallowed, monks again emerged to play a leading opposition role. Twenty thousand monks participated in a 'spiritual boycott' to protest at the Government's annulling of the elections. In response, the Government implemented a programme of systematic closure of hundreds of monasteries. Matthews (1993: 419) suggests that probably '80 per cent of Burma's monks directly support or have sympathy for the pro-democracy movement . . . Activist monks act as moral chastisers . . . offering quiet but visible leadership in the name of their cause'. It has been essential to offer 'quiet' leadership because from 1990 the SLORC embarked on a crackdown of 'illegal' monks' organizations, including ABYMU (Tin Maung Maung Than 1993: 39). Raids took place at over 100 monastries in Rangoon alone and dozens of monks were arrested and detained. The Government claimed to have seized 'subversive' literature and weapons in the raids. More than 200 monks and novices were later expelled from the *sangha* as a result of their alleged involvement with illegal organizations. By 1991 the *sangha* appeared to have been cowed into submission. Dissident monks were obliged to keep a very low profile. But it was not all 'stick', the 'carrot' was also employed: the State-controlled media carried frequent reports at this time of 'senior army officers offering colour televisions to monasteries and paying respects to senior monks' (*Far Eastern Economic Review* 29 August 1991: 16).

Uncertainty about the social position of the *sangha* under the military regime may, along with stress due to political and economic change, have resulted in an increased popular reliance on the supernatural or magical in contemporary Burma. As Matthews (1993: 418) notes, this is a reaction which has been noticed elsewhere in the Theravada Buddhist world, including, in the form of new Buddhist movements, Thailand. The root cause is probably linked to political and economic uncertainty and social change. However, some members of the Burmese *sangha* maintain that the reason for these developments had nothing to do with the SLORC regime *per se*, but with the general impact of modernity and the loosening of traditional values. There is a perceived deterioration in public spirit and honesty – cheating and prostitution are increasingly common – probably indicative of worsening economic conditions. In addition, because many people are poor there is less willingness to give to the monks. Overall, however, the role of Buddhism as the hallmark of Burmese civilization has not appreciably diminished; rather, religious changes may primarily reflect a lowering of capacity to carry on a traditional spiritual life because of harsh political and economic conditions.

Four main conclusions emerge from this account of religion and politics in Burma. First, the country has had a long tradition of politicized and even militant Buddhism. Second, there seems to have been no compromise in most people's faith in what Buddhism has to offer pertaining to salvation and culturally. Third, Buddhism is not by itself an urgent element in political choice in Burma. Fourth, Buddhism in Burma does not appear to be intellectually old-fashioned and out of touch with the rapidly changing world.

Cambodia

Theravada Buddhism became a prominent religion in Cambodia from the fourteenth century. Prior to this, Hinduism and local cults provided not only the dominant forms of religious belief but also the cultural system upon which the ideology of the State and mode of government was based (Somboon 1993: 110). Cambodia was colonized by the French between 1863 and 1954.

After independence, 'Khmer Buddhism', Somboon (1993: 137) claims, was 'continuously mobilized to achieve the political goals of the ruling élite'. Like the first post-colonial regime in Burma, Cambodia's ruler, Sihanouk,[11] also used the rhetoric of a somewhat hazy 'Buddhist socialism'. Sihanouk claimed, like U Nu in Burma, that 'Buddhist socialism' was characterized by a desire to 'establish equality, promote the well-being of the poor in . . . society, and to strive towards national identity' (Somboon 1993: 137). Yet the concept of Buddhist socialism for Sihanouk was unlike other kinds of socialism, both of the West and of the East, in that it was inspired far more by Buddhist morality and the religious traditions of Khmer national life than by doctrines imported from abroad. He claimed that his attempted policy of political neutrality was conceived of in terms of the Middle Path in accordance with the Buddha's teaching. In the unsuccessful battle against communism in the early 1970s, Sihanouk invoked Buddhism to support his campaign (Somboon 1993: 138).

As in both Thailand and Burma the relationship of Buddhism to politics since the late 1960s in Cambodia has been firmly located in the conflict between a desire for modernization and a cohesive national identity, which, for these countries, is primarily based on religious values. However, as Vickery (1984: 9) explains, Cambodian Buddhism – like its Burmese counterpart – also contains many syncretic elements, including 'prejudices peculiar to the [Cambodian] society, special relationships with ruling classes, and the ability to rationalise the pursuit of material gain'.

No longer widely regarded as the axiomatic Khmer ruler, Sihanouk was deposed by Lon Nol in March 1970. The latter justified his dethronement by accusing him not only of mismanagement of the economy and inability to maintain political stability but also of 'committing serious crimes against the national religion' (Somboon 1993: 140). It appears that Sihanouk's Buddhist socialism offered little in the way of a solution to overcome the increasingly serious political and economic crises which were emerging from the late 1960s. While the policy of the Lon Nol Government was not presented in Buddhist terms, it did strive to give Cambodians the impression that it respected Khmer tradition; moreover, it continued the former government's role as protector and patron of the national religion. In Lon Nol's regime not only was the *sangha* assured of its prestige and status, but also the change of political rule was meant to be beneficial to Buddhism. With the country already immersed in a rebel insurrection, Lon Nol declared 'holy war' against the indigenous communists, the Khmer Rouge.

The ensuing civil war was fought in terms of 'atheist devilry' versus 'Buddhism as the opiate of the people' which, the Khmer Rouge alleged, impaired the people's talent and power both physically and mentally (Chandler 1992). The teachings of the Buddha were said by the Khmer Rouge to make people see life negatively – that is, 'Buddhist passivity' – and accept suffering without making any effort to improve their own fate, thus perpetuating poverty and exploitation. Members of the *sangha* were accused by the Khmer Rouge of being unproductive members of society, social parasites. Popular merit-making undertakings, including contributing to the maintenance and construction of monasteries and religious places and catering

---

11. King from 1941, Sihanouk abdicated in 1955, but played an important political role until 1970 and again from the early 1980s after the Khmer Rouge had been ousted.

to the needs of monks, were pronounced by the Khmer Rouge as no more than a profligate squandering of the 'people's wealth in unproductive programmes which weakened national economic growth' (Somboon 1993: 140).

On coming to power in 1975, the Khmer Rouge lost no time in seeking to elim-inate Buddhism from Cambodia. Ironically, many Buddhist monks had previously been recruited by the Khmer Rouge because, like numerous students and teachers, they were highly vulnerable to its moral appeal to build a better, less polarized society (Chandler 1992: 65). By the end of 1975, Buddhism was declared to be a 'reactionary' religion and banned (Sam 1987: 70–2). Monasteries were destroyed and monks and novices, even those in the base areas that the Khmer Rouge already controlled, were compelled to disrobe (Keyes 1994: 55–6). Some were forced to get married – which went against their monkly vows – and to do hard labour in the fields or to work in the construction of roads and irrigation systems (Somboon 1993: 141). The few permitted to remain in the monkhood had to undergo political re-education and were henceforward treated as laity. It was later estimated that five out of every eight monks were killed by the State during the five years of Khmer Rouge rule: 'Within a period of four years of the rule of the Khmer Rouge, Bud-dhism almost disappeared' (Keyes 1994: 56).

But such fears were groundless. Buddhist renewal in Cambodia can be divided into two phases: from 1979 to the late 1980s, and from the late 1980s. The invasion by Vietnamese troops and the taking of the capital, Phnom Penh, in January 1979 marked the end of Khmer Rouge rule. A new government under Heng Samrin was installed. One of its first acts was to permit the – albeit partial and controlled – restoration of Buddhism. As Keyes (1994: 61) puts it, 'the new government was allowing the people to reclaim some of the ritual landscape'. Ordination into the monkhood was once again permitted within strict limits; the new government was seeking to ensure that Buddhist institutions operated in accordance with the State's wishes (Hunter 1989). By 1981, however, the Government was making it difficult for Buddhism to be restored in the form in which it had existed before 1970. 'It started restricting ordinations, permitting only those over 50 years of age to enter the *sangha*' (Keyes 1994: 61–2). In 1985–9 there were between 6,500 and 8,000 monks, that is, less than 10 per cent of the number of pre-Khmer Rouge times (Keyes 1994: 62). As in Burma, this restrictive policy towards Buddhism also reflected the State's desire to ensure that the *sangha* did not emerge as an independ-ent institution capable of focusing opposition. However, by 1989 there were nearly 2,500 Buddhist temples in the country, that is about two-thirds of the pre-1970 num-ber, although there were only, on average, between two and four monks attached to each.

Clearly, the Government was, on the one hand, torn between encouraging the re-emergence of a vibrant, culturally relevant Buddhism, and, on the other, anxious not to facilitate the development of a potential political challenger. However, around 1988 there was a clear policy shift in favour of encouraging Buddhism. As the leaders of the Government began to foresee a time when they would have to com-pete in elections, they must have felt that the need to develop a broader popular appeal outweighed the potential dangers of developing political rivals among the *sangha*. Consequently, restrictions on ordinations of men under the age of 50 were removed, while in April 1989 the National Assembly voted to amend the constitution to make Buddhism once again the national religion of Cambodia (Keyes 1994: 62–3). State leaders became conspicuous in their public support of Buddhism.

The restoration of Buddhism was strengthened in late 1991 when government and opposition representatives – including the Khmer Rouge – agreed to accept United Nations-supervised settlement of the Cambodian conflict. As a consequence, Sihanouk returned to chair the transitional Supreme National Council. Monks played high profile roles in festivities associated with Sihanouk's return, while he reassumed his erstwhile royal role as the *sangha*'s supreme patron (Keyes 1994: 64). More generally, the peace accords made it possible for the return of Cambodian refugees from camps in Thailand, including hundreds of monks and novices. While the final outcome of the generations of political upheaval in Cambodia is still unclear – the Khmer Rouge is still active and low-level civil war continues – it seems likely that Buddhism will once again become central to the nation-building project.

Conclusion

Buddhism has played an important political role in each of the three South-east Asian countries discussed in this chapter. Traditionally, when secular authorities – as in Thailand – were able to exercise considerable control over the *sangha*, Buddhism was an invaluable asset in the task of State building and State legitimation, useful in encouraging compliance to the political authorities. This was a pattern also present in colonial Burma and evident in attempts by the Heng Samrin regime to recreate a pliable Buddhism after 1979 in Cambodia.

Where the *sangha* was able to achieve some degree of autonomy, whether through a history of struggle against an occupying power or against an illegitimate regime as in Burma, it periodically posed a significant threat to the prevailing order because the centrality of Buddhism to millions of people gave the monks scope for influencing popular opinion. Fearful of the power of the monks, governments have sought to limit their freedom and independence.

Where political discontent emerges, often hand in hand with modernization and change, novel currents in Buddhist teaching and practice – most clearly in Thailand – have emerged. Such currents often incorporate criticism not only of the existing *sangha* structures and their relationship with the State but also of the wider political order. In Burma in particular, where their efforts have posed significant threats to State legitimacy, groups of monks played a direct role in challenging ruling elites, sometimes resorting to violence in pursuit of their aims. On the other hand, the brutal Khmer Rouge regime was able for a brief period almost to crush Buddhism; however, the religion's enduring popular appeal and cultural importance soon became apparent in the post-Khmer Rouge period.

Finally, the alleged passivity of Buddhists – making them indifferent to political changes – has been shown to be myth. In fact, Buddhists, often led by their monks, are anything but passive when it comes to changing an unjust status quo. Monks are *not* the unquestioning allies of temporal rulers. Instead, there is a clear division between the normally conservative senior figures in the *sangha* and more radical, often youthful elements. It is the latter who have played the pivotal role in the pursuit of political changes in both the colonial and post-colonial periods in Buddhist South-east Asia.

Chapter 11

Conclusions

This book has sought to provide a global perspective on the relationship between religion and politics since the early 1970s, a period of history when, according to the secularization thesis, the public role of religion would inevitably decline. However, during the course of the preceding chapters, it emerged that the relationship of religion with temporal power frequently changes over time, but it is not by any means inevitable that its public role would be downgraded. Consequently, it is necessary to be concerned with the historical and comparative complexities of secularization. In particular, how best to explain religious resistance to secularization: is it more than an irrational refusal to accept the consequences of modernization? Is there a legitimate religious resistance to depolitization that is more than a clinging to inherited privileges by religious professionals? Further, how best to understand what some call a religious 'resurgence'? Is it really a proper account of what has been happening since the early 1970s? Finally, what is the interplay of levels of analysis – ranging from the personal and community to institutional and national arenas – when it comes to religion and politics in the contemporary period? In this, the final chapter, I want to discuss these issues and suggest some conclusions.

Catalysed by the epochal 1979 revolution in Iran, the high global public profile of Islam has been one of the main developments thrusting religion into international attention. But, as the chapters of this book have shown, the last quarter century has also seen increasing socio-political profiles for the other so-called 'world' religions, that is, Buddhism, Christianity, Hinduism and Judaism. How best to understand this development? The evidence of the foregoing chapters suggests that very often these religious traditions are increasingly unwilling to be confined to the private sphere, where theories of secularization, especially in the case of Christianity, had long sought to condemn them. Instead, they are either seeking to re-enter the public sphere – if already privatized or are making strenuous efforts, especially in the Third World, to *prevent* privatization at the hands of the State. Fighting religious privatization is carried forward at three analytically separate levels: (a) at the *State* level, that is, in the context of relations between religious institutions and the State; (b) at the *political society* level, that is, where religion seeks to use or ally itself with political parties and/or movements to pursue goals; and (c) at the *civil society* level, that is, where religious actors, on their own or with other groups, work to change the status quo, the prevailing power equation, in their favour.

In sum, many religious actors are creating novel yet significant political pressures in a variety of national contexts. I have argued in the chapters of the book that the socio-political importance of religion shows up most clearly in the realm of political culture, in core assumptions about governance. Treated as communities of believers, religion has often had particular relevance to the study of group conflict and electoral cleavages.

Postmodernism and the socio-political salience of religion

But all this has been a surprise. Thirty years ago it would have taken a brave person to predict that by the end of the century there would be an apparent revitalization of religion, with new places of worship being built in profusion and new religious sects emerging in great numbers. But what are the origins of the religious efflorescence? Of considerable importance, I believe, is the fact that popular faith in progress – via *secular* modernization – has widely collapsed. Instead, the post-modern condition – the contemporary *zeitgeist* – reflects widespread undermining of the certainties by which people, especially in the West, have lived for decades. This explains why the book has been concerned with the quarter century since the early 1970s: during this time, the forces and processes of modernization, by threatening the survival of traditional religious forms and religio-cultural identities, has helped to stimulate their efflorescence. States have aimed for the cultivation and maximization of both political legitimacy and power, very often by the pursuit of an increasingly secular State of affairs. Political legitimacy, we should recall, is necessary for states to maintain themselves in power without too frequent a resort to coercion. It refers to particular combinations of rights embodied in authority and political institutions, enabling the rulers to be acceptable to the ruled. Legitimacy is also related to a set of conceptions held by significant members of the polity about the rightness of a political pattern, which, in turn, provides the pattern with a set of properties. Legitimacy is thus often determined by the goal of the polity. If legitimacy is *not* achieved, authority will be weakened, and opposition movements will rise up. A political system or a regime acquires legitimacy when the belief becomes widespread that its political institutions and procedures are right and proper for the society and that its decisions should be accepted and rules obeyed as a matter of moral obligation. However, in recent years, as states have sought to modernize – and normally to secularize – they have increasingly impinged upon issues which were once the sole domain of religion. This has stimulated conflict and, in many cases, diminished their legitimacy in the eyes of many citizens, especially if they are religious.

The crises which have emerged are consistent with what is widely known as the 'post-modern condition'.[1] The term, post-modernism was invented, it is widely

---

1. While, strictly speaking, the conditions of post-modernism can only logically apply to 'modern' societies, I have extended the use of the term to include countries that are not 'yet' modern, but are still modernizing.

believed, by J.-F. Lyotard (1979) who defined it as: incredulity toward meta-narratives, that is, a rejection of absolute ways of speaking truth. The term has been applied in and to many diverse spheres of human life and activity, including art, literature, architecture, politics and religion. But post-modernism is a rather enigmatic concept. Yet this very ambiguity reflects the confusion and uncertainty inherent in contemporary life for many people. Socially, post-modernism refers to changes in everyday practices and experiences of people and groups, who develop new means of orientation and identity structures. In short, 'post-modernism . . . directs our attention to changes taking place in contemporary culture' (Featherstone 1988: 208). It is important for politics and religion as it decisively reflects the end of belief in the Enlightenment project, the assumption of universal progress based on reason, and in the 'modern Promethean myth of humanity's mastery of its destiny and capacity for resolution of all its problems' (Watson 1994: 150).

The fact of the post-modern era, I want to argue, is of major significance for the importance of public religion.[2] This is because post-modernism encourages the rejection of centres and systems of power, especially the State, while engendering the growth of local identities. Put another way, post-modernism reflects the declining grip that all-encompassing systems of thought – that is, secularized ideologies and world views – exercise over their adherents. In addition, as a result of the communications revolution, more information is made available, teaching people, for example, in Eastern Europe during the communist era, to demand their rights, including their religious rights (Ahmed 1992: 129). The consequence of all this is widespread disaffection with the scientific rationalism of Western thought, a development represented by numerous – especially so-called 'fundamentalist' – religious formulations. In short, post-modernism offers opportunities for religion to pursue a public role, a position facilitated by a feeling of widespread socio-political instability, a time 'turbulent, traumatic and dislocating, yet also . . . potentially creative' (De Gruchy 1995: 5). One of the most important aspects of post-modernism is the cultural/interpretive dimension,[3] with religious 'fundamentalism' one of its chief manifestations (Simpson 1992, Cox 1984). It is the post-modern rejection of de-politization and privatization – in an epoch widely regarded as both amoral and increasingly despiritualized – that has facilitated the rise of fundamentalist and other religious imperatives.

As a reflection of group concerns, religion has had a growing impact upon politics in many regions of the world over the last few decades. What this indicates is that the belief that societies would *inevitably* secularize as they modernized has not turned out to be well-founded. Instead, the combined impact of modernization

2. For a discussion of post-modernism and Christianity, see Simpson (1992) and in relation to Islam, see Ahmed (1992).

3. The fall of the Berlin Wall in 1989, followed by the sudden, unexpected demise of communist systems in the Soviet Union and Eastern Europe in 1990–91, exemplifed other – socio-political and human rights – dimensions of the post-modern era. These events marked a fundamental historical change from one epoch to another, helping to fuel widespread, albeit transitory, optimism that a benign 'New World Order' would follow the ideological divisiveness and malignity of the Cold War. Optimism was expressed with regard to the spread of liberal democracy, pluralism and human rights to nondemocratic countries.

(urbanization, industrialization and swift technological development), coupled with a lack of faith in secular developmental ideologies, has left many people with a feeling of loss rather than achievement. By undermining 'traditional' value systems and allocating opportunities in highly unequal ways within and among nations, modernization produced in many people a deep sense of alienation stimulating a search for an identity to give life meaning and purpose. In addition, the rise of a global consumerist culture has led to an awareness of relative deprivation that people may believe they can deal with most effectively if they present their claims as a group, perhaps a religiously oriented group. A result of these developments has been a wave of socio-political religiosity, with far-reaching implications for social integration, political stability and, some argue, international security. Whether we look at Europe, North America or the Third World it is not the case, as some have maintained, that such movements only attract the poor and marginalized segments of society; many people with Western-style further or higher education also find them attractive. But they are most prevalent in urban centres, that is, areas with a particularly high degree of modernization. The foregoing chapters have shown that religion's political involvement is taking place in a variety of countries with differing political systems and ideologies, at various levels of economic development and with diverse religious traditions. But all have been subject to the destabilizing pressures of either a pursuit of modernization or modernity itself; in other words, all are experiencing to some degree the post-modern condition, characterized by a lack of clarity about the future direction of society.

There is a further dimension of the contemporary high public profile of religion worth noting. Samuel Huntington (1993) believes that an era of cultural conflict is dawning between the West and the 'antidemocrats' of the Third World, especially those of the Islamic persuasion. It is widely accepted that the Muslim world is one of the areas about which the secularization thesis was wrong: during the twentieth century the hold of Islam over Muslims has not diminished; on the contrary, for many it has probably increased. It is a striking counter-example to the secularization thesis.

The core of Huntington's argument is that the 'Christian', democratic West is finding itself in conflict with a group of Muslim countries, united in their antipathy to the West, and inspired by the nondemocratic religious and cultural dogma of 'Islamic fundamentalism'. He believes that the post-Cold War order will be one in which conflict between the West and Islam is almost inevitable, notwithstanding the trend towards the creation and consolidation of broadly democratic political systems in many areas of the world, but not, unfortunately, to any great degree in the Islamic heartland of the Middle East.

While Islam, according to Huntington, is the chief threat to international stability, Christianity, on the other hand, is said with some justification to spawn a culture highly efficacious to the growth of liberal democracy, an important foundation of global order. As we have seen, the Roman Catholic Church was an important catalyst and actor in the introduction of democracy in a number of regions from the 1970s. The collapse of dictatorships in southern and eastern Europe and Latin America was followed by the introduction of liberal democratic political norms, including the rule of law, free elections and civic rights. This is regarded by Huntington as conclusive proof of the synergy between Christianity and liberal democracy. This is a view also held by Francis Fukuyama, another who believes in the 'Islamic threat'. He argues (1992: 236) that 'Islamic fundamentalism' has a 'more than superficial resemblance to European fascism'.

Now it is one thing to argue that various brands of political Islam have qualitatively different perspectives on liberal democracy than some types of Christianity but it is quite another to claim that the Islamic countries *en masse* are poised to enter into a period of conflict with the West. In my view, the raising of the Muslim 'threat' has more to do with the bigotry of some Western analysts than with the threat of Islam *per se*. Instead, I believe it is important to see the struggle of Islamist groups primarily against their own secularizing and modernizing rulers. It is the support of some Western states – especially France – for certain anti-Islamist regimes, especially the military junta in Algeria, which has served to export domestic struggles in the Middle East to the streets of Europe. The point is that since the beginning of Islam, critics of the status quo have periodically emerged to oppose what they perceive as unjust rule. Contemporary Islamists are the most recent example, characterizing themselves as the 'just' involved in struggle against their modernizing rulers, the 'unjust'. The dichotomy between 'just' and 'unjust' in the promotion of social change throughout Islamic history parallels the historic tension in the West between the State and civil society.

The goal of the 'just' in Islamic history has been to form popular consultative mechanisms (*shura*) in line with the Quranic idea that Muslim rulers must not only be open to popular pressure but also seek to settle problems brought by subjects to a common satisfaction. However, the concept of *shura* should not be equated closely with the Western notion of popular sovereignty because to Muslims sovereignty resides with God alone. Instead, *shura* is a way of ensuring unanimity from the *umma*, the community of Muslims, which allows for no legitimate minority position. Some – but not all – Islamists oppose Western interpretations of democracy, because it is seen as a system which negates God's own sovereignty. It is partly for this reason that Islamists (in conflict with conservative, 'unjust' Islamic establishments) are often conspicuous by their absence in demands for Western-style democratic change. Yet, despite an unwillingness to accept any sovereignty other than God's, most Islamists nevertheless accept the need for earthly rulers to seek a mandate from their constituency (Dorr 1993: 151).

A wider point is that the contemporary rise of Islamism throughout the Middle East and beyond is the result of the failure of modernization and nationalism to deliver on their promises. Etienne and Tozy (1981: 251) argue that Islamic resurgence in Morocco is a result of 'disillusionment with progress and the disenchantments of the first 20 years of independence'. This type of analysis could be extended to the entire Muslim world. Faced with State power seeking to destroy – or at the least control – the former communitarian structures in the name of nationalism and national progress and to replace them with an idea of a national citizenry based on the link between State and individual, radical-popular, as opposed to State-controlled, Islam has emerged as an often significant vehicle of political opposition. This turn of events should be seen in relation to the capacity of popular Islam to oppose the State and frustrate its designs, but it is primarily at the domestic level one sees Islam at work. This form of radical Islamic organization does not, it seems to me, translate into a wider threat to *global* order. Suggesting great religious passion, a defiance of modernization, and a response to secularizing forces, it is, above all, a reaction against post-modernist *uncertainty*. And uncertainty is a condition that many people find impossible to tolerate. *Any* movement – not only religious ones, but also those, *inter alia*, pursuing goals of ethnic autonomy or advancement – promising to provide or renew certainty will have a ready following in the current era of instability and uncertainty. An undiluted secular view of reality, with its principal social location in the elite culture of the political leadership is, not surprisingly, resented by large numbers of people who are not part of it, but who nevertheless must live under its influence. A wider point can be made: there is a legitimate religious resistance to depolitization that is more than a clinging to inherited privileges; instead, it is a means to deny the State the level and degree of power that it requires to pursue its goal of hegemony.

The complexities of secularization in the post-modern world

I do not believe that it is accurate to describe what is happening as a global religious *resurgence*. This is because tens of millions of people – especially, but by no means exclusively, in the Third World – have been staunchly religious throughout their lives, just like their parents, grandparents, great grandparents, and so on; consequently, it is implausible that they have suddenly *rediscovered* religion. Millions of other people in other parts of the world also have what might be called the religious impulse. This involves a quest for meaning that goes beyond the restricted empirical existence of the here and now. It is an enduring feature of humankind that goes back over millenia.

Yet, despite the clear evidence of religion's widespread tenacity, a few sociologists of religion have been trying to salvage the secularization theory by arguing that we are witnessing no more than its last, dying gasp. Their claim is that modernization does indeed secularize and that religious actors' contemporary efforts merely represent a last-ditch attempt to triumph in a war that will turn out to be unwinnable. Ultimately, secularization will achieve victory. But this argument seems to me to be unsatisfactory, not least because the very range, power and numbers of extant contemporary religious actors – some of which I have described and examined in this book – seem to me fatally to undermine the argument. Can one really easily perceive American Christian fundmentalists, Egyptian and Algerian Islamists, or Hindu nationalists suddenly becoming non-religious? I strongly doubt it.

But the development of religious ideologies of opposition targeting secular rulers certainly goes against the grain of recent sociological thinking. Since the 1960s sociologists have predicted that modernization would automatically lead to secularization. The idea of secularization theory is traceable to the Enlightenment: modernization, it was assumed, would *always* lead to a decline of religion, at the levels both of individuals and of society. The hypothesis that modernity necessarily leads to a decline of religion is, in principle, 'value free', but in fact it is filled with a number of normative notions. Enlightenment thinkers and those who followed very often thought that the decline of religion would be 'A Good Thing' because it would do away with 'backward', 'superstitious' and/or 'reactionary' religious phenomena. However, with the exception of much of Western Europe, the secularization thesis has not come to pass. Today, with some exceptions, the world is as strongly religious as it ever was. The assumption that we would all soon live in a secularized world was false. This means that a body of literature written by historians and social scientists, labelled 'secularization theory', was, by and large, mistaken.

The question of what is the nature of this largely unexpected interposition of religion in politics has not only both troubled and puzzled many seeking to analyse the phenomenon but has also necessitated a rethinking of the secularization theory. But all who assess the situation bring their own perceptions and prejudices. Basically, however, views can be dichotomized thus: those who are not religious believers – like the current author – are charged with assigning every cause but the divine to religious movements and effects. On the other hand, those with religious faith perceive the hand of God behind the religious efflorescence. Unfortunately, there is no way of arriving at a satisfactory compromise on this issue between such implacably opposed world views.

But what can be agreed upon is that the historic decline in the social and political importance of religion in Western Europe is solidly grounded in mainstream social science. As Shupe (1990: 19) points out, 'the demystification of religion inherent in the classic secularization paradigm posits a gradual, persistent, unbroken erosion of religious influence in urban industrial societies'. Secularization is said to be a unidirectional process, whereby societies move from a sacred condition to successively areligious states. As a result, the sacred becomes socially and politically marginalized. The commanding figures of nineteenth-century social science – Durkheim, Weber, Marx – all maintained that secularization is an integral facet of modernization, a global trend. As modernization extended its grip, so the argument went, religion would be privatized everywhere. Consequently, it would lose its grip on culture, becoming a purely personal matter, no longer a collective force with significant mobilizing potential for social change. In short, secularization, as Donald Eugene Smith proclaimed in 1970, was 'the most fundamental structural and ideological change in the process of political development' (1970: 6), a one-way street whereby societies gradually move away from being focused around the sacred and a concern with the divine to a situation characterized by a significant diminution of religious power and authority.

But the secularization thesis was not wrong everywhere. Undoubtedly secularization has proceeded a long way in Western Europe. Falling income levels for mainline Churches, declining numbers and quality of religious professionals, and diminishing Church attendance collectively point to 'a process of decline in the *social* significance of religion' (Wilson 1992: 198, emphasis added). Nearly everywhere, institutional religion in Western Europe has lost most of the functions it once fulfilled for other social institutions. Once it provided legitimacy for secular authority in a number of ways. It not only endorsed public policy while sustaining with 'a battery of threats and blandishments the agencies of social control', but also claimed to be the only font of 'true' learning (Wilson 1992: 200). It was also largely responsible for socializing the young and sponsoring a range of recreational activities.

In much of Western Europe the old secularization thesis still seems to hold. Under the conditions prevailing, the hold of religion over society and many individuals has diminished; there has been an increase in the key indicators of secularization: on the level of expressed beliefs; on the level of Church-related behaviour such as attendance at services of worship, adherence to Church-dictated codes of personal behaviour on social issues of sexuality, reproduction and marriage; recruitment into the clergy, and so on. These phenomena have long been observed in the northern segment of the region, but over the last 30 years they have also been increasingly clear in the predominantly Catholic south. For example, both Italy and Spain have experienced rapid decline in Church-related religion, put down to the liberalizing effects of Vatican II by Catholic conservatives. However, the fact that there has also been a similar decline in orthodox Greece rather cuts the ground from under the conservatives' feet in this regard (Moore 1989).

But while such facts are not seriously in dispute, recent works on the sociology of religion concerned with several highly secularized societies in Europe – France, England and Scandinavia – point out that 'secularization' may not be the right term to apply to what has happened. There is overwhelming evidence of strongly surviving belief, most of it Christian or quasi-Christian, despite widespread alienation from mainline Churches. What seems to be happening is a shift in the institutional location of religion, rather than secularization *tout court*. Further, although societies may become secular individuals frequently do not. How to explain this seeming paradox? The point is that religious institutions may have lost power and influence in many Western European societies, but varying religious beliefs and practices continue to be important in the lives of millions of individuals, sometimes taking new institutional forms, sometimes leading to great explosions of religious fervour. Further, religiously identified institutions – like the Anglican and other mainline Churches in England – can play social or political roles even when declining numbers of people believe or practise the religion they represent.

Religious resistance to secularization

A point made earlier is that the conditions of post-modernism have helped to stimulate publicly oriented religious movements, including those which pursue a public agenda and are often in conflict with the State. Yet the example of Western Europe indicates that under some circumstances secularization *does* occur. What seems to be happening is that secularization proceeds *except* when religion finds or retains work to do other than relating people to the supernatural. In much of the world, it does. Religion normally seems to retain a high place in people's attentions and in their politics when it does something other than mediate between the individual and

God. In other words, as many of the case studies of this book have illustrated, religion normally shrinks in social significance during modernization except under two, highly important and consequential, sets of circumstances. First, when religion is a component of a group's *cultural defence* against unwelcome encroaching influences it will be of political salience. This occurs when a source – usually the State – promotes, or at least does not stand in the way of, either an alien religion or rampant secularism. But groups seeking to protect their culture negatively value such onslaughts because they are perceived to threaten group culture, identity and, hence, a group sense of worth. Examples discussed in this book include the Sikhs of India, galvanized by the re-emergence of Hindu chauvinism, religious Jews in Israel, Islamists in the Middle East and Islamic activists in Britain and France.

The second circumstance is where religion is also an aspect of group solidarity, utilized in its defence in the context of *cultural transition*. This occurs when a group's identity is threatened in the course of a major cultural transition, common during modernization. Examples discussed in the foregoing chapters include Christian fundamentalists in both Northern Ireland and the USA and Buddhist and Hindu activists in South-east Asia and India respectively. The rigours of cultural transition, where identity is seriously threatened, both underpin and galvanize such a religious reaction. There is also the effect of political crises, the importance of growing communications networks and the social upheavals and economic dislocations characteristic of the previously discussed 'post-modern condition'. In circumstances where the defence of culture and tradition are deemed highly important, religion may well furnish resources for asserting a group's claim to a sense of worth and to fight the perception that changes which seem to be occurring are not conducive to the long-term well-being and progress of the group. In sum, the key to understanding the contemporary socio-political role of religion is that it regularly furnishes the resources for groups to try to deal with the effects stemming either from the processes of modernization or the contradictions of post-modernity.

Many religious people have understood a link between modernity and secularity, and most have not liked what they see. Two reactions have been common: some, as already noted, have defined (post)-modernity as the enemy to be fought. Others – like some senior Catholics – seem to have believed modernity to be invincible; religious beliefs and practices would, of necessity, be forced to adapt. The global struggle with modernity in the Roman Catholic Church illustrates the difficulties of rejection and adaptation strategies. Following the Enlightenment and the multiple revolutions of late eighteenth and early nineteenth centuries, the Church's first response was to reject what was happening. In 1870, the first Vatican council (Vatican I) was organized at the time of Italy's unification when the Church rightly considered itself under threat from the forces of nationalism. The main task of Vatican I was both to proclaim papal infallibility and to urge that physical force should not be used within Vatican City by any organization (including the Italian State). It also suggested that henceforward religious and secular power should be separated in Italy. Vatican I also marked the emergence of the Roman Catholic Church as a transnational and international body with no overt interest in tandem with any government, while organizationally it confirmed the development of the

Church into a centralized, supranational body with a strongly hierarchical structure. At this time the Church had a transubstantiated form as a kind of State almost without physical substance, but significantly with an unparalleled international network of interests and influence.

Nearly a century later, in 1965, the second Vatican council (Vatican II) considerably modified the earlier rejectionist approach. The Church's declaration of religious freedom at Vatican II and the subsequent acceptance of the constitutional separation of Church and State in newly established democratic regimes in Southern Europe – Spain and Portugal in the early 1970s, and later throughout the Catholic world – offered confirmation of the 'providential' character of this modern structural trend, not only in Western Christendom but also in its former colonial outposts. Thus, over time, the Vatican was forced to adapt to what was happening outside of its control, in effect, to admit that the world was changing and that the Church must adapt.

Looking away from the Roman Catholic Church at the wider religious scene, it is clear that conservative and orthodox movements are on the rise in a large number of countries. These movements reject a deal with modernity as defined by progressive intellectuals. On the other hand, religious movements and institutions that have made the greatest efforts to conform to a perceived modernity are on the wane almost everywhere. In the USA and England, for example, this is exemplified by the decline of mainstream Protestantism and the corresponding rise of evangelicalism. It is widely assumed that the conservative thrust of the Roman Catholic Church under John Paul II from the early 1980s explains why it has not suffered the same fate as its mainline Protestant rivals. Rather, Catholicism enjoys growing numbers of converts and a renewed enthusiasm among native Catholics especially in non-Western countries. Other conservative religions have also done well. Following the collapse of the USSR there is a strong popular revival of the Orthodox Church in Russia while the last few years saw the emergence of Islamic groups and movements in its erstwhile Central Asian republics. There has also been an upsurge of conservative religious movements among other religious traditions, including Buddhism, Hinduism, Judaism and Sikhism. In sum, the success of conservative religious movements refutes the idea that modernization leads inevitably to secularization. At the very least one can say that, in the 1990s, counter-secularization is as important in the contemporary world as secularization.

Of course, it is possible to reject any number of modern ideas and values in theory. But to make this rejection stick in practice is more difficult. To accomplish such a goal to an ultimate degree – establishing a religious society or a theocracy – it would be necessary to take over a society and make your counter-modern religion obligatory for all. But this is a difficult task, as General Franco found in Spain when he tried it after the civil war; the Islamists of Iran and Sudan are currently trying to do the same but without much apparent success. It is so difficult because modernization not only has the effect of creating very heterogeneous societies but also leads to a huge increase in intercultural and international communications. Both developments favour religious pluralism and religious monopolies find it very difficult – perhaps impossible – to establish or re-establish their hegemony. Putative religious monopolists can alternatively seek to establish religious cultures in enclaves to keep at bay the influences of the outside world. But, as we saw in the case of American Protestant fundamentalists, such a project is immensely difficult to pursue to a satisfactory conclusion, not least because modern culture is an immensely powerful force that fails to recognize self-proclaimed religious entities and hence penetrates and changes them.

The only other tactic to maintain religious purity is to try to change the world. Then it is necessary to enter the secular world of politics to fight for power via one's chosen party or, alternatively, to lobby hard for the election of politicians who can be trusted to take fundamentalist concerns seriously. But such a strategy is also doomed to failure because in all societies there seems to be a relatively low limit to the numbers of people attracted to a religiously fundamentalist message, perhaps one fifth or a quarter of voting-age adults at the most. Why? Because fundamentalist regimes promise no fun! They are restrictive of personal freedoms and inhibit what many people – especially, and understandably, women – see as their right to self-development and personal progress. This is as true in the United States – as evidenced by the failure of Pat Buchanan to make inroads in the 1996 presidential campaign – as it is in Iran. In the latter the landslide presidential victory of the moderate Ayatollah Khatemi in May 1997 was judged by knowledgeable observers to be a 'sharp break with the harsher aspects of Islamic fundamentalism' (Evans 1997). It appears that Khatemi's victory was facilitated by the high level of support he attracted from those desiring as much change as possible, especially women, young people and the intelligentsia. These are groups widely judged not to have benefited during nearly 20 years of Islamic revolution. What they wanted was greater freedom of speech and an easing of the strict regulations governing most aspects of social life. Khatemi, they believed, was the man to deliver such an outcome. Interestingly, whereas in Iran – an Islamic State for nearly 20 years – it is the daughters of the professionals and the intelligentsia most keen to cast off their veils, in Egypt and Turkey it is their counterparts who seem most keen to put them on.

What this underlines is that Islamic conservatism means different things in various countries. Where there is a high degree of institutionalized religious conservatism, as in, say, Iran or Saudi Arabia, there is correspondingly little public discussion allowed. Consequently, opposition to the status quo can be expressed merely by adopting dress codes out of line with official preferences. Similarly, if a self-proclaimed modernizing regime deems Islamic dress to be unacceptable, then it is a badge of rebellion to wear it. But as one moves away from the Middle East, the heartland of Islam, the symbols of opposition and support for regimes take other forms. For example, in Indonesia, a country that wears its Muslim culture lightly, Islam is the vehicle of a powerful movement, *Nahdatul Ulama*, stridently pro-democracy and propluralism, opposed to the 30-plus years of *Golkhar* dominance. Put another way, when and where political circumstances allow it, there will be lively discussion about the relationship of Islam to various modern realities, even among individuals who are equally committed to the faith. But what is rarely on the agenda is the desirability of secularism. This is because in Islam secularism is believed to be incompatible with the religion's well-being.

However, it would be accurate to say that Islamist movements in the main have difficulties in coming to terms with key modern institutions like liberal democracy, religious pluralism and the market economy. But it would be a basic error to view the global Islamist upsurge as simply denoting a focus on political concerns. For these are movements – with an impressively wide geographical scope, affecting societies across thousands of kilometres from North Africa to South-east Asia – which also emphatically proclaim and seek to revive Muslims' *religious* commitments during an era activists regard as increasingly areligious. Moreover, Islam continues to gain new converts, notably in Sub-Saharan Africa where it is in direct competition with Christianity. It is also becoming increasingly visible in the burgeoning Muslim communities in Europe and, to a lesser extent, in North America. This high contemporary profile of Islam is not necessarily about winning political power alone, it is also widely concerned with the survival of Islamic beliefs in alien or modernizing societies. The same could be said of Hindu and Buddhist revivalist movements. The wider point is that they want to ensure not only that the young retain religious beliefs, but also that distinctive religiously oriented lifestyles endure in relation to moral codes governing everyday behaviour.

However, the election of Khatemi indicates that even in the closed society that is the Islamic republic of Iran, the pressures associated with (post)-modernity and its accompaniment, globalization, may be almost irresistible. But, to underline the point again, such a development does not automatically lead to secularization. Many religious communities have survived and flourished to the extent that they have *not* tried to adapt themselves to the perceived requirements of an increasingly secularized world. Religious movements – such as evangelical born-again Christianity or Islamism – with beliefs and practices 'dripping with "religious supernaturalism"' have good records of success (Berger 1997: 33). Such groups may or may not involve themselves in the secular world of politics – often at the corporate level they will not. But once again exceptions exist, as noted earlier in the case of Brazil where left wing evangelicals lobby and strive to keep welfarist issues on the political agenda and to seek the election of politicians to push through such policies.

While contemporary religious movements with an interest in socio-political issues display a number of common features across cultural boundaries, there are also wider differences not only *between* them but also *within* religious traditions more generally. But we should not be surprised by this. Throughout history, the world religions have functioned as 'terrains of meaning', subject to radically different interpretations and conflicts, often with profound social and political implications. Islam, Judaism, Hinduism, Christianity and Buddhism all have long traditions of reformers, populists and 'protestants', seeking to give the religion contemporary meaning and social salience. The post-modern era, rather than being dominated by fundamentalism alone, is a period of wider religious reinterpretation, spurred by changes both within individual countries and at the universal level, like globalization. What this points to is that those who neglect religion in their analyses of contemporary and comparative politics do so at their peril.

References

Abdurazakova, D. (1992) Black holes of Central Asia's history, *Central Asia Survey*, 11, 4, pp. 85–92.

Abramsky, S. (1996) Vote redneck, *The Observer, Life Magazine*, 27 October, pp. 16–19.

Africa Confidential (1992) Malawi: referring to the opposition, 6 November 1992, p. 7.

Africa Watch (1991) *Kenya. Taking Liberties*, New York: Africa Watch.

Aguilar, E., Sandoval, J., Steigenga, T. and Coleman, K. (1993) Protestantism in El Salvador: conventional wisdom versus survey evidence, *Latin American Research Review*, 28, 2, pp. 119–40.

Ahmed, A. (1992) *Postmodernism and Islam: Predicament and Promise*, London: Routledge.

Ahmed, I. (1996) Religious nationalism and Sikhism, in D. Westerlund (ed.) *Questioning the Secular State. The Worldwide Resurgence of Religion in Politics*, London: Hurst, pp. 259–83.

Akiner, S. (1989) Muslims of the USSR, in S. Mews (ed.) *Religion in Politics. A World Guide*, Harlow: Longman, pp. 281–5.

Aquaviva, S. (1979) *The Decline of the Sacred in Industrial Society*, Oxford: Blackwell.

Archbiship of Canterbury's Commission on Urban Priority Areas (1985) *Faith in the City*, London: Church House.

Asad, T. (1986) *The Idea of an Anthropology of Islam*, Washington DC: Center for Contemporary Arab Studies, Georgetown University, Occasional Papers.

Atkin, M. (1989) The survival of Islam in Soviet Tajikistan, *Middle East Journal*, 43, 4, pp. 605–18.

Auda, G. (1993) The Islamic movement and resource mobilization in Egypt: a political culture perspective, in L. Diamond (ed.) *Political Culture and Democracy in Developing Countries*, Boulder, CO: Lynne Rienner, pp. 379–407.

Aughey, A. (1990) Recent interpretations of Unionism, *Political Quarterly*, 61, 2, pp. 188–99.

Ayubi, N. (1991) *Political Islam. Religion and Politics in the Arab World*, London: Routledge.

Barrett, D. (1982) *World Christian Encyclopedia*, Nairobi: Oxford University Press.

Barylski, R. (1994) The Russian Federation and Eurasia's Islamic crescent, *Europe–Asia Studies*, 46, 3, pp. 389–416.

Bastian, J.-P. (1993) The metamorphosis of Latin American protestant groups: a sociohistorical perspective, *Latin American Research Review*, 28, 2, pp. 33–61.

Bayart, J.-F. (1993) *The State in Africa*, London: Longman.

Beeley, B. (1992) Islam as a global political force, in A. McGrew and P. Lewis (eds) *Global Politics. Globalization and the Nation State*, Oxford: Polity Press, pp. 293–311.

Bellah, R. (1964) Religious evolution, *American Sociological Review*, 29, pp. 358–74.

Bellah, R. (1965) *Religion and Progress in Modern Asia*, New York: Free Press.

Bellah, R. (1967) Civil religion in America, *Daedalus*, 96, pp. 1–21.

Bellah, R. (1975) *The Broken Covenant*, New York: Seabury.

Bellos, A. and White, M. (1997) Churches slate all parties, *The Guardian*, 9 April.

Benningsen, A. (1981) Islam in the Soviet Union, in P. Stoddart et al. (eds) *Change and the Muslim World*, Syracuse, NY: Syracuse University Press, pp. 119–38.

Benningsen, A. and Lemercier-Quelquejay, C. (1967) *Islam in the Soviet Union*, London: Pall Mall Press.

Berger, P. (1997) Against the current, *Prospect*, no. 17, pp. 32–36.

Bernal, V. (1994) Gender, culture and capitalism, *Comparative Studies in Society and History*, 36, 1, pp. 36–67.

Berryman, P. (1994) The coming of age of evangelical Protestantism, *NACLA Report on the Americas*, 26, 6, pp. 6–10.

Betto, F. (1983) *CEBs: Rumo a Nova Sociedade*, Sao Paulo, Brazil: Paulinas.

Bhatia, S. (1995) Bombay's McCarthyite terror, *The Observer*, 23 April.

Bhatia, S. (1996) A dark shadow descends on Israel, *The Observer*, 2 June.

Bidwas, P. (1991) The Sena VHP offensive. Disintegrative politics of identity, *The Times of India*, 25 October.

Bill, J. and Springborg, R. (1994) *Politics in the Middle East* (4th edn), New York: Harper Collins.

Black, I. (1996) The hard noes [sic] leader, *The Observer*, 2 June.

Black, J. K. (1993) Elections and other trivial pursuits: Latin America and the new world order, *Third World Quarterly*, 14, 3, pp. 545–54.

Boff, L. (1981) Theological characteristics of a grassroots Church, in S. Torres and J. Eagleson (eds) *The Challenge of Basic Christian Communities*, Maryknoll, NY; Orbis, pp. 25–43.

Bone, D. (1982) Islam in Malawi, *Journal of Religion in Africa*, 13, 2, pp. 126–38.

Boron, A. (1995) *State, Capitalism, and Democracy in Latin America*, London and Boulder, CO: Lynne Rienner.

Boudewijnse, B., Droogers, A. and Kamsteeg, F. (eds) (1991) *Algo más que opio: Una lectura antropológica del pentecostalismo latino-americano y caribeno*, San José, Costa Rica: Departamento Ecuménico de Investigaciones.

Boyle, P. (1992) Beyond self-protection to prophecy: the Catholic Church and political change in Zaire, *Africa Today*, 39, 3, pp. 49–66.

Bozarslan, H. (1989) Islam and the Turkish community in West Germany: Religion, identity and politics, *Contemporary European Affairs*, 2, 4, pp. 115–28.

Bratton, M. (1994) International versus domestic pressures for 'democratization' in Africa. Paper presented to conference: 'The End of the Cold War: Effects and Prospects for Asia and Africa', School of Oriental and African Studies, London, October.

Bromley, S. (1994) *Rethinking Middle East Politics*, Cambridge: Polity Press.

Bruce, S. (1988) *The Rise and Fall of the New Christian Right: Conservative Protestant Policies in America, 1978–88*, Oxford: Clarendon Press.

Bruce, S. (1990) Modernity and fundamentalism: the New Christian Right in America, *British Journal of Sociology*, 41, pp. 477–96.

Bruce, S. (1992) Introduction, in S. Bruce (ed.) *Religion and Modernization*, Oxford: Clarendon Press, pp. 1–7.

Bruce, S. (1993) Fundamentalism, ethnicity and enclave, in M. Marty and R. Scott Appleby (eds) *Fundamentalisms and the State. Remaking Polities, Economies, and Militance*, Chicago and London: University of Chicago Press, pp. 50–67.

Bruneau, T. (1974) *The Political Transformation of the Brazilian Catholic Church*, London: Cambridge University Press.

Bruneau, T. (1982) *The Church in Brazil*, Austin: University of Texas Press.

Bunting, M. (1996a) Church in a State, *The Guardian*, 15 February.

Bunting, M. (1996b) Shopping for God, *The Guardian*, 16 December.

Burdick, J. (1993) *Looking for God in Brazil: the Progressive Church in Urban Brazil's Religious Arena*, Berkeley: University of California Press.

Burdick, J. (1994) The progressive Catholic Church in Latin America: Giving voice or listening to voices?, *Latin American Research Review*, 29, 1, pp. 184–97.

Callaghy, T. (1993) Vision and politics in the transformation of the global political economy: lessons from the Second and Third Worlds, in R. Slater, B. Schutz and S. Dorr (eds) *Global Transformation and the Third World*, Boulder, CO: Lynne Rienner, pp. 161–258.

Caplan, L. (ed.) (1987) *Studies in Religious Fundamentalism*, Albany, NY: State University of New York.

Carnoy, M. (1984) *The State and Political Theory*, Princeton, NJ: Princeton University Press.

Casanova, J. (1994) *Public Religions in the Modern World*, Chicago and London: University of Chicago Press.

Chai-Anan, Samudavanija (1993) The new military and democracy in Thailand, in L. Diamond (ed.) *Political Culture and Democracy in Developing Countries*, Boulder, CO: Lynne Rienner, pp. 269–94.

Chandler, D. (1992) *Brother Number One: A Political Biography of Pol Pot*, Boulder, CO: Westview Press.

Chilton, P. (1995) Mechanics of change: social movements, transnational coalitions, and the transformation processes in Eastern Europe, in T. Risse-Kappen (ed.) *Bringing Transnational Relations Back In*, Cambridge: Cambridge University Press, pp. 189–226.

Chiriyankandath, J. (1994) The politics of religious identity: a comparison of Hindu nationalism and Sudanese Islamism, *Journal of Commonwealth and Comparative Politics*, 32, 1, pp. 31–53.

Chiriyankandath, J. (1995) Hindu nationalism and Indian regional political culture: a study of Kerala. Paper prepared for the workshop: 'Political Culture and Religion in the Third World', European Consortium for Political Research Joint Sessions of Workshops, Bordeaux, April–May 1995.

Chiriyankandath, J. (1996a) The 1996 Indian general election, London: The Royal Institute of International Affairs, Briefing Paper, No. 31.

Chiriyankandath, J. (1996b) Hindu nationalism and regional political culture in India: a study of Kerala, *Nationalism and Ethnic Politics*, 2, 1, pp. 44–66.

Chrypinski, V. C. (1989) Poland, in S. Mews (ed.) *Religion in Politics. A World Guide*, Harlow: Longman, pp. 218–27.

Clapham, C. (1989) Ethiopia, in S. Mews (ed.) *Religion in Politics. A World Guide*, Longman: London, p. 73.

Clark, F. (1992) Religion and State in Europe, in J. Nielsen (ed.) *Religion and Citizenship in Europe and the Arab World*, London: Grey Seal Books, pp. 39–55.

Cleary, E. (1985) *Crisis and Change: The Church in Latin America Today*, Maryknoll, NY: Orbis.

Clévenot, M. (1987) *L'Etat des Religions dans le Monde*, Paris: La Decouverte/Le Cerf.

Coleman, S. (1996) Conservative Protestantism, politics and civil religion in the United States, in D. Westerlund (ed.) *Questioning the Secular State. The Worldwide Resurgence of Religion in Politics*, London: Hurst, pp. 24–47.

Colombo, F. (1984) *God in America. Religion and Politics in the United States*, New York: Columbia University Press.

Comaroff, J. (1994) Epilogue. Defying disenchantment. Reflections on ritual, power, and history, in C. Keyes, L. Kendall and H. Hardacre, (eds) *Asian Visions of Authority. Religion and the Modern States of East and South-east Asia*, Honolulu: University of Hawaii Press, pp. 301–14.

Copley, A. (1993) Indian secularism reconsidered: from Gandhi to Ayodhya, *Contemporary South Asia*, 2, 1, pp. 47–65.

Coulon, C. (1983) *Les Musulmans et le Pouvoir en Afrique Noire*, Paris: Karthala.

Cox, H. (1984) *Religion in the Secular City. Toward a Postmodern Theology*, New York: Simon and Schuster.

Crahan, M. (1990) Religion, revolution, and counter-revolution: the role of the religious right in Central America. Paper presented at the Annual Meeting of the Association for the Sociology of Religion, Washington, D.C., 9–11 August.

Cruise O'Brien, D. (1986) Wails and whispers: the people's voice in West African Muslim politics, in P. Chabal (ed.) *Political Domination in Africa*, Cambridge: Cambridge University Press, pp. 71–84.

D'Antonio, M. (1990) *Fall from Grace. The Failed Crusade of the Christian Right*, London: Andre Deutsch.

Dabashi, H. (1987) Symbiosis of religious and political authorities in Islam, in T. Robbins and R. Robertson (eds) *Church–State Relations*, New Brunswick, NJ and London: Transaction Books, pp. 183–203.

Daudelin, J. (1992) Corporatist intermediation in the religious field: Protestants and the State in revolutionary Nicaragua. Paper presented at the Annual Meeting of the Canadian Association of Latin American and Caribbean Studies, Ottawa, Canada, 22–25 October.

Davie, G. (1994) Unity in diversity. Religion and modernity in Western Europe, in J. Fulton and P. Gee (eds) *Religion in Contemporary Europe*, Lewiston, NY: Edwin Mellen, pp. 52–65.

De Gruchy, J. (1995) *Christianity and Democracy. A Theology For a Just World Order*, Cambridge: Cambridge University Press.

Deeb, M.-J. (1989a) Egypt, in S. Mews (ed.) *Religion in Politics. A World Guide*, Harlow: Longman, pp. 62–66.

Deeb, M.-J. (1989b) Algeria, in S. Mews (ed.) *Religion in Politics. A World Guide*, Harlow: Longman, pp. 6–8.

Deiros, P. (1991) Protestant fundamentalism in Latin America, in M. Marty and R. Scott Appleby (eds) *Fundamentalisms Observed*, Chicago: University of Chicago Press, pp. 142–96.

Della Cava, R. (1989) The 'People's Church', the Vatican, and *abertura*, in A. Stepan (ed.) *Democratizing Brazil*, New York: Oxford University Press, pp. 143–67.

Demerath III, N. (1991) Religious capital and capital religions: cross-cultural and non-legal factors in the separation of Church and State, *Daedalus*, 120, 3, pp. 21–40.

Diamond, L. (1993) The globalization of democracy, in R. Slater, B. Schutz and S. Dorr (eds) *Global Transformation and the Third World*, Boulder, CO: Lynne Rienner, pp. 31–70.

Dieckhoff, A. (1991) The impact of Jewish religious parties in the State of Israel. Paper prepared for the workshop: 'Religion and International Politics', European Consortium for Political Research Joint Sessions of Workshops, University of Essex, March 1991.

Dodd, V. (1996) Jews fear rise of the Muslim 'underground', *The Observer*, 18 February.

Dorr, S. (1993) Democratization in the Middle East, in R. Slater, B. Schutz and S. Dorr (eds) *Global Transformation and the Third World*, Boulder, CO: Lynne Rienner, pp. 131–57.

Duke, J. and Johnson, B. (1989) Religious transformation and social conditions: a macrosociological analysis, in W. Swatos, Jr. (ed.) *Religious Politics in Global and Comparative Perspective*, New York: Greenwood Press, pp. 75–110.

Durning, A. (1989) *Action at the Grassroots*, Washington, DC: Worldwatch Institute, Worldwatch Papers no. 88.

Earnshaw, G. (1996) Xinjiang bosses step up fight against 'splittists', *The Guardian*, 6 June.

Edwards, D. (1990) *Christians in a New Europe*, London: Routledge.

Eisenstadt, S. N. (1993) Religion and the civilizational dimensions of politics, in S. A. Arjomand (ed.) *The Political Dimensions of Religion*, Albany, NY: State University of New York Press, pp. 13–42.

Ellis, J. (1990) Hierarchs and dissidents: conflict over the future of the Russian Orthodox Church, *Religion in Communist Lands*, 18, 4, pp. 307–18.

Engels, D. and Marks, S. (eds) (1994) *Contesting Colonial Hegemony. State and Society in Africa and India*, London: German Historical Institute/British Academic Press.

Etienne, B. (1989) Islamic Associations and Europe, *Contemporary European Affairs*, 2, 4, pp. 29–44.

Etienne, B. and Tozy, M. (1981) Le glissement des obligations islamiques vers le phenomene associatif à Casablanca, in Centre de Recherches et d'Etudes sur les Sociétés Méditerranénnes, *Le Maghreb Musulman en 1979*, Paris: Centre de Recherches et d'Etudes sur les Sociétés Méditerranénnes, pp. 235–51.

Evans, K. (1997) New era for Iran as moderate triumphs, *The Observer*, 25 May.

Featherstone, M. (1988) In pursuit of the post-modern. An introduction, in M. Featherstone (ed.) *Theory, Culture and Society*, special issue, 5, 2/3, pp. 195–216.

Fine, R. (1992) Civil society and the politics of transition in South Africa, *Review of African Political Economy*, 55, pp. 71–83.

Fletcher, M. (1994) Mullah of Chicago's Mean Streets, *The Guardian*, 17 February.

Flint, J. (1993) Sudan cracks down on Muslim rivals, *The Guardian*, 11 June.

Fogarty, M. (1992) The Churches and public policy in Britain, *Political Quarterly*, 63, 3, pp. 301–16.

Frankland, M. (1992) Wretched Tajiks turn to Iran for inspiration, *The Observer*, 10 May.

Freedland, J. (1996) Cardinals lambast Clinton on abortion, *The Guardian*, 18 April.

Freston, P. (1996) Evangelicalism and politics: a comparison between Africa and Latin America. Paper presented at the African Studies Association of the UK biennial conference, University of Bristol, 9–11 September.

Fukuyama, F. (1992) *The End of History and the Last Man*, London: Penguin.

Furedi, F. (1994) *Colonial Wars and the Politics of Third World Nationalism*, London: I. B. Tauris.

Gaffney, P. (1994) *The Prophet's Pulpit. Islamic Preaching in Contemporary Egypt*, Berkeley: University of California Press.

Gardell, M. (1996) Behold I make all things new! Black militant Islam and the American apocalypse, in D. Westerlund (ed.) *Questioning the Secular State. The Worldwide Resurgence of Religion in Politics*, London: Hurst, pp. 48–74.

Garrard-Burnett, V. (1996) Resacralization of the profane. Government, religion, and ethnicity in modern Guatemala, in D. Westerlund (ed.) *Questioning the Secular State. The Worldwide Resurgence of Religion in Politics*, London: Hurst, pp. 96–116.

Gharabaghi, K. (1994) Development strategies for Central Asia in the 1990s: in search of alternatives, *Third World Quarterly*, 15, 1, pp. 103–119.

Gifford, P. (1992) Bishops for Reform, *The Tablet*, 30 May, pp. 672–3.

Gifford, P. (1994) Some recent developments in African Christianity, *African Affairs*, 93, 373, pp. 513–34.

Gitari, D. (1988) The Church's witness to the living God: seeking just political, social and economic structures in contemporary Africa, *Transformation*, 5, 2, pp. 13–20.

Gittings, J. (1996) Tibet faces an atheist crusade, *The Guardian*, 26 October.

Glasman, M. (1996) *Unnecessary Suffering. Managing Market Utopia*, London: Verso.

Gooch, A. (1996) Spanish Church denies leading flock to polls, *The Guardian*, 22 February.

Gott, R. (1973) *Rural Guerrillas in Latin America*, Harmondsworth: Penguin.

Goulborne, H. and Joly, D. (1989) Religion and the Asian and Caribbean Minorities in Britain, *Contemporary European Affairs*, 2, 4, pp. 77–98.

Gravers, M. (1996) Questioning autocracy in Burma, in D. Westerlund (ed.) *Questioning the Secular State. The Worldwide Resurgence of Religion in Politics*, London: Hurst, pp. 297–322.

Gray, J. (1996) If the fez fits, *The Guardian*, 8 January.

Guardian (1995) Private morals, 27 March.

Guardian (1996) Egyptian Islamists, 17 May.

Günes-Ayata, A. (1994) Roots and trends of clientelism in Turkey, in L. Roniger and A. Günes-Ayata (eds) *Democracy, Clientelism and Civil Society*, Boulder, CO and London: Lynne Rienner.

Gustafsson, G. (1989) Denmark, in S. Mews (ed.) *Religion in Politics. A World Guide*, Harlow: Longman, p. 59.

Gutiérrez, G. (1981) The irruption of the poor in Latin America and the Christian Communities of the common people, in S. Torres and J. Eagleson (eds) *The Challenge of Basic Christian Communities*, Maryknoll, NY: Orbis, pp. 54–78.

Gyimah-Boadi, E. (1994) Associational life, civil society, and democratization in Ghana, in J. Harbeson, D. Rothchild and N. Chazan (eds) *Civil Society and the State in Africa*, Boulder, CO and London: Lynne Rienner.

Hackel, S. (1989) Union of Soviet Socialist Republics, in S. Mews (ed.) *Religion in Politics. A World Guide*, Harlow: Longman, pp. 270–9.

Haddad, Y. (1985) Islam, women and revolution in twentieth century Arab thought, in Y. Haddad and E. Findly (eds) *Women, Religion and Social Change*, Albany, NY: State University of New York, pp. 275–306.

Hadden, J. (1989) Religious broadcasting and the mobilization of the New Christian Right, in J. Hadden and A. Shupe (eds) *Secularization and Fundamentalism Reconsidered*, New York: Paragon House, pp. 236–53.

Hallencreutz, C. and Westerlund, D. (1996) Anti-secularist policies of religion, in D. Westerlund (ed.) *Questioning the Secular State. The Worldwide Resurgence of Religion in Politics*, London: Hurst, pp. 1–23.

Hansen, T. Blom (1995) Democratisation, mass-politics and Hindu identity: the communalisation of Bombay. Paper prepared for the workshop: 'Political Culture and Religion in the Third World', European Consortium for Political Research Joint Sessions of Workshops, Bordeaux, April–May 1995.

Harris, I., Mews, S., Morris, P. and Shepherd, J. (1992) *Contemporary Religions: A World Guide*, Harlow: Longman.

Hastings, A. (1979) *A History of African Christianity, 1950–75*, Cambridge: Cambridge University Press.

Haynes, J. (1993) *Religion in Third World Politics*, Buckingham: Open University Press.

Haynes, J. (1995) *Religion, Fundamentalism and Identity: A Global Perspective*, Discussion Paper no. 65, Geneva, United Nations Research Institute for Social Development.

Haynes, J. (1996a) *Religion and Politics in Africa*, London: Zed Books.

Haynes, J. (1996b) *Third World Politics. A Concise Introduction*, Oxford: Blackwell.

Hearst, D. (1996) Orthodoxy raises barriers, *The Guardian*, 16 December.

Hearst, D. (1997) Tajik leader survives grenade that kills two, *The Guardian*, 1 May.

Hellman, E. (1996) Dynamic Hinduism: towards a new Hindu nation, in D. Westerlund (ed.) *Questioning the Secular State. The Worldwide Resurgence of Religion in Politics*, London: Hurst, pp. 237–58.

Helweg, R. (1989) Sikh politics in India: the emigrant factor, in N. Barrier and V. Dusenbery (eds) *The Sikh Diaspora: Migration and the Experience Beyond Punjab*, Delhi: Chanakya Publications, pp. 301–27.

Hertzke, A. (1989) United States of America, in S. Mews (ed.) *Religion in Politics. A World Guide*, Harlow: Longman, pp. 298–317.

Hewison, K. (1993) Of regimes, states and pluralities: Thai politics enters the 1990s, in K. Hewison, R. Robison and G. Rodan (eds) *South-east Asia in the 1990s*, St Leonards: Allen and Unwin, pp. 161–73.

Hiro, D. (1993) Islamist strengths and weaknesses in Central Asia, *Middle East International*, 443, 5 February, pp. 20–3.

Hooper, J. (1996a) John Paul's critical mass, *The Observer*, 6 April.

Hooper, J. (1996b) Turkey's new beginning turns into a false dawn, *The Guardian*, 7 August.

Hunter, A. (1989) Cambodia, in S. Mews (ed.) *Religion in Politics. A World Guide*, Harlow: Longman, p. 34.

Hunter, J. D. (1987) Religious elites in advanced industrial society, *Contemporary Studies in Society and History*, 29, 2, pp. 360–74.

Huntington, S. (1991) *The Third Wave. Democratization in the Late Twentieth Century*, Norman: University of Oklahoma Press.

Huntington, S. (1993) The clash of civilisations?, *Foreign Affairs*, 72, 3, pp. 22–49.

Husain, M. Z. (1995) *Global Islamic Politics*, New York: HarperCollins.

Hyman, A. (1993) Moving out of Moscow's orbit: the outlook for Central Asia, *International Affairs*, 69, 2, pp. 288–304.

Jacobs, L. (1992) Contemporary Judaism, in I. Harris, S. Mews, P. Morris and J. Shepherd (eds) *Contemporary Religions. A World Guide*, Harlow: Longman, pp. 31–8.

Jaffrelot, C. (1995) The Vishva Hindu Parishad. Structures and Strategies. Paper prepared for the workshop: 'Political Culture and Religion in the Third World', European Consortium for Political Research Joint Sessions of Workshops, Bordeaux, April–May 1995.

James, H. (1991) The German revolution and the legacy of German nationalism, in G. L. Geipel (ed.) *The Future of Germany*, Indianapolis: Hudson Institute, pp. 106–25.

Jenkins, K. (1991) Christian Churches in Africa: agents of change or supporters of the status quo?, *Geonomics*, 3, 5, pp. 6–10.

Johnson, W. (1988) Theravada Buddhism in South-east Asia, in S. Sutherland, L. Houlden, P. Clarke and F. Hardy (eds) *The World's Religions*, London: Routledge, pp. 726–38.

Johnston, H. (1992) Religious nationalism: six propositions from Eastern Europe and the former Soviet Union, in B. Misztal and A. Shupe (eds) *Religion and Politics in Comparative Perspective*, Westport, CT and London: Praeger, pp. 67–78.

Johnston, H. (1993) Religio-nationalist subcultures under the communists: comparisons from the Baltics, Transcaucasia and Ukraine, *Sociology of Religion*, 54, 3, pp. 237–55.

Joseph, R. (1993) The Christian Churches and democracy in contemporary Africa, in J. Witte, Jr. (ed.) *Christianity and Democracy in Global Context*, Boulder, CO: Westview, pp. 231–47.

Joshi, R. (1970) The Shiv Sena: a movement in search of legitimacy, *Asian Survey*, 10, 11, pp. 967–78.

Jowitt, K. (1993) A world without Leninism, in R. Slater, B. Schutz and S. Dorr (eds) *Global Transformation and the Third World*, Boulder, CO: Lynne Rienner, pp. 9–27.

Juergensmeyer, M. (1989) India, in S. Mews (ed.) *Religion in Politics. A World Guide*, Longman: Harlow, pp. 98–107.

Juergensmeyer, M. (1993) *The New Cold War? Religious Nationalism Confronts the Secular State*, Berkeley and London: University of California Press.

Juree, Namisirichai and Vicharat Vichit-Vadakan (1979) American values and research on Thailand, in C. Neher (ed.) *Modern Thai Politics* (2nd edn), Cambridge MA: Schenkman, pp. 419–35.

Kamrava, M. (1993) *Politics and Society in the Third World*, London: Routledge.

Kane, O. (1990) Les mouvements religieux et le champ politique au Nigeria septentrional, *Islam et Societés au Sud du Sahara*, 4, pp. 7–24.

Keddie, N. (1995) *Iran and the Muslim World*, London: Macmillan.

Kelley, D. (1986) *Why Conservative Churches are Growing: a Study in Sociology of Religion*, New York: Harper and Row.

Kelley, M. (1987) *A State in Disarray. Conditions of Chad's Survival*, Boulder, CO: Westview.

Kepel, G. (1994) *The Revenge of God*, Cambridge: Polity.

Keyes, C. (1989) Buddhist politics and their revolutionary origins in Thailand, *International Political Science Review*, 10, 2, pp. 121–42.

Keyes, C. (1994) Communist revolution and the Buddhist past in Cambodia, in C. Keyes, L. Kendall and H. Hardacre (eds) *Asian Visions of Authority. Religion and the Modern States of East and South-east Asia*, Honolulu: University of Hawaii Press, pp. 43–73.

Keyes, C., Kendall, L. and Hardacre, H. (1994) Introduction. Contested visions of community in East and South-east Asia, in Keyes, C. *et al.* (eds) *Asian Visions of Authority. Religion and the Modern States of East and South-east Asia*, Honolulu: University of Hawaii Press, pp. 1–16.

Klaiber, J. (1992) The Church in Peru: between terrorism and conservative restraint, in E. Cleary and H. Stewart–Gambino (eds) *Conflict and Competition: The Latin American Church in a Changing Environment*, Boulder, CO: Lynne Rienner, pp. 87–103.

Korolov, M. (1994) Religious warriors ready to avenge human rights abuses, *The Guardian*, 7 June.

Lalive d'Epinay, C. (1969) *Haven of the Masses*, London: Lutterworth Press.

Lapidus, I. (1988) *A History of Islamic Societies*, Cambridge: Cambridge University Press.

Lease, G. (1993) Delusion and illusion, false hopes and failed dreams: Religion, the Churches and East Germany's 1989 'November revolution', in L. Martin (ed.) *Religious Transformations and Socio-Political Change. Eastern Europe and Latin America*, Berlin and New York: Mouton de Gruyter, pp. 161–76.

Lehmann, D. (1994) God's own poor, *The Guardian*, 26 July.

Lernoux, P. (1982) *Cry of the People*, New York: Penguin.

Lernoux, P. (1989) *People of God. The Struggle for World Catholicism*, New York: Viking.

Levine, D. (1990) The Catholic Church and politics in Latin America, in D. Keogh (ed.) *Church and Politics in Latin America*, London: Macmillan, pp. 25–48.

Lewis, H. D. and Slater, R. L. (1969) *The Study of Religions*, Harmondsworth: Penguin.

Liebman, C. and Eliezer, D.-Y. (1983) *Civil Religion in Israel*, Berkeley: University of California Press.

Lima, L. Gonzaga de Souza (1979) *Evoluço Política dos Católicos e da Igreja no Brasil*, Petrópolis, Brazil: Vozes.

Lincoln, C. E. (1973) *The Black Muslims in America*, Boston: Beacon Press.

Ling, T. (1993) Introduction, in T. Ling (ed.) *Buddhist Trends in South-east Asia*, Singapore: Institute of South-east Asian Studies, pp. 1–6.

Luckmann, T. (1969) The decline of Church-oriented religion, in R. Robertson (ed.) *The Sociology of Religion*, Baltimore, MD: Penguin, pp. 141–51.

Luneau, R. (1987) *Laisse Aller mon Peuple! Eglises Africaines au-delà des Modèles?*, Paris: Karthala.

Lustick, I. (1993) Jewish Fundamentalism and the Israeli–Palestinian impasse, in L. Silberstein (ed.) *Jewish Fundamentalism in Comparative Perspective. Religion, Ideology and the Crisis of Modernity*, New York: New York University Press, pp. 104–16.

Lyotard, J.-F. (1979) *The Post-Modern Condition: a Report on Knowledge*, Manchester: Manchester University Press.

MacGaffey, J. (1991) *The Real Economy of Zaire*, London/Philadelphia: James Currey/ University of Pennsylvania Press.

Madan, T. (1987) Secularism in its place, *The Journal of Asian Studies*, 46, 4, pp. 740–53.

Madeley, J. (1991) Politics and religion in Western Europe, in G. Moyser (ed.) *Religion and Politics in the Modern World*, London: Routledge, pp. 28–66.

Mainwaring, S. (1986) *The Catholic Church and Politics in Brazil, 1916–85*, Stanford, CA: Stanford University Press.

Mamiya, L. (1982) From Black Muslim to Bilalian. The evolution of a movement, *Journal of the Scientific Study of Religion*, 2, 6, pp. 138–51.

Martin, D. (1978) *A General Theory of Secularization*, Oxford: Blackwell.

Martin, D. (1990) *Tongues of Fire. The Explosion of Protestantism in Latin America*, Oxford: Blackwell.

Martin, D. (1994) Religion in contemporary Europe, in J. Fulton and P. Gee (eds) *Religion in Contemporary Europe*, Lewiston, NY: Edwin Mellen, pp. 1–16.

Marty, M. and Scott Appleby, R. (1993) Introduction, in M. Marty and R. Scott Appleby (eds) *Fundamentalism and the State. Remaking Polities, Economies, and Militance*, Chicago, University of Chicago Press, pp. 1–9.

Matthews, B. (1993) Buddhism under a military regime. The iron heel in Burma, *Asian Survey*, 33, 4, pp. 408–23.

McCargo, D. (1992) The Political Ramifications of the 1989 'Santi Asoke' Case in Thailand. Paper presented at the Annual Conference of the Association of South-east Asian Studies, School of Oriental and African Studies, University of London, 8–10 April.

McCargo, D. (in preparation) The politics of Buddhism in South-east Asia, in J. Haynes (ed.) *Religion, Globalization and Political Culture in the Third World*, London: Macmillan.

McCrystal, C. (1996) Orange flames of bigotry, *The Observer*, 8 December.

McEwan, D. (1989) Germany, Federal republic of, in S. Mews (ed.) *Religion in Politics. A World Guide*, Harlow: Longman, pp. 83–6.

McGreal, C. (1996) Racist leader plans SA trip, *The Guardian*, 20 January.

Medhurst, K. (1981) Religion and politics. A typology, *Scottish Journal of Religious Studies*, 2, 2, pp. 115–34.

Medhurst, K. (1989) Chile, in S. Mews (ed.) *Religion in Politics. A World Guide*, Harlow: Longman, pp. 39–43.

Medhurst, K. (1991) Politics and religion in Latin America, in G. Moyser (ed.) *Politics and Religion in the Modern World,* London: Routledge, pp. 189–219.

Meek, J. (1995) Islamic Russia forms own party, *The Guardian*, 2 September.

Meek, J. (1996) Orthodox schism looms, *The Guardian*, 5 March.

Mews, S. (1989) England, in S. Mews (ed.) *Religion in Politics. A World Guide*, Harlow: Longman, pp. 286–92.

Michel, P. (1991) *Politics and Religion in Eastern Europe*, Oxford: Polity.

Michel, P. (1994) Religion and democracy in Central Eastern Europe, in J. Fulton and P. Gee (eds) *Religion in Contemporary Europe*, Lewiston, NY: Edwin Mellen, pp. 34–42.

Mickulsky, D. (1993) Muslim fundamentalism in Soviet Central Asia. A social perspective, in L. Martin (ed.) *Religious Transformations and Socio-Political Change. Eastern Europe and Latin America*, Berlin and New York: Mouton de Gruyter, pp. 141–8.

Migranyan, V. (1992) Migranyan looks at ex-Soviet republics, future, *Current Digest of the Post-Soviet Press*, 43, pp. 10–14.

Miles, W. (1996) Political para-theology: rethinking religion, politics and democracy, *Third World Quarterly*, 17, 3, pp. 525–35.

Mitra, S. K. (1991) Desecularising the State: religion and politics in India after independence, *Comparative Studies in Society and History*, 33, 4, pp. 755–77.

Moore, P. (1989) Greece, in S. Mews (ed.) *Religion in Politics. A World Guide*, Harlow: Longman, p. 88.

Moran, E. and Schlemmer, L. (1984) *Faith for the Faithful?*, Durban, South Africa: Centre for Applied Social Studies.

Morris, P. (1989) Israel, in S. Mews (ed.) *Religion in Politics. A World Guide,* Harlow: Longman, pp. 123–37.

Moyser, G. (1991) Politics and religion in the modern world: an overview, in G. Moyser (ed.) *Politics and Religion in the Modern World*, London: Routledge, pp. 1–27.

Mushaben, J. C. (1983) Cycles of peace protest in West Germany: Experiences in three decades. Paper presented at the Annual Meeting of the American Sociological Association, Detroit, September.

Narayan, N. (1996) Muslims set schools spiritual test, *The Observer*, 25 February.

Naumkin, V. (1992) Islam in the states of the former USSR, *The Annals of the American Academy of Political and Social Science*, 524, pp. 131–42.

Nielsen, J. (1992) Muslims, Christians and loyalties in the nation-State, in J. Nielsen (ed.) *Religion and Citizenship in Europe and the Arab World*, London: Grey Seal Books, pp. 1–18.

Neuhaus, J. (1984) *The Naked Public Square: Religion and Democracy in America*, Grand Rapids, MI: Eerdmans.

Nonneman, G. (1996) Muslim communities in post-Cold War Europe: themes and puzzles, in I. Hampsher-Monk and J. Stanyer (eds) *Contemporary Political Studies 1996, Volume One. Proceedings of the Annual Conference of the Political Studies Association held at Glasgow, 10–12 April, 1996*, pp. 381–94.

Nuttall, C. (1997) Military rattles Turkey's Islamists, *The Guardian*, 28 April.

Nyang, S. (1988) Islam in North America, in S. Sutherland, L. Houlden, P. Clarke and F. Hardy (eds) *The World's Religions*, London: Routledge, pp. 520–9.

O'Connor, R. (1993) Interpreting Thai religious change: temples, sangha reform and social change, *Journal of South-east Asian Studies*, 24, 2, pp. 330–9.

O'Donnell, G. (1973) *Modernization and Bureaucratic Authoritarianism*, Berkeley: Institute of International Studies.

Okullu, J. (1978) Church–State relations: the African situation, in World Council of Churches, *Church and State. Opening a New Ecumenical Discussion*, Geneva: World Council of Churches, pp. 79–89.

Olcott, M. B. (1990) Soviet Central Asia: does Moscow fear Iranian influence?, in J. Esposito (ed.) *The Iranian Revolution: Its Global Impact*, Miami: Florida International University Press, pp. 205–225.

Olcott, M. B. (1992) Central Asia's post-empire politics, *Orbis*, Spring, pp. 253–68.

Oosthuizen, G. (1985) The African independent Churches centenary, *Africa Insight*, 15, 2, pp. 70–80.

O'Shaughnessy, L. (1990) What do the evangelicals want?, in E. Sahliyeh (ed.) *Religious Resurgence and Politics in the Contemporary World*, Albany, NY: State University of New York Press, pp. 81–105.

Owen, R. (1992) *State, Power and Politics in the Making of the Modern Middle East*, London: Routledge.

Oz. A. (1996) A fantasy returns, *The Observer*, 2 June.

Özbudun, E. (1993) State elites and democratic political culture in Turkey, in L. Diamond (ed.) *Political Culture and Democracy in Developing Countries*, Boulder, CO and London: Lynne Rienner, pp. 247–68.

Papousek, D. (1993) John Paul II and Mikhail Gorbachev: the process of globalization in multidimensional comparison, in L. Martin (ed.) *Religious Transformations and Socio-Political Change. Eastern Europe and Latin America*, Berlin and New York: Mouton de Gruyter, pp. 97–108.

Parrinder, G. (1977) *Comparative Religion*, London: Sheldon Press.

Peterson, A. (1996) Religion and society in Latin America: ambivalence and advances, *Latin American Research Review*, 31, 2, pp. 236–51.

Phillips, H. (1979) Some premises of American scholarship on Thailand, in C. Neher (ed.) *Modern Thai Politics* (2nd edn), Cambridge, MA: Schenkman, pp. 436–56.

Philps, A. (1997) Bible-burning cloud over Russian freedom, *Daily Telegraph*, 3 March.

Pieterse, J. (1992) Christianity, politics and Gramscism of the right: introduction, in J. Pieterse (ed.) *Christianity and Hegemony. Religion and Politics on the Frontiers of Social Change*, Oxford: Berg, pp. 1–31.

Piscatori, J. (1986) *Islam in a World of Nation-States*, Cambridge: Cambridge University Press.

Poliakov, S. (1992) *Religion and Tradition in Central Asia*, Armonk, NY: M. E. Sharpe.

Prins, G. (ed.) (1990) *Spring in Winter. The 1989 Revolutions*, Manchester: Manchester University Press.

Pugh, D. (1994) Militants claim responsibility for attack on train in Egypt, *The Guardian*, 21 February.

Ram-Prasad, C. (1993) Hindutva ideology: extracting the fundamentals, *Contemporary South Asia*, 2, 3, pp. 285–309.

Ramet, S. P. (1991) Politics and religion in Eastern Europe and the Soviet Union, in G. Moyser (ed.) *Politics and Religion in the Modern World*, London: Routledge, pp. 67–96.

Ramet, S. P. (1995) Spheres of religio-political interaction: Social order, nationalism, and gender relations, in S. P. Ramet (ed.) *Render Unto Caesar. The Religious Sphere in World Politics*, Lanham, MD: The American University Press, pp. 51–70.

Ranger, T. and Vaughan, O. (1993) Postscript, in T. Ranger and O. Vaughan (eds) *Legitimacy and the State in Twentieth Century Africa*, Basingstoke: Macmillan, pp. 255–61.

Ray, A. (1996) Religion and politics in South Asia, *Asian Affairs*, 1, 1, pp. 9–12.

Reid, M. (1990) Centre-right ahead in Guatemala, *The Guardian*, 13 December.

Robbins, T. and Anthony, D. (eds) (1982) *In God We Trust: New Patterns of Religious Pluralism in America*, New Brunswick, NJ: Transaction Books.

Roberts, B. (1968) Protestant groups and coping with urban life in Guatemala City, *American Journal of Sociology*, 73, pp. 753–67.

Roberts, H. (1991) A trial of strength: Algerian Islamism, in J. Piscatori (ed.) *Islamic Fundamentalisms and the Gulf Crisis*, Cambridge: Cambridge University Press, pp. 131–54.

Roberts, H. (1992) The Algerian State and the challenge of democracy, *Government and Opposition*, 27, 4, pp. 433–54.

Rocha, J. (1991) Catholicism falls from grace as Indians seek alternative salvation, *The Guardian*, 24 April.

Rostas, S. and Droogers, A. (eds) (1993) *The Popular Use of Popular Religion in Latin America*, Amsterdam: Centro de Estudios y Documentacion Latinoamericanos.

Rudolph, S. and Piscatori, J. (eds) (1997) *Transnational Religion and Fading States*, Boulder, CO: Westview.

Rueschemeyer, D., Stephens, E. and Stephens, J. (1992) *Capitalist Development and Democracy*, Cambridge: Polity.

Rugman, J. (1994a) Turks fear big shift to Islam, *The Guardian*, 21 February.

Rugman, J. (1994b) City-dwellers of Turkey choose Islamist mayors, *The Guardian*, 30 March.

Rugman, J. (1994c) Muslim radicals challenge nation's secular, European self-image, *The Guardian*, 2 April.

Rugman, J. (1995a) Tajik struggle is lethal brew for Moscow, *The Guardian*, 11 February.

Rugman, J. (1995b) Religion's sweet stolen fruit turns sour for Tajik Muslims, *The Guardian*, 14 February.

Rugman, J. (1995c) Islam advances in land of Ataturk, *The Guardian*, 23 December.

Ryall, D. (1994) The Roman Catholic Church and socio-political change in South Africa, 1948–90. Unpublished manuscript, University of Wales, Swansea.

Sadowski, C. (1993) Autonomous groups as agents of democratic change in communist and post-Communist Eastern Europe, in L. Diamond (ed.) *Political Culture and Democracy in Developing Countries*, Boulder, CO and London: Lynne Rienner, pp. 163–95.

Sahliyeh, E. (1990) Religious resurgence and political modernization, in E. Sahliyeh (ed.) *Religious Resurgence and Politics in the Contemporary World*, Albany: State University of New York Press, pp. 1–16.

Salame, G. (1993) Islam and the West, *Foreign Policy*, Spring, pp. 22–37.

Sam, Y. (1987) *Khmer Buddhism and Politics, 1954–84*, Newington, CT: Khmer Studies Institute.

Sarin, R. (1990) *The Assassination of Indira Gandhi*, New Delhi: Penguin Books.

Schatzberg, M. (1988) *The Dialectics of Oppression in Zaire*, Bloomington: Indiana University Press.

Schober, J. (1995) The Theravada Buddhist engagement with modernity in South-east Asia: whither the social paradigm of the galactic polity?, *Journal of South-east Asian Studies*, 26, 2, pp. 307–25.

Scott, J. (1985) *Weapons of the Weak. Everyday Forms of Peasant Resistance*, New Haven, CT: Yale University Press.

Serra, L. (1985) Ideology, religion and class struggle in the Nicaraguan revolution, in R. Harris and C. Vilas (eds) *Nicaragua: a Revolution under Siege*, London: Zed, pp. 151–74.

Shaikh, F. (1989) Turkey, in S. Mews (ed.) *Religion in Politics. A World Guide*, Harlow: Longman, pp. 269–70.

Shepard, W. (1987) 'Fundamentalism' Christian and Islamic, *Religion*, 17, pp. 355–78.

Shupe, A. (1990) The stubborn persistence of religion in the global arena, in E. Sahliyeh (ed.) *Religious Resurgence and Politics in the Contemporary World*, Albany: State University of New York Press, pp. 17–26.

Sigmund, P. (1993) Christian democracy, liberation theology, and political culture in Latin America, in L. Diamond (ed.) *Political Culture and Democracy in Developing Countries*, Boulder, CO and London: Lynne Rienner, pp. 329–45.

Silberstein, L. (1993) Religion, ideology, modernity: theoretical issues in the study of Jewish fundamentalism, in L. Silberstein (ed.) *Jewish Fundamentalism in Comparative Perspective. Religion, Ideology, and the Crisis of Modernity*, New York and London: New York University Press, pp. 3–26.

Simmons, M. (1992) Church leaders tell of massacre horrors in Kenya's Rift Valley, *The Guardian*, 22 December.

Simpson, J. (1992) Fundamentalism in America revisited: the fading of modernity as a source of symbolic capital, in B. Misztal and A. Shupe (eds) *Religion and Politics in Comparative Perspective. Revival of Religious Fundamentalism in East and West*, Westport, CT and London: Praeger, pp. 10–27.

Sisson, R. (1993) Culture and democratization in India, in L. Diamond (ed.) *Political Culture and Democracy in Developing Countries*, Boulder, CO: Lynne Rienner, pp. 37–66.

Slater, W. and Engelbrekt, K. (1993) Eastern orthodoxy defends its position, *RFE/RL Research Reports*, 2, 35, 3 September, pp. 48–58.

Smart, N. (1989) *The World's Religions*, Cambridge: Cambridge University Press.

Smith, B. (ed.) (1978) *Religion and Legitimation of Power in Thailand, Laos and Burma*, Chambersburg, PA: ANIMA Books.

Smith, Br. (1982) *The Church and Politics in Chile*, Princeton, NJ: Princeton University Press.

Smith, D. E. (1965) *Religion and Politics in Burma*, Princeton, NJ: Princeton University Press.

Smith, D. E. (1970) *Religion and Political Development*, Boston: Little Brown.

Smith, D. E. (1990) Limits of religious resurgence, in E. Sahliyeh (ed.) *Religious Resurgence and Politics in the Contemporary World*, Albany, NY: State University of New York Press, pp. 33–44.

Smith, M. (1991) *Burma: Insurgency and the Politics of Ethnicity*, London: Zed Books.

Somboon, Suksamran (1982) *Buddhism and Politics in Thailand: A Study of Socio-Political Change and Political Activism of the Thai Sangha*, Singapore: Institute of South-east Asian Studies.

Somboon, Suksamran (1993) Buddhism, political authority, and legitimacy in Thailand and Cambodia, in T. Ling (ed.) *Buddhist Trends in South-east Asia*, Singapore: Institute of South-east Asian Studies, pp. 101–53.

Sparks, A. (1993) 'Coloureds' back their ex-tormentor, *The Observer*, 14 February.

Sprinzak, E. (1993) Fundamentalism, ultranationalism, and political culture: the case of the Israeli radical right, in L. Diamond (ed.) *Political Culture and Democracy in Developing Countries*, Boulder, CO and London: Lynne Rienner, pp. 247–78.

Steele, J. (1992) The Tajiks next door watch Massoud's Kabul, *The Guardian*, 5 May.

Stein, A. (1992) Religion and mass politics in Central America. Paper presented at the Meeting of the New England Council of Latin American Studies, Boston, 24 October.

Stenberg, L. (1996) The revealed word and the struggle for authority, in D. Westerlund (ed.) *Questioning the Secular State. The Worldwide Resurgence of Religion in Politics*, London: Hurst, pp. 140–66.

Stepan, A. (1988) *Rethinking Military Politics. Brazil and the Southern Cone*, Princeton, NJ: Princeton University Press.

Stoll, D. (1990) *Is Latin America Turning Protestant? The Politics of Evangelical Growth*. Berkeley: University of California Press.

Storkey, A. (1997) Dealing with God – the stuff of politics, *The Guardian*, 26 April.

Suwanna, Satha Anand (1990) Religious movements in contemporary Thailand, *Asian Survey*, 30, 4, pp. 395–408.

Swearer, D. (1987) The Buddhist tradition in today's world, in F. Whaling (ed.) *Religion in Today's World*, Edinburgh: T. & T. Clark, pp. 55–75.

Tahi, M. S. (1992) The arduous democratisation process in Algeria, *The Journal of Modern African Studies*, 30, 3, pp. 400–20.

Talbot, I. (1991) Politics and religion in contemporary India, in G. Moyser (ed.) *Politics and Religion in the Modern World*, London: Routledge, pp. 135–61.

Tambiah, S. (1976) *World Conqueror and World Renouncer*, Cambridge: Cambridge University Press.

Taylor, J. L. (1990) New Buddhist movements in Thailand: An 'individualistic revolution', reform and political dissonance, *Journal of South-east Asian Studies*, 21, 1, pp. 130–43.

Therborn, G. (1994) Another way of taking religion seriously. Comment on Francis G. Castles, *European Journal of Political Research*, 26, 1, pp. 103–10.

Thomas, C. (1995) Hindu extremists take over Bombay, *The Times*, 15 March.

Thomas, S. (1995) Religion and International Society. Paper prepared for the workshop: 'Political Culture and Religion in the Third World', European Consortium for Political Research Joint Sessions of Workshops, Bordeaux, April–May 1995.

Tin Maung Maung Than (1988) The *sangha* and *sasana* in socialist Burma, *Sojourn: Socialist Issues in South-east Asia*, 3, 2, pp. 26–61.

de Tocqueville, A. (1969) *Democracy in America*, New York: Anchor.

Triaud, J.-L. (1982) L'Islam et l'état en republique du Niger, *Le Mois en Afrique*, 194–5, pp. 10–25, 35–48.

Tully, M. and Jacob, S. (1985) *Amritsar: Mrs Gandhi's Last Battle*, London: Cape.

United Nations Development Programme (UNDP) (1996) *Human Development Report 1996*, Oxford: Oxford University Press for the UNDP.

Vatikiotis, P. J. (1987) *Islam and the State*, London: Routledge.

Venugopal, C. N. (1990) Reformist sects and the sociology of religion in India, *Sociological Analysis*, 51 (Summer), pp. 77–88.

Vickery, M. (1984) *Cambodia 1975–82*, Sydney: Allen and Unwin.

Voll, J. (1991) Fundamentalism in the Sunni Arab World, in M. Marty and R. Scott Appleby (eds) *Fundamentalisms Observed*, Chicago: University of Chicago Press, pp. 345–402.

von der Mehden, F. (1989) Burma (Myanmar), in S. Mews (ed.) *Religion in Politics. A World Guide*, Harlow: Longman, pp. 32–3.

Vulliamy, E. (1995) US at war over life and death issue abortion issue, *The Observer*, · 19 February.

Wald, K. (1991) Social change and political response: the silent religious cleavage in North America, in G. Moyser (ed.) *Religion and Politics in the Modern World*, London: Routledge, pp. 239–84.

Walker, M. (1996) Born-again lose faith in Dole, *The Observer*, 27 October.

Wallis, R. and Bruce, S. (1992) Secularization: the orthodox model, in S. Bruce (ed.) *Religion and Modernization*, Oxford: Clarendon Press, pp. 8–30.

Walls, A. (1987) The Christian tradition in today's world, in F. Whaling (ed.) *Religion in Today's World*, Edinburgh: T. & T. Clark, pp. 74–107.

Walsh, M. (1989) Spain, in S. Mews (ed.) *Religion in Politics. A World Guide*, Harlow: Longman, pp. 249–50.

Watson, M. (1994) Christianity and the green option in the new Europe, in J. Fulton and P. Gee (eds) *Religion in Contemporary Europe*, Lewiston, NY: Edwin Mellen, pp. 148–59.

Webber, M. (1992) Angola: continuity and change, *Journal of Communist Studies*, 13, 2, pp. 317–33.

Weber, M. (1969) Major features of world religions, in R. Robertson (ed.) *Sociology of Religion*, Baltimore, MD: Penguin, pp. 19–41.

Weber, M. (1978) *Economy and Society*, Berkeley: University of California Press.

Weiner, M. (1992) Peoples and states in a new ethnic order?, *Third World Quarterly*, 13, 2, pp. 317–33.

Westerlund, D. (ed.) (1996) *Questioning the Secular State. The Worldwide Resurgence of Religion in Politics*, London: Hurst.

Wiebe, V. (1989) Guatemala, in S. Mews (ed.) *Religion in World Politics*, Harlow: Longman, pp. 89–90.

Willems, E. (1967) *Followers of the New Faith*, Nashville, TN: Vanderbilt University Press.

Williams, H. (1992) *International Relations in Political Theory*, Milton Keynes: Open University Press.

Wilson, B. (1982) *Religion in Sociological Perspective*, Oxford: Oxford University Press.

Wilson, B. (1992) Reflections on a many sided controversy, in S. Bruce (ed.) *Religion and Modernization*, Oxford: Clarendon Press, pp. 195–210.

Witte, J., Jr. (1993) Introduction, in Witte, J. Jr. (ed.) *Christianity and Democracy in Global Context*, Boulder, CO: Westview, pp. 1–21.

World Bank (1995) *World Development Report 1995*, Oxford: Oxford University Press for the World Bank.

Wuthnow, R. (1988) *The Restructuring of American Religion*, Princeton, NJ: Princeton University Press.

Zotz, V. (1993) Personal spiritual orientations and religiousness in (former) Soviet society, in L. Martin (ed.) *Religious Transformations and Socio-Political Change. Eastern Europe and Latin America*, Berlin and New York: Mouton de Gruyter, pp. 83–96.

Zubaida, S. (1989) *Islam, the People and the State*, London: Routledge.

Index